COPING
WITH
CRISIS

D1070297

COPING WITH CRISIS

Government Reactions to the Great Recession

Nancy Bermeo and
Jonas Pontusson
Editors

Russell Sage Foundation
New York

The Russell Sage Foundation

The Russell Sage Foundation, one of the oldest of America's general purpose foundations, was established in 1907 by Mrs. Margaret Olivia Sage for "the improvement of social and living conditions in the United States." The Foundation seeks to fulfill this mandate by fostering the development and dissemination of knowledge about the country's political, social, and economic problems. While the Foundation endeavors to assure the accuracy and objectivity of each book it publishes, the conclusions and interpretations in Russell Sage Foundation publications are those of the authors and not of the Foundation, its Trustees, or its staff. Publication by Russell Sage, therefore, does not imply Foundation endorsement.

BOARD OF TRUSTEES
Robert E. Denham, Esq., Chair

Kenneth D. Brody	Nicholas Lemann	Richard H. Thaler
W. Bowman Cutter III	Sara S. McLanahan	Eric Wanner
John A. Ferejohn	Nancy L. Rosenblum	Mary C. Waters
Larry V. Hedges	Claude M. Steele	
Lawrence F. Katz	Shelley E. Taylor	

Library of Congress Cataloging-in-Publication Data

Coping with crisis : government reactions to the great recession / Nancy Bermeo and Jonas Pontusson, editors.
   p. cm.
  Includes bibliographical references and index.
  ISBN 978-0-87154-076-8 (pbk. : alk. paper)   1. Economic policy. 2. International economic relations. 3. Financial crises. 4. Global Financial Crisis, 2008–2009. 5. Economic policy—Case studies.   I. Bermeo, Nancy Gina, 1951–   II. Pontusson, Jonas.
  HD87.C667 2012
  338.9—dc23   2012014046

Copyright © 2012 by the Russell Sage Foundation. All rights reserved. Printed in the United States of America. No part of this publication may be reproduced, stored in a retrieval system, or transmitted in any form or by any means, electronic, mechanical, photocopying, recording, or otherwise, without the prior written permission of the publisher.

Reproduction by the United States Government in whole or in part is permitted for any purpose.

The paper used in this publication meets the minimum requirements of American National Standard for Information Sciences-Permanence of Paper for Printed Library Materials. ANSI Z39.48-1992.

Text design by Genna Patacsil.

RUSSELL SAGE FOUNDATION
112 East 64th Street, New York, New York 10065
10 9 8 7 6 5 4 3 2 1

Contents

vi   Contents

Contributors |

NANCY BERMEO is Nuffield Professor of Comparative Politics at Oxford University.

JONAS PONTUSSON is professor of comparative politics at the University of Geneva, Switzerland.

BEN W. ANSELL is associate professor of political science at the University of Minnesota.

KLAUS ARMINGEON is professor of comparative and European politics at the University of Bern, Switzerland.

LUCIO BACCARO is professor of sociology at the University of Geneva, Switzerland.

LUCY BARNES is Prize Postdoctoral Research Fellow in politics at Nuffield College, Oxford.

DAVID R. CAMERON is professor of political science at Yale University and director of the Yale Program in European Union Studies.

ERIC HELLEINER is professor of political science and CIGI Chair in International Political Economy at the University of Waterloo, Canada.

TORBEN IVERSEN is Harold Hitchings Burbank Professor of Political Economy at Harvard University.

JOHANNES LINDVALL is associate professor of political science at Lund University, Sweden.

NOLAN MCCARTY is Susan Dod Brown Professor of Politics and Public Affairs at the Woodrow Wilson School at Princeton University.

DAVID RUEDA is professor of comparative politics at Oxford University and fellow at Merton College.

WALTRAUD SCHELKLE is senior lecturer of political economy at the European Institute at the London School of Economics.

DAVID SOSKICE is research professor of political science at Duke University and research professor of comparative political economy at Oxford University.

YVES TIBERGHIEN is professor of comparative politics at the University of British Columbia.

ANNE WREN is research associate of the Institute for International Integration Studies at Trinity College Dublin

Chapter 1 | Coping with Crisis: An Introduction

Nancy Bermeo and Jonas Pontusson

THE CHINESE IDEOGRAPH for *crisis* combines the image of danger with the image of opportunity. This makes good sense. Crises are surely periods of peril, but they also facilitate change. This simple observation is the essence of the punctuated equilibrium model in economics. It is also the foundation of the social science literature on critical junctures. Whether they take the form of wars, depressions, deep recessions, or natural disasters, crises give leaders the opportunity to turn policies, and sometimes polities, in new directions.

Thus, crises threaten but they also enable, and the economic crisis that erupted in 2007 and 2008 was no exception. When the toxic assets of the U.S. mortgage market began to weaken financial institutions in the United States, Ireland, Germany, and Britain in 2007, policymakers in each state swiftly crafted a variety of policy reforms. Ruling party ideology proved a poor predictor of what transpired as the staunchly pro-market Bush administration engineered the largest government intervention in capital markets in U.S. history. Yet, on this occasion, as on so many others, reform opportunities were neither unconstrained nor uniformly utilized. As the financial crisis spread and morphed into the Great Recession, different governments responded in different ways, reacting to a mix of domestic and international pressures and incentives.

What forms did government responses take? How might they best be explained and who, if anyone, has seized the opportunity for change thus far? The essays in this volume address these questions from a variety of perspectives. Taken as a whole, the volume maps the varied nature of national responses, sheds light on the extent to which policies were shaped by international actors and international coordination and explores how

1

responses were affected by institutional complementarities, party politics, and organized interests. This opening chapter previews what lies ahead and sets government responses to the Great Recession in historical perspective through a comparison with government responses to the global economic crisis running from 1974 to 1982. The Long Recession, as we shall call it here, provides an appropriate comparison for the contemporary crisis, for it too was an extraordinarily sharp economic downturn that called into question core features of prevailing growth models in the advanced industrial (or postindustrial) economies.

Although our authors were not constrained by a single analytic framework, the collection as a whole highlights three major themes. The first is that international institutions have generally failed to play the ameliorative role that many envisioned: international financial institutions proved incapable of preventing the U.S. mortgage crisis from becoming a global recession; the EU failed to take the early measures that might have prevented the crisis from growing worse, and its inability to foresee and then forestall a series of sovereign debt crises has severely curtailed the autonomy of decision-making in debt-ridden member states and generated political disenchantment with the European project in general. The collection's second theme emerged when we, as editors, set the policy responses outlined by our authors in historical perspective. Comparing the responses to the Great Recession with the responses to the Long Recession of the 1970s and early 1980s, we found that the contemporary menu of policy choices had not only narrowed considerably but also changed in content. The third theme is that economic policymaking between 2008 and 2011 is only partially explained by the factors invoked to explain economic policymaking in better times and in previous crises: the institutional complementarities of liberal versus coordinated market economies, the ideology of ruling parties, and pressures from traditional interest associations carry less explanatory weight than the current literature in comparative political economy would lead us to expect.

Our themes have been shaped, no doubt, by our project's regional and temporal boundaries. Geographically, the volume deliberately focuses on advanced capitalist democracies. Its essays trace and explain policy responses in the EU, Britain, France, Germany, Greece, Ireland, Japan, Portugal, Spain, the Nordic countries, and the United States, and include references to Italy as well. Although the Great Recession has certainly been felt globally, the crisis started in the most developed economies, and much is to be gained by beginning our inquiry where the crisis began. In addition, an extensive literature exists on government responses to previous economic crises in advanced capitalist democracies, providing us with the opportunity to engage in cross-temporal as well as cross-national comparisons (see Gourevitch 1986; Scharpf 1991).

The temporal focus of this collection is on policy responses crafted before the first quarter of 2011. Defining the term *recession* conventionally, as two consecutive quarters of GDP contraction, our time frame encompasses the entire period in which these advanced democracies were technically in recession (Stiglitz and Walsh 2006). Of course, the Great Recession followed somewhat different trajectories in different places. Ireland was the first to enter into recession and then experienced more recessionary quarters than any of the other country cases. Sweden was among the last and then experienced fewer. Despite this variation, all our cases save Greece had managed to restore growth for at least one quarter before the end of 2010, and even Greece managed a short-lived rebound in the first quarter of 2011.

This said, it is quite clear that the negative consequences of the Great Recession are still being felt at the time of this writing (February 2012). Stock prices have not reached their pre-recession level in Britain or the United States and are in decline again in both the eurozone and Japan.[1] The United States, Ireland, Spain, and Greece are continuing to struggle with crises in their housing sectors, and unemployment remains much higher than before the Great Recession in most countries (see table 12.7). The full effects of the sovereign debt crises have yet to be felt, and that Portugal and Japan entered new recessionary cycles in 2011 seems ominous.[2] The policy reactions we analyze here are thus government reactions to what is probably only the first phase of an extended economic crisis with multiple components. This makes our task more difficult but also more important: the policy changes made between 2007 and 2010 will be the foundation for coping responses in the future.

THE ROLE OF INTERNATIONAL INSTITUTIONS IN THE ORIGINS AND MANAGEMENT OF THE CRISIS

It is hardly necessary to underline the international nature of the Great Recession. The subprime mortgage crisis in the United States spread across the global economy by virtue of the fact that financial institutions in all major countries proved unable to control their direct and indirect exposure to the high-risk lending that drove global finance from the early 1990s onwards. In the first quarter of 2009, twenty-five of the twenty-seven member states of the European Union experienced negative GDP growth (see table 4.2). Just as unprecedentedly high levels of trade interdependence, particularly among EU states, contributed to the depth and spread of the recession, unprecedentedly high levels of financial interdependence contributed to the depth and spread of the negative fallout from sovereign debt crises. Sovereign debt problems now pose the major threat to global recovery as well as a major political challenge for the European Union.

Torben Iversen and David Soskice illuminate the association between interdependence and the origins of the Great Recession in chapter 2. They argue that the crisis of 2008 to 2010 is the manifestation of a two-fold regulatory failure at the international level: first, the failure to regulate high-risk lending activities by a small number of very large (and interdependent) financial institutions; and, second, the failure to regulate global trade imbalances. As Iversen and Soskice point out, the flow of capital from countries with trade surpluses to countries with large financial markets and high rates of return on financial assets (most notably, of course, the United States and the United Kingdom) made possible the persistence of trade imbalances in the ten to fifteen years before the crisis. In the absence of these capital flows, surplus countries would have lost and deficit countries would have gained trade through real exchange-rate adjustments. At the same time, cross-national capital flows fuelled speculative activities in countries without strong financial regulations and exposed countries with stricter regulations to increased systemic risk. The United States or the United Kingdom may well have experienced a financial crisis in the absence of global trade imbalances, but the crisis and its repercussions for the global economy would have been far less severe.

Reflecting lessons learned during the Long Recession of 1974 to 1982, the major industrial economies all embraced inflation targeting as the core principle of global macroeconomic management in the two decades prior to the onset of the crisis. Iversen and Soskice stress that this macroeconomic regime was never meant to regulate trade imbalances. Quite the contrary, it was designed precisely to accommodate the build-up of trade surpluses by export-oriented economies, such as Germany and China. By the same token, the institutional framework of global economic governance allowed the United States, the United Kingdom, and other liberal market economies to boost their comparative advantage in financial services by engaging in financial deregulation in the 1980s and 1990s. For Iverson and Soskice, then, the twofold regulatory failure at the heart of the economic crisis can be directly linked to an international framework based on national sovereignty over the rules governing finance and the accommodation of divergent national approaches to trade and macroeconomic management.

Although Iversen and Soskice conclude by suggesting that "lessons have been learned about the operation of the financial system that may limit the dangers of a future crisis," their core argument is that the major players on the global stage continue to have divergent preferences with respect to financial regulation as well as macroeconomic management. Emphasizing the determinant role of each country's "variety of capitalism" for domestic and foreign economic policies, Iversen and Soskice argue that domestic policymakers' preferences reflect the interests of the dominant economic sector in each state (Hall and Soskice 2001). This means the financial sector in the (Anglophone) liberal market economies and the manufacturing sector in coordinated, export-oriented economies. In Iversen and Soskice's framework, international coordination boils down to bargaining among governments representing different national models of capitalism and there is little reason to believe that the economic crisis will engender new forms of multilateral or supranational regulation.

Whereas Iversen and Soskice's chapter explores how tensions between international and national institutions played a role in the origins of the economic crisis, the four chapters that follow explore the role of international institutions during the crisis. In chapter 3, Eric Helleiner emphasizes the limits of multilateral crisis management and in so doing offers an important corrective to the commonly held view that extensive international cooperation distinguishes the experience of 2007 through 2010 from that of the Great Depression. Heilleiner's argument is nuanced: he recognizes that the G20 of November 2008 legitimated fiscal stimulus as a national response to the crisis while the World Trade Organization (WTO) restrained protectionist impulses around the world. He also notes that the central banks of the major industrial countries coordinated among themselves to achieve financial stabilization. However, Helleiner downplays the role of the International Monetary Fund (IMF) as an arena for crisis resolution and argues that domestic pressures were more important than the G20 in bringing about the reorientation of fiscal policy in most industrial countries.

Perhaps most decisively, Helleiner stresses the absence of a dollar crisis as the main reason the financial crisis of 2007 and 2008 did not lead to the kind of global collapse of trade and economic activity that occurred in the early 1930s, and points out the lack of any evidence whatsoever of bilateral or multilateral coordination to shore up the dollar in 2007 and 2008. Echoing the Iversen and Soskice emphasis on domestic structures, Helleiner argues persuasively that the absence of a dollar crisis can and should be analyzed in terms of unilateral, self-interested decisions by governments and financial institutions holding large dollar reserves. In addition, he suggests that the economic crisis has hampered rather than stimulated ongoing efforts to strengthen the international regulation of finance. Again consistent with Iversen and Soskice, he emphasizes conflicts between national models in this realm but also points out that financial regulation has become a hotly contested issue in domestic politics in the wake of the crisis. In his words, the ultimate legacy of the Great Recession "is likely to be a more decentralized international regulatory order, one that gives more autonomy to national and regional authorities to set their own regulatory priorities."

Because much of our volume deals with crisis responses in western Europe, the role played by the European Union as a multilateral organization and supranational actor receives special attention. Although the EU is discussed in all chapters that deal with crisis responses in Europe, this subject features most prominently in those on European fiscal policy responses (chapter 4), France, Germany, and the EU (chapter 5), and sovereign debt crises (chapter 6). Taken together, these chapters bring out the Janus-faced quality of the EU's role in crisis management. In relation to fiscally solvent member states, its influence on responses to the crisis has been very limited. In relation to debt-ridden member states, however, the EU has come to assume formidable new powers of surveillance and policy constraint.

As chapters 4 and 5 both show, the EU provided a forum for member states to discuss and coordinate fiscal policy responses to the economic downturn, but the Recovery Plan adopted by the European Council in December of 2008 amounted to little more than a summation of stimulus measures that had already been decided by national governments in the member states. Wielding a budget of only 1 percent of the EU's GDP, and legally prevented from issuing its own debt, the capacity of the EU itself to engage in expansionary fiscal policy was strictly limited. As Waltraud Schelkle notes in chapter 5, German opposition effectively preempted any serious discussion of strengthening the fiscal capacity of the EU and the German government vetoed a general EU-wide reduction of value-added taxes proposed by the Commission. The Recovery Plan shied away from any attempt to impose a more expansionary policy stance on member states that were reluctant to engage in fiscal stimulus, and the EU did not initiate further coordination of expansionary policies when it became clear, in the spring of 2009, that its initial economic projections were overly optimistic.

David Cameron argues in chapter 4 that the Growth and Stability Pact, which imposes limits on the ability of euro members to run deficits, was an important constraint, particularly for those member states that were already in deficit when the crisis started. More broadly, Cameron suggests that the EU experience of 2008 through 2010 illustrates the vexing collective action problem that fiscal expansion entails under conditions of interdependence. Simply put, national governments worried that demand stimulus would benefit other member states by boosting demand for imports and, at the same time, reduce the competitiveness of their own exports. In Cameron's assessment, the member states of the EU ended up engaging in less-than-optimal fiscal expansion in the absence of effective policy coordination.

Schelkle makes a similar point about weak policy coordination in her analysis of Germany and France. She shows that the EU proved weak as an autonomous actor when faced with pressure from two powerful core members, yet her analysis of the EU's first responses to the Greek and Irish sovereign debt crises of 2010 and 2011 highlights a different and much stronger face of the EU. In its relations to these debt-ridden countries, the EU has emerged as a powerful and remarkably unitary supranational actor, dictating the imposition of draconian austerity measures in return for financial support. As Schelkle explains, this new EU role has involved significant institutional changes, with the creation of the European Financial Stability Facility and new mechanisms of budgetary surveillance. Perhaps most important, recent developments have shattered the carefully crafted separation of fiscal and monetary policy within the EU.

Schelkle argues persuasively that the EU's management of sovereign debt crises corresponds to the French vision of a more "political Europe," but the common policy that the European Central Bank and strong member states such as France and Germany have agreed on represents a surrender to bond markets and, thus, to finance capital. The long-term implications for the democratic legitimacy of the EU, in the eyes of German taxpayers as well as (unemployed) Greek workers, are potentially very serious.

In chapter 6, Klaus Armingeon and Lucio Baccaro complement Schelkle's arguments about both the power of the EU over its economically weaker members and about the implications of EU actions for democratic legitimacy. Their study of post-crisis policymaking in Greece, Ireland, Portugal, and Spain does not confine itself to the role of the EU and shows how the political economies of peripheral states are being shaped by the International Monetary Fund as well. Their central point, however, is about the constraints brought on by membership in the eurozone. Use of the euro deprives countries of the option of currency devaluation. In so doing, it deprives them of the standard means of buffering austerity by boosting external demand while domestic demand is compressed. The deep budget cuts required by debt crises have "worsened rather than ameliorated prospects for financial solvency" and, to make matters worse, the peripheral countries' austerity packages "are by no means distributionally neutral." They will scale back welfare states that are already modest by most measures and further deregulate key parts of the labor market and industrial relations system.

Armingeon and Baccaro argue further that the overwhelming disparity in power revealed by the recent debt crises will sow disenchantment not simply with the integration of European democracies but with democracy itself. Trust in national governments has already receded dramatically as citizens come to believe that neither domestic parties nor collective action affect policy outcomes. Austerity budgeting to cope with crisis may "profoundly change the social contract in the countries in question, and possibly in Europe as a whole."

Taken together, these internationally focused essays illustrate that international organizations have often fallen short of expectations. Helleiner argues persuasively that decisions taken by national governments were more consequential for crisis control than decisions taken through international coordination. Cameron, Schelkle, and Armingeon and Bacarro highlight a variety of coordination problems that compromised institutional effectiveness in the EU, and Iverson and Soskice situate the origins of the crisis itself in international coordination problems intrinsic to different varieties of capitalism.

COMPARING POLICY RESPONSES: CROSS-NATIONAL AND CROSS-TEMPORAL PERSPECTIVES

Three facts about policy responses to the Great Recession stand in sharp relief. First, states not in danger of default relied overwhelmingly on fiscal stimulus packages to cope with the crisis. Second, the size and composition of fiscal stimuli varied considerably across states. Third, the heavy reliance on fiscal stimulus, plus a radically different industrial policy, distinguished the reactions to the Great Recession from reactions to its predecessor. The other mechanisms used to cope with crisis in the Long Recession, including protectionism, devaluation, and nationalization, were, for the most part, absent in the Great Recession. The menu of policy options that governments considered in 2008 through 2010 appears to have been much narrower than the menu considered during the crisis of the 1970s and early 1980s.

Macroeconomic Policy

The United States, Japan, and nearly all countries in Europe reacted to the Great Recession with some form of fiscal stimulus. Even Portugal and

Spain attempted stimulus packages before their debt crises began. Yet, as the contributions to this volume demonstrate (most notably chapters 4 and 11) cross-national variation in the extent to which different governments engaged in fiscal stimulus was substantial. Although Ireland from the very beginning stands out for its procyclical fiscal policy, the United States, Britain, and Japan pursued decidedly more expansionary fiscal policies than eurozone members, particularly if we restrict the comparison to discretionary policy measures. The Nordic and core continental countries relied more heavily on *automatic stabilizers* (that is, budget deficits automatically generated by increased spending and declining tax revenues due to the decline of economic activity and the rise of unemployment). However, the Nordic countries also undertook discretionary measures to boost aggregate demand (see chapter 8).

Cross-national differences in the size of fiscal stimulus packages sometimes took surprising turns. Contrary to what we might have expected based on policy legacies and public rhetoric, Germany adopted a more expansionary policy stance than France (see chapter 5). And, contrary to what we might have expected on purely ideological grounds, chapter 6 shows that the first fiscal responses adopted by ruling socialist parties in southern Europe ran the gamut from highly expansive in Spain to moderately expansive in Portugal and countercyclical in Greece. Contradicting expectations that liberal economies might react with a uniform response, chapter 10 illustrates an even starker contrast between Ireland and Britain: Ireland cut spending dramatically while Britain increased it sharply in 2008 and 2009. Finally, the depth of a country's economic contraction and the strength of its stimulus package had at best only "a very slight relationship" (chapter 4).

Evidence presented in chapters 4, 8, and 11 shows that the composition of fiscal stimulus packages also varied significantly across countries. Some governments relied primarily on tax cuts whereas others also increased spending. Within the first of these two broad categories, countries varied substantially in the sorts of tax cuts passed: Spain and the United States, for example, focused primarily on cutting individual income taxes, Germany on cutting payroll taxes, and the United Kingdom cutting consumption taxes (chapter 11).

The nature of spending-based stimuli varied greatly as well. For example, though nearly all the countries included in this study subsidized scrapping programs to boost automobile sales, the programs ranged in size from the relatively ambitious initiatives of Germany, Japan, Spain, and the United States to the more modest initiatives of Britain and France (see chapters 5 and 9; see also Haugh, Mourougane, and Chatal 2010). Countries varied as well in the extent to which they invested in public employment maintenance. In Sweden, both government and opposition agreed to maintain public sector employment via large transfers from the central government to municipal governments (chapter 8). In the much more polarized United States, however, public-sector employment dropped considerably, despite federal government transfers to regional and local authorities (chapter 11). In the peripheral countries of the EU, a third pattern eventually emerged in which public-sector employment was deliberately slashed as part of centralized austerity measures.

Compared with the Great Recession, the fiscal policy responses to the recessions of 1974 to 1976 and 1980 to 1982 were less expansionary and even less uniform. It is also noteworthy that monetary policy was generally quite restrictive from 1974 to 1982, in marked contrast to the 2007 to 2010 period. American and German governments responded to the recession of 1974 to 1976 with fiscal stimulus, but in both cases monetary policy counteracted the effects of fiscal policy, and in stark contrast to 2008 to 2009, both countries responded to the recession of 1980 to 1982 in a decidedly non-Keynesian manner (on Germany, see Scharpf 1991). Faced with rampant inflation and mounting public debt, British Labour governments of 1974 through 1979 pursued restrictive fiscal policies, anticipating the policy stance adopted by Mrs. Thatcher's government during the recession of the early 1980s. Portugal and Spain pursued expansionary and then restrictive policies at different times. France weathered these earlier recessions relatively well and avoided extensive reliance of fiscal stimulus over the entire 1974 to 1982 period. Only for Sweden and a few other countries can we say without qualification that the macroeconomic policy response to the recession of the mid-1970s was decidedly more expansionary than that to the Great Recession.

Although the countries coping with the recent crisis all adopted more restrictive fiscal policies as soon as signs of economic recovery appeared in 2009 and 2010, the comparison with the recessions of 1974 to 1976 and 1980 to 1982 suggests that reliance on fiscal stimulus represents a distinctive feature of government responses to the Great Recession—Ireland, Greece, and later Italy and the Iberian countries being major exceptions.[3] In our view, this feature is particularly noteworthy because so much of the existing literature on macroeconomic management emphasizes the ascendancy of monetarist ideas from the early 1980s onwards (for example, Mc-Namara 1998). Over the last few years, we have learned that fiscal stimulus remains an economically effective and politically viable policy option for governments coping with economic crisis.

At the same time, the modalities of fiscal activism appear to have changed relative to the golden age of Keynesiasm in the 1960s and 1970s, at least in western Europe. In the 1970s, fiscal stimulus primarily involved increases in government spending and when governments subsequently sought to restore a balanced budget they did so by raising the rate of taxation. In the recent period, in contrast, governments relied more heavily on tax cuts to stimulate the economy and on spending cuts to achieve fiscal consolidation. Following Jonas Pontusson and Damian Raess (2012), we might think of this as a shift from social Keynesianism to liberal Keynesianism.

Protectionism, Devaluation, and Compensation

The comparison with the 1970s also serves as a useful reminder of what governments did not do in response to the Great Recession. From an historical perspective, the absence of protectionist responses to the Great Recession is striking. Though the United States and the EU both imposed antidumping duties on certain imports, the percentage of total imports affected by such measures increased by less than one percentage point from 2008 to 2009 (Kee, Neagu, and Nicita 2010). By contrast, the share of U.S. manufactured imports affected by nontariff barriers increased from 5.6 percent in 1974 to 18.4 percent in 1979. Increases of similar magnitude over this period occurred in all the major European countries as well (Page 1981).

Several European countries engaged in devaluation as a strategy to boost exports (and curtail imports) in the 1970s. In contrast, European hard-currency commitments remained remarkably firm between 2007 and 2010. Japan and the United States reacted differently from their European counterparts on currency issues but not as differently as sometimes portrayed. The use of "quantitative easing" in the United States drove dollar values down, but the dollar had been losing value against almost every other global currency for ten years, as Iversen and Soskice point out (see also Landon Thomas Jr., "Some See Rise Ahead for Dollar," *New York Times*, May 17, 2011). In any case, quantitative easing was aimed not at devaluation but at driving down long-term interest rates. Likewise, Japan sold the yen against the dollar under pressure from business leaders to boost exports, but it took this action only in September 2010, after the Great Recession had technically subsided in Japan's trading partners.[4]

Yet another point of contrast between the 1970s and the Great Recession concerns government efforts to compensate the jobless and protect workers against rising unemployment. In most of the advanced capitalist democracies, governments increased the generosity of unemployment insurance and other forms of compensation for the unemployed in response to rising unemployment in the second half of the 1970s. Many European countries also increased regulations that made it more difficult, or expensive, to shed workers during economic downturns (Pontusson and Raess forthcoming). In contrast, neither employment protection nor unemployment compensation appears to have been a prominent feature of government responses to the Great Recession. Quite the contrary, several of our authors show that even the maintenance of existing unemployment compensation provisions has been problematic in many states. Britain made eligibility for the jobseekers allowance decidedly more restrictive (chapter 12). Ireland lowered unemployment benefits and decreased access, and Spain extended benefits at first but then retreated (chapter 6). The Obama administration did increase spending on passive labor market policies after a long struggle and painful concessions to Republicans on tax cuts (chapter 7), and Japan's new government dramatically expanded unemployment insurance eligibility and benefits (chapter 9), but the United States and Japan are clearly outliers in this respect. As David Rueda shows in chapter 12, the general shift toward an emphasis on "demanding workfare" that occurred in the ten to fifteen years before the crisis continued through the crisis, both in liberal economies such as Britain, and in coordinated economies such as Germany. Exploring whether the Great Recession led countries to expand either their active or passive labor market policies, Rueda finds only marginal changes. Controlling for the rate of unemployment, only two countries, Italy and the Netherlands, saw government spending on unemployment compensation increase by more than 0.05 percent of GDP from 2007 to 2009 (table 12.8).

Industrial Policy

In the mid-1970s and early 1980s, European governments engaged in various selective interventions to deal with the economic difficulties of specific industrial sectors. Some of these interventions involved government subsidies to industry, but by no means all of them took this form. As John Zysman stresses, French industrial policy in the 1970s relied heavily on selective intervention in the allocation of long-term credit by private and para-public financial institutions (1983). In Britain, Sweden, France, Portugal, and Greece, industrial policy in this earlier period also involved a significant expansion of state enterprise.

The Great Recession also prompted a number of governments to use industrial policies to cope with the economic crisis. Thus industrial policy might be seen as a dimension on which government responses to the Great Recession were similar to those of the Long Recession. However, we are struck by how differently these types of targeted policy measures have been used in the more recent period. Three contrasts in industrial policy stand out. The first involves a markedly different role for the state in creating employment. To the extent that governments in the Great Recession took an active role in employment creation at all, they did so mostly indirectly. They worked either through tax breaks for potential employers, as in Sweden's construction industry (chapter 8), or through temporary subsidies for short-term work in the private sector (chapters 5 and 9). Japan and a number of continental European countries, most notably Germany, introduced temporary subsidies for short-term work as a way to dampen unemployment in 2008 and 2009 (Schmitt 2011). These coping mechanisms did dampen unemployment but the contrast with the past is noteworthy. Rather than providing jobs directly, governments worked largely at the margins of the labor market, changing the incentives of potential employers with no guarantees that jobs would actually be created and no attempt to ensure long-term employment.

The second difference in industrial policy concerned the framing of the direct sectoral interventions that did occur. As several of these chapters show, the crisis prompted a number of governments to intervene in their automotive industries. In addition to the scrapping programs mentioned above, the United States provided some $80 billion in assistance to General Motors and Chrysler (Edmund Andrews, "Bailout Set to Ride Off into Sunset," *New York Times*, September 11, 2009). France provided $7.8 billion to Renault and Peugeot-Citroen, and Germany provided 4.5 billion euro to Opel. In some respects, these interventions mirrored actions taken in the earlier recessions. After all, Chrysler was bailed out in 1979 as well. Yet throughout the interventions of 2008 and 2009, governments went to great lengths to insist that their actions were only temporary measures and neither a challenge to free market principles, nor an expansion of state activities. Although European Commission leaders such as Mario Monti point out that industrial policy is no longer "taboo" (European Commission on Enterprise and Industry 2010), sectoral interventions are now invariably framed as a means to strengthen market mechanisms. Long-term spending programs and market substitution are no longer on the agenda. The European Commission's October 2010 Communication on Industrial Policy conveys the contemporary vision of industrial policy nicely:

> Whilst the economic and financial crisis shifted the focus of industrial competitiveness policies towards short-term rescue and recovery actions . . . the attention of policy makers has to focus on long-term structural challenges, in particular maintaining global competitiveness, . . . In the context of fiscal consolidation, *competitiveness strategies cannot be built on major spending programmes, but are more likely to address structural reforms in areas such as improving the business environment.* (2010, 30, emphasis added)

Thus, the role of industrial policy is to boost market competition through environmental changes rather than state spending. This very different framing of intervention dovetails with the different policy reactions to rising unemployment highlighted above. Despite a continued employment crisis in several EU countries, the European Commission endorses a limited role for government in the labor market. Its official position on industrial policy states explicitly that "excess capacities in some industries require tailor-made responses *at the company level . . . Companies and social partners have the primary responsibility for restructuring*" (European Commission 2010, 21, emphasis added).

The third and most consequential contrast between industrial policy in the Great Recession and industrial policy in the 1970s concerns the targets of state intervention. During the Long Recession, the targets of industrial policy were concentrated in manufacturing. In the Great Recession, the targets of intervention were overwhelmingly outside the manufacturing sector and in the financial sector instead. As Ben Ansell documents in chapter 11, all the countries considered in the volume engaged in massive bailouts of failing financial institutions. These bailouts focused primarily on the banking sector but many governments provided massive bailouts to the insurance industry as well. In Europe, for example, FORTIS was bailed out at a cost of $16.1 billion in September, 2008. In the United States, the Bush administration purchased $40 billion in preferred stock and provided a $30 billion credit line to bail out the American International Group (AIG). Although policymakers have so far shied away from using the infusion of public funds as a means to extend government involvement in the governance of financial institutions, the scale of these government interventions was historically unprecedented.

EXPLAINING POLICY RESPONSES

We now turn to the question of how government responses to the Great Recession might be explained. The contributors to this volume set a lively research agenda in developing a number of different causal arguments. We begin this section with an overview of the explanations they offer.

Explaining Current Cross-National Variation

Several factors help explain cross-national variation in macroeconomic policy responses. For peripheral countries with sovereign debt crises, policy responses were dictated almost exclusively by the demands of the EU and the IMF. For our other cases, however, domestic factors carry the greatest explanatory weight. Even Helleiner, who in chapter 3 explores the role of international coordination and supranational actors in the politics of crisis management, points to the limits of "internationalist" explanations. What domestic factors stand out?

A first factor concerns the role of *ideological divisions among lawmakers*. Although crisis might, in theory, have led to convergence, Nolan McCarty shows in chapter 7 that economic crisis did little to dampen elite polarization in the United States and that the country's response to the crisis was profoundly shaped (and hampered) by ideologically driven politics as a result. Johannes Lindvall's analysis in chapter 8 focuses on an opposite outcome but makes a similar point. He illustrates how, by the time of the Great Recession, the main Swedish parties had converged when it came to the size of the public sector and that elite consensus facilitated a swift and effective crisis response as a result.

Focusing on the environment in which political elites operate, a number of our authors illustrate how crisis responses can be deeply affected by *domestic political institutions*. Despite winning the 2009 election by a landslide, Japan's Democratic Party (DPJ) was unable to use the crisis as an opportunity for a major expansion of universal welfare because it had only weak cabinet control of the parliamentary agenda and, by 2010, no majority in the Upper House (chapter 9). Likewise, in the United States, the Democratic Party was forced to make dramatic cuts to its original stimulus proposal because supermajoritarianism and other institutional veto points allowed it no alternative (chapter 7).

Not surprisingly, a number of this volume's authors find that *electoral considerations* shaped responses to crises. Schelkle argues persuasively in chapter 5 that Germany's response to the crisis largely followed the logic of electoral politics, and Lindvall points out in chapter 8 that politicians' support for reforms will always be partially contingent on their projected effects on electoral prospects. McCarty shows in chapter 7 how the U.S. crisis response was deeply affected by the short-run electoral calculations of a presidential election year.

Without denying the role of political variables, several of our essays point to the pivotal role of economic conditions and policy legacies as explanations for government responses to the Great Recession. As David Cameron demonstrates in chapter 4, the government's *budgetary position* at the onset of the crisis is a strong predictor of the extent of fiscal stimulus in 2008 and 2009: EU member states that entered the recession with budget surpluses engaged in significantly more fiscal stimulus than those that entered the recession with budget deficits. (This association holds for both aggregate and discretionary measures.) In chapter 12, David Rueda highlights the implications of budgetary deficits, arguing that the need for austerity was used to justify the decrease in the generosity of the welfare state before and during the Great Recession. Tiberghien's analysis in chapter 9 complements Rueda's in showing how Japan lacked "the fiscal scope for a major expansion of universal welfare," despite being governed by a party that genuinely sought expansion. The chapters dealing with Ireland, Greece, Portugal, and Spain show how budget deficits have affected not only reactions to the crisis but the autonomy of domestic political elites vis-à-vis international organizations.

Closely related to arguments about pre-crisis budgets are a series of reinforcing arguments about *pre-crisis tax policies*. Asking what enabled certain countries to amass a budgetary surplus in the years immediately prior to the Great Recession, Cameron finds income-elastic forms of revenue and, in particular, taxes on personal incomes to be pivotal. The countries that had the greatest latitude in crafting a response to crisis were those that used personal income taxes to build a budget surplus in good times. Barnes and Wren's chapter 10 analysis of Ireland shows how a very different set of tax policies ultimately led to a situation in which policymakers had little choice about crisis response. Ireland was forced to implement austerity measures in part because the government had routinely offered income tax reductions in exchange for wage restraint in the years before the crisis hit. The country's "over-reliance on other, more cyclical taxes exacerbated the fiscal impact of the crisis" and sharply limited policy options.

Finally, the *sectoral foundations of economic growth* over the two decades preceding the Great Recession feature as an explanatory variable in several of the chapters. For instance, Barnes and Wren argue in chapter 10 that Britain and Ireland reacted to the Great Recession in contrasting ways because Ireland's growth model was much more heavily reliant on the construction and housing sectors. Ireland was forced into a countercyclical response because it experienced a greater shock to output, employment, and revenue when the housing bubble burst. The weight of the housing sector looms large as an explanatory variable in Ansell's chapter 11 argument as well. His analysis of crisis reactions in thirty OECD countries concludes that "countries that had housing booms see a very strong effect of partisanship on the types of discretionary tax and spending policies" formulated—with the Right cutting more taxes and the Left initiating more spending programs. In countries without housing bubbles, "demands from homeowners for tax relief or spending measures to maintain demand were largely absent." In these cases, "neither the *opportunity* for parties to engage in politically attractive shifts in policy nor the *compositional* motivation produced by changing demands from parties' voting bases was in play." Without "a large group of politically active homeowners, partisan responses were constrained."

Updating Past Perspectives

How do the arguments in this volume relate to the existing literature? It is commonplace to distinguish three, sometimes overlapping, theoretical traditions and research agendas within the field of comparative political economy. One strand of this literature emphasizes institutional differences among advanced capitalist political economies and notes that different sorts of institutional arrangements cluster together. A second tradition focuses on the role of government partisanship, typically postulating that parties of the Left and the Right have different core constituencies and, as a result, different distributive objectives. Finally, a third tradition emphasizes the role of organized interests and coalitions among different segments of labor and capital. This typology of CPE traditions provides a convenient way to assess the contribution these essays make to the larger literature on the domestic determinants of policy choice.

Varieties of Capitalism   The varieties of capitalism (VOC) approach referred to in our discussion of chapter 2 provides a prime example of the institutionalist tradition and is arguably the dominant approach to comparative political economy today (Soskice 1999; Hall and Soskice 2001; Hall and Gingerich 2009). Emphasizing complementarities among the different components of political-economic systems (industrial relations, skill formation, corporate governance, and inter-firm relations), this theoretical perspective identifies the coordinating capacities of business as the key dimension on which capitalist political economies differ. As a consequence, it draws a sharp distinction between liberal market economies (LMEs), exemplified by the United States, the United Kingdom, and the other Anglophone countries, and coordinated market economies (CMEs), exemplified by Japan, Germany, and the small states of northwestern Europe. Each variety of capitalism entails distinct comparative advantages, promoting different economic sectors and encouraging firms to pursue different innovation and production strategies. National governments will strive to maintain existing comparative advantages and, in so doing, serve the interests of dominant economic sectors.

As discussed, chapter 2 treats the Great Recession as a manifestation of the conflicting regulatory logics of different national models of capitalism. The discussion of the origins of the contemporary crisis is compelling, but leaves open the question of how far the VOC approach takes us in explaining government responses to the crisis itself. The VOC approach did not derive from an effort to explain policy reactions to economic crisis per se. It derived instead from an effort to explain "economic adjustment" to the "challenge of globalization" and to changes in "technology, products and tastes" (Hall and Soskice 2001, 60, 62–63) , Recognizing this, we as editors believe that the experience of the Great Recession provides an opportunity to examine some the core elements of the VOC framework in a different setting. The chapters in this volume advance this opportunity by bringing out important commonalities among LMEs and CMEs, important differences within each cluster of countries, and explanatory factors not yet incorporated in the VOC model.

In the realm of commonalities across varieties of capitalism, the phenomenon of housing booms has not been confined to LMEs. Japan experienced a huge housing bubble in the 1980s (chapter 9) and housing booms also occurred in Scandinavia and southern Europe (chapter 11). In the period leading up to the Great Recession, speculative increases in the price of financial assets appear to have been widespread in CMEs, LMEs, and the Mediterranean economies. Perhaps most important, financial institutions based in CMEs became deeply involved in high-risk lending in this period, which explains why the sovereign debt crises of relatively small economies such as Ireland and Greece have had such grave implications for the financial sectors in Germany, France, and elsewhere. Clearly, the Great Recession has had an important financial dimension in CMEs as well as LMEs, which has led to certain similarities in policy responses.

Among these similarities, the reliance on fiscal stimulus stands out. Beyond showing that fiscal stimulus was the weapon of choice across system types, chapter 4 indicates that a number of export-oriented CMEs—Japan as well as Sweden, Denmark, and Germany—adopted much larger discretionary stimulus packages than the United Kingdom or France, let alone procyclical Ireland, in 2008 through 2010.[5] Looking beyond fiscal policy measures, and to other policy similarities, other chapters show that Germany, the United States, and France all provided direct assistance to their automobile industries and that an equally broad range of economies bailed out failing banks (chapters 5, 7, and 11).

This collection also brings out important policy differences within the clusters of states that are conventionally categorized as LMEs or CMEs. Without contradicting the basic tenets of the varieties of capitalism approach, chapter 10 highlights substantial variation within the liberal category in a detailed contrast of crisis responses in Ireland and the United Kingdom. Chapter 12 also points out differences among LMEs in noting that the United States increased spending on passive labor market policies significantly while other liberal economies made marginal changes or no changes at all. Ansell's chapter 11 argument points to the significance of heterogeneity among both CME and Mediterranean states, showing that the presence or absence of housing booms (rather than institutional models) proved determinant in certain policy areas. Those who know the VOC literature well will not be surprised by these internal differences. Peter Hall and David Soskice noted from the start that "significant variations can be found" within the LME and CME categories (2001, 33). This project has brought several variations to light, inviting more work on how the differences might best be explained.

Several of the essays in this volume illustrate that policy differences within LMEs and CMEs can be explained by the relative importance of different sectors (for example, construction), suggesting that more scholarly attention to sectoral weighting might be fruitful. Another suggestion is that comparative political economists need to pay more attention to questions concerning state capacity and, in particular, the fiscal capacity of states (see also Beramendi 2010). Discussions of state capacity loomed large in the literature on industrial policy in 1970s and 1980s (for example, Katzenstein 1978; Zysman 1983), but faded in importance as comparative political economists increasingly focused attention on the coordinating capacities of private actors. This collection illustrates that the explanatory power of various aspects of state capacity merit more attention. Established state fiscal structures feature prominently in Cameron's chapter 4 explanation for the relatively successful response to the Great Recession in the Nordic countries: the Nordic countries were in an "advantageous position" largely because they relied on large automatic stabilizers and "forms of revenue—in particular, taxes on personal incomes—that are income elastic and tend to increase markedly during good times." Ireland's very different fiscal structure—with its heavy reliance on revenues tied to housing, corporate tax, and VAT—meant that it entered the recession greatly disadvantaged. In a related vein, Greece, Spain, Italy, and Portugal struggle with debt today in part because their states have historically lacked the capacity to stem tax evasion.

The experience of the Great Recession also suggests that comparative political economists need to pay more attention to the regulatory capacity of the state. Although U.S. policymakers have been generally reluctant to control high-risk financial activities, the efforts they have made in this domain were hampered by weak regulatory capacity (chapter 7). By contrast, the sense of stability that prevails in the Japanese bond markets, despite the highest debt to GDP ratio in the OECD, derives in part from continued confidence in regulatory state institutions (chapter 9). The question of how fiscal and regulatory state capacities relate to varieties of capitalism strikes us as a very important topic to explore further, extending and enriching the institutionalist tradition in comparative political economy.

Parties and Government Partisanship   Several of the chapters in this volume focus on the role of partisan politics in shaping government reactions to the Great Recession. Whether government partisanship matters to policy outcomes and economic performance—or under what conditions and for what policies it matters—have long been central preoccupations of comparative political economists. The existing literature on partisan effects typically asks whether governments run by center-left parties consistently make different policy choices from governments run by center-right parties and suggests that the answer to this question depends on electoral systems (for example, Iversen and Soskice 2006) as well as the interplay of external constraints and domestic political pressures (for example, Garrett 1998; Kwon and Pontusson 2010). However, this literature has not given systematic attention to the question of how recessions or economic crises affect the role of partisanship in policymaking. Some authors (such as Pierson 2001) have suggested that economic downturns generate policy convergence between left and right governments because they restrict the ability of governments to increase public spending, but it seems equally plausible to suppose that it is precisely under conditions of scarcity that governments have to make hard choices and end up showing their true colors, catering to the distributive interests of their core constituencies.

Taken together, the discussions of partisan politics in this volume bring out an important conceptual distinction that the existing literature has tended to overlook. The topic of partisan politics involves two separate questions. The first concerns the extent to which the major parties disagree over policies or, for present purposes, over how to meet current economic challenges. To use McCarty's language, this is the question of "partisan polarization." The second question is whether it matters which of the major of the parties hold the reins of government—this we should see as the question of "government partisanship."

The partisan polarization question is analytically prior in the sense that we would not expect government partisanship to matter greatly if policy consensus among the major parties is strong, but partisan polarization does not necessarily mean that government partisanship matters. As McCarty makes clear in chapter 7, the deep polarization that has come to characterize American parties since the 1980s persisted in the face of the financial crisis of 2007 and 2008 and the ensuing recession. There can be little doubt that a Republican administration would have pursued different policy priorities from those of the Obama administration, but partisan polarization in the context of American political institutions, most notably the supermajoritarian rules of the Senate, effectively constrained the effects of government partisanship even before the Republicans gained a House majority in the 2010 midterm election. Put simply, the partisan identity of the ruling party mattered less than ideology alone would have led us to expect.

The Japanese story recounted in chapter 9 is strikingly similar to the American on the partisanship dimension. In this case too, a Left-leaning and reform-minded government elected by a landslide in the wake of the global economic crisis has been constrained by institutional intricacies and subsequent electoral setbacks. The story of Ireland and southern Europe, as recounted in chapter 6, is also one where government partisanship had little effect on policymaking, though in these cases, the constraints came less from domestic institutions than from external pressures. Finally, the chapter 5 comparison of France and Germany shows the policy contrasts between two governments run by center-right parties.

In light of these case studies, it is remarkable that Ansell's comparative analysis of fiscal and financial government responses to the Great Recession reveals significant partisan effects. Chapter 11 usefully distinguishes between spending increases and tax cuts as alternative means to achieve fiscal stimulus and indicates that the partisan composition of government only matters for fiscal policy responses in countries that experienced major housing booms in the period leading up to the Great Recession. In these countries, right-leaning governments cut taxes more and increased spending less than left-leaning governments. With regard to the financial sector, chapter 11 suggests that government bailouts and new regulatory measures are linked and involve partisan politics too. Relative to governments dominated by centrist or left-leaning parties, governments dominated by right-leaning parties have not only regulated less but also provided less money to the financial sector (at least in the form of liquidity injections and upfront financing). Recognizing that the quantitative analysis in chapter 11 is preliminary, the question of how its results are to be reconciled with the case studies presented in this volume deserves further research and thinking. Setting this task of reconciliation aside, it seems clear that government partisanship alone provides relatively little leverage on the question of why government responses to economic crises differ.

Organized Interests and Class Coalitions   Organized interests are certainly part of the causal stories told here but are not a focal point for any of the essays. This may be due, in part, to the authors' individual research questions (or to the relatively short time frame of the study), but it is noteworthy in the context of a larger literature in comparative political economy. After all, the seminal *Politics of Hard Times* concluded with the observation that the mobilization of organized interests had increased markedly by the 1970s and 1980s and that "their role in explaining outcomes" had increased as well (Gourevitch 1986, 230).

In comparison with the literature on crisis politics in the 1970s, the absence of any sustained discussion of the role of labor unions in this volume is particularly noteworthy. Although Lindvall argues in chapter 8 that Sweden's successful crisis reaction derived (in part) from the fact that unions and employers had established a new, more cooperative, labor regime, the role of unions in shaping crisis responses in our other cases appears less obvious. Schelkle asserts in chapter 5 that the corporatist structures that should have brought class actors together in Germany "played no discernible role" in the crafting of policy there and that in France, "a get-together of social partners" was simply "staged" to legitimate the government's plan. In chapter 10, Barnes and Wren point out that Ireland's public-sector unions proved unable to maintain their sheltered position after 2008, despite their long-standing pre-crisis consensus with the country's financial and construction sectors. In chapter 6, Armingeon and Bacarro go further and argue that in Ireland and southern Europe, trade unions were reduced to either mobilizing for fights that were "unlikely to produce results" or to making concessions that brought them "nothing" beyond symbolic recognition.

In chapters 12 and 9, Rueda and Tiberghien make the point that labor market outsiders were even more powerless than unionized workers both before and after the Great Recession occurred. These outsiders—immigrants, the unskilled, first-time job seekers, and the precariously employed—had few political resources and (in the period of this study) little if any effect on policymaking. Much of the shock of the Great Recession was borne (and continues to be borne) by those who are not incorporated in class associations at all.

The social actors that figure most prominently in our collection's causal stories are the financial sector and homeowners. Chapter 7 highlights the extraordinary and lasting influence of the financial sector in the United States (see also Hacker and Pierson 2010), but the financial sector is a key player in cases from Japan to Ireland. Chapter 9 shows the strong association between government aid to the financial sector and the sector's contribution to GDP, but massive bank bailouts were undertaken (as noted) in LMEs, CMEs, and mixed cases as well. As long as EU and other government officials continue to give primacy to the goal of "improving the business environment" (European Commission 2010, 30), supporting the financial and insurance industries on which the business environment depends will continue to be a top policy priority.

Homeowners do not figure in our collection as formally organized interests, but the political implications of the growth in their numbers are profound. They were obviously integral to the housing boom that sustained the liberal growth model and fuelled the crisis in the first place (chapter 10). However, their increased numbers may be most consequential for the crafting and maintenance of coalitions in the aftermath of the boom itself. As easy credit made homeownership more accessible, a sizeable group of homeowners has emerged even among people with below median income. In the liberal economies, homeowners came to constitute 65 percent of the population by 2002 (chapter 11) and grew significantly in number after that. In Ireland and the United Kingdom, "half the poor" came to own their own home (chapter 10), but homeownership also became a cross-class phenomenon in nonliberal economies in southern Europe and Scandinavia (chapter 11). As citizens of various income levels become owners of wealth, the maintenance of associations and alliances based on class and sector becomes more difficult. The sorts of associations and coalitions that loomed large in the literature on earlier economic crises may well play a muted role in this project because their role in society has changed over time. We expand on this point as we turn to explaining why responses to the Great Recession differed from responses to the Long Recession.

Explaining Cross-Temporal Variation

Peter Gourevitch's classic treatment of crisis politics in the 1930s and 1970s makes no reference whatsoever to homeowners or even to the housing sector more generally (1986). Rather, it focuses on collective actors representing classes and (or) manufacturing sectors. The contrast here is emblematic of how profoundly the political landscapes of advanced capitalist societies have changed in the past three to four decades. The differences between crisis responses across time are rooted in these changed political landscapes. Contemporary government leaders adopted a narrower and substantively different set of policy options because their institutional environment presented them with a very different set of constraints and incentives.

The narrowing of the menu of policy options must be attributed in part to the emergence and strengthening of international organizations. The emergence of the WTO in 1995 and of the ECB and EMU in 1998 constrained government choices in concrete ways. As chapters 3 and 5 stress, WTO and EU obligations curtailed the ability of governments to engage in protectionist measures and to provide subsidies to domestic producers. The EMU prevented devaluations in all its member states. The ECB controlled (and controls) monetary policy in the eurozone and, for the countries with sovereign debt crises, economic policy more generally. None of these constraints existed in the 1970s and early 1980s.

Just as these institutional changes made certain options less likely, other changes made the new reliance on fiscal stimulus more likely. Low levels of inflation, and a new confidence in government capacity to control it, made fiscal Keynesianism a much more attractive option than it had been in the past. The institutional practices that allowed for the moderation of price inflation (or the Great Moderation as it came to be called) were not in place during the Long Recession. Quite the contrary, according to Ben Bernanke (2004), they actually resulted from "the lessons of the 1970s"—but the fact that price inflation had been substantially lower for decades (chapter 11) made the nearly universal reliance on fiscal stimuli possible. That the 1970s left lessons for economic policymakers illustrates Lindvall's chapter 8 argument that governments (sometimes) learn from the past. To the extent that these lessons result in changed institutions or, at least, changed behaviors, we should not expect consistency over time.

We certainly have not seen consistency over time in the use of industrial policy, and this is is also due to a changed political landscape. The focus of state intervention switched to the financial sector in part because the Great Recession began as a financial crisis. But the different origins of the more recent recession cannot explain why sectoral interventions were consistently framed as temporary and market enhancing, or why governments often failed to initiate a broader set of interventions in the face of lasting unemployment and increasing inequality. Differences in origins also fail to explain why contemporary crisis responses have done so little to expand either active labor market policies or welfare support programs more generally.

To understand the differences in the scope and framing of crisis responses we have to turn to at least four major changes that have transpired since the Long Recession. First, organized labor, which was pivotal in shaping industrial and labor market policies in the 1970s, has been weakened dramatically by both neoliberalism and deindustrialization. The weakening is most obvious in liberal economies but affects many hybrid and coordinated economies as well. These structural changes, plus the implications of ownership just discussed, help explain why very few governments involved trade unions in managing the Great Recession (Hassel 2011).

Beyond weakening trade unions, deindustrialization has altered the relative power of manufacturing versus finance capital in a broad range of countries. This second change has, in turn, weakened the sector-specific coalitions of employers and unionized workers that shaped industrial policy interventions in the past. Ireland provides a classic example of the displacement of manufacturing by nontradables but the decline of manu-

Figure 1.1   Manufacturing versus Financial Sector Value Added as a
Percentage of GDP

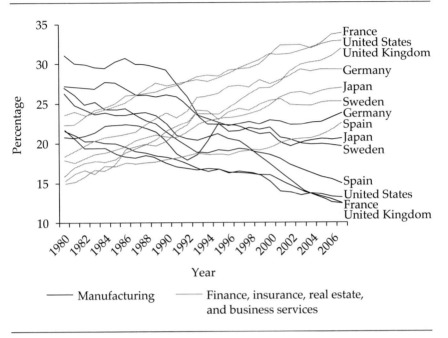

Source: Authors' compilation based on OECD (2011).

facturing in countries that have been export leaders has sometimes been dramatic as well. Figure 1.1 illustrates the widespread nature of the trend.

As Tiberghien notes in chapter 9, Japan's manufacturing sector decreased by 18 percent between 1999 and 2005 alone. In most of our cases, manufacturing has decreased so much that it provides 20 percent or less of all employment (Thelen 2011, 16). As a result, the cross-class coalitions that were central to crisis responses in the past are "no longer is a position to exercise leadership for the economy as a whole" (Thelen 2011, 38; Martin and Thelen 2007). That the automotive sector benefitted from intervention in 2008 and 2009 while other manufacturing industries did not is due in large part to the sector's almost unique ability to maintain sector-specific cross-class coalitions despite deindustrialization.

The growth of new social divisions that cross-cut class identities is a third change that helps explain historical differences in crisis reactions. The sectors of society that would have benefitted from more activist employment programs, or an expansion of welfare services in the aftermath of the Great Recession, were unable or unwilling to mobilize in broad coalitions in favor of a different outcome in the period we studied. Why? First, the divisions between labor market insiders and outsiders have grown over time and made coalitions more difficult. Second, massive immigration has transformed the political landscape in all but a few rich democracies since the 1980s. Divisions around immigration have complicated the task of mobilization further, divided the labor movement as a whole and, in countries such as France, turned traditional left-wing constituents toward the xenophobic right. Finally, the growth of what Ansell in chapter 11 calls *asset dominance* has also complicated the creation of constituencies that might have pressed for more redistributive crisis reforms. Beginning in the early 1980s, precisely when the welfare state was being challenged by neoliberalism and when inequality began to rise, citizens in many advanced capitalist countries increasingly came to depend, in Ansell's words, "on the value of their assets both for day-to-day income (using the value of their asset as collateral) and for unemployment or retirement" income.

Coupled with home ownership, stocks, bonds, and other financial assets have come to play an increasing role in people's retirement plans through pension funds and direct purchase. Research in the United States suggests that ownership of even small stock holdings has the potential to transform people's beliefs about their fundamental political interests (Rahn 2011). Whether this is true elsewhere remains to be seen. We can be certain, however, that the decline of organized labor, the decline of manufacturing, massive immigration, and what Colin Crouch (2009) has aptly called the privatization of Keynesianism makes the political identities of today's citizens decidedly different from those of their predecessors in the 1970s. No wonder their political behavior differs as well.

The near extinction of political parties that offer a challenge to capitalism marks a fourth consequential change from the 1970s. The days when communist parties could mobilize and successfully force the state to play a more active role in the economy have waned, at least for now. This situation serves the interests of those who benefit most directly from the contemporary varieties of capitalism but it also serves the interests of center-right and center-left parties. These facts together explain why government responses to the Great Recession have been framed, and indeed crafted, as market enhancing. As Lindvall reminds us in chapter 8, parties generally "prefer to maintain the status quo rather than agreeing to change institutional equilibriums in ways that might do damage to their long-term political interests." Economic reforms that "might be expected to have" even "indirect effects on how these institutions operate" are unlikely to garner party support. Thus, crisis responses were framed (and designed) as they were precisely to underscore (and ensure) institutional continuity. But why was this the case? In other words, why was more discontinuity not possible? This question brings us full circle, back to our opening discussion of crisis and opportunity and to our concluding section.

CONCLUSION

It is commonplace in the comparative political economy literature to view economic crises as critical junctures, characterized by electoral realignments, the emergence of new social coalitions, institutional change, and policy innovation. It is also common to argue that these dynamic processes are driven partially by international factors, but largely by domestic interests and institutions. This perspective is developed most forcefully in Gourevitch's analysis of political realignments in response to the three main crises of industrial capitalism prior to the Great Recession (1986).

The chapters in this volume reveal politics that bear only a partial resemblance to the politics of crises past. Two partial similarities and one major difference stand out. In terms of partial similarities, the politics of the Great Recession are still largely shaped by domestic factors in the United States, Japan, and the wealthier countries of the EU. However, this is not the case for countries struggling with sovereign debt crises. In Ireland, Portugal, Spain, Greece, and possibly Italy, international politics and institutions have trumped even fundamental democratic institutions such as political parties, at least in the short term.

A second partial similarity concerns policy innovations and institutional change. Governments have certainly responded to the Great Recession with some of both. Even in the United States, the financial sector is now subject to somewhat more stringent regulations and, in the institutional realm, a major new agency to protect financial consumers has been created (on paper, if not in fact). Yet, by and large, governments did not respond to the Great Recession with either striking policy innovations or dramatic institutional changes. In the United States, Japan, and the wealthier countries of the EU, governments responded with tax cuts and temporary, narrowly targeted relief programs, in many cases followed quickly by dramatic fiscal austerity measures. In countries with sovereign debt crises, policy innovation took the form of harsh austerity programs almost immediately.

The absence of either radical policy innovation or dramatic institutional change is due to what appears to be a major difference between the Great Recession and its predecessors: no powerful new social coalitions seem to have emerged to take advantage of the opportunity for dramatic change.

Old coalitions have certainly broken down. In Japan, the coalition of business and banking interests around the LDP broke down and dislodged the party that had ruled Japan for most of the postwar period (chapter 9). In Ireland, the coalition of developers and bankers around Fianna Fail also collapsed (chapter 10). But no truly new coalition has filled the void in either case. Japan's center-left party got elected by a landslide but never got the support it needed for its redistributive agenda. Ireland's Labor Party increased its mandate in the 2011 general election but fell far short of the victory forecast in opinion polls, leaving the center-right Fianna Gael as the dominant party in the new coalition government.

Those who hoped that the Great Recession might provide the opportunity for the forging of new coalitions to lessen economic inequality must be sorely disappointed. Though an assortment of actors are mobilizing sporadic protests in the United States, Europe, and Japan, no successful new redistributive coalitions have yet emerged.[6] What we have seen instead is an increase in inequality, both within states and between states. We have also seen that not all the resistance to redistributive change has come from economic elites. The chapters that follow illustrate that more ambitious policy reactions to the Great Recession were often constrained by popular opinion. In the United States, only a bare majority of the public supported even the watered down version of the 2009 stimulus package and strong majorities did so only because of its tax cuts rather than its spending increases (chapter 7). In Japan, the redistributive programs sought by the JDP were stymied in part by popular resistance to an increase in consumption tax (chapter 9). Even in Sweden and the Nordic countries, it is likely that "a more comprehensive, prolonged program of government intervention in the economy" would not have been politically possible (chapter 8).

Of course the ultimate political impact of the Great Recession may be different from what we have observed so far. It is noteworthy that the electoral realignments and policy reorientations that we commonly associate with the crisis in the 1970s came about several years after the crisis began. The Long Recession started in 1973 and 1974, but it was not until 1979 through 1982 that its political ramifications were realized, with the path-breaking election victories of Margaret Thatcher in Britain, Ronald Reagan in the United States, and François Mitterrand in France as well as the shift to a center-right coalition under Helmut Kohl in Germany.[7]

Should current economic difficulties persist, new coalitions with a redistributive agenda may yet emerge, but if they do, they will have to confront an already established and powerful cross-class coalition that resists a more activist role for the state. This coalition is dominated by finance capital but it is clearly supported by more modest and more numerous property owners who seek shelter from taxes and from state control more generally. With governments in many rich democracies now implementing harsh austerity programs, this is the coalition that seems to have seized the latest opportunity for change.

The ideas in this introductory chapter were generated through a series of discussions that also included Larry Bartels. We thank Larry for his many intellectual insights and for his leadership role in organizing this project. We also thank the Russell Sage Foundation, the John Fell Fund of Oxford University, and Princeton's Institute for International and Regional Studies for funding as well as Matthew Powell and Nahyun Yoo for research assistance.

NOTES

1. As measured by Dow Jones indices, U.S. industrial stocks have recovered, but stocks in general have not.
2. Japan's change in GDP in the first quarter of 2011 was surely affected by the earthquake of March 11, 2011, but the economy had already slipped in the last quarter of 2010.
3. This generalization seems to hold even if we take into account the fact that GDP contracted more sharply in 2008 and 2009 than between 1974 and 1976 or 1980 and 1982 (see Pontusson and Raess 2012).
4. Toru Fujioka and Aki Ito, "Japan May Sell Yen for Second Day to Protect Economy," *Bloomberg*, September 15, 2010.
5. For an empirical analysis questioning the idea that varieties of capitalism were associated with distinctive macroeconomic policies in the period from 1980 to 2002, see Amable and Azizi 2011.
6. As a follow-up to this study, Larry Bartels and Nancy Bermeo are examining citizen reactions to the economic crisis in an edited volume tentatively titled *The Costs of Crisis: Popular Reactions to the Great Recession*.
7. Similarly, a recent paper shows that in many countries center-right parties did well in the first elections after the onset of the Great Depression, and that that crisis did not produce a swing of the Left until the second round of elections (Lindvall 2011).

REFERENCES

Amable, Bruno, and Karim Azizi. 2011. "Varieties of Capitalism and Varieties of Macro-economic Policy." *MPIfG* discussion paper 11/6. Köln: Max-Planck-Institute für Gesellschaftsforschung.

Beramendi, Pablo. 2010. "Fiscal Legacies and Tax Policy Responses to the Financial Crisis." Paper presented to the Princeton University conference on Comparative Responses to the Economic Crisis. Princeton, N.J. (March 27–29, 2010).

Bernanke, Ben. 2004. "The Great Moderation." Remarks by Governor Ben S. Bernanke, Meetings of the Eastern Economic Association. Washington, D.C. (February 20, 2004).

Crouch, Colin. 2009. "Privatised Keynesianism: An Unacknowledged Policy Regime." *British Journal of Politics & International Relations* 11(August): 382–99.

European Commission. 2010. "An Integrated Industrial Policy for the Globalisation Era: Putting Competitiveness and Sustainability at Centre Stage." Brussels: European Commission, October 28, 2010.

European Commission on Enterprise and Industry. 2010. "2nd High Level Conference on Industrial Competitiveness: The Role of Policy and Markets in Difficult Times." Brussels (April 26, 2010).

Garrett, Geoffrey. 1998. *Partisan Politics in the Global Economy*. New York: Cambridge University Press.

Gourevitch, Peter. 1986. *Politics in Hard Times*. Ithaca, N.Y.: Cornell University Press.

Hacker, Jacob, and Paul Pierson. 2010. *Winner-Take-All Politics*. New York: Simon & Schuster.

Hall, Peter A. forthcoming. "The Political Origins of Our Economic Discontents: Contemporary Adjustment Problems in Historical Perspective." In *Politics in the New Hard Times*, edited by Miles Kahler and David Lake. Ithaca, N.Y.: Cornell University Press.

Hall, Peter A., and Daniel Gingerich. 2009. "Varieties of Capitalsm and Institutional Complementarities in the Political Economy." *British Journal of Political Science* 39(3): 449–82.

Hall, Peter, and David Soskice, eds. 2001. *Varieties of Capitalism*. Oxford: Oxford University Press.

Hassel, Anke. 2011. "Universalism and Segmentalism: Adjustment Patterns of Economic Interests in Postindustrial Economies." Paper presented at the Swiss Federal Institute of Technology conference The Future of Democratic Capitalism. Zürich (June 16–19, 2011).

Haugh, David, Annabelle Mourougane, and Olivier Chatal. 2010. "The Automobile Industry in and beyond the Crisis" *OECD Economics Department* working papers no. 745. Paris: Organisation for Economic Co-operation and Development.

Iversen, Torben, and David Soskice. 2006. "Electoral Institutions and the Politics of Coalitions: Why Some Democracies Redistribute More Than Others." *American Political Science Review* 100(2): 165–81.

Katzenstein, Peter, ed. 1978. *Between Power and Plenty*. Madison: University of Wisconsin Press.

Kee, Hiau Looi, Cristina Neagu, and Alessandro Nicita. 2010. "Is Protectionism on the Rise? Assessing National Trade Policies During the Crisis of 2008." *Policy Research* working paper 5274. Washington, D.C.: The World Bank.

Kwon, Hyeok Yong, and Jonas Pontusson. 2010. "Globalization, Labour Power, and Partisan Politics Revisited." *Socio-economic Review* 8(2): 251–81.

Lindvall, Johannes. 2011. "The Political Effects of Two Great Crises." Paper presented at the 18th International Conference of Europeanists. Barcelona (June 20–22, 2011).

Martin, Cathie Jo, and Kathleen Thelen. 2007. "The State and Coordinated Capitalism: Contributions of the Public Sector to Social Solidarity in Post-industrial Societies." *World Politics* 60(October): 1–36.

McNamara, Kathleen. 1998. *The Currency of Ideas*. Ithaca, N.Y.: Cornell University Press.

Organisation of Economic Co-operation and Development (OECD). 2011. *Structural Analysis (STAN) Databases C15T37, C65T74*. Available at: http://stats.oecd.org (accessed September 2011).

Page, S. A. B. 1981. "The Revival of Protectionism and Its Consequences for Europe." *Journal of Common Market Studies* 20(1): 17–40.

Pierson, Paul. 2001. "Coping with Permanent Austerity." In *The New Politics of the Welfare State*. Oxford: Oxford University Press.

Pontusson, Jonas, and Damian Raess. 2012. "How (and Why) Is This Time Different? The Politics of Economic Crisis in Western Europe and the US." *Annual Review of Political Science* 15: 13–33.

Rahn, Wendy. 2011. "A Ticket to Ride: Citizen Investors' Political Response to the Market Roller Coaster." Paper presented at Princeton University, February 3.

Scharpf, Fritz. 1991. *Crisis and Choice in European Social Democracy*. Ithaca, N.Y.: Cornell University Press.

Schmitt, John. 2011. "Labor Market Policy in the Great Recession." Washington, D.C.: Center for Economic Policy and Research.

Soskice, David. 1999. "Divergent Production Regimes." In *Contemporary Capitalism*, edited by Herbert Kitschelt, Peter Lange, Gary Marks, and John D. Stephens. New York: Cambridge University Press.

Stiglitz, Joseph E., and Carl E. Walsh. 2006. *Economics*, 4th ed. New York: W. W. Norton.

Thelen, Kathleen. 2011. "Varieties of Capitalism: Trajectories of Liberalization and the New Politics of Social Solidarity." *Annual Review of Political Science* (online version) 15(December): 1–23.

Zysman, John. 1983. *Governments, Markets, and Growth: France and the Politics of Industrial Change*. Ithaca, N.Y.: Cornell University Press.

PART I | International Origins, Organizations, and Constraints

Chapter 2 | Modern Capitalism and the Advanced Nation State: Understanding the Causes of the Crisis

Torben Iversen and David Soskice

WE ARGUE IN this chapter that the crisis illuminates the relationship between modern capitalism and the advanced nation state. Advanced nation states are deeply concerned—in a world in which they can no longer use protection, direct intervention, or subsidies—with promoting the interests of their high value-added sectors, which are central to their innovation and human capital investment systems, as well as the source of well-paid employment and tax revenue. In relation to the crisis, comparative institutional advantages led the U.S. and U.K. governments to be concerned with regulatory environments that promoted, among other things, their innovative and high-risk financial sectors; they also led Germany and Japan to fashion or maintain regulatory environments that promoted high value-added export sectors. As we develop the argument, powerful domestic high value-added sectors increase the power of the advanced nation state in the global knowledge economy, just as the differences between those sectors across nation states explain why governments have not been and are not interested in pooling economic sovereignty. Rather, they have wanted to hone relevant regulatory systems for the benefit of their advanced economic sectors.

Two central regulatory systems were key to the crisis. The first was the system of financial regulation, and in particular the set of rules governing the leverage of so-called highly leveraged financial institutions (HLFIs) and the systemic monitoring of these institutions. The second was the system governing macroeconomic regulation, including the operation of fiscal and monetary policy. The financial regulatory system failed to prevent major HLFIs from developing exceptionally high leverage multiples in financial systems in which major HLFIs were systemically interdependent. And the macro regime failed—indeed was not designed—to prevent the development of global imbalances.

That these two regulatory systems, however, should have proved dysfunctional would have been surprising to many commentators through the two decades before the crisis, the two decades in which the systems took concrete shape. The systems imposed something like international uniformity on macroeconomic management and national financial regulation for the first time since Bretton Woods. In the system of inflation targeting, independent central banks were given responsibility for macroeconomic management and used interest rates to return deviations of inflation and unemployment to their target or equilibrium values. They did so within a more or less common macroeconomic framework, that of the so-called New Keynesian macroeconomic model. Many policy-oriented macroeconomists agreed with Ben Bernanke's assessment that this system was responsible for the Great Moderation in inflation and unemployment since the early 1990s. In addition, that inflation targeting should be carried out without international coordination was not disputed. Indeed, inflation targeting within the New Keynesian framework and without international coordination is still generally accepted.

Equally, the broad regulatory system of financial liberalization and international mobility of financial assets and financial institutions became widely agreed upon over the last two decades. As with the macroeconomic system, the regulators were primarily national, minor qualifications for the EU being the exception. Again, this was widely endorsed by professional economists, at least in relation to the advanced economies. With hindsight, one can be critical of these arrangements, but many in the business community saw, and still see, financial liberalization as a positive development for at least three reasons. First, it generated competition for domestic banks and led to reductions over time in borrowing costs. This reflected the oligopolistic structure of much domestic commercial and retail banking that had developed since the 1930s. Second, the great rise in international competition in goods and services associated with the development of the global knowledge economy led large companies to use financial markets to pressure employees, including management, to become more flexible. Third, and as a consequence of this, risk, openness, and the complexity of business investment increased, generating the need for complex financial derivatives to hedge risks.

In broad terms, then, these two key regulatory systems were accepted and approved by the governments of the advanced countries, as well as by their business communities. But the systems were not internationally administered, nor were there detailed international agreements on their rules. For example, as far as banking regulation was concerned, the attempts to do this via the Bank for International Settlements (BIS) and Basel II were unsuccessful; and the story, though unending, of the International Accounting Standards Board (IASB) and common accounting standards is similar. The broad principles were accepted internationally, but both the detailed rule-making and regulatory authorities were at the national level. Interpretation of rules in specific cases, monitoring of financial institutions, sanctions, and assessment of systemic risk, as well as interest rate setting and fiscal policy choices that affected external imbalance, all took place at the national level.

The basic argument of this chapter is that national control of these systems was not accidental. Instead, in our view, national governments—especially of advanced countries—are deeply concerned with promoting the high value-added sectors of their economies, in which they enjoy comparative institutional advantage. Because these sectors vary across countries, governments want to control the detailed operations of regulatory systems in their own environments.

There is now little dispute that the U.K. and the U.S. governments allowed a lax interpretation of the financial regulations governing leverage, both in the valuation of the risky assets that HLFIs owned and in the assessment of bank capital; we argue that they took this position because they saw it as beneficial to one of the most important economic sectors in which the United States and the United Kingdom had comparative institutional advantage. It was certainly true that the large banks were politically powerful in the United States, but this was far less so in the United Kingdom with its centralized and disciplined political system—yet Thatcher had made the first move to the liberalization of the City with the Big Bang in 1985 and Blair had enthusiastically supported light-touch financial regulation.

Analogously, in terms of external surpluses, the governments of Germany, Japan, China, and other nations whose leading high value-added sectors are export oriented were not and are still not prepared to accept constraints on external surpluses. Such constraints would imply expansionary fiscal or monetary policies generating real exchange rate appreciation, thus damaging the interests of the sectors in which they have comparative institutional advantage. The precise arguments are spelled out in the following sections.

HOW THE CRASH OCCURRED

How did the combination of global imbalances and loose regulation of leverage of systemically interdependent financial institutions lead to the crash? The crash was not simply financial and not simply confined to the two epicenters of the original implosion, Wall Street and the City of London. It was also a most dramatic recession of the real economy, and both financial and economic collapse was propagated internationally. We sketch out how the financial crash was the initiating event.

Let us first look at the financial implosion. In a simple model, assets can be divided up into risky assets and safe short-term assets, such as treasury bills or short-term loans to financial institutions. The key institutions in the initial story are the big investment banks located in Wall Street and the City, including the investment banking subsidiaries of the major European and Japanese banks. Hedge funds play a quite subsidiary role with generally much lower leverage. The big investment banks undertake a wide range of activities, but a large part of their profits are earned from borrowing on a short-term basis and earning a higher rate of return by using these funds to buy risky and typically longer-term assets. A simple example of an HLFI balance sheet with some numbers is presented in table 2.1.

Here the leverage is ten—the capital is multiplied up ten times. A critical issue is the value of the institution's capital and how it changes. Suppose the HLFI starts up by raising equity of $10; that is its initial capital. It then borrows $90, and buys 100 risky assets at a price of $1 each. We assume $90 is the maximum that can be borrowed given capital of $10, and the known risk attached to the risky assets. For a risk-neutral HLFI, the leverage is the maximum that short-term lenders will allow—assuming the HLFI is making a positive marginal return with the maximum leverage. At the end of a year, it earns 7 percent on the risky assets and pays 3 percent on the short-term borrowing; assume the value of the risky assets has not changed; then profits are 4.3, so the return on capital is 43 percent. If no dividend is paid, profits are added to existing capital and that capital increases to $14.30. If investors adopt similar principles as before, they are now prepared to lend $130, and the HLFI buys additional risky assets so that its holding of risky assets is now $144.30. The next year it distributes all its profits so that its retained earnings are zero; hence capital remains at $14.30, still assuming the value of a risky asset stays at $1.

A critical element is what happens if, for whatever reason, the price of the risky assets changes. Work by John Geanakoplos (2010) and Hyun Shin (2010) has greatly increased understanding of the joint determination of risky asset prices and leverage ratios, and how big covarying swings in leverage and prices arise. The mechanics are as follows. If, for whatever

Table 2.1   Sample HLFI Balance Sheet

Assets	Liabilities
Risky assets 100	Short-term borrowing 90
	Capital 10

Source: Author's compilation.

reason, the price rises (basically some news that leads to a positive re-evaluation of their profitability or risk, hence to a generalized rise in their demand from HLFIs and other investors, hence to a higher price), HLFI accounting implies that the capital gain on existing risky assets is added to the existing capital. In the last example, if the risky asset price rises by 10 percent, then the capital gain is $14.40, and the HLFI's capital doubles to $28.70. There is now a multiplier process, because with a constant leverage the demand for risky assets by HLFIs will increase. Because the relative demand by HLFIs has now risen, risky assets will be sucked in from other investors to the HLFIs. This process continues until a new equilibrium is reached at multiplied-up prices and a higher leverage, reflecting the rise in the quantity of risky assets in the HLFIs.

If the reverse happens and the price falls by 10 percent, then the HLFI makes a capital loss of $14.40. Again the initial price fall, on the receipt of bad news, leads to a multiplied reaction. Of course, the asymmetry be-tween upward and downward cycles is that in the latter bankruptcy is possible. In this example the HLFI's capital is in fact wiped out with the initial price decline: and once this happens, the HLFI is bankrupt. The higher the leveraging of the capital, the smaller the price fall needed to bring about bankruptcy: a leverage of twenty requires a fall of only 5 percent, of forty (roughly the Lehmann multiplier), 2.5 percent.

The risky assets are in general not quite so dangerous as this makes them sound; they are typically complex loans or derivatives ultimately to households or companies at least partially secured against collateral, rather than equity. When initially sold, they were priced in terms of the available statistical information on past micro as well as macro risk patterns. Moreover, two financial instruments had been rapidly developing over the previous two decades, which had radically reduced the riskiness of individual assets. Securitization—through the use of collateral debt obligations (CDOs)—bundled loans such as mortgages, credit card debt, student loans, and bank loans, thus minimizing individual default risk, and cut the securitized packages into different risk tranches. Credit default swaps (CDSs) "insured" assets against a wide range of defaults.[1] These instruments were not new—in some form or other they had always existed—but they had expanded in a massive and increasingly complex way over the previous two decades. In turn both CDSs and CDOs were or could be rated by the rating agencies. As long as individual risks were idiosyncratic, at least not hugely positively correlated, these instruments acted effectively to reduce aggregate risk.

The two major problems with the development of this system were both based on the weight of a limited number of very large HLFIs, all of which invested in similar classes of risky assets, including CDOs and CDSs, and the relatively shallow market for these assets outside the HL-FIs. First, if the price of a class of assets fell exogenously, and we will see why it might, even without provoking a bankruptcy, it required all the HLFIs to sell risky assets to restore their desired leverage ratios; this, though, implied significant price falls across their asset classes because they were the major buyers of these assets—there was no elastic outside market for them. This in turn generated a multiplier process of further asset sales, further price falls, and so on, to restore a leverage at which short-term borrowers would be prepared to lend. Second, *if* a large HLFI did get forced into bankruptcy, the system as a whole came under risk. This was directly because each major HLFI was engaged in the hugely profitable CDS business, so that a HLFI bankruptcy set to zero the value of all the CDSs it had issued and were held through the system. Next, it put under pressure the issuers (counterparties) of CDSs contingent on the bankruptcy of that HLFI—Lehmann's collapse was the major hit on AIG. In addition, the market was flooded with its erstwhile risky assets leading to further price falls in the relevant asset classes. Finally, it necessarily defaulted on some portion of its liabilities, of which a proportion came from other HLFIs, with knock on effects on the assets of the other HLFIs.

All of this was in principle consistent with agreed values of the risky assets. But a further and massive complication was the uncertainty of their value, which was a consequence of the absence of monitoring and detailed surveillance of the relevant markets. Now it became unclear whether other HLFIs might go bankrupt. And this led to an effective freezing of the market for short-term borrowing, as no financial institution was prepared to lend overnight without exceptionally high interest. This situation was unsustainable without the government support then forthcoming. In this sense, all the major HLFIs were probably too big to fail.

Global imbalances hugely magnified this process. The external surpluses of the net exporters played a dual role. On the one hand, they allowed U.S. consumers to spend above U.S. GDP, and U.S. consumers had to dissave to finance this deficit. On the other hand, the external surpluses provided short-term loans to the HLFIs to cover the acquisition of a large proportion of the risky assets—that is, securitized loans—that financed the consumption. They were of course also used, for example, by German banks in Germany to purchase the risky assets themselves.

The first point follows from the basic macroeconomic equation requiring that aggregate demand be equal to equilibrium output (GDP) in the medium term. In a simple model assume that all domestic expenditure is on consumption, C:

$$y^e = C + X - M$$

Equilibrium GDP, y^e, is equal to total demand for domestically produced goods and services, consumer expenditure, C, and exports, X, less that part of demand produced abroad, imports, M. Household savings, S, are $y^e - C$, so that

$$S = X - M$$

With $S < 0$, dissavings are exactly equal to the external deficit, $-S = X - M$. (With net investment, I, that is, gross investment less business savings, and a public sector deficit $G - T$, $X - M = (I - S) + (G - T)$, the foreign surplus is equal to the net private sector deficit and the public sector deficit.) With net investment and the public sector deficit zero, an external deficit is necessary to allow net household sector dissavings. Absent an external deficit, household dissavings would have required a public sector surplus or a surplus of business savings (retained earnings) over investment. Given the public sector deficit in much of the 2000s in both the United Kingdom and the United States, and only recently positive net business savings, global imbalances were central to the build-up to the crisis from a macroeconomic perspective.

The external surpluses had a second function: they provided short-term loans to the HLFIs to cover the acquisition of a large proportion of the risky assets (securitized loans) that financed the consumption "permitted" by the global imbalances. The surpluses of the exporting countries to the United States were possible only if the exporting countries were able to use the dollar proceeds such that they did not end up on the foreign exchanges. If no one had been prepared to hold the dollars, then the value of the dollar would have fallen until the surplus had been eliminated. Alternatively, traders might have absorbed the dollars when the depreciation was such as to generate expectations of an appreciation. The maintenance of a surplus therefore required that the dollars were used to purchase in-effect American assets. This could have taken many forms: direct investment in property or purchase of companies, investment in equities, and so on; and considerable investment took place in all these assets. But a major attraction of Wall Street was the safety of investing in short-term treasury bills and in short-term loans, at slightly higher rates, to the investment banks. The short-term market had very low transaction costs and was highly liquid; London offered similar opportunities on a smaller scale. Both London and Wall Street offered risky assets that appeared safe because of validation by the major rating agencies and the possibility of insurance through CDSs. Demand for loans from the housing, credit card, and automobile finance markets combined with a correspondingly massive supply of funds in the form of short-term loans to HLFIs and in purchases of securitized risky assets.

Had there been no global imbalances, a minor crash might have taken place. Hyman Minsky shows how on several occasions in the United States from the 1970s forward the collapse of a significant financial institution led to a downturn in the economy, albeit minimized by government deficits and lender-of-last-resort action by the Federal Reserve (1986). The scale of the financial crash in 2007 to 2009 was of a different order of magnitude than those of 1974 to 1975 and the early 1980s; here the global imbalances played a major role and despite the massive interventions of the authorities, the financial crash led to the worst crash in the real economy since the 1930s. The major effects of the real crash were felt primarily and initially in the United States and the United Kingdom, and spread through much of the world economy as American and British imports declined sharply, and as exporting countries felt financial pressures from their own bank failures as a result of investing in risky U.S. and U.K. assets.

Why did the financial crash lead to a crash in the real economy? The real economy crashed because consumer expenditure and business expenditure both collapsed. Three separate shocks hit both households and companies. First, bank and to a lesser extent mortgage lending, including trade credit, seized up. The reason was straightforward: as the interbank borrowing and lending market became inoperative for reasons we have seen in the financial crisis, banks became desperate to hold onto liquid assets, and thus cut lending sharply and called in loans. This move was reinforced by their concern with building up capital to avert the risk of bankruptcy, all the while facing the threat from hitherto reliable creditors of cutting lending to the banks. As bank lending dried up, both household expenditure and business expenditure, a proportion of which depended on trade credit, were sharply cut back. Second, household wealth fell as house and stock prices fell. Because it was in part on growing household wealth that households had based dissaving decisions, believing that they could rely on rising property and equity values for their pensions, the decline of all three led households to switch from dissaving into saving. Third, expectations in the business community about the future growth of markets changed dramatically and investment activity came close to a halt unless the costs of stopping were too great.

Finally, in the event of a serious financial crisis, inflation targeting loses some of its efficacy as the leading tool of demand management. The direct reason is a minimum (short-term) real rate of interest a central bank can impose. The nominal rate of interest is bounded below by zero; hence the real rate of interest—equal to the nominal rate less the expected rate of inflation—can never be set below minus the expected rate of inflation. Negative real rates of interest are thus quite possible with high inflation—precisely when the central bank does not want them. But in a serious crisis, expected inflation (well proxied by existing inflation) is close to zero, if not negative; and aggregate demand has typically fallen enough that only a negative real interest rate would push activity above the equilibrium level.

This weakness of the interest rate instrument is reinforced by two other factors. As bank lending dries up for the reasons we have seen, so households and companies cannot find willing lenders. In any case, the switch from dissaving into saving reflects the wealth effect dominating the substitution effect, so that for the relevant households a low interest rate now works in the opposite direction: the lower the interest rate, the more a household has to save to attain its pension target level of wealth.

Finally, how was the financial and real crash in the epicenter countries, the United States and the United Kingdom, propagated to the exporting countries? The collapse of aggregate demand in the epicenters transmitted itself directly by a collapse in epicenter imports, hence exporting country exports. It involved two mechanisms. Most important and obvious, the fall in epicenter GDP reduced household consumption and business investment, both implying a decreased demand for exports. More subtly, the prospect of low interest rates in the epicenters for some years led foreign exchange markets to depreciate the dollar and sterling against the euro and the yen in nominal and real terms, reinforcing the downward pressure on exports.

But a major factor limited the deflationary effect in the EU exporters and in Japan—the strength of the welfare state in these countries. In Japan, this took the form of a guarantee of lifetime employment in the more highly skilled parts of the economy; in more informal ways similar arrangements, though less widespread, operated in South Korea and Taiwan. In the formal welfare states of northern Europe, skilled workers either got high replacement rates if they became unemployed, were protected by employment protection, or benefitted from part-time arrangements that underwrote a high proportion of their full-time net disposable income; they were also protected by collective bargains from falling wages. We would argue that the availability of these mechanisms—formal welfare states or less formal understandings—is a consequence of the co-specificity of skill investments in skill-intensive exporting sectors (Iversen 2005; Estevez-Abe, Iversen, and Soskice 2001). We explain subsequently why countries like Germany did and do not make significant use of discretionary fiscal policy, and how that reluctance also reflected the institutional incentive structures of export-oriented economies.

Thus fiscal policy becomes the more effective instrument for stimulating demand, at least for a period. But where the necessary fiscal policy is discretionary, as in the United States and the United Kingdom, there is both a political lag in gaining the consent of the legislature, and an implementation lag because government expenditure cannot easily be turned on like a tap. A period therefore elapses before either monetary or fiscal policy becomes operative and effective, and during this period aggregate demand is likely collapsing, adding to adverse expectations of both households and companies.

EXPORT-ORIENTED CAPITALISM: MECHANISMS OF DOMESTIC RESTRAINT AND EXPORT PROMOTION

In this section, we argue that the institutions of coordinated market economies (CMEs) generate restraint in the use of resources in a variety of ways. The argument is not that these are the intentional consequences of these institutions (they may be or may have been), but that they are the consequences of strong institutional complementarities.

Restrictive Monetary Policy and Real Wage Restraint in the Traded Sector

A number of studies have shown empirically that where wage bargaining is coordinated, central banks are conservative. In line with a number of papers in the political economy and macroeconomics literature, we explain why that is the case (Hall and Franzese 1998; Iversen 1998; Soskice and Iversen 2000). In terms of inflation targeting, what does this mean? In inflation targeting, central banks primarily target inflation, target inflation rates are broadly similar across inflation targeting regimes (2 percent to 2.5 percent), and it is an accepted part of the model that optimal unemployment (output) for central bankers is equilibrium unemployment (output), the unemployment (output or activity) rate at which inflation is stable. Although this much is common, the difference between more conservative and more accommodating central banks rests on the sharpness with which central banks respond with interest rate changes to inflation or output shocks that push the economy off its target combination of target inflation rate and equilibrium output rate. The conservative central bank will aim to move the economy quickly back to equilibrium after a positive inflation shock, for example, implying the use of the short-term real interest rate to push up unemployment enough above equilibrium to bring inflation back down rapidly.

Unions in the traded sectors of the economy are sensitive to the increased interest rate because it pushes up the real exchange rate, putting export- or import-competing employment at risk. Export sector companies are similarly sensitive and for related reasons. The objective function of a central bank is generally modeled as a loss function, say

$$-L_0 = -\sum_{t=0} \mu^t [(Y_t - Y^e)^2 + \beta(\pi_t - \pi^T)^2],$$

where Y_t is output in period t, Y^e is equilibrium output, π is the inflation rate in t, and π^2 is the target rate of inflation. The central bank's goal is to minimize over time divergences from its target combination. In principle, if the conservatism of a central bank is defined by its preferences, it will have a high β (more concerned to get inflation back to target) and a high μ (concerned to get back to target quickly). But the political economy argument relates to central bank behavior and does not depend on central bank preferences. The behavior of central banks is manifested in the *monetary rule* (or Taylor rule) it adopts: this tells us how the central bank will change the short-term real interest rate in response to an inflation shock.

The argument is that the choice of central bank accommodation is endogenous to the coordination of wage bargaining. At first sight paradoxically, if the number of uncoordinated wage and price setters in an economy is high, the central bank adopts a more accommodating response to above-target inflation, though its response is more conservative when wage bargaining is coordinated. With many wage and price setters, a potentially sharper response to an increase in aggregate inflation by the central bank has no dampening effect on the individual wage or price setter because they know that their individual wage or price increase will have no effect on aggregate inflation and hence on the central bank response. The central bank will therefore tend to the accommodating end of interest rate policy. But where wage bargaining is highly coordinated, where unions and business organizations are large and powerful, the individual union or employer group will pay considerable attention to how sharply the central bank will respond to its wage increases because these will have a noticeable effect on the rate of inflation. Hence coordinated wage bargaining will lead central banks to adopt non-accommodating positions: this turns out to be the case (Soskice and Iversen 2000; Iversen 1998).

The form of the Taylor rule in an open economy is $r = r^* + \gamma (\pi - \pi^T)$, where r is the domestic short-term real rate of interest and r^* is the world short-term real rate of interest. In the standard derivation, the central bank takes the Phillips curve as given and chooses its optimal Taylor rule. The standard derivation shows the central bank interest response to an inflation shock, with

$$\gamma = \frac{1}{a\left(\alpha + \dfrac{1}{\alpha\beta}\right)},$$

increases in β, the conservativeness parameter in the CB loss function, in α, the responsiveness of inflation to labor market conditions in the Phillips curve, and decreases in a the responsiveness of future output to the interest rate. Once the central bank faces a small number of large wage and price setters, however, we are in a Stackelberg game: the central bank makes the first move by choosing a Taylor rule; wage and price setters optimize wage-setting based on that—the larger γ, the more restrained the wage setting—and this determines the Phillips curve with the response coefficient in the Phillips curve as a function of γ; and the CB then chooses γ to minimize its loss function.

Restrictive Fiscal Policy and Real Wage Restraint in Sheltered Sectors

It has been noted by many commentators that CMEs are relatively fiscally restrained, measured in a variety of ways, notably in terms of the public sector deficit (for example, Soskice 2007). This is not a statement about the size of the government sector nor about the extent of transfers. In the European CMEs, the general tendency for center-left government has led to relatively high provision of public services or public-private services operating within a publicly defined framework. This is even more the case for transfer payments both in terms of insurance and redistribution. Why then the seemingly paradoxical fiscal restraint?

First, public sector labor markets are both unionized and heavily protected. That a relatively large proportion of the skilled workforce is in the traded sector has reduced the pool of available labor for the public sector. Indeed, in some countries, centralized unions presided deliberately over wage compression between traded and sheltered sectors, aided in the sheltered sectors by the relative tightness of these labor markets. Given relatively strong public-sector unionism, perceived fiscal restraint has been important in holding down public-sector wages to avoid raising taxes.

But second, and explaining the significance of fiscal conservatism in addition to monetary conservatism, conservative monetary policy set up quite different incentives for unions in the sheltered sector in comparison to those in the export sectors. Whereas export-sector unions saw the threat of increased interest rates in response to rising inflation as raising the exchange rate and generating unemployment, public-sector unions were relatively well protected against redundancies and saw an appreciating exchange rate primarily in terms of lower import prices. Hence, for public-sector unions a restrictive monetary policy regime generates positive rather than negative incentives for high wage settlements.

These factors stretched beyond the public sector into many other parts of the private sheltered sector. The nature of decision-making, both in the economy and in the polity of these societies, has been one of coordination and neo-corporatism. In the private sheltered sector, even when unions are not strong, associational principles apply to business. Hence government needs fiscal restraint to deal with well-organized lobbies. Switzerland is a good example of this.

Thus we argue that fiscal and monetary conservatism reinforce each other in export-oriented economies, especially when wage- and price-setters are well organized in both open and sheltered sectors of the economy. The only exception is when wage bargaining is so centralized that a single union can internalize all the potential externalities of wage bargaining. As we have shown elsewhere (Iversen 1998; Soskice and Iversen 2000), this explains the relatively accommodating behavior of Scandinavian governments over a long period. But because collective bargaining has become relatively more decentralized since the 1990s in the Scandinavian economies, these economies have adopted more conservative monetary and fiscal policies.

Real Wage Restraint in the Traded Sector and the Development of Skills

Export-oriented capitalism has operated at the national level over many decades through a complex set of coalitions to ensure that a suitably large proportion of the workforce is trained in the relatively specialist skills needed in high-quality export sectors (Iversen and Soskice 2010). One co-alition, between organized business and coordinated unions in the export sectors, and possibly—in the case of unions—in the sheltered sector as well, held down real wage growth sufficiently to expand export demand to create employment for newly trained skilled workers. Absent such re-straint in liberal economies, company-level unionization would push up real wages to prevent absorption of newly trained workers, and the incen-tive for training would be impeded. A second, political, coalition between left and center parties in the form of center-left governments, dominant in the European CMEs, supplied the resources for public-private sector train-ing in implicit exchange for the wage compression that came about as an increasing proportion of the workforce shifted into the export sector. Thus this mechanism conjointly generated wage restraint to shift out export sector demand and the training to enable a corresponding increase in the necessary supply of specialist export-sector skills.

Private Savings

As noted, the skills and assets characteristic of export-oriented econo-mies—for example, the skills needed to work with particular technologies and the particular technologies themselves—are specialized and may not be easily or fully redeployable outside a particular range of markets. This is basic to the Krugman view of trade. On the one hand, it provides a pow-erful incentive to develop as many export markets for the goods or ser-vices as possible (Krugman's economies of scale). On the other hand, it requires insurance in various forms to meet demand fluctuations. These incentives reinforce each other. Companies and employees, for example, will want some guarantee of long-term finance to tide over bad times without companies being forced to close and employees move elsewhere. This reflects in one form or another a guarantee of access to long-term bor-rowing. Second, as we have seen, export-oriented economies have devel-oped relatively strong insurance-based welfare states. Finally, and funda-mentally, companies and employees have a strong incentive to build up private wealth to cover fluctuations. This may take many forms: compa-nies may develop quasi-private systems of unemployment insurance or pensions or also have rules about limits on gearing or leveraging of assets in the case of financial institutions; households may build up their private wealth to supplement the perceived resources of companies and of the state.

The Positive Externalities of Exports

More generally in the export-oriented countries, exports produce positive externalities. The functioning of the vocational training system—of the technical universities and of tertiary professional and technical education more generally, of the technology transfer and innovation systems, of the surrounding business associations, as well as of the high value-added sectors that feed into the export sectors—depends on the size and profitability of the export sectors in the export-oriented economies. Benefits are less quantifiable but equally important in terms of the cooperation of workforces with long-term company tenure and co-specific skills, where aligning the incentive structure of skilled employees with their companies depends on longer-term export viability. For these more general reasons, governments may be cautious about expansionary domestic demand that has the effect—as described in the next section—of appreciated real exchange rates.

THE SURPLUS EXTERNAL BALANCE BIAS AND MODERN MACROECONOMICS

In the previous section, we argued that the institutions of the export-oriented advanced economies generated restraint in the use of domestic resources and promote the supply side of exports. This is not true in liberal economies where wage-setting and training policies do not favor the export sector, and where macroeconomic policies are geared toward maintaining demand. Here we show how, in equilibrium, export-oriented economies not only exhibit high exports but also tend to run a surplus on the external balance, and that the opposite is true for liberal countries. This produces capital exports to the liberal countries, which fuelled the high leverage in those countries. This is an inherent feature of the current international economic regime because there is no reason to think that any government would find it in its interest to promote a balanced trade constraint. In this sense, the roots of the current crisis are structural.

To make our case, we first establish that the rules of the game increasingly being adopted for governing macroeconomic policymaking, namely inflation targeting, are in fact neutral with respect to the deficit-surplus bias: persistent surpluses and deficits are possible in the current global economy. This is a necessary condition for the current equilibrium to be sustainable. We then suggest why the imbalance takes the particular form it does: liberal countries absorbing surpluses from elsewhere. This gets us back to institutional differences and establishes the sufficient condition for the global equilibrium. We briefly consider a country that currently does not play by the established rules—China.

We start by framing the argument in national income accounting terms. This explains how surpluses and deficits are related to capital movements, and provides the background for understanding the effects of macroeconomic policies. The external surplus (on the balance of trade in goods and services), exports minus imports, $X - M$, is equal to the difference between GDP and expenditure by domestic residents (households, companies, and government) where Y is GDP or domestic output, C is consumer expenditure, I is investment expenditure, and G is government expenditure:[2]

$$X - M \equiv Y - (C + I + G)$$

The right hand side measures total domestic net savings, public and private. The equation can be rewritten to reflect the separate impacts of the public and private net savings on the external surplus. The difference between domestic output Y, which is also equal to domestic income, and household consumption C must go to private savings, S, and taxation, T:

$$X - M \equiv (Y - C) - I - G \rightarrow X - M \equiv (S + T) - I - G = (S - I) + (T - G)$$

In terms of financial flows this is identical to:

Acquisition of foreign financial assets = External balance = Private sector financial surplus + Public sector financial surplus

where financial surplus is acquisition of financial assets by a sector. So, when there is a surplus on the external balance, capital will be exported, but if there is a deficit on the trade balance, it will be imported.

We now put the key elements of wage restraint identified in the previous section into a simple medium-term open economy equilibrium model to show the role of macroeconomic policies. In characterizing this model a small open economy, which takes as given the world real interest rate, r^*, is assumed; we modify this subsequently.

The equilibrium of this model is based on a New Keynesian New Open Economy Model (NOEM), which posits a number of relationships that permit the macroeconomic equilibrium to be identified. The first is that aggregate demand in reduced form can be written as the sum of autonomous private spending, $\bar{A} - ar$, government expenditure G, and the external balance B:

$$Y = \bar{A} - ar + G + B(q,Y)$$

This is effectively the same as the national income identity, but private spending is now a function of the interest rate, r; q is the real exchange rate.

The second relationship is the *external balance equilibrium schedule*:

$$B(q,Y) = X\,(q,Y^*) - qM(q,Y)$$

where q is defined as the real exchange rate in competitiveness terms (that is, unit labor costs in manufacturing). This shows that the external balance depends on the real exchange rate and domestic demand. The Marshall Lerner condition, implying that a real appreciation of the currency worsens the external balance, is realistically assumed to hold.[3]

The next equation establishes that wages are bargained and that an increase in economic activity increases the bargaining power of labor—the *real wage bargaining condition*:

$$w = w^B(Y),\, w^{B\prime} > 0$$

But though wages are set through bargaining, it is also true that firms set wages through their pricing behavior, so the wage is also equal to the price-determined wage. Because a real depreciation raises the real cost of imports and hence reduces the real wage, the price-determined wage is a rising function of the real exchange rate:

$$w = w^P(q),\, w^{P\prime} < 0$$

In equilibrium, the bargained and price-determined wage must be identical:

$$w^B(Y) = w^P(q) = w,$$

which is the set of combinations of Y and q that generate stable inflation, where real wage demands made in the labor market are equal to real wages implied by pricing behavior of companies; a real depreciation requires a fall in Y for stable inflation; thus a real depreciation cutting the price-determined real wages is consistent with stable inflation only if there is a corresponding fall in economic activity levels reducing the bargaining power of labor in a corresponding way.

Finally, the model assumes an *uncovered interest parity condition*, which requires the difference between the domestic and world short-term interest rates to be equal to the expected depreciation of the currency, $q^E - q$ (expressed in real terms here).

The implication of the New Keynesian NOEM is that stable trade deficits and surpluses are possible when the macroeconomic authority follows an accepted inflation target strategy, the necessary condition. In turn, whether the external balance is in surplus or deficit depends on how fiscally conservative the macroeconomic regime is relative to other countries, and on the degree of real wage restraint. High real wage restraint is implied by, among other things, conservative central banks, so that conservatism of monetary and fiscal policy then increases the likelihood of external surplus. We can show this with some simple diagrams, implied by the relationships outlined.

The equilibrium is defined by $q^E - q$ implying $r = r^*$; the stable inflation condition $w^B(Y) = w^P(q) = w$; and the aggregate demand schedule $Y = \bar{A} - ar + G + B(q)$. With $r = r^*$, the aggregate demand equation becomes $Y = \bar{A} - ar^* + G + B(q,Y)$, and we have two conditions to determine the equilibrium values of q and Y. The aggregate demand condition with $r = r^*$ is a downward sloping line in (q,Y) space, with a depreciation of the real exchange rate increasing aggregate demand; the stable inflation condition is an upward sloping line with an increase in Y pushing up the real wage and forcing an appreciation of the real exchange as domestic prices rise relative to the world price.

This equilibrium is shown in figure 2.1.

In equilibrium we have to be on the *AD* schedule with $r = r^*$. If $r \neq r^*$, then the model is inconsistent with rational expectations in the financial markets. If we are not on the *AD* schedule. then we have either rationing or businesses unable to sell what they produce. The requirement of the stable inflation line speaks for itself. An interesting and important aspect of medium-term equilibrium in these NOEM models is that changes in fiscal policy or private autonomous expenditure shift the *AD* schedule and hence the equilibrium.

Figure 2.1　Medium-Term Equilibrium

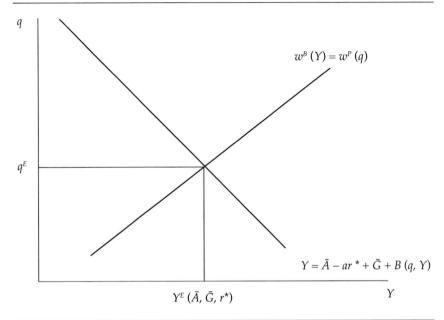

$$w^B(Y) = w^P(q)$$

$$Y = \bar{A} - ar^* + \bar{G} + B(q, Y)$$

$Y^E(\bar{A}, \bar{G}, r^*)$　　　　　　　Y

(axis labels: q, q^E, Y)

Source: Authors' calculation.

Figure 2.2 introduces the external balance schedule into the diagrammatic apparatus. Above the *EB* schedule, the economy is in deficit: take any point on *EB* and holding q constant, an increase in Y increases imports and hence moves the economy into deficit; likewise holding Y constant an appreciation of the exchange rate worsens the external balance via the Marshall-Lerner condition. Vice versa, we have a surplus below the *EB* schedule. A key element in the diagram is that the *EB* schedule is always flatter than the *AD* schedule: a depreciation increases income via its effect on aggregate demand by less than would be needed to increase imports by enough to restore the external balance to zero.

The only feasible equilibrium in figure 2.2 is *c*, where the *AD* and $w^B w^P$ schedules intersect. At *a*, inflation rates are not stable (they are falling); at *b*, we are off the *AD* schedule (there is rationing). The economy can always in principle be restored to external balance, but that requires a shift in one or more of the three schedules.

The economy always has to be at a point such as *c* in medium-term equilibrium, but where *c* is depends on government policy. If such fiscal and monetary policies are common knowledge, financial agents can ratio-

Figure 2.2   The External Balance

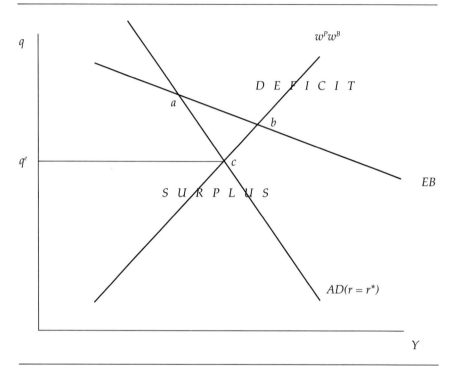

Source: Authors' calculation.

nally work out the value of q in equilibrium. If the policy rule is inflation targeting, and not the exchange rate, then the Central Bank has no instruments at its disposal to shift the equilibrium. It has to make sure, through short-term movements in the rate of interest (its only "permitted" instrument in normal times), that the economy is on the stable inflation $w^B w^P$ line, and at the target inflation rate; we will see how this is done. If the economy is small and open, as is for the moment assumed, the rate of interest in equilibrium is pinned down to the world rate of interest r^* that it takes as given (we loosen this assumption momentarily, but doing so does not change the basic argument). The central bank cannot shift the AD schedule given $r = r^*$ in equilibrium. $\bar{A}$, the autonomous expenditure of the domestic private sector is taken as given in equilibrium by the central bank; the central bank will of course engineer an adjustment to the economy in the short to medium term in response to an increase in $\bar{A}$, and this will result in an appreciated exchange rate in equilibrium. It is not the central bank that brings about the equilibrium appreciation—that hap-

Figure 2.3   Building Up a Surplus

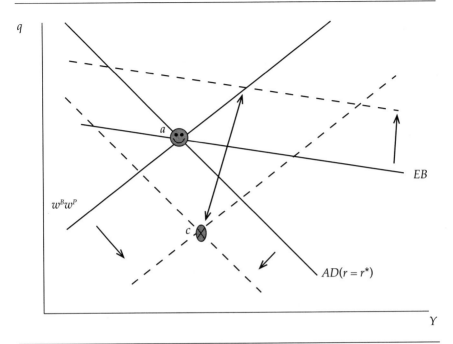

Source: Authors' calculation.

pens anyway. Nor can the central bank shift the $w^B w^P$ line, though that will vary with its conservatism preference, β, as we have seen. More generally, the rules of the game of inflation targeting do not allow targeting the exchange rate (except under exceptional circumstances), do not say anything about fiscal policy (especially if public sector deficits and debt are held in order), and simply require the central bank to be on the $w^B w^P$ line at the target rate of inflation in equilibrium.

Thus the real exchange rate is given in the equilibrium defined by c. The central bank takes the parameters of the $w^B w^P$ and the $AD(r = r^*)$ schedules as given. It accepts the consequence for the external balance of the economy in medium-term equilibrium. This is key for our argument because if the central bank and the fiscal authorities in export-oriented economies choose conservative policies to induce wage restraint and exports in the context of coordinated bargaining and high investment in skills, the equilibrium will lead to a surplus on the external balance. The logic is illustrated in figure 2.3.

In figure 2.3, a represents an equilibrium in which the external balance is zero. There are happily no global imbalances at a. Now we see how the institutional factors shift each of the three schedules toward a growing export surplus.

1. Real wage restraint shifts the $w^B w^P$ and the AD schedules. The $w^B w^P$ schedule shifts down as a result of the bargained real wage being lower at each level of output. The AD schedule shifts down in a deflationary direction as a consequence of a reduction in real household income from earnings relative to profits, the former implying a bigger reduction in consumption than the latter.

2. Skill formation shifts the EB schedule up as an increase in exports is permitted. Wage restraint comes into the EB schedule indirectly through the effect of wage restraint on the real exchange rate.

3. Finally, a higher level of private precautionary savings and perhaps restrictive fiscal policy directly also shift the AD schedule down.

The export-oriented economy moves then from a to c. The export surplus is shown by the double-arrowed dashed line.

What this indicates is that the net effects of parameter shifts, each individually justified in relation to exports, end up by producing an export surplus. The reverse logic holds for liberal economies because the key concern in an economy without coordinated bargaining or heavy investment in skills is to maintain the highest possible aggregate demand consistent with stable prices. This leads to a deficit on the external balance. With two blocks of countries, one running surpluses and one running deficits, surplus capital flows toward the deficit countries. This ensures the median-term persistence of the system, but it is also an important element in understanding the concentration of financial assets in countries with an emphasis on investment in risky assets.

These arguments do not depend on the small country assumption. Take a world of two large economies, and we can write down the four equations defining the equilibria in the two economies:

$$Y_L = \bar{A}_L - ar^* + \bar{G}_L - B(q)$$
$$Y_{EO} = \bar{A}_{EO} - ar^* + \bar{G}_{EO} + B(q)$$
$$w^B(Y_L) = w^P(q)$$
$$w^B(Y_{EO}) = w^P(q^{-1})$$

If we substitute out for Y_L and Y_{EO}, which we can do uniquely, we have two equations in the two unknowns r^* and q. In very large economies, it is appropriate to assume a unique equilibrium output or unemployment rate, that is, that the $w^B w^P$ stable inflation schedules are vertical (vertical Phillips curve). On that basis, adding the two AD conditions, we can see that r^* is determined by the world balance of the exogenous components of net public and private savings:

$$r^* = \frac{1}{2a}[(\bar{A}_L + \bar{G}_L - Y_L^e) + (\bar{A}_{EO} + \bar{G}_{EO} - Y_{EO}^e)]$$

Given that we were looking at a low real rate interest through the 2000s, this is then consistent with the view that net exogenous savings from the export-oriented countries drove down real interest rates. The real exchange rate between the two blocs is then given by the value of q, which generates a surplus equal to the difference between exogenous net savings in the export-oriented and those in the liberal bloc.

$$2B(q) = (Y_{EO}^e - \bar{A}_{EO} - \bar{G}_{EO}) - (Y_L^e - \bar{A}_L - \bar{G}_L)$$

Again, there is no mechanism in this system of equations to prevent one block running an external surplus equal to the deficit of the other bloc.

What we have shown is that it is perfectly consistent, within the rules of the game of the inflation-targeting regime, for economies to run external surpluses (and deficits) in medium-term equilibria. The inflation-targeting regime is of interest in part because it is not based on an international agreement. There are therefore no explicit or legal rules of the game at the supra national level, apart from the eurozone, although typically quite detailed national legal rules govern the behavior of individual national central banks. Our argument is that the large advanced economies were not prepared to operate on the basis of any set of rules that penalized either surpluses or deficits; and therefore no such regime emerged. This does not mean that there are no accepted rules: a basic rule is that central banks use short-term interest rates to bring inflation into equality with target inflation. No rules about fiscal policy exist, outside the Maastricht rules for the eurozone; neither the United States nor the United Kingdom believes other countries could credibly prevent them from using expansionary fiscal policy; nor do European export-oriented economies accept that they be required to reflate their economies or use more expansionary fiscal policies; certainly a country that pursues a conservative fiscal policy in terms of the public-sector deficit and debt cannot be forced to change it within the current regime.

Figure 2.4   China and a Low Real Exchange Rate Target

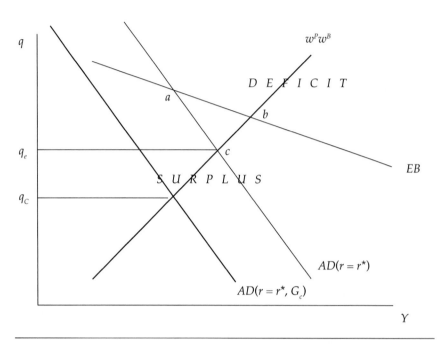

Source: Authors' calculation.

Thus we conclude that inflation targeting is a nation-based system that allows two very different types of advanced economies the freedom they each want to run surpluses and deficits. However problematic this is in the particular system of financial deregulation developed over the past two decades, it is unlikely that agreement on macroeconomic management will be international if our argument about government goals is correct.

China does not adhere to the accepted rules because Chinese authorities appear to wish to maintain a particular real exchange rate, say q_C, in figure 2.4. Although the institutional conditions leading to external surpluses in other export-oriented economies are missing, by targeting a low real exchange rate China has exacerbated the global imbalance problem.

To understand this, assume that q_C is believed by the financial operators, because they believe that the Chinese central bank is ready to enforce it. But it will be credible only if it corresponds to the intersection of the aggregate demand and the stable inflation schedule $w^B w^P$. In effect, given

$w^B w^P$, such correspondence requires sufficiently reduced aggregate demand—shown here by $AD(G_c)$—if inflationary pressures are to be avoided. Thus financial markets will have to take a view of the likelihood that China will adopt sufficiently demand-restraining measures.

The wider question is whether the maintenance of a real exchange rate target, even if only implicit, is consistent with the wider rules of the game. The United States believes it is not. And, at a certain stage, financial markets may decide that Chinese exchange rate policies are unsustainable. In the medium term, however, the Chinese real exchange rate is maintained at a stable inflation rate and a stable output or growth rate because it is consistent with the intersection of the $w^B w^P$ and the aggregate demand curve. The former guarantees stable inflation and the latter stable output-growth. Ultimately, then, the underlying real exchange rate depends on the operation (control) of labor markets and of an appropriate fiscal policy to keep aggregate demand at the right level.

In principle, the Chinese government can switch from real exchange rate targeting to inflation targeting. And it can de facto maintain a low real exchange rate at least within broad limits by a sufficiently tough fiscal policy. It is plausible that the Chinese government believes that there are positive externalities from export-led growth: this has been the lesson of the most readily available models, South Korea and Taiwan. More speculatively, export-led growth may be the most effective driver of the systems of education and training and of technology transfer and ultimately innovation, and key to relatively egalitarian growth in a developing country where government remains powerful. Thus it may be useful to think of China as not fundamentally different in its basic motivations from the advanced export-oriented nations—at least from a longer-term perspective.

To summarize, the effects in the export-oriented nations of labor market institutions on monetary and fiscal policy have generated external surpluses. These have been reinforced by the general operation of export-oriented systems of training and technology transfer, and have been quite consistent with inflation targeting. This is not to say that the surplus is a policy goal: the goal is to promote exports and the high value-added sectors that in one form or another feed into the export sectors, with their attendant externalities.

POLITICAL UNDERPINNINGS OF THE IMBALANCE EQUILIBRIUM

If the persistent imbalance is a cause of the current crisis, why do we not—leaving aside China for the moment—see attempts to reform the current system toward a balanced trade regime? Such a shift would involve export-oriented economies adopting a more accommodating macroeconomic regime, and liberal countries adopting a more restrictive regime. The reason this does not happen, we argue, is that it is inconsistent with the domestic political coalitions that sustain the current policies in the two types of economies. We base our argument on Iversen and Soskice (2010).

Consider first the export-oriented economies. Because the most productive and skill-intensive firms are concentrated in the export sector—as implied by the now universally accepted Melitz model of trade—a large export sector goes together with high investment in public training so that the supply of skilled workers will meet the demand. This in turn requires that unions in the export sector hold down their wages to allow for newly trained workers to be priced into jobs, and a key mechanism in ensuring this, as we have argued, is a nonaccommodating macroeconomic regime.

Assume now that policies become more accommodating in order to eliminate the trade surplus. This leads to a decline in the demand for skilled workers, so if the government continues to train at the previous level, there will be redundancies among skilled workers. The government would not want that, of course, but the alternative of reducing training intensity runs up against the interests of two very different constituencies. First, and most obvious, export-oriented firms will be opposed because they would face an increase in labor costs and will have to scale back their operations. Second, the relative supply of low-skilled workers will rise, which will cause a corresponding decline in their relative wages. Although this will be somewhat compensated for by a higher real exchange rate and cheaper imports, the compensation is less than 100 percent, and much less in large countries. From this it follows that low-skilled workers will block lower funding for training if they are represented by a party in government. Insofar as PR electoral systems—which all export-oriented countries in Europe adopted in the early twentieth century—produce more center-left governments, it would be hard for such governments to agree to a balanced trade international rule. This would also be true of center-right governments in these export-oriented countries, since the interests of export sectors dominate business and employer organizations.

Now consider the situation from the perspective of liberal countries. Because wage-setting is decentralized, governments in liberal countries cannot induce restraint through nonaccommodating macroeconomic policies. Such policies can instead affect demand only by reducing government spending and, if the economy is large, by raising interest rates. This will lead to lower wages, which in turn boosts exports and reduces the real exchange rate, cutting domestic demand. Both skilled and semi-skilled workers would both be worse off under these policies, except if the government substantially boosted subsidies for training and thereby reduced the supply of low-skilled workers. But in majoritarian political sys-

Table 2.2   Game Theoretic Context

		Export-Oriented Bloc			
		Balanced Trade		Fiscal Conservatism	
Liberal bloc	Balanced trade	Medium	Medium	Low	High
	Fiscal accommodation	High	Low	High—C	High—C

Source: Authors' compilation.
Note: Entries are the payoffs to the liberal and export-oriented blocs, respectively. "C" means high risk of a crisis.

tems, which are linked historically to liberal economic systems, the median voter is likely to be a skilled worker and would not support such a policy. Hence, governments in liberal countries will also not see it in their interest to back a balanced trade international regime.

It might be useful to think of the current nation-based macroeconomic management system in game theoretic terms. Readers may find it useful to see it as a prisoners' dilemma (PD) type game: each bloc can choose balanced trade (as the cooperative strategy), fiscal conservatism or fiscal accommodation being the defection strategies of the export-oriented and the liberal blocs respectively; the equilibrium defect-defect outcome is Pareto-inferior for the dominant political coalitions in the two blocs of economies on account of the significant probability that it leads to financial crisis (see table 2.2).

For this game to be a PD, make the (provisional) assumption that High—C < Medium. Given that assumption the current international regime is Pareto-inferior to a regime of balanced trade. To move to balanced trade requires some way of reaching an agreement whereby the losers are compensated by the winners of a new regime. Two major problems are evident.

The first is that, quite apart from the difficulty of writing an appropriate enforceable contract, analogous to Bretton Woods, it is unclear who the winners from a more stable international regime would be—whether it is really the dominant political coalitions who lose when the current system leads to major crises like the one we are in now. The crisis cost for the dominant political coalitions may be much less than the long-term costs for society as a whole. If the C for the political coalitions is such that, for them, High—C > Medium, then no balanced trade agreement is possible because they are the coalitions with the political power to make such an agreement.

The second problem for an international balanced trade agreement is different. Politicians in the liberal bloc believe that the likelihood of a future crisis can be tackled by changing the financial rules of the game in relatively small ways, most notably by more careful monitoring of the effective leverage ratios of HLFIs, and in particular those who pose a systemic risk. And the dominant political coalitions in the export-oriented economies also believe that changing the financial rules is preferable to adopting a more relaxed attitude to fiscal policy; indeed the latter is close to anathema for them. Financial rule-changing may be over-optimistic as a way of reducing the probability of future crises under nation-based inflation targeting, but it suggests a more attractive route to both parties than trying to work out a balanced trade agreement.

CONCLUSION

We have tried to put the crisis in the context of the relationship between the dominant political coalitions of advanced nation states and modern capitalism. We take as our starting point that the crisis was generated by the conjoint failure of two of the key regulatory systems that govern the economy: financial regulation and macroeconomic regulation. The former led to dangerously high leverage of the large investment banks in Wall Street and the City of London but not taking account of their system-threatening interrelationships. The latter allowed global imbalances to build up that fuelled the high leverage and stimulated the demand for risky assets in the United States and the United Kingdom. Although the principles of both regulatory systems are accepted through the advanced world, their detailed operation is at the national level.

Our contention is that the governments of advanced nation states attach high importance to the success of those high value-added sectors in which—along varieties of capitalism lines—they have comparative institutional advantages. For the United Kingdom and the United States, the innovative financial sector was and is of great importance. Both governments—independent of their partisan affiliations—were increasingly committed to light touch regulation and giving wide latitude to choice of financial activity areas. This was not primarily because of the political influence of the financial sector. It is of course true that large financial institutions were closely politically involved in the United States, given the operation of Congress and its agencies as well as relatively loose party discipline, but they were not politically involved in the United Kingdom; indeed, Thatcher's initial Big Bang in 1986 was followed enthusiastically by Blair and Brown. For CMEs, the export sectors and the sectors that supported them were the high value-added sectors, and these nations were opposed to using domestic demand through fiscal policy to reduce external surpluses because it would have meant real appreciation in medium-term equilibrium with inflation targeting, and hence damaging directly or indirectly to exports, as explained earlier.

From our perspective of modern capitalism and the governments of advanced nation states, it is difficult to see governments in either group of nations changing their positions on these regulatory systems fundamentally, especially as the crisis recedes over time. The pre-crisis regulatory systems remain today very attractive to both groups of governments. Because change will only come about in the modern post-hegemonic world if major governments agree, major change is unlikely.

Does this mean that governments are unconcerned about a future crisis? It is true that policy responses, even if uncoordinated, have so far been greatly more successful in response to the recent crisis than they were in the 1930s. This is partly due to monetary policy and discretionary fiscal policy, partly to central banks and governments intervening as lenders of last resort to a range of institutions, partly to quantitative easing, and in wide measure especially in the export-oriented economies to the existence of an effective welfare state. Governments have less to fear from another massive crisis than they might have thought based on the experience of the 1930s. But we are not proposing a theory of endemic crisis. If it was really clear that a continuation of broadly similar regulatory systems would lead to crisis, then doubtless agreement to change would have been reached, as it was in the 1930s. But a great deal has been learned from the crisis, in particular about why it developed. The reason now accepted by many economists is excessive leverage cycles of the large investment banks, and inadequate tools to monitor the systemically threatening implications of this, as we saw earlier. Part of the answer lies in requiring financial institutions to build up capital, which will be embodied in some form in Basel 3. More important will likely be rules governing leverage cycles and monitoring of their systemic implications. In both respects, national regulatory interpretation of rules and innovative practices will be decisive.

Whatever our personal views, it is unlikely that the U.K. or the U.S. governments will overly constrain the innovative activities of their financial systems, or that export-oriented economies will stimulate domestic demand to reduce global imbalances. But it is likely that, just as macroeconomics is today quite different as a result of the lessons of the Great Crash, so lessons have been learned about the operation of the financial system that may limit the dangers of a future crisis.

NOTES

1. Not technically insurance because the insuree did not need to own the asset.
2. If we add income to domestic residents from abroad (profits, dividends, and

interest) to both sides, the LHS is now the current account surplus and Y is redefined as GNP.

3.   Note that we are defining q as the intuitive way, the inverse of the standard economics definition.

REFERENCES

Estevez-Abe, Margarita, Torben Iversen, and David Soskice. 2001. "Social Protection and the Formation of Skills: A Reinterpretation of the Welfare State." In *Varieties of Capitalism: the Institutional Foundations of Comparative Advantage*, edited by Peter Hall and David Soskice. Oxford: Oxford University Press.

Geanakoplos, John. 2010. "The Leverage Cycle." In *NBER Macroeconomics Annual 2009*, vol. 24, edited by Daron Acemoglu, Kenneth Rogoff, and Michael Woodford. Chicago: University of Chicago Press.

Hall, Peter A., and Robert J. Franzese. 1998. "Mixed Signals: Central Bank Independence, Coordinated Wage Bargaining, and European Monetary Union." *International Organization* 52(Summer): 505–36.

Iversen, Torben. 1998. "Wage Bargaining, Central Bank Independence, and the Real Effects of Money." *International Organization* 52(3): 469–504.

———. 2005. *Capitalism, Democracy, and Welfare*. Cambridge: Cambridge University Press.

Iversen, Torben, and David Soskice. 2010. "Real Exchange Rates and Competitiveness: The Political Economic Foundations of Comparative Advantage." *American Political Science Review* 104(3): 601–23.

Minsky, Hyman. 1986. *Stabilizing an Unstable Economy*. New Haven, Conn.: Yale University Press.

Shin, Hyun. 2010. "Discussion of 'The Leverage Cycle' by John Geanakoplos." In *NBER Macroeconomics Annual 2009*, vol. 24, edited by Daron Acemoglu, Kenneth Rogoff, and Michael Woodford. Chicago: University of Chicago Press.

Soskice, David. 2007. "Macroeconomics and Varieties of Capitalism." In *Beyond Varieties of Capitalism: Conflict, Contradictions, and Complementarities in European Economies*, edited by Bob Hancke, Martin Rhodes, and Mark Thatcher. Oxford: Oxford University Press.

Soskice, David, and Torben Iversen. 2000. "The Non-neutrality of Monetary Policy with Large Wage and Price Setters." *Quarterly Journal of Economics* 115(1): 265–84.

Chapter 3 | Multilateralism Reborn? International Cooperation and the Global Financial Crisis

Eric Helleiner

POLICYMAKERS HAVE CONGRATULATED themselves for the cooperative ways in which they responded to the 2007 to 2009 global financial crisis. States worked together to manage the crisis through activities such as macroeconomic stimulus programs, supporting markets and firms in distress, enhancing the lending capacity of official international financial institutions, and restraining protectionism. Cooperation of this kind is credited with helping to prevent the crisis from becoming as severe as that in the early 1930s when international cooperation broke down. As International Monetary Fund (IMF) managing director Dominique Strauss-Kahn argued in the spring of 2010, "during the crisis, unprecedented cooperation allowed us to avert another Great Depression."

Particular praise has been given to the new G20 leaders' forum for its role in supporting various cooperative crisis management activities. As French President Nicolas Sarkozy put it in an August 2010 speech, the G20 "enabled the main economic powers to successfully weather the most severe crisis since the 1930s." These sentiments were echoed a few months later by the head of the European Commission, José Manuel Barroso, who suggested that the G20 had "prevented the boat from sinking" (quoted in Alan Beattie and Christian Oliver, "US Hits at Greenspan Comments on Dollar," *Financial Times*, November 12, 2010). Alongside its crisis management activities, the G20 has also been lauded for launching ambitious international regulatory reforms in the financial sector to prevent future crises. This forward-looking reform agenda has generated new international financial standards as well as institutional innovations such as the creation of the new Financial Stability Board.

These developments have understandably encouraged a widespread view that the crisis has catalyzed a strengthening of multilateral cooperation centered around the G20 in the post–Cold War world. This chapter sounds a more cautious note. In contrast to the self-congratulations of many policymakers, I argue that the significance of the G20, and international cooperation more generally, to both the management of the crisis and post-crisis regulatory reforms is easily overstated.

INTERNATIONAL DIMENSIONS OF CRISIS MANAGEMENT

How important was the G20 leaders' forum and international cooperation more generally in managing the crisis? The answer begins with a brief discussion of some reasons to be cautious in attributing too much importance to specific crisis management initiatives the G20 undertook after it was created in November 2008.

What Did G20 Do in Managing the Crisis?

The G20 leaders' forum is credited with managing the crisis effectively because of a number of initiatives it undertook after it was created in November 2008. The first was to encourage coordinated national macroeconomic stimulus programs. At their first summit in Washington, the G20 leaders prioritized the use of "fiscal measures to stimulate domestic demand to rapid effect, as appropriate" (2008). Many countries subsequently introduced national fiscal stimulus programs that are credited with lessening the severity of the crisis.

There is little question that the G20 commitment helped to boost support for fiscal stimulus programs in many countries. In addition to legitimizing Keynesian-style policies, this coordinated endorsement of fiscal stimulus helped ease fears, especially in small open economies, that the effectiveness of unilateral national fiscal expansions might be undermined by external leakages, as unilateral expansions often had been during the 1970s and 1980s. Support for stimulus programs may also have been boosted by policymaker desires to be seen as constructive international actors in the new forum. China's important stimulus program, for example, was announced just days before the first G20 meeting was held.

What is less clear, however, is how important the G20 endorsement of fiscal expansion was in explaining national fiscal stimulus policies. Politicians across the world were, after all, facing strong domestic pressures for more expansionary programs at this time because of the severity of economic shock experienced during the fall of 2008. Even in the absence of the G20, it is very likely that many countries would have introduced fiscal stimulus programs (and some already had before its creation). The timing of fiscal stimulus initiatives, in other words, may have been a product more of simultaneous domestic pressures induced by the global nature of the shock than of successful coordination. Indeed, as David Cameron and Waltraud Schelkle's contributions to this volume highlight, the size of stimulus programs depended very much on domestic circumstances (see chapters 4 and 5).

It is also worth noting that macroeconomic stimulus programs came not only in the form of fiscal policy but also through dramatic monetary easing during the crisis. Although the G20 leaders (2008) did "recognize the importance of monetary policy support, as deemed appropriate to domestic conditions" at their first summit, the G20's role in catalyzing monetary easing was much less significant. Key national initiatives in this area had been under way as far back as the fall of 2007 and the coordination that took place in this area was facilitated more by central bank networks including those within the Bank for International Settlements (Bayne 2008).

Alongside encouraging macroeconomic stimulus programs, the G20 leaders are credited with boosting financial market confidence through their joint commitment in November 2008 to "take whatever further actions are necessary to stabilize the financial system" (G20 2008). This statement certainly did help reassure markets that public authorities stood ready collectively to support firms and markets in distress. Once again, however, the role of the G20 in fostering cooperation vis-à-vis the provision of emergency liquidity should not be overstated because leading central banks had undertaken key cooperative initiatives in this area for months before the first G20 summit (Bayne 2008).

Even leaving aside the G20's role, it is also important more generally not to exaggerate the successes of international cooperation in providing emergency assistance to troubled firms during the crisis. Uncertainty was heightened during the crisis by governments' lack of clarity over the bailout responsibilities of host versus home governments. Similarly, the final catalyst for the collapse of Lehman Brothers—a key turning point in the worsening of the crisis—was the British government's last-minute decision to block Barclay's takeover of the U.S. institution, a decision that left U.S. officials "in amazement" and which was driven by the British desire not to "import" the U.S. "cancer" (quoted in Sorkin 2009, 348). A few weeks later, the shoe was on the other foot when British efforts to lead a coordinated international initiative to recapitalize banks failed to secure the cooperation of the United States and other foreign governments, forcing the country to launch this initiative in a highly risky unilateral manner.[1] Only after the markets responded positively to the British move did other countries begin to follow its lead. The recapitalization initiatives in October 2008 marked a crucial turning point in the management of the crisis, but they were not a product of successful cooperation (Brown 2010).

The G20 leaders are also credited with managing the crisis well because of their decision to boost dramatically the lending capacity of official international financial institutions, especially the IMF, at their second summit in April 2009. This decision helped bolster confidence and provided key financial assistance to various countries suffering balance of payments problems at the time. Again, however, it is important not to overstate its significance. For some countries, key balance of payments support during the crisis came not from the IMF but from less publicized swap arrangements created among central banks outside the G20 process. South Korea, for example, drew key support from a swap arranged with U.S. Federal Reserve in September 2008 (Moon and Rhyu 2010). The Fed arranged swaps with central banks from other developing countries at this time as well (Singapore, Brazil, and Mexico), as did monetary authorities from other leading financial powers such as China and Japan.

Finally, the G20 leaders have been praised for restraining trade protectionism during the crisis through their declaration at the first summit that "within the next 12 months, we will refrain from raising new barriers to investment or to trade in goods and services, imposing new export restrictions, or implementing World Trade Organization (WTO) inconsistent measures to stimulate exports" (2008). Although this agreement was not fully upheld, the international trading system did not experience anything like the turn to protectionism that was experienced during the Great Depression. The G20 leaders can take some credit for this result, but it is important not to overlook the role of the WTO and the constraints embodied in its agreements.

There is thus no question that the G20 leaders' forum played an important role in the management of the 2007 to 2009 global financial crisis. But the credit for successful cooperative crisis management needs to be shared with others, such as the WTO and especially central bank networks. The significance of cooperation—within the G20 and more generally—in generating policy outcomes that prevented "the boat from sinking" also should not be overstated. This is true not just in areas such as fiscal and monetary policy and emergency assistance to troubled firms but also in one other area that requires more extensive discussion because it is often overlooked.

The Dog That Didn't Bark: The Absence of a Dollar Crisis

Policymakers have applauded the various cooperative initiatives they undertook in managing the crisis of 2007 to 2009, but they rarely discuss the significance of international cooperation in preventing a dollar crisis at the time. At first sight, this neglect seems odd because one of the key reasons the crisis did not descend into another Great Depression was the absence of a crisis of the U.S. dollar. Moreover, many governments contributed directly to this outcome through their financial support of the United States at the time. The official neglect of this subject is more understandable, however, when we recognize that this foreign support had little to do with multilateral—or even bilateral—cooperation.

As bad as the 2007 to 2009 crisis was, it could have been much worse. The U.S. financial meltdown unfolded at a moment when the United States had become unusually dependent on foreign capital to fund large current account and fiscal deficits. If the meltdown had triggered capital flight from the United States and a dollar crisis, the financial and economic consequences would have been severe. A collapse of confidence in U.S. investments would have put upward pressure on U.S. interest rates, contributing further to the country's domestic financial troubles. The Federal Reserve might also have felt compelled to hike interest rates dramatically—as it did in 1979—to stem the dollar's depreciation. U.S. authorities would also have encountered greater difficulties in financing the massive bailouts and fiscal stimulus programs. In addition, these developments— U.S. dollar collapse, higher U.S. interest rates, U.S. fiscal problems—would have greatly exacerbated financial and economic instability in the world economy as a whole.

This scenario was far from hypothetical. Even before the crisis, the growing U.S. current account and fiscal deficits had generated widespread predictions of a looming dollar crisis. When the U.S. financial crisis began to unfold in 2007 and 2008, prominent analysts such as George Soros (2008) reiterated these predictions, and suggested that a dollar crisis was imminent. Even top policymakers, such as U.S. Treasury Secretary Hank Paulson, worried about this scenario throughout 2008 (Paulson 2009; Sorkin 2009). Given that the United States was at the epicenter of the financial turmoil, it seemed plausible that the crisis would provoke a loss of confidence in U.S. financial assets and the dollar. When U.S. policymakers responded to the crisis with dramatic interest rate cuts and larger fiscal deficits, the likelihood of this outcome only seemed to grow.

In the end, however, these fears proved misplaced. Not only was a dollar crisis avoided, but the dollar even strengthened after mid-2008, foreign investors showing greater enthusiasm for dollar investments as the crisis became more severe. This outcome made the U.S. financial crisis unfold in a completely different way from those in many emerging market countries over the previous two decades. Like them, the U.S. financial bubble of the precrisis years had been fueled in part by foreign capital inflows. But when the bubbles in emerging market countries burst, foreign (and domestic) investors withdrew their funds, thereby generating exchange rate crises, which only exacerbated the domestic financial troubles of these countries. In the United States, however, the opposite phenomenon occurred: foreigners helped ease the pain of the bursting of the financial bubble (Reinhart and Rogoff 2009).

For those interested in the role of international cooperation in crisis management, it is striking that much of the foreign support for the United States during the crisis came from foreign governments. During the half decade leading up to the 2007 to 2009 financial crisis, foreign governments had already emerged as major investors in U.S. dollar assets, particularly Treasury bills and the bonds issued by the two government-sponsored giant mortgage lending agencies, Fannie Mae and Freddie Mac ("Fannie and Freddie"), which these governments held mostly as foreign reserves. The scale of this investment was large: approximately half of the U.S. current account deficit between 2002 and 2007 was financed by foreign governments (Wolf 2008). The Chinese government emerged as the largest foreign official source of funding by the end of this period, but other governments also played a significant role such as those of Japan, the Gulf States, and other oil exporting countries (including Russia), as well as other developing countries, particularly in Asia.

Many of these same governments continued to support the U.S. financial position during the crisis and some even increased their support. This support came not just in the form of reserve holdings of Treasury bonds and "agency" bonds. Sovereign wealth funds (SWFs) from countries such as China, Singapore, and the Gulf States, even helped recapitalize U.S. financial institutions directly during the crisis, especially in its first phase. Indeed, Herman Schwartz notes that "ironically, developing country SWFs provided the US financial firms with more money—$24.8 billion— in the last quarter of 2007 than the IMF ever lent in any single quarter to bail out troubled LDCs" (2009, 211).

In some respects, the foreign official enthusiasm for financing the United States was puzzling. Before the crisis began, analysts had highlighted the growing costs to foreign governments of their investments in U.S. financial assets (Eichengreen 2006; Dieter 2007; Helleiner 2009; Kirshner 2008). One such cost was the risk of domestic inflation, as ever larger official dollar reserves proved difficult to sterilize. Another was the direct financial cost incurred from holding massive dollar reserves. This cost stemmed partly from the fact that investments in U.S. Treasury bills often earned much lower yields than investments at home. Equally important was the fact that the value of U.S. assets was undermined by the dollar's slow depreciation vis-à-vis the euro after 2002, a depreciation that looked set to continue because of growing U.S. external debt and current account deficits. For countries with enormous dollar reserves, such as China, the scale of the financial losses from the dollar's depreciation was huge; each 10 percent decline in the U.S. dollar generated a loss equivalent to approximately 3 percent of China's GDP (Cohen 2008, 462).

Before the crisis, analysts also warned of the possibility of the selling of dollars being triggered by collective action problems among the larger reserve holders (for example, Eichengreen 2006; Helleiner 2009). As the costs of reserve holdings rose, one country might be tempted to sell first to minimize their losses before others made the same move, a process that might then trigger a herd-like selling of dollars. This collective action problem seemed all the more serious given the existence of a new credible and attractive alternative reserve currency, the euro. The prospect of disorderly dumping of the dollars was said to be further enhanced by the absence of close ties and intergovernmental networks of officials among the main reserve holders as well as between them and the United States.

Indeed, some scholars even noted that large reserve holding countries might consider strategic reserve selling as a weapon to achieve political goals, as had sometimes been done in the past (Kirshner 2008). The prospect seemed even higher at this time because some of the largest dollar holders—such as China and Russia—were strategic rivals of the United States. Before the crisis, Juliet Johnson (2008) highlighted how Russian officials were in fact already reducing their large dollar reserves as a part of a broader distancing from U.S. foreign policy. In the summer of 2007, Chinese analysts were also speculating that their country's enormous dollar reserves could be used as a political bargaining chip with or regarding the United States (quoted in Helleiner 2009).

In light of these considerations, a number of analysts argued before the crisis that foreign official support for the United States was increasingly fragile. Some had even predicted that a major U.S. recession or financial crisis could spark a withdrawal from U.S. dollar investments (Kirshner 2008; Dieter 2007; Murphy 2006, 62). As the crisis unfolded, these fears intensified. Particular attention was focused on the Chinese government's intentions because of the scale of its reserves, which totaled close to $2 billion at the start of the crisis, of which approximately 70 to 80 percent was in dollar-denominated assets.

Some analysts highlighted the parallel between China's position as the major creditor during the crisis and that of the United States during the Great Depression. After emerging as the main creditor to the world economy during the 1920s, the United States chose, for a variety of political reasons, not to support the old European powers when financial crisis struck. The U.S. failure to act as a stabilizer at this moment intensified the depth of the Great Depression. Scholars highlighted various political reasons why Chinese authorities might make the same choice during the crisis. One reason was that China policymakers were already facing growing domestic criticism for investing the country's wealth in the low-return U.S. investments rather than at home to meet pressing domestic needs (Chin and Helleiner 2008; Drezner 2009, 32–33). Harold James also wondered whether Chinese officials might see the crisis as a moment for a kind of "payback for the American bungling of the 1997 to 1998 East Asia crisis" (2009, 224).[2] More generally, he also speculated about whether Chinese authorities might be tempted to turn back toward a more inward-looking development path in light of the global economic uncertainty and worries about their lack of influence with U.S.-controlled global economic institutions (James 2009, 227).

In the end, however, China and many other foreign governments acted as stabilizers rather than destabilizers during the crisis, maintaining and even increasing their investments in U.S. financial assets. Was their behavior the product of yet another example of successful cooperative crisis management during the crisis? For example, did it reflect the ability of reserve holdings to overcome the collective action problems among themselves identified by precrisis scholarship? Or was it a result of agreements with the United States hashed out in either multilateral forums such as the G20 or bilateral channels?

Did International Cooperation Generate This Outcome?

There does not appear to have been much effort among the major reserve holding countries to cooperate in preventing individual states from dumping dollars unilaterally in late 2007 or throughout 2008. Indeed, the one story that has surfaced publicly concerning cooperation on reserve policy among U.S. creditors involved a Russian initiative in the summer of 2008 to encourage China to cooperatively sell dollar reserves to force the United States to prop up Fannie and Freddie. This Russian initiative, reported in U.S. Treasury Secretary Hank Paulson's memoirs, appeared to raise the prospect not of cooperation to prevent a dollar crisis but rather of strategic reserve selling to induce one.

This initiative—which Paulson described as "deeply troubling" (2009,

161)—was a potentially significant one because the Chinese did share the Russian concerns about Fannie and Freddie at the time. Both countries had a large portion of their reserves invested in the agencies' bonds (approximately 25 percent in China's case). Like many other foreign investors, they had purchased the bonds under the assumption that the bonds were implicitly backed by the U.S. government, despite repeated denials from U.S. officials (Thompson 2009; Setser 2008, 28). As Fannie and Freddie's financial problems mounted in mid-2008, the Chinese government became increasingly worried about whether the U.S. government would in fact back the companies up. Prominent Chinese analysts such as Yu Yongding were even warning at the time, "If the US government allows Fannie and Freddie to fail and international investors are not compensated adequately, the consequences will be catastrophic. If it is not the end of the world, it is the end of the current international financial system" (quoted in David Hirst, "China Goes the Big Squeeze," *The Age*, August 30, 2008).

Why did the initiative not proceed further? Once again, international cooperation seems to have played little role. According to Paulson, Chinese officials rebuffed the Russian overtures. A number of reasons are outlined later for why Chinese policymakers chose unilaterally to continue supporting the United States during the crisis. But the risk of strategic selling of dollars was also minimized by a U.S. decision to place Freddie and Fannie under a public conservatorship in early September. That decision may have been influenced by U.S. fears about whether China and Russia would stop buying and holding Fannie and Freddie bonds (for these fears, see Sorkin 2009, 222; Drezner 2009, 34–35). But there have been no indications that it was a product of any explicit negotiated agreement between the United States and these reserve-holding states; indeed, although the decision eased Chinese worries about the safety of their investments, Daniel Drezner notes that the U.S. government still refused to provide an explicit guarantee of the agencies' debts despite Chinese pressure (2009). Rather than seeing this move as a product of cooperation, evidence points to the decision being taken unilaterally by U.S. authorities with many domestic considerations also in mind, just as were other U.S. bailout decisions that foreign investors favored, such as the rescue of Bear Sterns and AIG and the introduction of the Troubled Asset Relief Program (TARP) (for foreign official interest in these decisions, see Tett 2009, 211; Paulson 2009, 233, 318; Sorkin 2009).

Looking beyond this particular episode, no evidence has surfaced of any other negotiated deals either between the United States and its creditors that helped generate foreign financial support for the U.S. position. It is certainly true that U.S. officials did make efforts throughout the crisis to keep in touch with their major foreign official creditors, encouraging their investments in U.S. troubled financial institutions, and welcoming support for the dollar (Paulson 2009, 161, 242, 318; Sorkin 2009, 269–74, 444–53, 469–70, 482, 509, 518). But these discussions do not appear to have resulted in any formal arrangements between U.S. officials and their foreign counterparts to encourage support for the United States. And the issue certainly never made an appearance as a formal negotiation item in any of the multilateral forums at the time, including the new G20 leaders' forum created in November 2008, whose final communiqué focused almost exclusively on international regulatory issues.

To explain the unilateral decisions of governments to support the United States during the crisis, it is useful to recall why they had invested so heavily in the United States during the precrisis years (Helleiner 2011). One reason that foreign investors—both public and private—had been so attracted to invest surplus funds in the United States was the unique depth, liquidity, and security of U.S. financial markets, especially the U.S. Treasury bill market. Despite exchange rate risks and low yields, there were simply no other markets in the world to provide equivalent benefits for foreigners with large sums to invest. The development of equivalent financial markets within most of the creditor states had long been inhibited by policies of "financial repression" designed to serve a variety of goals such as monetary policy autonomy, state-led growth, or export success (Schwartz 2009). Even the eurozone lacked an equivalent to the U.S. Treasury bill market because of the absence of a single European fiscal authority.

The rapid accumulation of dollar reserves by China and many other developing countries has also been linked to their export-led growth strategies. As Torben Iversen and David Soskice note in chapter 2 of this volume, governments built up reserves to keep their country's exchange rate low as a tool to bolster the competitiveness of national exporters. The recycling of reserves into dollar assets then helped keep their major export market—the United States—economically buoyant. Analysts drew a parallel to the strategy of many western European countries and Japan during the 1960s when they built up dollar holdings in the 1960s as a result of their export-led strategies under the Bretton Woods exchange rate system (Dooley, Folkerts-Landau, and Garber 2003). More sophisticated versions of this Bretton Woods II explanation for the growth of dollar reserves identified the domestic interests in the reserve-accumulating countries that backed this policy, such as China's coastal elite involved in the export sector (Schwartz 2009).

Finally, other scholars have argued that rapid growth of dollar reserves was less a by-product of export-oriented exchange rate objectives than a goal designed to reduce national vulnerability to external influences. In the wake of the 1997 to 1998 East Asian financial crisis, many developing countries are said to have amassed large dollar reserves as a kind of war chest to defend themselves against volatile international capital flows as well as dependence on the IMF, whose role in that crisis was widely criticized. This desire for "self-insurance" produced a kind of "supercharged export-led growth strategy" to earn reserves after 1998 (Rajan 2010, 82; see also Wolf 2008).

Given these motivations, it is easier to see why the crisis did not lead to a foreign pullout. None of these motivations for reserve accumulation were changed by the crisis and some were even reinforced. To begin with, the crisis highlighted very starkly the relative attractiveness of dollar assets vis-à-vis others. Despite the U.S. financial difficulties from 2007 to 2009, the U.S. Treasury bill remained the investment of choice for financial institutions and investors scrambling for liquidity and safety (Reinhart and Rogoff 2009, 222). As one Chinese official, Luo Ping, put it in early 2009 when explaining why China continued to buy U.S. Treasury bills, "Except for U.S. Treasuries, what can you hold? . . . U.S. Treasuries are the safe haven. For everyone, including China, it is the only option. . . . Once you start issuing $1 trillion–$2 trillion . . . we know the dollar is going to depreciate, so we hate you guys but there is nothing much we can do" (quoted in Henry Sender, "China to Stick with U.S. Bonds," *Financial Times*, February 12, 2009).

Confidence in the euro was undermined not just by the absence of an equivalent to the Treasury bill markets but also by the fact that the crisis revealed its fragile political foundations very starkly. Because the Maastricht Treaty had failed to specify clear procedures for the prevention and resolution of eurozone financial crises, European financial institutions in trouble were forced to turn to national governments for support. When some national governments initially responded unilaterally, financial analysts wondered whether European financial integration could unravel and whether the eurozone unity itself might be threatened (see, for example, David Oakley and Gillian Tett, "Credit Markets Point to Strains in Rich Economies," *Financial Times*, October 8, 2008). This failure of international cooperation within Europe made the crisis more severe within that region, but had the effect of reducing the likelihood of a wider global financial instability by boosting foreign support for the U.S. dollar.

Turning to the Bretton Woods II story, foreign governments whose economies were heavily dependent on exports to the United States—particularly China—also faced strong incentives to maintain and even increase dollar reserves during the crisis. Given the global economic downturn, countries were more concerned than ever to keep their major foreign market afloat financially and to prevent exchange rate appreciation from undermining the competitiveness of their export sector. As Schwartz puts it, "steering a different course would have required painful changes in the domestic political structures of U.S. foreign creditors" (2009, 172). This Bretton Woods II logic trumped any collective action problems that might have encouraged individual reserve-holding countries to dump reserves for short-term financial gain. As long as China kept accumulating reserves, other developing countries involved in export competition with Chinese firms felt compelled to follow in order to prevent exchange rate appreciation vis-à-vis the renminbi. As Brad Setser put it, "there has been little coordination between debtors and creditors in this crisis. Emerging markets bought U.S. bonds as a result of their ongoing commitment to managing their own exchange rates against the dollar, not as a result of a negotiated agreement with the United States" (2008, 29).

Finally, the self-insurance rationale for reserve holdings was also strengthened during the crisis. The 2007 to 2009 global financial meltdown represented a moment when the war chest of reserves was finally proving its worth as a bulwark against external instability. Rather than dumping reserves, governments thus sought to preserve and even increase them. Indeed, policymakers across the developing world took note of the fact that countries with large reserves were less badly affected by the crisis, such as those in East Asia, than those that had not, such as many countries in eastern and central Europe. Foreign financial support for the United States during the crisis thus ironically partly stemmed from the opposite of cooperative sentiments: developing countries' desire for national autonomy and their lingering distrust of the IMF.

In addition to reinforcing these foreign rationales for supporting the United States financially, the crisis also reduced some of the costs associated with this support. The global economic downtown diminished worries about the inflationary impact of reserve sterilization. Concerns about low returns on dollar investments were also offset by the troubles in the eurozone as well as the rising value of the dollar after mid-2008. In the Chinese case, one further motivation to support the United States financially also deserves mention. That China had so much invested in dollar assets already reduced its room for maneuver. Any effort to diversify its reserves out of dollars risked triggering market reactions that undercut the value of its remaining investments. Its claims on the United States equal to approximately one-third of the Chinese GDP near the start of the crisis (Cohen 2008, 462), China found itself entrapped with its economic well-being tied up with that of the United States.

In sum, international cooperation—either multilateral or bilateral— played little role in generating one of the most important international dimensions of the official response to the crisis: the support that foreign governments provided for the dollar. This support reflected unilateral government decisions made for distinct national political reasons rather than cooperative arrangements between the United States and its creditors or among the creditor governments themselves. On the U.S. side, the willingness of U.S. authorities to bail key financial institutions had the consequence of assuaging foreign official creditors who were concerned about the safety of their assets. On the creditor side, the crisis reinforced the attractiveness of dollar assets with respect to the alternatives, as well as the Bretton II and self-insurance logics for reserve holdings. Interestingly, to push the point even further, some of the creditor behavior was itself a reaction to failures of international cooperation, notably the inability of European governments to make the euro a more attractive reserve asset and East Asian distrust of the IMF.

LIMITS OF INTERNATIONAL REGULATORY COOPERATION

If we need to be cautious when assessing the significance of the G20 and international cooperation more generally in crisis management, what about their role in driving regulatory reform? G20-centred cooperation has without question played a key role in the regulatory reform process. Indeed, the emergence of the G20-led, high-profile, internationally coordinated regulatory reform agenda has been one of the most striking features of the official response to the 2007 to 2009 crisis. In this section, however, I argue that the limitations of international cooperation in this sphere have become increasingly apparent.

International Regulatory Reform Agenda

The emergence of the international regulatory reform agenda began very soon after the financial crisis broke out. At their October 2007 meeting, the G7 finance ministers and central bank governors asked the Financial Stability Forum (FSF) to develop proposals that could address regulatory and supervisory weaknesses revealed by the crisis. By April 2008, the FSF had developed more than sixty recommendations in consultation with international financial institutions such as the IMF and Bank for International Settlements (BIS) as well as various international standard-setting bodies (SSBs) such as the Basel Committee on Banking Supervision (BCBS), the International Organization of Securities Commissions (IOSCO), the International Association of Insurance Supervisors (IAIS), the Committee on Payment and Settlement Systems (CPSS), and the International Accounting Standards Board (IASB). The G7 quickly endorsed these recommendations, which were subsequently refined in the fall of 2008.

The FSF's lead role in the initial phase of this reform process significantly boosted its profile. The body had been created by the G7 countries in 1999 as part of their ambitious effort to develop and promote international financial standards across sectors ranging from accounting to bank supervision after the 1997 to 1998 East Asian financial crisis. The principal rationale for the construction of this 'international standards regime' was the G7's view that the 1997 to 1998 crisis had emanated primarily from developing countries whose domestic financial regulation and supervision needed to be improved to meet international best practices (Walter 2008). As one of its first tasks, the FSF had compiled in 1999 a compendium of existing international financial standards developed by the SSBs, from which it identified twelve as priority to be promoted worldwide. The IMF and World Bank were then assigned the task of assessing and monitoring national compliance with these standards—which covered issues ranging from bank supervision to corporate governance—through their voluntary Financial Sector Assessment Program (FSAP) and Reports on the Observance of Standards and Codes (ROSCs).

The G7 initially had high hopes that the FSF would not just coordinate this new international standards regime but also "assess issues and vulnerabilities affecting the global financial system and identify and oversee the actions needed to address them, including encouraging, where necessary, the development or strengthening of international best practices and standards and defining priorities for addressing and implementing them" (1999, para. 15). To facilitate this role, its membership brought together for the first time representatives of the central bank, finance ministry, and regulatory and supervisory authority from each G7 country and the European Central Bank, relevant international financial institutions, and key international standard-setting bodies. After an ambitious start, however, the FSF played a much more marginal role in global financial governance than many of its founders had hoped. In the words of Howard Davies and David Green, the FSF came to act primarily "as a clearing house for initiatives and ideas emerging elsewhere" and it was not able to "carve out a distinctive position, integrating the various perspectives of the diverse membership, as was originally hoped" (2008, 223, 118).

The FSF's role in setting the agenda for international regulatory reform in 2007 and 2008 gave new life to the organization. When the G20 leaders held their first summit in November 2008, they took over from the G7 the role of driving regulatory reform. They used the bulk of their final communiqué to outline a roadmap for international regulatory reform that closely mirrored the FSF's recommendations. At their second summit, in

April 2009, the G20 leaders then transformed the FSF into the Financial Stability Board (FSB) with a wider membership including all G20 countries, plus some others,[3] and a more robust organizational capacity, including a larger secretariat, full-time secretary general, and steering committee. The mandate of the new FSB was also strengthened to include activities such as early warning exercises, strategic reviews of the work of international standard-setting bodies, and the creation and guidance of supervisory colleges for all major cross-border financial institutions. In addition, the FSB's role in encouraging compliance with international standards was boosted by imposing obligations on members to adopt the standards endorsed by the body, undergo FSAPs and ROSCs, and participate in a FSB-led mandatory peer review process. The FSB also immediately launched a process to encourage worldwide compliance with some minimum international standards among nonmember countries (Helleiner 2010a).

The G20 leaders assigned the FSB a leadership role—along with the SSBs and other international financial institutions—in carrying out detailed priorities for international regulatory reform they outlined at their various summits after April 2009. In some instances, new standards were developed to cover activities and sectors that had previously fallen outside the orbit of international regulatory initiatives. For example, the FSB created new Principles for Sound Compensation Practices in 2009 designed to restrict excessive private sector risk-taking by significant financial institutions. Regulators also worked to develop new kinds of official regulation over sectors such as hedge funds and over-the-counter derivatives that had been covered only by private international standards before the crisis (Helleiner and Pagliari 2010).

In other instances, existing official international standards were reformed, the most important initiative being the effort to update the 2004 Basel II agreement regulating international banks. This Basel III agreement, approved by the G20 leaders at their November 2010 summit in Seoul, involved tougher capital standards, new leverage ratios and liquidity rules, and improved risk management and disclosure standards. The G20 leaders also backed new macro-prudential goals that went beyond the precrisis micro-prudential focus on the stability of individual banks to look out for the stability of the system as a whole. One example was the goal to create countercyclical capital buffers—that is, firms would boost their capital in good times in order to have a protective buffer available during the economic downturns. Another example was the goal to subject "systemically important financial institution" (SIFI) to tighter regulation, which was, in the words of the G20 leaders, "commensurate with the costs of their failure" (2009, 9).

The Limits of International Regulatory Reform

This agenda has generated a number of reforms (for an overview, see Helleiner 2012), but policymakers are finding it increasingly difficult to reach
agreement in a number of key areas. The G20 commitment to converge on
a single global accounting standard looks unlikely to be achieved soon
(Rachel Sanderson and Nikki Tait, "Accounts Bodies Revise Standards
Workplan," *Financial Times*, June 25, 2010). Officials have also had trouble
constructing detailed rules for a global cross-border resolution regime to
wind down a failing international financial institution. The Basel III negotiations also revealed important national disagreements, prompting prominent policymakers to declare that they may need to fine-tune the agreement to meet local circumstances, such as the European Parliament, or
may set national standards well above Basel III levels, such as Switzerland
and the United Kingdom (see, for example, Nikki Tait, "European Policymakers Urged to Fine-Tune Basel III," *Financial Times*, October 8, 2010;
Haig Simonian, "'Swiss Finish' to Top Basel III Rules," *Financial Times*,
October 4, 2010; Brooke Masters and Patrick Jenkins, "U.K. Signals
Tougher Bank Capital Regime," *Financial Times*, September 22, 2010).

Disagreements about the central issue of how to treat SIFIs have been
particularly intense. Some policymakers favor size limits, others prefer to
restrict these firms from high-risk financial activities, and still others argue
that the institutions should simply be subject to tighter regulation and
supervision and be forced to prepare "living wills" that outline how they
will be wound down in times of trouble. Disagreements also exist on the
question of whether and how the private financial sector should be forced
to pay for bailouts of these firms, or whether there should be a "bail-in" of
private creditors when banks get in trouble. In the face of these disagreements, a number of countries have simply marched ahead with their own
legislative initiatives. The Dodd-Frank bill passed in U.S. Congress in July
2010, for example, contained provisions on which no international consensus existed, such as the Volcker rule restricting banks' proprietary trading, and provisions concerning the forced liquidation of troubled firms.
Various countries have also unilaterally introduced various kinds of levies
on large banks designed to help pay for past or future bailouts.

Because of these various disagreements, the content of international
standards being set through the G20 process has often been diluted to focus on rather general principles that give countries considerable latitude
to make their own policy choices. A key goal of the macro-prudential
agenda—the boosting of capital buffers in times of excess credit growth
—has also been left up to the discretion of national authorities. In addition, international disagreements have also been paved over by provid-

ing for very long implementation deadlines of the new Basel III capital standards.

Even in other financial sectors where international consensus has been reached, implementation of international agreements at the national (or regional, in the case of the EU) level has been uneven. For example, the results of the FSB's peer review process concerning its new compensation standards revealed quite inconsistent adoption and enforcement of the new standards across the member countries. Some aspects of the derivatives provisions of the Dodd-Frank bill also fall short of the G20 commitments, such as exemptions from clearing requirements for end-users of over-the-counter (OTC) derivatives, yet others go beyond, such as position limits on commodity derivatives (Clapp and Helleiner 2012). The European regulatory proposals have also departed from the international script in areas such as hedge fund regulation.

These difficulties surrounding implementation highlight one further weakness of the post-crisis international reform initiatives: the international standards regime remains remarkably toothless. Even after the creation of the FSB, international financial standards remain entirely voluntary. Although the international trade law has "hardened" since the creation of the WTO, the international financial standards regime still relies entirely on what is called soft law. U.S. Treasury Secretary Tim Geithner has described the FSB as a new fourth pillar of the architecture of global economic governance alongside the IMF, World Bank, and WTO (quoted in Helleiner 2010a), but the institution has not been ratified by any national legislature and its charter acknowledges that membership "is not intended to create any legal rights or obligations" (FSB 2009, 7). There is, in other words, no bite behind FSB's new membership obligations to implement international standards and undergo FSAPs, ROSCs, and peer reviews. Even the threat of expulsion from the FSB is not credible since the body's Plenary works on a consensus basis, thus allowing a non-complying country to veto any attempt to revoke its membership (Helleiner 2010a).

Toward a Weakening of International Standards

What explains these limitations of post-crisis international regulatory cooperation? Although the crisis acted as the impetus for international regulatory reform, it also unleashed a number of political developments that have undermined the prospects for cooperation. To begin with, the crisis politicized financial regulatory issues to an unprecedented extent, particularly within the countries that experienced massive public bailouts of private financial institutions such as the United States and countries within the European Union. Previously obscure topics such as the regulation of credit default swaps suddenly became the subject of legislative debates and lively public discourse. In this new political environment, regulators have faced much greater constraints on their ability to negotiate new international rules or delegate sovereignty to international institutions.

Although elite technocrats were able initially to drive the content of regulatory reform through the FSF and SSBs, other actors—legislators, heads of state, domestic societal actors—increasingly gained influence over direction of the regulatory change after the autumn of 2008. This influence reflected not just the domestic politicization of regulatory issues but also that many of the ambitious agreements reached at the international level could be implemented only through major legislative changes. This had been much less true in the precrisis period, when scholars had been able to argue that "regulators who initiate international negotiations over harmonization do not face a ratification requirement and therefore can conduct themselves in a relatively opaque and seemingly apolitical environment" (Singer 2007, 119). When they were forced to enter the legislative political arena, technocrats quickly discovered that the ideas around which consensus had formed with the G20, FSF/B, and SSBs were not necessarily shared by domestic politicians and interest groups whose support was needed to implement them into law (Helleiner and Pagliari 2010, 2011).

The ambition of many of the post-crisis regulatory initiatives also has brought the distinctive functioning of different national economies and financial systems to the surface. For example, European parliamentarians have highlighted how the initiative to raise capital requirements in the Basel III negotiations imposed higher costs on European companies that depended more on bank loans than did their U.S. counterparts, who relied more on capital markets, for their funding (Nikki Tait, "European Policymakers Urged to Fine-Tune Basel III," *Financial Times*, October 8, 2010). Contrasting national perspectives on international standards relating to issues such as accounting, corporate governance, credit rating, and hedge fund regulation have also been shown to reflect distinct features of national varieties of capitalism (Fioretos 2010; Nölke 2010; Walter 2008; Zimmermann 2009). The new macro-prudential goals with respect to SIFIs also raise unique political-economy issues across countries. As a November 2009 report from the FSB, IMF, and BIS highlighted, even the task of identifying SIFIs inevitably involves "a high degree of judgment and flexibility to reflect national and conjunctural circumstances" (2009, 4–5). The choice of how to regulate them only raised additional political issues that differ significantly according to national circumstances.

The ability of officials to reach consensus at the international level was undermined not just by these new domestic political constraints but also by the fact that the epicenter of the crisis was in the U.S. and British financial markets. Since the late 1990s, U.S. and British officials had been the leaders of the project to construct the international standards regime, and Anglo American regulatory and supervisory practices had served as models for the development of international best practices (Walter 2008). The crisis shattered the prestige of the practices, forcing the reform of international standards to take place without such a clear focal point at the technocratic level.

The erosion of Anglo American prestige was paralleled by the new post-crisis influence of emerging market countries in international regulatory discussions. Their influence came not just from their being included in the FSB and G20 leaders' forum, and its wresting of the control of regulatory debates away from the G7 from November 2008 onward. Encouraged by the G20 leaders, most of the major SSBs also reformed their governance arrangements to give these countries more formal voice in 2009. More generally, these countries also saw their power in world finance enhanced by the increased international significance of their financial institutions and investors, a significance that was particularly apparent during the crisis when U.S. and European financial institutions turned to them for financial assistance (Helleiner and Pagliari 2011).

The growing influence of developing countries has further complicated the task of reaching consensus on international regulatory issues. Over the previous decade, developing countries had often complained not only about their exclusion from the FSF and SSBs but also about the content of the international standards. The latter was seen to reflect developed countries' interests in ways that either disadvantaged developing countries, such as by favoring the interests of sophisticated firms from developed countries, or were inappropriate to their needs (see Porter 2005, 127, 134). Now that many of them are members of the standard-setting clubs, they have had an opportunity to bring their distinctive preferences to the negotiating table. As Stéphane Rottier and Nicolas Véron wrote in a 2010 *Financial Times* article, "emerging countries are asserting themselves in global financial rule-making, and increasingly resist standards proposed by members of the old north Atlantic consensus" ("The New Disintegration of Finance," September 10).

Some of these post-crisis political constraints on international regulatory cooperation may lessen in the coming years, such as the intense politicization of regulatory issues within the United States and Europe. But others will endure, such as distinct varieties of capitalism and macroprudential priorities, and some are likely to become more pronounced, such as the diffusion of power in the interstate system. These latter developments may lead states to increasingly disregard international standards either overtly or through more subtle forms of "mock compliance" (Walter 2008). They are also likely to make new international standards more difficult to create and more likely to assume the form of principles-based standards than rules prescribing detailed harmonization.

Resistance to harmonization may also take the form of greater use of host country regulation in which international firms are forced to transform branches into separately capitalized subsidiaries governing by national rules (Helleiner 2010a; Persaud 2010). This trend toward greater "ring fencing" of international businesses along national lines is likely to be reinforced if countries continue to be unable to agree on the creation of a substantial cross-border resolution regime or international burden-sharing arrangements to fund future bailouts. Some aspects of the macroprudential regulatory agenda may also encourage this kind of segmentation of global financial business along national lines such as the requirement for SIFIs to establish "living wills" or the introduction of countercyclical capital charges for banks that vary according to country-specific credit cycles. In the wake of the crisis, European policymakers have also turned to greater host country control in areas such as derivatives clearing and credit rating regulation as a way of reducing Europe's dependence on, and vulnerability to, U.S. regulatory practices (Helleiner and Pagliari 2011).

These various trends suggest that the ultimate legacy of the 2007 to 2009 crisis is likely to be a more decentralized international regulatory order, one that gives more autonomy to national and regional authorities to set their own regulatory priorities. Rather than as a catalyst for the strengthening of the one-size-fits-all international standards regime that began to be constructed after the late 1990s, the crisis may thus be viewed by future historians as a turning point that led to a weakening of that regime. This is not to say that international regulatory cooperation is likely to wane completely. In a world of more differentiated national regulations, the FSB could still have an important role to play in facilitating the development and promotion of broad principles-based international regulatory standards as well as activities such as information-sharing, research collaboration, international early warning systems, and capacity building. But the constraints imposed by domestic politics and changing interstate power relations in the post-crisis era are likely to ensure that the international cooperation increasingly serves national priorities rather than the other way around (Helleiner and Pagliari 2011).

CONCLUSION

Has the global financial crisis of 2007 to 2009 catalyzed a strengthening of multilateral cooperation centered around the new G20? The official response to the crisis certainly involved a great deal of G20-led cooperation in the areas of both crisis management and regulatory reform. But this chapter has argued that the significance of this cooperation should not be exaggerated. In the realm of crisis management, although politicians such as Gordon Brown may argue that the G20 "averted a second global depression" (2010, 129), we need to acknowledge that some of the key successes of cooperation were facilitated through other channels, such as the WTO and especially central bank networks. It is also easy to overstate the significance of international cooperation itself in generating national policies that averted the crisis, such as macroeconomic stimulus programs, emergency support to troubled firms, and especially prevention of a dollar crisis at the height of the financial meltdown. Staff members of the IMF may believe that "the international community's response to the crisis was successful because it was based to a large extent on global collaboration" (Mateos y Lago and Yang 2010, 223), but that line of argument may assign too much credit to the role that international collaboration actually played in the managing the crisis.

In the regulatory realm, international cooperation in the G20 and other multilateral bodies certainly did play a major role in generating the initial stage of reforms in response to the crisis. But the crisis also generated political trends that have made cooperation increasingly difficult, such as a widespread politicization of regulatory issues within leading states, reform agendas that cut to the core of distinctive varieties of capitalism, the erosion of the international prestige of Anglo American standards, and growing influence of emerging market countries. If these trends continue, the result is likely to be a weakening—rather than a strengthening—of international regulatory cooperation in the coming years.

This analysis thus suggests that scholars must be careful not to get too swept up in the idea that the crisis has generated an important revival of G20-led multilateral cooperation (for a similar conclusion regarding the revival of the IMF`s role, see Woods 2010; for a critique of the idea that the crisis represented a Bretton Woods moment, see Helleiner 2010b). Some of the key outcomes of the crisis were a product more of a lucky alignment of domestic politics and national priorities of key countries than multilateral—or even bilateral—cooperation. Even in areas where multilateral cooperation was extensive, domestic politics and power diffusion have placed growing limits on that cooperation. In short, though official responses to the crisis provide some backing for liberal internationalist understandings of global financial governance, they also suggest support for analytical approaches that focus more on the enduring influence of domestic and comparative political economy as well as interstate power politics (see in particular chapters 2 and 4, this volume).

This analysis also has some important policy implications. Those who have lauded the G20 for preventing a repeat of the Great Depression risk setting up unrealistic expectations of what the G20 can achieve in the post-crisis period, expectations that may then lead to disillusionment with the G20 when they are not met. Indeed, this disillusionment was already clearly in evidence in the wake of the two G20 summits in Toronto and Seoul in 2010, the results of which were deemed less spectacular than those of summits at the height of the crisis. The harsh criticisms of the G20 at that time often exaggerated what the G20 had in fact achieved during what British Prime Minister David Cameron called the more "heroic" crisis phase (quoted in Beattie and Oliver, "U.S. Hits at Greenspan Comments on Dollar," *Financial Times*, November 12, 2010).

The analysis in this chapter provides the basis for a more measured assessment of some key challenges facing supporters of multilateral cooperation in the coming years. The enduring foreign support for the United States during the crisis suggests that global imbalances are unlikely to disappear if the root political sources of that support are not addressed. At their September 2009 summit, the G20 leaders initiated a new multilateral framework to encourage more balanced growth involving mutual assessment of each other's medium-term policy frameworks. This initiative too is unlikely to be successful if some of the underlying causes of the imbalances discussed in this chapter are not addressed, such as the lack of an attractive alternative to dollar assets, the logic of Bretton Woods II, the demand for self-insurance, and China's dollar entrapment.

Policymakers also need to recognize the limits of international regulatory cooperation in finance. Instead of trying unrealistically to create harmonized regulations on a worldwide scale, they would do better to acknowledge that national regulatory differences are likely to persist, and even widen. Cooperation to support a more decentralized and pluralistic regulatory order need not result in a less stable global financial order; indeed, this kind of cooperative decentralization may usher in a more stable one (Helleiner and Pagliari 2011). As Dani Rodrik wrote in the *Economist*, "the world economy will be far more stable and prosperous with a thin veneer of international co-operation superimposed on strong national regulations than with attempts to construct a bold global regulatory and supervisory framework. The risk we run is that pursuing an ambitious goal will detract us from something that is more desirable and more easily attained" ("A Plan B for Global Finance," March 12, 2009).

One further rationale for this less ambitious vision of international cooperation is that it will help to minimize international constraints on national policy experimentation during future crises. In this chapter, I have focused on the enabling role of international cooperation. But in the era of the Great Depression, international cooperation—in the form of efforts to maintain the international gold standard—acted as a key constraint on governments' policy space to experiment with measures to address the crisis (Eichengreen 1992). This kind of constraint was less present for most countries in the financial realm during the 2007 to 2009 crisis because contemporary global financial governance—in contrast to trade governance—is characterized largely by informal networks and soft law of the kind that the G20, the FSB, and the various SSBs embody. Even in the one area where more formalized hard-law financial commitments exist—the IMF's Articles of Agreement—the constraints on exchange rate policy have become very loose since the breakdown of the Bretton Woods exchange rate regime in the 1970s. Only in regional contexts, notably Europe, has international financial cooperation assumed a much more constraining form in the current era (see chapters 4 and 6, this volume). But the European experience of the crisis is unlikely to be one that other countries will want to emulate.

For their helpful comments, I am very grateful to Ben Ansell, Nancy Bermeo, Jonas Pontasson, Waltraud Schelkle, and two anonymous reviewers.

NOTES

1. The risks were considered so high that British Prime Minister Gordon Brown told his wife to be prepared to leave the prime minister's residence within hours if markets responded badly to the initiative (Brown 2010).
2. The logic of this payback argument was strengthened by the fact that U.S. policymakers—some of whom had been involved in the management of the East Asian crisis—were now responding to the U.S. crisis with much more lenient policy measures than they had demanded of East Asia a decade earlier (for this double standard, see, for example, Stiglitz 2010, 221–22; Sheng 2000, 39).
3. Other members included Hong Kong, the Netherlands, Singapore, and Switzerland, each of which, along with Australia, had become members of the FSF after its founding, as well as Spain and the European Commission.

REFERENCES

Bayne, Nicholas. 2008. "Financial Diplomacy and the Credit Crunch." *Journal of International Affairs* 61(1): 1–16.

Brown, Gordon. 2010. *Beyond the Crash*. New York: The Free Press.

Chin, Gregory, and Eric Helleiner. 2008. "China as a Creditor: A Rising Financial Power?" *Journal of International Affairs* 61(2): 87–102.

Clapp, Jennifer, and Eric Helleiner. 2012. "Troubled Futures? The Global Food Crisis and the Politics of Agricultural Derivatives Regulation." *Review of International Political Economy* 19(2): 181–206.

Cohen, Benjamin. 2008. "The International Monetary System." *International Affairs* 84(3): 455–70.

Davies, Howard, and David Green. 2008. *Global Financial Regulation: The Essential Guide.* Cambridge, Mass.: Polity.

Dieter, Heribert. 2007. "The U.S. Economy and the Sustainability of Bretton Woods II." *Journal of Australian Political Economy* 55(1): 48–76.

Dooley, Michael, David Folkerts-Landau, and Peter Garber. 2003. "An Essay on the Revived Bretton Woods System." *NBER* working paper 9971. Cambridge, Mass.: National Bureau of Economic Research.

Drezner, Daniel. 2009. "Bad Debts: Assessing China`s Financial Influence in Great Power Politics." *International Security* 34(2): 7–45.

Eichengreen, Barry. 1992. *Golden Fetters.* Oxford: Oxford University Press.

———. 2006. *Global Imbalances and the Lessons of Bretton Woods.* Cambridge, Mass.: MIT Press.

Financial Stability Board (FSB). 2009. "Charter." Basel: Financial Stability Board, Bank for International Settlements. Available at: http://www.financialstability board.org/publications/r_090925d.pdf (accessed April 14, 2012).

Financial Stability Board, International Monetary Fund, Bank for International Settlements. 2009. "Guidance to Assess the Systemic Importance of Financial Institutions, Markets, and Instruments: Initial Considerations." *Bank for International Settlements.* Available at: http://www.bis.org/publ/othp07.htm (accessed April 14, 2012).

Fioretos, Orfeo. 2010. "Capitalist Diversity and the International Regulation of Hedge Funds." *Review of International Political Economy* 17(4): 696–723.

G7. 1999. "Communique of G7 Finance Ministers and Central Bank Governors," February 20. Bonn, Germany. Available at: http://www.g8.utoronto.ca/finance/fm022099.htm (accessed April 14, 2012).

G20. 2008. "Declaration of the Summit on Financial Markets and the World Economy." November 15, Washington D.C. Available at: http://www.g20.utoronto .ca/2008/2008declaration1115.html (accessed May 24, 2012).

———. 2009. "Leaders Statement, The Pittsburgh Summit." September 24–25, Pittsburgh. Available at: http://www.g20.utoronto.ca/2009/2009communique 0925.html (accessed May 24, 2012).

Helleiner, Eric. 2009. "Enduring Top Currency, Fragile Negotiated Currency." In *The Future of the Dollar,* edited by Eric Helleiner and J. Kirshner. Ithaca, N.Y.: Cornell University Press.

———. 2010a. "The Financial Stability Board and International Standards." *CIGI G20 paper no.1.* Waterloo, Canada: Centre for International Governance Innovation.

———. 2010b. "A Bretton Woods Moment? The 2007–08 Crisis and the Future of Global Finance." *International Affairs* 86(3): 619–36.

———. 2011. "Understanding the Global Financial Crisis: Lessons for IPE?" *Annual Review of Political Science* 14(June): 67–87.

———. 2012. "The Limits of Incrementalism: The G20, FSB, and the International Regulatory Agenda." *Journal of Globalization and Development* 2(2): 1–19. ISSN (Online) 1948–1837. DOI 10.1515/1948-1837.1242.

Helleiner, Eric, and Stefano Pagliari. 2010. "The End of Self-Regulation?" In *Global Finance in Crisis*, edited by Eric Helleiner, Stefano Pagliari, and Hubert Zimmermann. London: Routledge.

———. 2011. "The End of an Era in International Financial Regulation?" *International Organization* 65(3): 169–200.

James, Harold. 2009. *The Creation and Destruction of Value.* Cambridge, Mass.: Harvard University Press.

Johnson, Juliet. 2008. "Forbidden Fruit: Russia's Uneasy Relationship with the Dollar." *Review of International Political Economy* 15(3): 379–98.

Kirshner, Jonathan. 2008. "Dollar Primacy and American Power." *Review of International Political Economy* 15(3): 418–38.

Mateos y Lago, Isabelle, and Yongzheng Yang. 2010. "The IMF and a New Multilateralism." *Global Policy* 1(2): 223–25.

Moon, Chung-in, and Song-Young Rhyu 2010. "Rethinking Alliance and the Economy: American Hegemony, Path Dependence, and the South Korean Political Economy." *International Relations of the Asia-Pacific* 10(3): 441–64.

Murphy, R. Taggart. 2006. "East Asia's Dollars." *New Left Review* 40(1): 39–64.

Nölke, Andreas. 2010. "The Politics of Accounting Regulation." In *Global Finance in Crisis*, edited by Eric Helleiner, Stefano Pagliari, and Hubert Zimmermann. London: Routledge.

Paulson, Hank. 2009. *On the Brink.* New York: Business Press.

Persaud, Avinash. 2010. "The Locus of Financial Regulation: Home versus Host." *International Affairs* 86(3): 637–46.

Porter, Tony. 2005. *Globalization and Finance.* Cambridge, Mass.: Polity.

Rajan, Rajhuram. 2010. *Fault Lines.* Princeton, N.J.: Princeton University Press.

Reinhart, Carmen, and Ken Rogoff. 2009. *This Time Is Different.* Princeton, N.J.: Princeton University Press.

Sarkozy, Nicolas. 2010. "Speech by the President of the Republic." 18th Ambassadors' Conference, Elysée Palace. Paris. (August 25, 2010). Available at: http://www.diplomatie.gouv.fr/en/ministry_158/events_5815/speech-by-the-president-of-the-republic_14177.html (accessed April 14, 2012).

Schwartz, Herman. 2009. *Subprime Nation*. Ithaca, N.Y.: Cornell University Press.

Setser, Brad. 2008. "The New 'Westphalian' International Financial System." *Journal of International Affairs* 62(1): 17–34.

Sheng, Andrew. 2009. *From Asian to Global Financial Crisis*. Cambridge: Cambridge University Press.

Singer, David. 2007. *Regulating Capital*. Ithaca, N.Y.: Cornell University Press.

Sorkin, Andrew. 2009. *Too Big to Fail*. New York: Viking.

Soros, George. 2008. *The New Paradigm for Financial Markets*. New York: Public Affairs.

Stiglitz, Joseph. 2010. *Freefall*. New York: W. W. Norton.

Strauss-Kahn, Dominique. 2010. "Economic Policy Challenges in the Post-Crisis Period." Speech at Inaugural Conference oft the Institute for New Economic Thinking. Cambridge (April 10, 2010). Available at: http://www.imf.org/external/np/speeches/2010/041010.htm (accessed April 14, 2012).

Tett, Gillian. 2009. *Fool's Gold*. New York: Free Press.

Thompson, Helen. 2009. "The Political Origins of the Financial Crisis." *Political Quarterly* 80(1): 17–24.

Walter, Andrew. 2008. *Governing Finance*. Ithaca, N.Y.: Cornell University Press.

Wolf, Martin. 2008. *Fixing Global Finance*. Baltimore, Md.: The Johns Hopkins University Press.

Woods, Ngaire. 2010. "Global Governance after the Financial Crisis: A New Multilateralism or Last Gasp of the Great Powers." *Global Policy* 1(1): 51–63.

Zimmermann, Hubert. 2009. "Varieties of Global Financial Governance? British and German Approaches to Financial Market Regulation." In *Global Finance in Crisis*, edited by Eric Helleiner, Stefano Pagliari, and Hubert Zimmermann. London: Routledge.

Chapter 4 | European Fiscal Responses to the Great Recession

David R. Cameron

BEGINNING IN LATE 2007 with the collapse of the construction, real estate, and housing booms in Ireland and Spain, in 2008 and 2009 one European country after another experienced the most severe economic contraction since the 1930s. The effects of the contractions were amplified, of course, because they were synchronized and continent-wide, and part of a larger global economic and financial collapse (Krugman 2009; Münchau 2010; Rajan 2010; Roubini and Mihm 2010; Stiglitz 2010). Thus, by the late winter of 2008–2009, twenty-five of the twenty-seven member states of the European Union—all but Poland and Slovakia—were in recession, according to the conventional definition of two consecutive quarters of negative growth. In the three Baltic states, the contraction was so great as to warrant the term *depression* rather than *recession*.

In November 2008, the European Commission proposed a recovery program that would involve a fiscal stimulus of €200 billion in 2009 and 2010, equivalent to about 1.5 percent of the EU-wide GDP. Because the EU institutions themselves have very little fiscal capacity—the entire EU budget is equivalent to roughly 1 percent of the EU-wide GDP—and are greatly limited in the purposes for which they can issue debt, 85 percent of the proposed stimulus would come from the budgets of the member states. The plan was approved by the European Council at its meeting in December 2008.

Less than two months later and one month after President Barack Obama took office, the Congress approved and the president signed into law the American Recovery and Reinvestment Act (ARRA). The act was expected to introduce a fiscal stimulus in 2009 and 2010 of $787 billion in revenue and spending measures, equivalent to roughly 5 percent of the

U.S. GDP (on the ARRA, see chapters 7 and 11, this volume). Soon after, a heated debate arose between the EU, on one hand, and the United States, the International Monetary Fund (IMF), and the Organisation for Economic Co-operation and Development (OECD), on the other, about whether Europe should do more to respond to the deepening crisis. Despite the accelerating contraction of the European countries, the EU and its member states resisted the calls to pursue an additional fiscal stimulus. The predictable result was a contraction that was more severe, lasted longer, and imposed greater costs in terms of lost output and unemployment than might otherwise have been the case. In the absence of any further coordinated EU-wide response to the contraction, the member states inevitably responded in different ways. Some adopted expansionary fiscal measures whereas others relied almost exclusively on the countercyclical "automatic stabilizers" in their budgets. Some moved quickly to assume control over large financial institutions and to regulate the financial sector while others left the financial system largely unregulated. (On the varying responses to the financial crisis, see chapters 2 and 10, this volume.) Some —most notably, Germany—introduced or expanded schemes for part-time and flexible work to dampen the inevitable increase in unemployment while others allowed unemployment to drift upward into double digits (on Germany's use of short work, see chapter 5, this volume.) As a result, some were able to initiate a recovery by mid- to late 2009 and achieve relatively high rates of growth and lower rates of unemployment in 2010 and beyond, whereas others remained mired in recession and continued to experience low rates of growth and high rates of unemployment.

This chapter discusses the fiscal responses of the EU and its member states to the economic crisis of 2007 to 2009. After presenting data indicative of the breadth, depth, and timing of the contraction, it describes the EU's 2008 recovery plan, notes the extent to which it underestimated the magnitude of the economic contraction, and discusses some of the reasons it subsequently refused to inject a larger fiscal stimulus into the economy. That discussion highlights the lack of fiscal capacity within the EU, the constraining effect of its Stability and Growth Pact, and the constraining effects of the widely held assumptions that, among countries with open economies and high levels of trade dependence, a large part of any fiscal stimulus would "leak" abroad and that the ample countercyclical automatic stabilizers in the member states' budgets would bring the recession to an end and fuel a recovery. In addition, the discussion highlights a profound coordination problem in the EU in the domain of fiscal and economic policy that impedes its ability to respond in a timely and effective manner to an economic crisis—a problem that became glaringly apparent in the subsequent eurozone debt crisis (see chapter 6, this volume; Cameron 2012) but was evident before that crisis in the response to the contraction of 2007 to 2009.

The chapter then turns to the fiscal responses of the member states and considers the extent to which and the reasons why they differed in the extent to which the aggregate budget of all levels of government had an expansionary or contractionary effect on the economy, the extent to which their budgets were sensitive to cyclical changes in the economy and could offset the effect of a contraction in output with automatic stabilizers, and the extent to which they introduced discretionary measures to reduce taxes or increase spending. The analysis suggests that, contrary to conventional wisdom, the extent to which the aggregate fiscal balance of all levels of government changed from year to year—for example, the extent to which the overall budget deficit increased—did not have a significant effect in promoting a recovery from the 2007 to 2009 contraction, perhaps because the countercyclical automatic stabilizers in the countries' budgets and the discretionary measures adopted by some governments constituted only a small portion of the fisc and were offset by other components that are either noncyclical or procyclical.[1]

Nevertheless, the analysis does suggest that both the automatic stabilizers in the countries' budgets and the discretionary fiscal measures that some governments adopted had an expansionary impact on the economy and contributed to an early recovery from the 2008 to 2009 contraction. The analysis suggests that discretionary fiscal measures—in particular, reductions in taxes—had a significant effect in generating an early and robust recovery from the trough of the contraction. That finding suggests that some European countries recovered from the contraction earlier and more robustly than others in part because they were better situated, in terms of fiscal policy before the crisis, to enact expansionary discretionary measures once the crisis hit. In particular, those countries which, despite having well-developed and well-funded welfare states, accumulated significant budget surpluses in good times, in large part because they rely more extensively than other countries on sources of revenue—most notably, taxes on personal and corporate income—that are income elastic and increase in good times, were better situated to undertake expansionary fiscal measures—most notably, reducing taxes—in hard times.

In concluding, the chapter notes that, because the ability to enact such measures was not randomly distributed but instead depended on certain structural and political attributes that appear to be regionally concentrated, the varying responses to the economic contraction resulted in a substantial regional difference within the EU in postcontraction growth rates. However, it also notes that the prolonged debt crisis in the eurozone, accompanied as it has been by the widespread pursuit of austerity and deficit reduction, not only in Greece, Ireland, and Portugal but in Germany, France, Italy, Spain, Britain, and other countries as well, has undone much of the recovery that occurred in 2010 and 2011 and made it likely that Europe as a whole will experience low rates of growth—on average, 1 to 2 percent a year—and high levels of unemployment—on average, around 10 percent—for some time.

BREADTH, DEPTH, AND DURATION OF THE ECONOMIC CONTRACTION

Table 4.1 presents the quarter-by-quarter rates of change in "real" or constant-price GDP since the first quarter of 2007. The data indicate that the economic slowdown began in Europe in the second quarter of 2008 and accelerated noticeably in the fourth quarter of that year. Europe experienced the sharpest contraction in the first quarter of 2009, after which the economy contracted very slightly in the second quarter and increased very slightly in the third and fourth quarters and again in the first quarter of 2010. It was only in the second quarter of 2010 that the quarter-on-quarter rate of growth returned to levels experienced before the contraction of 2007 to 2009. However, that rate was not sustained and dropped by 50 percent in the third quarter of 2010.

Table 4.2 presents the results of the quarter-by-quarter change in GDP in the member states of the EU between the first quarter of 2007 and the third quarter of 2010. The table indicates simply whether a country's economy expanded or contracted or contracted in the quarter, not the extent of change. Only one member state—Denmark—experienced a contraction of its economy in the first quarter of 2007. Denmark and Ireland experienced contractions in the second quarter but expanded in the third quarter, during which Portugal's and Luxembourg's contracted. Using the conventional definition of a recession as two consecutive quarters of negative growth, the table suggests the first onset of recession occurred in four countries—Denmark, Ireland, Estonia, and Latvia—in the fourth quarter of 2007. In 2008, however, the recession broadened into an EU-wide phenomenon. By mid-2008, nine member states were in recession and by the end of the year twenty-two were. By the first quarter of 2009, twenty-five member states—all but Poland and Slovakia—were in recession.[2] As 2009 went on, one country after another began to experience at least moderate economic growth, and by the end of the year only eight member states were still in recession. By the end of the second quarter of 2010, only one country—Greece—was still in recession.

As a whole, the EU economy contracted by 4.2 percent in 2009 (European Commission 2011a, 206, table 1). The economies of several coun-

Table 4.1   Change in GDP

	EU 27	Eurozone	Year-on-Year
2007			
Q1	0.8	0.7	
Q2	0.5	0.3	3.2
Q3	0.8	0.7	
Q4	0.5	0.4	
2008			
Q1	0.5	0.6	
Q2	–0.1	–0.2	0.3
Q3	–0.3	–0.2	
Q4	–1.5	–1.6	
2009			
Q1	–2.4	–2.5	
Q2	–0.2	–0.1	–4.2
Q3	0.3	0.4	
Q4	0.3	0.2	
2010			
Q1	0.4	0.4	
Q2	1.0	1.0	2.0
Q3	0.5	0.4	
Q4	0.2	0.3	
2011			
Q1	0.7	0.8	
Q2	0.2	0.2	
Q3	0.3	0.2	

Source: Author's compilation based on European Commission (2011b; 2011a, 206, table 1, year-on-year data for EU 27).

tries—Ireland, Slovenia, and Finland—contracted by 7 to 8 percent. Those of the Baltic states contracted so much as to warrant the term depression rather than recession: in Estonia by 14 percent, in Lithuania by 15 percent, and in Latvia by 18 percent after a 3 percent drop in 2008. The overall level of unemployment in the EU, which had dropped to 7.1 percent of the civilian labor force in 2008, increased by almost 2 percentage points to 9 percent in 2009 and continued to increase, to 9.7 percent, in 2010 (217, table 23). In 2009, the unemployment rate rose to 10 percent in Hungary, 12 percent in Ireland and Slovakia, 14 percent in Estonia and Lithuania, 17 percent in Latvia, and 18 percent in Spain. In 2010, unemployment rose to 12 percent in Portugal, almost 13 percent in Greece, 14 percent in Ireland, 17 percent in Estonia, 18 percent in Lithuania, 19 percent in Latvia, and 20

Table 4.2   Quarters in Which the Economy Contracted

	2007				2008				2009				2010			
	1	2	3	4	1	2	3	4	1	2	3	4	1	2	3	4
Denmark	x	x		x	x		x	x	x	x						x
Ireland		x		x	x	x		x	x	x	x	x		x		x
Portugal			x				x	x	x			x				x
Luxembourg			x				x	x	x	x			x			
Estonia				x	x	x	x	x	x	x	x					
Latvia				x	x	x	x	x	x	x	x	x				
Italy				x		x	x	x	x	x		x				
Sweden					x	x	x	x	x							
Hungary						x	x	x	x	x	x					
Netherlands						x	x	x	x	x						
Germany						x	x	x	x							
France						x	x	x	x							
Finland						x	x	x	x	x						
Lithuania						x	x	x	x	x		x	x			
Spain						x	x	x	x	x	x	x				
Malta						x	x	x	x	x				x		
United Kingdom						x	x	x	x	x	x					
Belgium							x	x	x							
Austria							x	x	x							
Czech							x	x	x							
Slovenia							x	x	x				x			
Romania							x	x	x			x	x		x	
Cyprus								x	x	x	x	x				
Greece								x	x	x	x	x	x	x	x	x
Bulgaria											x	x	x			
Slovakia									x							
Poland																

Source: Author's compilation based on European Commission (2011b).
Note: Quarterly data not reported for Bulgaria prior to 2009:Q3.

percent in Spain. As Robert Zoellick, the president of the World Bank, said—appropriately, in an interview with a Spanish newspaper—"what began as a great financial crisis and became a great economic crisis is now becoming a great crisis of unemployment."[3]

Figure 4.1 presents measures for the twenty-seven EU member states of the cumulative contraction in the economy in 2007 to 2009 and the increase in the rate of unemployment between 2008 and 2010.[4] There is, as one would expect, a strong inverse relationship between the two; the greater the contraction in the economy, the greater the increase in unem-

Figure 4.1   Change in GDP, 2008 and 2009, and Change in
            Unemployment, 2008 to 2010

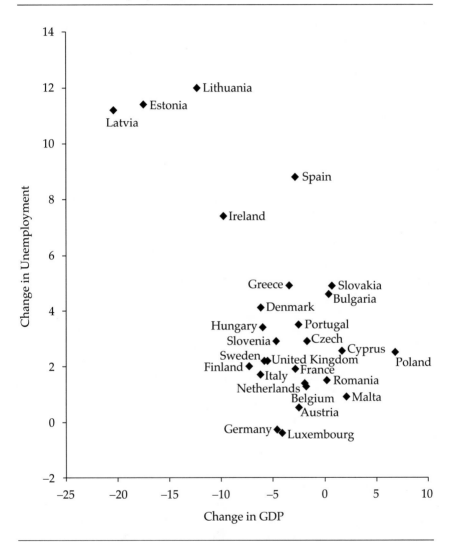

Source: Author's calculations of data from Economic Commission (2011a, table 1, p. 206 and table 23, p. 217).

ployment.[5] What is perhaps most notable about the array is, on the one hand, the extent to which most of the members of the EU are clustered together, in terms of the magnitude of the economic contraction and the increase in unemployment and, on the other, the extent to which Spain and Ireland and especially the Baltic states stand out in both the magnitude of the economic contraction and the increase in unemployment.

THE EU'S 2008 RECOVERY PLAN

In November 2008, as it became apparent that Europe would not be spared the economic contraction that had appeared in the United States with its subprime mortgage crisis, the European Commission formulated a recovery plan that featured a fiscal stimulus of €200 billion in 2009 and 2010, equivalent to 1.5 percent of the EU-wide GDP. Eighty-five percent of it, €170 billion, would be provided by the member states through their budgets and the remaining €30 billion would come from the European Investment Bank in the form of loans for small and medium enterprises, renewable energy, and clean transportation. The plan proposed that the EU would simplify the procedures for, and distribute more quickly, some €6 billion in spending for programs financed by its Cohesion Fund and Structural Funds, and would use its Agricultural Fund for Rural Development to strengthen investment in infrastructure. It would also fund up to €5 billion in specific projects to strengthen investment in energy interconnections and infrastructure, including, through regulatory incentives, broadband infrastructure in areas that are poorly served. Additionally, it would promote employment in key sectors of the economy through its Globalization Adjustment Fund, allow member states wishing to do so to reduce value-added tax (VAT) rates in certain sectors, and provide a temporary two-year exemption in the maximum state aid for small and medium enterprises.

The European Council adopted the plan in December 2008 (5–7). Taking into account the downturn in the European economy in 2009 and 2010, the European Commission (2009b, p. 45) estimated that these and all other discretionary measures would result in a fiscal stimulus over the two years equivalent to 1.8 percent of the 2008 EU GDP, with 1.1 percent occurring in 2009 and 0.7 percent in 2010. By way of comparison, it also estimated that the two-year fiscal stimulus proposed by the Obama administration and approved by the U.S. Congress in February 2009 was equivalent to 4.5 percent of the U.S. GDP, with 2.1 percent occurring in 2009 and 2.4 percent in 2010.

It is, of course, easy with hindsight to second-guess the EU regarding the fiscal stimulus it provided with its December 2008 plan. Those who

Table 4.3   EU Forecasts of Growth and Unemployment in 2009

		Growth	Unemployment
January 2009 forecast	EU 27	–1.8	8.7
	eurozone	–1.9	9.3
Spring 2009 forecast	EU 27	–4.0	9.4
	eurozone	–4.0	9.9
Actual 2009	EU 27	–4.2	9.0
	eurozone	–4.2	9.6

Source: Author's compilation based on European Commission, (2009a, 2009b, 2011a).

formulated the plan were doing so in the midst of an unfolding crisis and in a context of great uncertainty. Nevertheless, it can be argued that by November and December of 2008 it was apparent the contraction was accelerating, it would be very severe, and no turning point was in sight.

One reason the EU adopted a recovery plan that envisioned a fiscal stimulus equivalent to only 1.5 percent of GDP is because the European Commission badly underestimated the magnitude of the contraction. That it did so is illustrated by the data in table 4.3 that compare its January 2009 and spring 2009 forecasts of growth and unemployment in the EU in 2009 with the actual results (2009a, 2009b, 2011a). The January forecast, prepared about the time the European Council adopted the recovery plan, anticipated that the economy would contract by 1.8 percent in the EU and 1.9 percent in the euro area in 2009. Unemployment would edge up to about 9 percent. Four months later, the European Commission recognized that the contraction in 2009 would be much greater—4 percent—and unemployment would rise more sharply, approaching 10 percent.

As it became apparent during the first quarter of 2009 that the rate of economic contraction was accelerating and the EU had badly underestimated the breadth, severity, and likely duration of the crisis, the IMF, the OECD, the Obama administration, and others urged the EU to do more to stimulate demand.[6] Taking into account the large amount of public revenues and expenditures relative to GDP in most European states, and hence the relatively large size of the automatic stabilizers that come into play in those countries during a contraction, both the IMF and the Obama administration urged the EU to aim for a two-year stimulus in the range of 4 percent of GDP, more than twice the amount provided in the EU's recovery plan. The OECD likewise urged that further stimulus measures be enacted quickly, especially measures that would have a short-term impact and would address the problem of increasing unemployment (2009).

The EU leaders would have none of it. After a meeting of the euro area finance ministers prior to the March 2009 meeting of the European Council, Jean-Claude Juncker, the prime minister and minister of finance of Luxembourg and chair of the Eurogroup finance ministers, said, "The 16 finance ministers agreed that recent American appeals insisting Europeans make an added budget effort were not to our liking."[7] At its March meeting, after following the advice of the finance ministers and rejecting any additional stimulus, the European Council expressed its confidence in the medium- and long-term outlook, asserted that "good progress has been made in implementing the European Economic Recovery Plan," and said that "although it will take time for the positive effects to work their way through the economy, the size of the fiscal effort (around 3.3 percent of EU GDP or over €400 billion) will generate new investments, boost demand, create jobs and help the EU move to a low-carbon economy" (2009, 3).

Reporting to the European Parliament on the meeting several days later in his capacity as the head of the government holding the rotating presidency, Mirek Topolánek, the prime minister of the Czech Republic, famously said, "The U.S. Treasury secretary talks about permanent action and we, at our spring council, were quite alarmed at that. . . . The U.S. is repeating mistakes from the 1930s, such as wide-ranging stimuluses, protectionist tendencies and appeals, the Buy American campaign, and so on. All these steps, their combination and permanency, are the road to hell."[8]

Several factors contributed to the EU's unwillingness to modify its initial recovery plan when the full magnitude of the economic contraction became apparent in early 2009. For one thing, the plan had been adopted only three months earlier and had not yet been fully implemented. Also, the January forecast had not yet been updated and the first quarter results were not yet in. In those circumstances, it was perhaps understandable that, rather than modifying the plan, the leaders would ask the finance ministers to evaluate the recovery plan and report back at the June 2009 European Council meeting, which they did.[9] Also, of course, it is obviously much easier to enact a substantial change in policy, as the United States did after January 20, 2009, in a single country in which the executive and legislative branches are controlled by the same party than in a union of twenty-seven states that vary widely in the extent to which they were adversely affected by the unfolding crisis and were willing and able to incur large budget deficits and additional debt to stimulate demand and promote growth and employment.

It is commonplace to assume, after the Great Depression and John Maynard Keynes (1936), that everyone understands and endorses the logic of countercyclical demand management. But that assumption is almost certainly incorrect (Hall 1989) and it is doubtful that all of those responsible for macroeconomic policy in the EU at the time were good Keynesians.

But even if they were, and even if the political leaders of the twenty-seven member states were of one mind about the need for and value of a fiscal stimulus, there is, of course, the problem that the EU itself has very little fiscal capacity. All of the EU's spending, taken together, comprises roughly 1 percent of the EU GDP. That stands in marked contrast to the much greater fiscal capacity of the member states. In 2009, for example, public expenditures of the EU member states averaged 51 percent of GDP (European Commission 2011a, 222, table 33). Also, the EU cannot issue debt except for very limited purposes and in very limited amounts. Taken together, those two factors go a long way in explaining why the December plan envisioned that 85 percent of the fiscal stimulus would be provided through the budgets of the member states and the EU itself would provide a very small portion of the €200 billion.

That the great bulk of any EU-mandated stimulus would, of necessity, come out of the budgets of the member states meant that any such stimulus would face the potential constraint of the EU's Stability and Growth Pact, which seeks to curb "excessive deficits"—deficits over 3 percent of GDP unless they are "exceptional and temporary" and "remain close" to that figure. That the pact loomed over the consideration of a possible fiscal stimulus at the December 2008 meeting of the European Council was evident when, after endorsing the European Commission's recovery plan, it stated,

> The European Council emphasizes that the revised Stability and Growth Pact remains the cornerstone of the EU's budgetary framework. It affords the flexibility for all the Recovery Plan measures to be implemented. Aware that the latter will temporarily deepen the deficits, the European Council reaffirms its full commitment to sustainable public finances and calls on the Member States to return as soon as possible, in accordance with the Pact and keeping pace with economic recovery, to their medium-term targets. (2008, 7)

That view, expressed in nearly identical words, appeared in the Presidency Conclusions issued after the March 2009 Council meeting (European Council 2009).

For member states that generally record substantial budget surpluses in good times—for example, Finland, Sweden, and Denmark—the pact does not pose a serious constraint on the ability to provide a substantial fiscal stimulus in a time of economic crisis; the governments in those countries can undertake a stimulus equivalent to several percentage points of GDP without exceeding the 3 percent limit on deficits. But for those that tend to run deficits in most years, even when experiencing average or better-than-average economic growth, the pact may constrain their ability to provide as much of a fiscal stimulus as is needed in times of crisis. By early 2009, Britain, France, Spain, Ireland, Latvia, Greece, and Malta had excessive deficits. The pact has been applied unevenly, its sanctions are limited, compliance has been occasional and, at best, partial, it has been ineffective in preventing or reducing large deficits, and member states more often than not ignore Council of the European Union declarations that an excessive deficit exists. Nevertheless, the declarations and European Commission reports do put them on notice that they are expected to restore fiscal balance—which, of course, means pursuing a budgetary policy that has a net contractionary impact—in the next two or three years.

An additional constraint on the ability of at least some of the member states to undertake an additional fiscal stimulus was the amount of existing public debt relative to GDP. Countries with relatively little debt obviously have more latitude to take on additional debt than those with relatively large stocks. Two member states—Italy and Greece—had debt-to-GDP ratios that exceeded 100 percent in 2008, and seven others—including Germany and France—had ratios that exceeded 60 percent, the maximum percentage allowed by the treaty for EU member states wishing to enter the third and final stage of Economic and Monetary Union (European Commission 2011a, 225, table 40).

If those constraints weren't enough, the perception is widespread that in a union of states highly dependent on trade a good deal of any stimulus will leak abroad. That is, because the countries import a great deal, a substantial portion of a stimulus in a country would go abroad, through payments for imports, and ultimately benefit the firms and workers in the countries that produced the goods, rather than firms and workers in the country that adopted the stimulus. Because the EU as a whole and its member states are in varying degrees "open economies," the OECD (2009, 115) and others have argued that any fiscal stimulus undertaken by a member of the EU would be less effective because it would, to some degree, leak abroad through spending on imports. The notion that a government might undertake a stimulus that benefited those in other countries, at least to some extent, no doubt acted as a disincentive for some who might otherwise have supported an additional stimulus.

Another widespread perception that, like the notion of leakage, may have operated less as a constraint and more as a rationalization for passivity was the view that the member states of the EU have relatively large automatic stabilizers. The term refers to the fact that certain components of the budget will change automatically—that is, without any change in policy—in a countercyclical direction in response to changes in output.

Thus, for example, when the economy contracts some revenues—personal income taxes, corporate taxes, and consumption taxes—will also contract, and some expenditures—those related to unemployment—will increase. Conversely, when the economy expands, some revenues will increase and some expenditures will decrease. The net effect of the automatic stabilizers, then, is to reduce revenues and increase expenditures when the economy contracts, providing a countercyclical stimulus, and to increase revenues and decrease expenditures when the economy expands, introducing a contractionary effect.

The magnitude of the automatic stabilizers in a budget depends on both the relative size and the composition of revenues and expenditures. Countries in which relatively large shares of GDP are absorbed by public revenues and expenditures, and in which revenues and expenditures are especially sensitive to changes in GDP, will have relatively large stabilizers compared with those in which public revenues and expenditures constitute a smaller portion of the GDP and in which revenues and expenditures are less sensitive with respect to changes in output. Table 4.4 presents measures of the output sensitivity of the fiscal balance and the impact of automatic stabilizers in 2008 and 2009 in twenty-five member states of the EU as well as the United States and Canada. The measure of the output sensitivity of the fiscal balance, calculated by Natalie Girouard and Christophe André (2005) and adapted by the European Commission (2005), consists of the product of the weighted elasticities of four types of revenue—personal income taxes, corporate income taxes, social contributions, and indirect taxes—and one type of expenditure—that related to unemployment—multiplied by the ratios of all current taxes or current expenditures to GDP. The measure represents the amount of change in the fiscal balance—that is, the aggregate budget surplus or deficit—as a percent of GDP due to a 1 percentage point change in GDP. The measures of impact are the product of the measure of the output sensitivity of the fiscal balance multiplied by the annual rate of growth.

The data in table 4.4 indicate that the output sensitivity of the fiscal balance—that is, the extent to which the aggregate fiscal balance changes because of automatic stabilizers with a 1 percentage point change in GDP—varies widely across the EU, from Denmark and Sweden as well as the Netherlands, Belgium, Germany, Italy, and Finland, on one hand, to the member states of central and eastern Europe—most notably, the Baltic states—on the other.[10] But taken as a whole, the member states of the EU do, as the conventional wisdom holds, have budgets that in the aggregate are more sensitive to changes in output than those of the United States and Japan. That means that the EU member states get, on average, a larger fiscal stimulus from the reductions in revenues and increases in expendi-

Table 4.4   Size and Impact in 2008 and 2009 of Automatic
            Stabilizers in Europe

	Output Sensitivity of Fiscal Balance	Impact of Automatic Stabilizers on Fiscal Balance (% of GDP)		
		2008	2009	2008 to 2009
Denmark	.65	0.7	3.4	4.1
Sweden	.58	0.3	3.0	3.3
Netherlands	.55	−1.0	1.9	0.9
Belgium	.54	−0.5	1.5	1.0
Germany	.51	−0.6	2.6	2.0
Italy	.50	0.6	2.6	3.2
Finland	.50	−0.5	4.1	3.6
Luxembourg	.49	−0.4	2.6	2.2
France	.49	0.1	1.3	1.4
Austria	.47	−0.7	1.8	1.1
Hungary	.46	−0.4	3.1	2.7
Portugal	.45	0.0	1.1	1.1
Slovenia	.44	−1.6	3.5	1.9
Spain	.43	−0.4	1.6	1.2
Greece	.43	0.1	1.4	1.5
United Kingdom	.42	0.5	1.8	2.3
Ireland	.40	1.3	2.8	4.1
Poland	.40	−2.0	−0.6	−2.6
Cyprus	.39	−1.4	0.7	−0.7
Malta	.37	−1.6	1.0	−0.6
Czech Republic	.37	−1.1	1.7	0.6
Estonia	.30	1.1	4.3	5.4
Slovakia	.29	−1.7	1.4	−0.3
Latvia	.28	0.9	5.0	5.9
Lithuania	.27	−0.8	4.0	3.2
United States	.34	0.1	1.2	1.3
Japan	.33	0.4	2.1	2.5

Source: Author's compilation based on Girouard and André (2005, table 9) and European Commission 2005 (table 2 and table 6).

Note: The measure of output sensitivity is the product of the weighted elasticities of four types of revenue—personal income taxes, corporate income taxes, social contributions, and indirect taxes—and of unemployment-related expenditures multiplied by the ratios of all current taxes or all current expenditures to GDP. The measure represents the amount of change in the fiscal balance as a percent of GDP due to a 1 percentage point change in GDP. The measures of impact are the product of the measure of output sensitivity and the annual percent change in GDP (European Commission 2011a, 206, table 1).

tures that occur automatically with a unit reduction in output. How large that fiscal stimulus will be depends, of course, on both the extent to which the fiscal balance is sensitive to a change in output and the extent to which the GDP contracts.

Table 4.4 includes measures of the extent and direction of the impact, as a percentage of GDP, on the economy in 2008 and 2009 of the automatic stabilizers in the budget. These data suggest that automatic stabilizers had an expansionary impact in 2008 and 2009 in most of the EU member states—indeed, in all but Poland, which experienced growth in both years, and Cyprus, Malta, and Slovakia, where the impact was negligible. In several—most notably, in Denmark and Sweden, because of the high sensitivity of their budgets to changes in output, and in Finland, Ireland, and the Baltic states, because of the magnitudes of their contractions—the automatic stabilizers generated a fiscal stimulus in the two years that ranged between 3 and 6 percentage points of GDP. In most of the other countries, however, the impact was considerably less, either because their budgets were less sensitive to changes in output or because the economic contractions were less severe.

In addition to the constraints posed by the Stability and Growth Pact, the difficulty of negotiating an agreement among twenty-seven governments, and the widely held assumptions that a substantial portion of any fiscal stimulus would leak abroad and that the automatic stabilizers in the budgets would largely suffice, a more fundamental constraint limited the ability of the EU to undertake a larger fiscal stimulus at a time when almost all of the member states were in the depths of the most severe economic contraction since the 1930s. That constraint is the absence of an effective institutional mechanism through which the member states can coordinate their fiscal and economic policies and, if need be, exercise collective authority over those policies. The absence of such a mechanism is most apparent in the case of the member states that constitute the euro area, and as the eurozone debt crisis unfolded in early 2010 there were frequent calls to introduce the old French idea, first advocated in the run-up to Economic and Monetary Union in the mid-1990s, of "economic government" or "economic governance" (Pisani-Ferry 2006).[11] A year and a half later, as negotiations over a second large bailout for Greece stalled and the crisis threatened to spread to Italy and Spain, those calls became increasingly insistent, and in the winter of 2011–2012 the eurozone leaders negotiated and signed a new treaty—a "fiscal compact"—that would enhance their ability to exercise some degree of collective authority over the national budgets of the participating member states and move the eurozone some distance toward a "fiscal union" (see chapter 6, this volume; Cameron 2012).

There can be no doubt that the member states that have joined the euro area constitute a monetary union, using as they do a single currency and having turned over responsibility for monetary policy to a single supranational entity. Yet despite the first word in Economic and Monetary Union, they do not constitute an economic or a fiscal union and have neither the authority nor the means to act collectively with respect to the fiscal policies of the participating member states. As Wolfgang Schäuble, the German finance minister, succinctly put it after a year of dealing with the debt crisis, "We have a common monetary union, but we don't have a common fiscal policy."[12] In a similar vein, in a speech titled "Building Europe, Building Institutions" delivered after receiving the International Charlemagne Prize in Aachen in June 2011, Jean-Claude Trichet (2011), the president of the European Central Bank, said, "confronting the challenges of the future requires strengthening the institutions of economic union— the E in EMU."

Lacking an effective mechanism through which they could coordinate their fiscal and economic policies, the EU member states agreed only that 85 percent of the stimulus in the 2008 recovery plan would be provided through their budgets. There was no designation of which states would provide how much of the stimulus, when they would provide it, and how it would be targeted. There was no recognition of the fact that, given the inability of some member states—for example, those with excessive deficits or debt-GDP ratios well above 60 percent—to incur substantially larger deficits, other member states would have to incur larger deficits than they otherwise would incur in order for the stimulus to be large enough to promote an EU-wide recovery.

As the IMF noted in its regional outlook for Europe in the spring of 2009, the conventional wisdom that some portion of a fiscal stimulus enacted in an open economy would leak abroad could be turned on its head through coordination of the fiscal policies of the member states (2009). Although the member states have relatively high levels of imports through which leakage can occur, they also have relatively high levels of exports. Moreover, in the EU those high levels of exports are concentrated to a great extent in the markets of the other member states. In 2009, for example, while exports of goods and services were equivalent to about 42 percent of the EU-wide GDP, two-thirds of all EU exports went to other member states (European Commission 2011a). In a union of open economies highly dependent on exports and in which the great majority of all exports go to the other countries in the union, a fiscal stimulus enacted simultaneously by all members would create demand for exports throughout the EU. Whereas a stimulus enacted by a single member state might leak abroad through its imports from other countries, a stimulus enacted by all of the members simultaneously would create demand for goods and services produced in all of the members, thereby offsetting the leakage. The problem, of course, was that for the EU to carry out a simultaneous fiscal stimulus, the member states would have not only to agree to pursue a stimulus but also to coordinate their fiscal policies in pursuit of that objective. And that would mean they would have to exercise some degree of collective authority over the fiscal policies of the member states.

FISCAL RESPONSES OF THE MEMBER STATES

In the absence of a coordinated EU response beyond the 2008 recovery plan, the member states responded in various ways as the magnitude of the 2007 to 2009 economic contraction became apparent. Some relied largely on the automatic stabilizers that provide a fiscal stimulus in periods of economic contraction, even if government enacts no discretionary fiscal measures, as revenues from taxes on personal and corporate incomes and on sales decrease and expenditures on unemployment-related policies increase. Others, however, supplemented the automatic stabilizers with discretionary fiscal measures—that is, measures resulting in reductions in taxes and other revenues and/or increases in spending—and, in so doing, introduced an expansionary impulse into the economy.

The aggregate effect on the economy of the automatic stabilizers, whatever discretionary fiscal measures are enacted, and all of the other changes in revenues and expenditures is reflected in the year-to-year change in the aggregate fiscal balance—that is, in the aggregate budget surplus or deficit—of all levels of government as a percentage of GDP. A year-to-year reduction in the aggregate surplus or increase in the aggregate deficit of all levels of government as a percentage of GDP—the result of a decrease in the revenues of all levels of government as a proportion of GDP and/or an increase in the expenditures of all levels of government as a proportion of GDP—has, by definition, an expansionary impact on the economy. Conversely, a year-to-year increase in the aggregate surplus or decrease in the aggregate deficit of all levels of government as a percentage of GDP—the result of an increase in revenues or decrease in expenditures—has, by definition, a contractionary impact.

Table 4.5 presents measures of the magnitude and direction of the year-to-year change as a percent of GDP in the aggregate fiscal balance of all levels of government in the member states of the EU from 2007 to 2010. The data indicate that, as one would expect given the 3.2 percent increase in GDP in 2007, the change in the aggregate fiscal balance from 2006 to 2007 was, with one notable exception—Ireland, slightly contractionary or very modestly expansionary (European Commission 2011a, 223, table 35).

But in 2008 and especially in 2009, the overall year-to-year change in the fiscal balance as a percentage of GDP was expansionary.[13] In 2008, the year-to-year changes in the budgets of the twenty-seven EU member countries had an expansionary impact equivalent to 1.5 percent of GDP, and in 2009 an expansionary impact equivalent to 4.5 percent of GDP. Especially large fiscal stimuli occurred in those two years, taken together, in Ireland (14.3 percent), Spain (13.1), Cyprus (9.6), Latvia (9.3), Greece (9.3), the United Kingdom (8.8), Lithuania (8.5), Finland (7.8), Denmark (7.5), and Portugal (7.0). Only in a handful of states—Italy (3.8), Germany (3.4), Austria (3.2), and Malta (1.3)—did the aggregate change in all revenues and all expenditures as a percentage of GDP in 2008 and 2009 introduce a stimulus of less than 4 percent of GDP, and only in one state—Hungary (–0.5)—did the aggregate change in those two years introduce a contractionary effect on the economy.[14] By way of comparison, the data in table 4.5 indicate that the expansionary effect of the aggregate change in revenues and expenditures as a percentage of GDP in the EU in 2008 and 2009 was, though substantial (6 percent), less than that in the United States (8.7 percent) and Japan (6.3 percent) in those two years.

If the aggregate effect of all of the changes in revenues and expenditures as a percentage of GDP was expansionary in almost all member states in 2008 and 2009, one might expect that the largest expansionary effects occurred where contractions of the economy were the largest, if only because one would expect the greatest reductions in government revenues and greatest increases in expenditures relative to GDP to occur where economic contractions were the greatest. Figure 4.2 suggests, however, that the relationship between the extent of the economic contraction in 2008 and 2009 and the extent to which the change in the aggregate fiscal balance in those years introduced a fiscal stimulus is at best only slight.[15] Although the array suggests that the magnitude of the aggregate fiscal stimulus tended to be, as one would expect, greater in the member states that experienced a severe economic contraction than in those that experienced only a modest contraction or no contraction at all (such as Poland), a number of member states are situated well away from an imaginary regression line running from Latvia to Poland. Most notably, the overall effect of fiscal policy in the Baltic states, especially in Latvia and Estonia, was, though expansionary, much less so than might have been expected given the magnitude of their economic contractions. Thus, for example, although expenditures as a percentage of GDP increased in Estonia from 34 percent of GDP in 2007 to 45.2 percent in 2009, their expansionary impact was diminished by the increase in revenues from 36.4 percent of GDP in 2007 to 43.2 percent in 2009 (European Commission 2011a, 222). As a result, despite a contraction in GDP of 3.7 percent in 2008 and 14.3 percent

Table 4.5   Annual Change in Aggregate Fiscal Balance of All Levels of Government as a Percentage of GDP

	2007	2008	2009	2010
Belgium	0.4	1.0	4.5	−1.7
Bulgaria	0.8	−0.5	6.0	−1.2
Czech Republic	−1.9	1.5	3.6	−1.0
Denmark	0.4	1.6	5.9	−0.1
Germany	−1.9	0.3	3.1	1.1
Estonia	−0.1	5.3	−0.9	−2.2
Ireland	2.8	7.4	6.9	17.1
Greece	0.7	3.3	6.0	−5.2
Spain	0.1	6.4	6.7	−1.9
France	0.4	0.6	4.2	−0.4
Italy	−1.9	1.1	2.7	−0.8
Cyprus	−4.6	2.6	7.0	−0.8
Latvia	−0.2	3.8	5.5	−1.4
Lithuania	0.6	2.3	6.2	−2.5
Luxembourg	−2.3	0.7	3.9	0.2
Hungary	−4.3	−1.4	0.9	−0.4
Malta	−0.4	2.2	−0.9	−0.1
Netherlands	0.3	−0.3	6.1	−0.5
Austria	−0.7	0.0	3.2	0.3
Poland	−1.7	1.8	3.6	0.5
Portugal	−1.0	0.5	6.5	−0.3
Romania	0.4	2.8	3.3	−2.1
Slovenia	−1.3	1.9	4.2	−0.3
Slovakia	−1.4	0.3	5.9	−0.3
Finland	−1.2	1.0	6.8	0.0
Sweden	−1.3	1.4	2.9	−0.9
United Kingdom	0.0	2.3	6.5	−1.2
EU 27	−0.6	1.5	4.5	−0.3
United States	0.8	3.6	5.1	−0.9
Japan	0.8	−0.2	6.5	−1.9

Source: Author's compilation based on European Commission (2011b, 223, table 35).

Note: A year-to-year reduction in an aggregate surplus or increase in an aggregate deficit is indicated by a positive value and is assumed to have an expansionary impact on the economy. A year-to-year increase in an aggregate surplus or decrease in an aggregate deficit is indicated by a negative sign and is assumed to have a contractionary impact on the economy.

Figure 4.2   Change in GDP, 2008 and 2009, and Aggregate Fiscal
Stimulus, 2008 to 2009

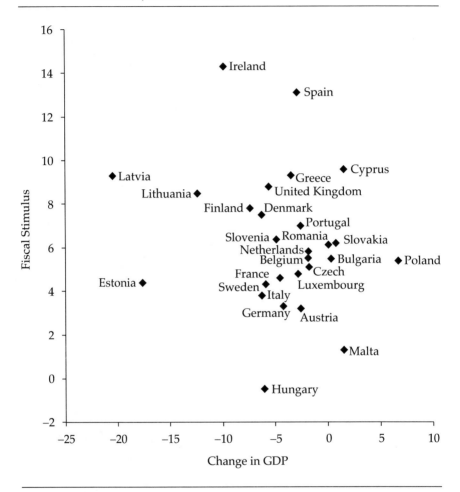

Source: Author's calculations of data from Economic Commission (2011a, table 1, p. 206 and table 35, p. 223).

in 2009, the aggregate fiscal balance changed only from a surplus of 2.4 percent of GDP in 2007 to a deficit of 2 percent in 2009. In contrast, the cumulative effect of the changes in revenues and expenditures as a share of GDP in 2008 and 2009 was exceptionally expansive, given the magnitude of the contraction, in Ireland and Spain. In Ireland, expenditures increased from 36.6 percent of GDP in 2007 to 48.9 percent in 2009, and revenues decreased from 36.7 percent in 2007 to 34.7 percent in 2009, resulting in a change from a surplus of 0.1 percent of GDP in 2007 to a deficit of 14.2 percent in 2009. Likewise, in Spain, expenditures increased from 39.2 percent of GDP in 2007 to 46.3 percent of GDP in 2009, and revenues decreased from 41.1 percent of GDP in 2007 to 35.1 percent in 2009, producing an aggregate change in the fiscal balance from a surplus of 1.9 percent in 2007 to a deficit of 11.2 percent in 2009.

One reason fiscal policy was, in the aggregate, more expansionary in some of the member states than in others was the greater ability of those countries to increase spending or reduce taxes, which was in part the result of their greater propensity to run substantial budget surpluses in good times. In 2007, the last year before the contraction and one in which the EU as a whole experienced a growth rate of 3.2 percent, Finland, Denmark, Sweden, Luxembourg, and Cyprus recorded aggregate budget surpluses of at least 3 percent of GDP (European Commission 2011a, 223). In Finland and Denmark, the surplus was roughly 5 percent of GDP—despite the fact that in both countries total government expenditures were equivalent to roughly 50 percent of GDP (222, table 35).

Figure 4.3 arrays the magnitude of the aggregate fiscal stimulus in 2008 and 2009 and the magnitude of the budget surplus or deficit in 2007 in the twenty-seven member states. Although the countries are scattered widely in the figure and there is, at best, only a modest relationship between the two measures,[16] the pattern does suggest that the existence of a surplus equivalent to several percentage points of GDP prior to the crisis provided some of the member states—Finland, Denmark, Sweden, Luxembourg, Cyprus, and Estonia—with enough fiscal latitude to enact, if they wished, expansionary fiscal measures without risking serious violation of the EU's 3 percent excessive deficit rule.[17] It was not necessary, of course, for countries to enter the crisis with large budget surpluses in order to increase the aggregate fiscal deficit in 2008 and 2009. Greece, in particular, but also the United Kingdom, Portugal, Ireland, Latvia, and Lithuania increased the aggregate deficit dramatically in 2008 and 2009 despite having had a significant deficit in 2007. But, not surprisingly, given their propensity to incur deficits even in years of relatively high growth, several of those—most notably, Greece, Ireland, Latvia, and Portugal—subsequently were forced, by downward pressure in the markets on the price of their bonds and upward movement in bond yields, to negotiate agreements with the IMF and EU that required, in exchange for many billions of euros in financial assistance, substantial reductions in their deficits.[18]

Although the data presented in table 4.5 pertaining to the aggregate year-to-year change in the fiscal balance are suggestive, because they reflect the combined effects of automatic stabilizers, whatever discretionary

Figure 4.3   Budget Surplus or Deficit as a Percentage of GDP, 2007, and Aggregate Fiscal Stimulus, 2008 and 2009

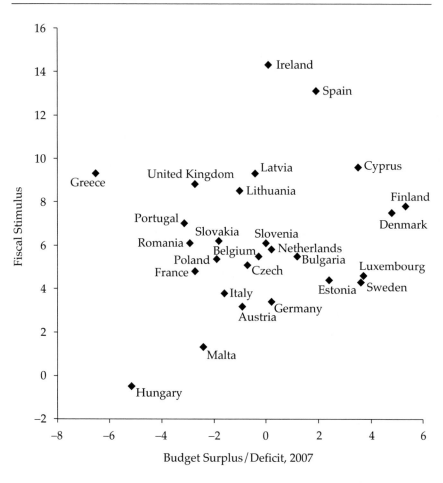

Source: Author's calculations of data from Economic Commission (2011a, table 35, p. 223).

fiscal measures the governments enacted, and all the other changes in revenues and expenditures relative to GDP, they provide less than ideal measures of the extent to which the governments deployed fiscal policy to introduce an expansionary impulse into the economy. Assuming that automatic stabilizers are indeed automatic and that the year-to-year change in the aggregate fiscal balance as a percentage of GDP reflects to a large extent the year-to-year change in GDP, the more interesting question con-

cerns the extent to which, if at all, the governments enacted and implemented discretionary measures designed to introduce a fiscal stimulus by
reducing taxes and other revenues and/or by increasing spending.

Data pertaining to the discretionary fiscal measures governments adopted in response to the crisis are few and far between. Nevertheless, the
OECD (2010a) has compiled such data for nineteen of the EU member
states as well as a number of other countries. Table 4.6 presents the OECD
data on the magnitude of decreases in taxes and increases in spending in
2008 through 2010 as a percentage of GDP in 2008. The data in table 4.6
indicate that six of the nineteen states—Spain, Luxembourg, Denmark,
Sweden, Finland, and Germany—enacted discretionary measures that
had a combined expansionary impact in 2008 through 2010 equivalent to
between 3 and 4 percent of their 2008 GDP. The Czech Republic, the Netherlands, and the United Kingdom adopted measures that had an impact of
between 1.5 and 3 percent of GDP. Those efforts fell well short of the discretionary tax and spending measures the United States adopted, which
taken together were estimated to represent 5.6 percent of the 2008 GDP.
Nevertheless, coming as they did on top of the substantially larger automatic stabilizers in Europe (see table 4.4), they are noteworthy. There were,
however, some notable foot-draggers among the EU member states;
France, Italy, Portugal, and Greece did very little, in terms of discretionary
measures, to counter the effects of the contraction. On the contrast between Germany, which enacted expansionary measures equal to 3.2 percent of its 2008 GDP, and France, which enacted expansionary measures
equal to 0.8 percent of its 2008 GDP, see chapter 5 in this volume. Two
countries, it should be noted—Hungary and Ireland—initiated substantial deficit-reducing measures. Hungary, which was forced to negotiate a
standby agreement with the IMF, EU, and World Bank in 2008, sharply
reduced its spending, and Ireland dramatically increased its revenues
through increases in personal income taxes, social contributions, and consumption taxes and reduced spending.[19]

There is good reason to suspect, from the data in table 4.5 and figure 4.3,
that the countries that made the greatest effort, through discretionary fiscal measures, to introduce an expansionary impulse into the economy
were those that, before the crisis, had sizeable budget surpluses. That suspicion is borne out by the array in figure 4.4, which presents the measure
of the magnitude of the discretionary fiscal measures enacted by the nineteen EU member states, relative to the 2008 GDP, and the size of the aggregate fiscal surplus or deficit in 2007. Excluding the two obvious outliers, the clustering of countries along an arc extending from Greece to
Denmark and Finland is fairly tight. The pattern suggests that, in general,
the countries in which government had a surplus in the years before the

Table 4.6   Magnitude of Expansionary Discretionary Fiscal Measures in 2008 through 2010 as Percentage of GDP in 2008

	Decreases in Taxes	Increases in Spending	Total Expansionary Impact
Spain	1.7	2.2	3.9
Luxembourg	2.3	1.6	3.9
Sweden	1.7	1.7	3.4
Denmark	0.7	2.6	3.3
Finland	2.7	0.5	3.2
Germany	1.6	1.6	3.2
Czech Republic	2.5	0.3	2.8
Netherlands	1.6	0.9	2.5
United Kingdom	1.5	0.4	1.9
Belgium	0.3	1.1	1.4
Slovakia	0.7	0.7	1.4
Poland	0.4	0.8	1.2
Austria	0.8	0.4	1.2
France	0.2	0.6	0.8
Portugal	0.0	0.8	0.8
Italy	−0.3	0.3	0.0
Greece	−0.8	0.0	−0.8
Hungary	−0.2	−7.5	−7.7
Ireland	−6.0	−2.2	−8.2
United States	3.2	2.4	5.6
Canada	2.4	1.7	4.1
Japan	0.5	4.2	4.7

Source: Author's compilation based on OECD (2010a).

crisis generally made a more substantial effort, in terms of the relative magnitude of the discretionary fiscal measures adopted, to introduce an expansionary impulse into the economy.

That some of the member states had substantial surpluses at the onset of the crisis and some others had, if not substantial surpluses, at least balanced budgets, whereas others had substantial deficits even in good times points to an important distinction among several clusters of European states. From a "varieties of capitalism" perspective, it was not simply coincidence or sheer luck that Finland, Denmark, and Sweden had substantial surpluses as the crisis hit Europe (Hall and Soskice 2001; Gourevitch 1986). They were in that advantageous position largely because they rely on forms of revenue—in particular, taxes on personal incomes—that are income-elastic and tend to increase markedly in good times. As a result,

Figure 4.4   Budget Surplus or Deficit as a Percentage of GDP, 2007, and Discretionary Fiscal Stimulus, 2008 to 2010

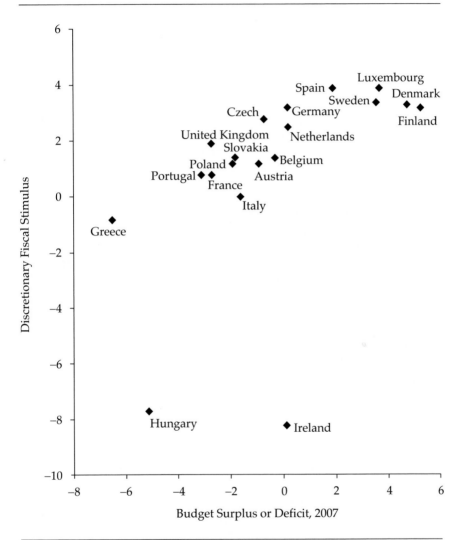

Source: Author's calculations of data from Economic Commission (2011a, table 35, p. 223) and OECD (2010a).

they generally run substantial surpluses in good times despite the fact that, as noted earlier, their public expenditures are unusually large relative to GDP. Moreover, because their revenues and expenditures are generally larger, relative to GDP, than those of other member states, they not only enjoyed greater latitude to undertake expansionary fiscal measures when the crisis hit but also benefited from relatively large automatic stabilizers. Interestingly, despite the many commonalities among the three Nordic countries, they did differ in the emphasis they gave to reducing taxes or increasing spending. Thus, as the data in table 4.5 indicate, Denmark relied mainly on increasing spending, Finland on reducing taxes, and Sweden on a balance of both. Even more interesting—and supportive of Lindvall's argument in this volume that the parties in those countries agree on the basic political-economic institutions and the contours of economic policy—is that the governments that undertook the relatively large expansionary fiscal measures were, in all three countries, controlled by the center-right parties. One might expect governments controlled by center-right parties to reduce taxes (on the effect of partisanship on the types of discretionary measures adopted by governments, see chapter 11, this volume). But the center-right governments of northern Europe—especially those in Denmark and Sweden—also increased spending.

The fiscal posture of the northern member states with respect to the aggregate fiscal balance of government in good times is, to some extent, a legacy of the decades of Social Democratic control of government—a legacy that is reflected not only in the magnitude of government spending on social programs but also in the means by which government raises revenue. The fiscal posture of a second group of states—Germany, Austria, and the Low Countries, which were not quite as well situated at the onset of the crisis as their northern neighbors, in part because they do not rely as heavily on income-elastic sources of revenue—may reflect, in contrast, the long-standing political weight of a large center-right, Christian Democrat *tendance* that often ruled, although often with a Social Democratic, Labor, or Liberal partner. Perhaps for that reason, although the discretionary measures enacted by those governments were not as expansionary in their impact, they nevertheless expanded existing labor market policies designed to encourage short work, part-time work, and furloughs, and in so doing kept the rate of unemployment at moderate levels throughout the crisis. Indeed, four of the five—all except Belgium—had lower rates of unemployment in 2010 and 2011 than Sweden, Denmark, and Finland (European Commission 2011a, 217, table 23; on the important German initiative to introduce and subsidize short work, see chapter 5, this volume.)

In contrast to those two clusters, another group of states—Italy, Greece, France, and Portugal—tend to rely to a lesser degree on taxes on personal income for their revenues and, partly for that reason, tend to incur budget deficits even in good times.[20] Government tends to spend almost as much, relative to GDP, in those countries as in the northern countries. But because they rely to a much greater degree on indirect taxes, impose low rates of taxation on income, and tolerate rampant tax avoidance, they inevitably incur substantial deficits, even in good times. As a result, they were less well situated, fiscally speaking, when the crisis hit and less able to adopt expansionary fiscal measures, especially tax reductions. Along with Hungary and Ireland, which had already adopted substantial deficit-reducing measures, those four are clustered at the bottom of table 4.6 in the extent to which the member states enacted discretionary fiscal measures designed to introduce an expansionary impulse into the economy. Moreover, because they have tended to run budget deficits even in good times, they have accumulated a large stock of public debt. Thus, in 2007, Greece and Italy had debt-to-GDP ratios in excess of 100 percent and France and Portugal had ratios in excess of 60 percent.

THE IMPACT OF FISCAL POLICY ON THE RECOVERY

As the quarterly data in table 4.1 indicate, the economic contraction in the EU, taken as a whole, ended in the third quarter of 2009. But, except for the second quarter of 2010, when the euro's exchange rate dropped in the wake of the eurozone crisis and gave a boost to exports, the rate of growth since then, though positive, has been modest. It is therefore perhaps too soon to ascertain the extent to which the automatic stabilizers in member states' budgets and discretionary fiscal measures adopted by some of them did in fact introduce an expansionary impulse into the economy that initiated a recovery. Nevertheless, given the considerable debate about the effectiveness of countercyclical fiscal policy (OECD 2009, 105–50; 2010b, 309–30; 2010c; 2010d), it is perhaps useful to consider whether the variation among the member states in the speed with which and the extent to which they began to recover from the crisis was related to the extent to which the automatic stabilizers in their budgets and the discretionary measures adopted by their governments introduced an expansionary impulse into the economy.

Table 4.7 presents the results of a series of regressions of two measures of the extent of economic growth in 2010 on measures of the magnitude of the stimulus provided by the year-to-year change in the aggregate fiscal balance as a percentage of GDP, the countercyclical automatic stabilizers in the budget, and the discretionary fiscal measures adopted by governments. The measures of growth are the annual rate of growth in 2010 and

Table 4.7   The Impact of Fiscal Policy on Growth in 2010

	Economic Growth	
	2010	2010-Q2 Versus 2009-Q2
Aggregate fiscal stimulus	−0.264**	−0.325**
2008 to 2009	(0.109)	(0.120)
	(t = 2.42)	(t = 2.73)
Automatic stabilizers	0.342	0.645
2008 to 2009	(0.552)	(0.637)
	(t = 0.62)	(t = 1.01)
Discretionary fiscal policy 2008 to 2010		
Tax reductions	0.493**	0.723***
	(0.234)	(0.223)
	(t = 2.11)	(t = 3.25)
Spending increases	0.175	0.354
	(0.225)	(0.232)
	(t = 0.78)	(t = 1.52)
Tax reductions + spending increases	0.226*	0.372**
	(0.137)	(0.130)
	(t = 1.66)	(t = 2.85)

Source: Author's calculations. Aggregate fiscal stimulus: table 4.5. Aggregate automatic stabilizers: table 4.4, expansionary discretionary measures, table 4.6. Rate of growth in 2010: European Commission (2011a, 206, table 1). Rate of growth in second quarter of 2010 versus second quarter of 2009: European Commission (2011b).

Note: Entries are regression coefficients and standard errors of separate regressions of each measure of growth on each measure of fiscal policy, controlling for the cumulative contraction of the economy in 2008 to 2009. The standard errors and t-statistics are in parentheses. For the regressions estimating the effect of the aggregate stimulus, N = 27; for those estimating the effect of automatic stabilizers, N = 25; for those estimating the effect of discretionary measures, N = 19. Asterisks indicate the probability the estimate would be as large if the null hypothesis (no effect) were true.

*p < .10; **p < .05; ***p < .01.

the rate of growth between the second quarter in 2009 and the second quarter of 2010. Both measures were regressed on each measure of fiscal stimulus controlling for the cumulative contraction of the economy in 2008 and 2009.[21]

The data in table 4.7 indicate that, while the change in the aggregate fiscal balance in 2008 and 2009 undoubtedly introduced a substantial expansionary impulse into the economy that slowed the contraction and caused it to bottom out, the magnitude of that impulse was not positively associated with the extent to which the economies grew in 2010 and from the second quarter of 2009—the trough of the contraction—to the second quarter of 2010. Obviously, one reason might be that the aggregate fiscal stimulus tended to be largest in the economies that experienced the greatest contraction during the crisis (figure 4.2) and those economies may have, for that reason, lagged behind the others in their recovery. But even after controlling for the extent of economic contraction, the regression coefficients for the aggregate fiscal stimulus in 2008 and 2009 are negative and statistically significant. Although one must be cautious about drawing any inferences from these results, they do suggest that the aggregate increase in the deficit as a percentage of GDP from 2007 to 2009 did not contribute to an early recovery. That, of course, does not exclude the possibility that the aggregate fiscal stimulus had the effect over the longer term of slowing and eventually bringing to an end the contraction that occurred in 2008 and 2009.

The regression results presented in table 4.7 indicate that, after controlling for the magnitude of the economic contraction in 2008 and 2009, the combined effect of the automatic stabilizers in 2008 and 2009, as a percentage of GDP, had an expansionary impact on the extent to which the economy recovered in 2010 ($b = 0.342$ for the equation estimating growth in 2010 and $b = 0.645$ for the equation estimating growth from the second quarter of 2009 to the second quarter of 2010). Interestingly, the coefficient is substantially larger in the regression estimating the impact of the automatic stabilizers on the rate of growth between the second quarter of 2009 and the second quarter of 2010, suggesting that they played an especially important role in promoting an early and relatively robust recovery from the trough of a contraction. However, as indicated by the relatively large standard errors and modest t-statistics, which are the ratio of the regression coefficient to the standard error, the magnitude of the impact of the automatic stabilizers varied widely after controlling for the extent to which the economy contracted in 2008 and 2009. One cannot assume with a great deal of confidence that a unit change in the stabilizers had a large expansionary effect on the rate of growth. One reason for this somewhat ambiguous finding is, of course, that the measure of the impact of the automatic stabilizers is the product of two components—the extent to which the fiscal balance is sensitive to a change in output and the extent to which output changed in 2008 and 2009.

The regression results in table 4.7 pertaining to the impact of discretionary fiscal measures indicate that the extent to which countries experienced a relatively high rate of growth in 2010 and a relatively high rate of growth from the second quarter of 2009 to the second quarter of 2010 was significantly associated with the magnitude of discretionary tax and spending measures. In particular, and contrary to every introductory macroeconomic textbook, these results indicate that the extent to which a country experienced an early and robust recovery from the economic contraction of 2008 and 2009 was strongly associated with the extent to which the government reduced taxes. It is possible that the countries that experienced the greatest growth in 2010 were those that experienced a relatively shallow contraction in 2008 and 2009, and that they experienced high growth in 2010 was for that reason rather than because the governments adopted discretionary fiscal measures. But, as noted earlier, the analysis in table 4.7 controls for the magnitude of the contraction in 2008 and 2009.

Perhaps the most intriguing result in table 4.7 concerns the strong effect of tax reductions, and thus overall discretionary fiscal measures, on growth from the trough of the contraction in the second quarter of 2009 to the second quarter of 2010. The large and statistically significant coefficients for the measures of the magnitude of discretionary reductions in taxes and all expansionary discretionary measures suggest that the best way to ensure an early and robust recovery from a severe contraction is not to increase discretionary spending, although that may help, but to reduce taxes. And as the OECD's disaggregation of the various discretionary tax and spending measures enacted from 2008 to 2010 suggests (see OECD 2009, 111, table 3.2; chapter 11, this volume), the largest discretionary reductions in taxes in most of the countries that enacted substantial expansionary fiscal measures involved taxes on personal income.[22]

The analysis in table 4.7 suggests that one reason the European recovery was sluggish at best in 2010 and continues to be sluggish was the failure of more governments to do more, in terms of enacting expansionary fiscal measures, especially tax reductions, to counter the contraction. Unfortunately, in the wake of the prolonged eurozone debt crisis and the turn to fiscal consolidation and austerity in much of Europe, it will be difficult, if not impossible, for most of the EU member states to adopt such measures in the near term, which means they are likely to experience relatively low rates of growth for some time to come.

If the EU as a whole faces the prospect of low growth in the near term, the analysis in table 4.7, coupled with the data in table 4.6 on the extent to which the governments enacted expansionary fiscal measures, suggests that the varied responses of the member states to the economic contraction of 2008 and 2009 resulted in a pronounced regional difference in the speed with which and extent to which they began to recover from the contraction. Table 4.8 presents the measure of the magnitude of the expansionary fiscal measures adopted in 2008 to 2010 and four measures of growth—the

Table 4.8 Magnitude of Expansionary Discretionary Fiscal Measures
and Rate of Economic Growth

	Magnitude of Expansionary Discretionary Measures	Economic Growth			
		2010: Q2 Versus 2009: Q2	2010	2011 Forecast	2012 Forecast
Luxembourg	3.9	5.3	2.7	1.6	1.0
Spain	3.9	0.0	–0.1	0.7	0.7
Sweden	3.4	4.5	5.6	4.0	1.4
Denmark	3.3	2.6	1.7	1.2	1.4
Germany	3.2	3.9	3.7	2.9	0.8
Finland	3.2	4.2	3.6	3.1	1.4
Czech Republic	2.8	2.3	2.7	1.8	0.7
Netherlands	2.5	2.2	1.7	1.8	0.5
United Kingdom	1.9	1.5	1.8	0.7	0.6
Belgium	1.4	2.7	2.3	2.2	0.9
Slovakia	1.4	4.3	4.2	2.9	1.1
Austria	1.2	2.2	2.3	2.9	0.9
Poland	1.2	3.6	3.9	.0	2.5
France	0.8	1.5	1.5	1.6	0.6
Portugal	0.8	1.4	1.4	–1.9	–3.0
Italy	0.0	1.5	1.5	0.5	0.1
Greece	–0.8	–3.1	–3.5	–5.5	–2.8
Hungary	–7.7	0.5	1.3	1.4	0.5
Ireland	–8.2	–1.9	–0.4	1.1	1.1
EU	—	2.0	2.0	1.6	0.6

Source: Author's compilation based on OECD (2010a); European Commission (2011a, 206, table 1; 2011b).

rate of growth between the second quarter of 2009 and that of 2010, the actual rate of growth in 2010, and the forecasted rates of growth in 2011 and 2012 (European Commission 2011a, 206, table 1). Six countries enacted expansionary fiscal measures equivalent to more than 3 percent of GDP. Five of these six—all but Spain—saw substantial increases in growth between the second quarters of 2009 and 2010. In three countries—Sweden, Germany, and Finland—the rate of growth exceeded 3 percent in 2010 and was forecast to come close to or exceed that rate in 2011. By contrast, another six countries enacted expansionary measures equivalent to less than 1 percent of GDP. In two of these—Greece and Ireland—contractions continued between the second quarter of 2009 and the second quarter of 2010 and in all of 2010. In the other four, rates of growth were relatively low, in the range of 0.5 to 1.5 percent. By 2011, four—Portugal,

Ireland, Italy, and Greece—had debt-to-GDP ratios that exceeded 100 percent, and four—Hungary, Greece, Ireland, and Portugal—had been forced to obtain financial assistance from the IMF and the EU in exchange for which they were required to implement a series of deficit-reduction measures and multiyear austerity programs that ruled out any expansionary fiscal measures for the foreseeable future. As a result and not surprisingly, all six experienced either further contraction of the economy or, at best, very modest growth in 2011 and 2012 and all appear consigned to years of economic stagnation and high unemployment.[23]

It would perhaps exaggerate to speak of a chasm between member states in northern Europe, which tend to run budget surpluses in good times and were able to enact substantial countercyclical fiscal policies in response to the contraction, and those in southern Europe, which tend to run budget deficits even in good times and were unable or unwilling to enact substantial countercyclical policies in response to the contraction. But the data in table 4.8 do suggest at least that leaving the response to the 2007 to 2009 contraction mostly to the member states accentuated regional divides between member states in northern and southern Europe.

It is, of course, much too soon to say whether the regional differentiation in growth between northern and southern Europe will remain as sharply defined as it was in the immediate aftermath of the economic crisis of 2008 and 2009. Unfortunately for those in northern Europe, the EU-wide and debt crisis-induced preoccupation with austerity and deficit reduction appears to have brought to an end the robust recoveries of 2010 and 2011 in Sweden, Finland, Germany, and other countries in northern Europe. Thus the EU projects that output in each will increase by less than 1.5 percent in 2012. On the other hand, the countries in southern Europe—especially Greece and Portugal, which have been required by the terms of their agreements with the IMF and the EU to carry out a series of very substantial reductions in spending and in their budget deficits—are expected to experience either substantial contractions in the GDP in 2012 or, at best, very low rates of growth, thereby perpetuating, at a lower overall rate of growth across Europe, the differentiation between North and South that appeared in the wake of the varied responses to the 2008 and 2009 contraction.

CONCLUSION

This chapter has examined the response of the EU and its member states to the economic contraction of 2008 to 2009. After adopting a recovery plan in December 2008, the EU subsequently resisted an additional fiscal stimulus as the contraction deepened in the spring of 2009. Several reasons for that resistance include the inherent difficulty in a union of twenty-seven states in agreeing on a change in policy in the midst of an unfolding crisis, the lack of fiscal resources available to the EU, the constraint on budget deficits posed by the Stability and Growth Pact and the high levels of debt in some member states, the widespread belief that, in trade-dependent economies, a fiscal stimulus will leak abroad, and the view, also widespread, that Europe's ample automatic stabilizers would suffice. As important as those factors were in accounting for the EU's failure to undertake a further stimulus, another reason is also significant: the absence of an effective mechanism—what some call "economic government" (Pisani-Ferry 2006) or, more recently, "fiscal union"—to coordinate the fiscal and economic policies of the member states and, if need be, to exercise some degree of collective authority over those policies.

Responsibility for enacting a stimulus was thus left almost entirely in the hands of the member states. The states introduced a fiscal stimulus either passively, as a result of the effect of the contraction of the economy on year-to-year changes in the aggregate fiscal balance between revenues and expenditures and the automatic stabilizers in the budget, or actively, by introducing expansionary fiscal measures involving tax reductions and spending increases. The extent to which a discretionary fiscal stimulus was introduced depended, in part, on the extent to which the state tended to generate budget surpluses in good times and thus had the capacity, after the contraction hit, to enact substantial expansionary fiscal policies without significantly exceeding the limits on deficits set by the Stability and Growth Pact. That tendency appears to depend in turn on some long-standing and regionally distinctive fiscal and political attributes such as the means by which governments raise revenues and the extent to which the governing parties understand the necessary prerequisites, in good times, for an effective countercyclical fiscal policy in bad times.

This chapter has considered the impact of year-to-year changes in the aggregate fiscal balance of all levels of government, the automatic stabilizers in the budget, and the discretionary fiscal measures enacted by governments on the timing and extent of the recovery from the economic contraction of 2008 and 2009. The analysis suggests that, although the fiscal stimulus resulting from the year-to-year changes in revenues and expenditures may have stabilized the economy, it had no discernible impact on the extent to which the economy recovered in 2010. In contrast, the automatic stabilizers in the budget had a positive impact on the recovery in 2010, although their magnitude and effect varied widely across the EU. In contrast, discretionary fiscal measures—especially reductions in taxes—

had a strong and consistently expansionary impact on the extent of the recovery. The discretionary measures appear to have been especially powerful in generating an early and robust recovery from the trough of the contraction in early 2009.

The propensity to enact substantial expansionary fiscal measures appears to have depended, at least in part, on the propensity to generate substantial budget surpluses in good times, and because the latter propensity appears to depend on certain long-standing and regionally concentrated fiscal and political attributes, the responses of the member states to the 2008 and 2009 contraction have accentuated a North-South division in the EU. Those in northern Europe that tend to generate budget surpluses in good times and were therefore able to respond with substantial expansionary fiscal measures experienced relatively strong recoveries while those in southern Europe, which tend to generate budget deficits and were unable to respond with substantial fiscal measures, experienced low rates of growth after the contraction. Rather than promoting a greater convergence in the economic performance of the member states, the net effect of the failure to undertake a substantial coordinated and EU-wide response to the contraction has been the creation of greater economic divergence among the member states. As the data in table 4.3 suggest, the eurozone debt crisis and the EU-wide preoccupation with deficit reduction and austerity have reduced rates of growth across all of Europe, and as this volume goes to press, the EU is edging toward another recession. Nevertheless, in the absence of fundamental structural change in the revenue-generating systems in southern Europe and the other countries that incur deficits even in good times, that differentiation in rates of growth is likely to remain, in part because those countries will be no more able than they were in 2008 and 2009 to undertake substantial expansionary discretionary fiscal measures when they are needed.

Earlier versions of this chapter were presented at Georgetown University, the School of Advanced International Studies of Johns Hopkins University, the University of Pennsylvania, Princeton University, Yale University, and the annual meeting of the American Political Science Association in Washington, D.C., in September 2010. For their comments and suggestions, I wish to thank Chris Achen, Jeffrey Anderson, Tassos Belessiotis, Nancy Bermeo, Peter Gourevitch, Niamh Hardiman, Isabela Mares, Gary Marks, Kate McNamara, Dennie Oude Nijhuis, Mitchell Orenstein, Jonas Pontusson, Wolfgang Proissl, Alberta Sbragia, Waltraud Schelkle, Aleksandra Sznajder Lee, Basak Taraktasl, and two reviewers of this volume.

NOTES

1. Even measures designed to stimulate the economy may of course fail to have that effect. For a discussion of the limited stimulative effect of the Obama administration's $787 billion ARRA, see chapter 7, this volume.

2. Slovakia experienced a contraction of the economy in only one quarter—the first quarter of 2009. However, the magnitude of the contraction in that quarter (–8.1 percent) qualifies as a recession because it resulted in a contraction of 4.8 percent for all of 2009 (European Commission 2011a, 206, table 1).

3. Quoted in *El País*, May 24, 2009.

4. The measures were calculated by the author from European Commission data (2011a, 206, table 1, 217, table 23).

5. The Pearson product-moment correlation between the two is $r = -69$.

6. See "Atlantic Rift over Stimulus Widens," *Financial Times*, March 11, 2009, p. 2.

7. Quoted in "Europe Rejects Extra Stimulus Appeal," *Financial Times*, March 10, 2009, p. 4.

8. Quoted in "EU Leader Condemns U.S. 'Road to Hell'," *Financial Times*, March 26, 2009, p. 1. Topolánek later acknowledged his phrasing may have been influenced by his having recently attended an AC/DC concert at which the group performed "Highway to Hell."

9. At their meeting on June 8–9, 2009, the finance ministers agreed that a majority of the measures were timely, targeted, and in line with the EU's long-term priorities, but they also noted the need to closely monitor their efficiency. At its meeting on June 18–19, 2009, the European Council did not consider an additional stimulus and focused, instead, on the need to restore fiscal balances.

10. As suggested, the correlation between the measure of the output sensitivity of the fiscal balance and the ratio of all public revenues to GDP across the twenty-five EU member states listed in table 4.4 is very strong ($r = .88$).

11. In March 2010, in the midst of the crisis triggered by Greece's deficit and debt problems, the heads of state and government of the euro area stated they were committed to promoting a "strong coordination of economic policies in Europe," believed the European Council "must improve the economic governance of the European Union and increase its role in economic coordination," and called for a task force to study the measures needed to ensure fiscal sustainability in the euro zone and enhance its capacity to act in crises. Herman Van Rompuy, the president of the European Council, created and chaired a Task Force on Economic Governance, which reported its conclusions and recommendations to the Council at its October 2010 meeting. (See Heads of State and Government of the Euro Area 2010; for a discussion of the causes and consequences of the eurozone debt crisis, see Cameron 2012.)

12. Quoted in "Financial Markets 'Do Not Understand the Euro,'" *Financial Times*, December 6, 2010, p. 4.

13. The exceptionally large increase in expansionary effect in Ireland in 2010 is a statistical artifact of EU accounting rules. In September 2010, the Irish government recapitalized the country's banks by buying their toxic assets at a substantial discount with promissory notes to be issued over the next ten years. By EU rules, such notes must appear as expenditures in the year issued and subsequently as debt. As a result, Ireland's deficit as a percentage of GDP increased from 14.2 percent in 2009 to 31.3 percent in 2010. It was projected to decrease to 10.3 percent in 2011. Had the banks not been recapitalized in that manner, the deficit would have been approximately 11 percent.

14. Hungary incurred large deficits in 2005 and 2006 (7.9 and 9.3 percent of GDP), despite growth rates of 3.5 percent and 4 percent, and was forced to undertake a substantial fiscal contraction in 2007 and negotiate a $25 billion standby arrangement with the IMF, the World Bank, and the EU in late 2008.

15. The correlation between the two measures in figure 4.2 is $r = -.22$.

16. The correlation between the two measures in figure 4.3 is $r = .20$.

17. As we shall see, at least four of those six—Denmark, Sweden, Finland, and Luxembourg—did in fact introduce expansionary fiscal measures. Data are unavailable for the other two. All of the member states of the EU are subject to the excessive deficit rules and procedures contained in the Stability and Growth Pact, regardless of whether they participate in the euro area.

18. In December 2008, Latvia received a total of €7.5 billion in assistance from the IMF (€1.7 billion), EU (€3.1 billion), World Bank (€400 million), and Denmark, Norway, Sweden, and Estonia (€2.3 billion). In May 2010, the euro area members and the IMF agreed to lend Greece €110 billion. In November 2010, the euro area members, the United Kingdom, Sweden, Denmark, and the IMF agreed to lend Ireland €67.5 billion. In May 2011, the EU and the IMF agreed to lend Portugal €78 billion. And in a series of meetings in July, October, and December 2011, the EU and the IMF agreed to lend Greece an additional €130 billion provided it negotiate a debt reduction agreement with private sector bondholders and institute a number of further reductions in the deficit (for discussions of the debt crisis, see chapter 6, this volume; Cameron 2012).

19. In November 2008, Hungary received a total of €20 billion in assistance from the IMF (€12.1 billion), EU (€6.5 billion), and World Bank (€1 billion).

20. Most would include Spain in this group and regard its position in table 4.5 as an anomaly. On the other hand, for most of the decade preceding the crisis, Spain, unlike the others, had either balanced budgets or small surpluses. It also tended to spend less, relative to GDP, than the other four. And it has a considerably lower debt-to-GDP ratio than the other four.

21. To simplify the presentation, the results in table 4.7 omit the constants, regres-

sions coefficients, and standard errors for the measure of economic contraction, and coefficients of determination.

22. In Spain, Luxembourg, Sweden, and Finland, all of which enacted discretionary measures that exceeded 3 percent of their 2008 GDP, the largest reductions in taxes involved those on personal incomes. However, in Germany, the Netherlands, and the Czech Republic, which enacted discretionary measures that ranged between 2.5 and 3.2 of their 2008 GDP, the largest reductions involved social contributions.

23. In the autumn of 2011, the EU estimated that unemployment in 2012 would be 8.2 percent in Italy, 10 percent in France, 11 percent in Hungary, 13.6 percent in Portugal, 14.3 percent in Ireland, and 18.4 percent in Greece (European Commission 2011a, 217, table 23).

REFERENCES

Cameron, David. 2012. "Stumbling Toward Fiscal Union: The Causes and Consequences of the Eurozone Debt Crisis." Unpublished manuscript. Yale University, New Haven.

European Commission. 2005. "New and Updated Budgetary Sensitivities for the EU Budgetary Surveillance." *Europa.eu*, September 20, 2005. Available at http://europa.eu/epc/pdf/budgetary_en.pdf (accessed March 5, 2012).

———. 2009a. "Interim Forecast: January 2009." *Europa.eu*, January 19, 2009. Available at: http://ec.europa.eu/economy_finance/pdf/2009/interimforecastjanuary/interim_forecast_jan_2009_en.pdf (accessed March 23, 2012).

———. 2009b. "Economic Forecast: Spring 2009." *Europa.eu*, May 5, 2009. Available at: http://ec.europa.eu/economy_finance/publications/publication15048_en.pdf (accessed March 7, 2012).

———. 2011a. "European Economic Forecast—Autumn 2011." *Europa.eu*, June 2011. Available at: http://ec.europa.eu/economy_finance/publications/european_economy/2011/pdf/ee-2011-6_en.pdf (accessed March 7, 2012).

———. 2011b. "Eurostat News Release: GDP up by 0.2% in euro area and by 0.3% in EU27." *Europa.eu*, December 6, 2011. Available at: http://epp.eurostat.ec.europa.eu/cache/ITY_PUBLIC/2-06122011-AP/EN/2-06122011-AP-EN.PDF.

European Council. 2008. "Presidency Conclusions—Brussels European Council, 11/12 December." 17271/1/08. *Consilium.europa.eu*, February 13, 2009. Available at: http://www.consilium.europa.eu/ueDocs/cms_Data/docs/pressData/fr/ec/104669.pdf (accessed March 23, 2012).

———. 2009. "Presidency Conclusions of the Brussels European Council, 19/20 March 2009." 7880/1/09. *Consilium.europa.eu*, April 29, 2009. Available at:

http://www.consilium.europa.eu/uedocs/cms_data/docs/pressdata/en/ec/106809.pdf (accessed March 23, 2012).

Girouard, Natalie, and Christophe André. 2005. "Measuring Cyclically-Adjusted Budget Balances for OECD Countries." *OECD Economics Department* working paper no. 434. Paris: Organisation for Economic Co-operation and Development.

Gourevitch, Peter. 1986. *Politics in Hard Times: Comparative Responses to International Economic Crises.* Ithaca, N.Y.: Cornell University Press.

Hall, Peter A., ed. 1989. *The Political Power of Economic Ideas: Keynesianism across Nations.* Princeton, N.J.: Princeton University Press.

Hall, Peter A., and David Soskice. 2001. "An Introduction to Varieties of Capitalism." In *Varieties of Capitalism: The Institutional Foundations of Comparative Advantage,* edited by Peter A. Hall and David Soskice. New York: Oxford University Press.

Heads of State and Government of the Euro Area. 2010. "Statement, March 25." *Europa.eu.* Available at: http://www.consilium.europa.eu/uedocs/cms_data/docs/pressdata/en/ec/113563.

International Monetary Fund (IMF). 2009. "Europe: Addressing the Crisis." World Economic and Financial Surveys: Regional Economic Outlook, May. Washington, D.C.: IMF.

Keynes, John Maynard. 1936. *The General Theory of Employment, Interest and Money.* London: Macmillan.

Krugman, Paul. 2009. *The Return of Depression Economics and the Crisis of 2008.* New York: W. W. Norton.

Münchau, Wolfgang. 2010. *The Meltdown Years: The Unfolding of the Global Economic Crisis.* New York: McGraw Hill.

Organisation for Economic Co-operation and Development (OECD). 2009. "OECD Economic Outlook: Interim Report." March. Paris: OECD.

———. 2010a. "OECD Factbook 2010: Economic, Environmental, and Social Statistics: StatExtracts." Paris: OECD. Available at: http://stats.oecd.org/Index.aspx ? DataSetCode=EO85_Main.

———. 2010b. "Economic Outlook 87." May. Paris: OECD.

———. 2010c. "Counter-cyclical Economic Policy." *OECD Economics Department* policy notes no. 1. Paris: OECD.

———. 2010d. "Fiscal Policy Reaction to the Cycle in the OECD: Pro- or Counter-cyclical?" *OECD Economics Department* working paper no. 763. Paris: OECD.

Pisani-Ferry, Jean. 2006. "Only One Bed for Two Dreams: A Critical Retrospective on the Debate over the Economic Governance of the Euro Area." *Journal of Common Market Studies* 44(4): 823–44.

Rajan, Raghuram G. 2010. *Fault Lines: How Hidden Fractures Still Threaten the World Economy.* Princeton, N.J.: Princeton University Press.

Roubini, Nouriel, and Stephen Mihm. 2010. *Crisis Economics: A Crash Course in the Future of Finance.* New York: Penguin.

Stiglitz, Joseph E. 2010. *Freefall: America, Free Markets, and the Sinking of the World Economy.* New York: W. W. Norton.

Trichet, Jean-Claude. 2011. "Building Europe, Building Institutions." Speech delivered on receipt of the Karlspreis [Charlemagne Prize]. Aachen, Germany (June 2, 2011). Available at: http://www.ecb.int/press/key/date/2011/html/sp11062en.html.

Chapter 5 | Policymaking in Hard Times: French and German Responses to the Eurozone Crisis

Waltraud Schelkle

TIMES ARE HARD for economic policymaking. A financial crisis of unprecedented scope shattered politicians' beliefs in the received economic wisdom that had informed two decades of continuous reform. After the demise of pump-priming Keynesianism in the late 1970s, governments tried to reduce their involvement in the direct provision of goods and services. They concentrated on setting regulatory frameworks and left the details to industry self-regulation or independent agencies; they came to follow rules in their budgetary policies and reduce discretionary interventions; and they established independent central banks that target inflation rather than the level of economic activity directly (Eichengreen 2007). The project of European integration was revived in the mid-1980s and became a major force in redefining what national government should and could do when intervening in markets. Yet, in 2008 and 2009, the international financial system would have collapsed had public authorities remained faithful to these hands-tying innovations instead of giving monetary and fiscal life support to banks.

A comparison of the French and German responses to a series of crises is of interest not least because the two have played a key role for the EU's concerted effort to combat recession and a meltdown of euro bond markets. The irony to be explored here is that what the two governments stated publicly, and at the EU level categorically, fitted the stereotype of *dirigiste* France and ordoliberal Germany, but it was the opposite of what they practiced at home. The French asked for decisive joint action, the

Germans proposed self-restraint and principled collective action only where absolutely necessary. In practice, the French government relied heavily on the built-in stabilizers of their tax-transfer system with largely symbolic extra spending that at least in one case was discriminatory against European partners. The German government, by contrast, topped up the built-in stabilizers with a sizeable subsidy to encourage labor hoarding by firms and generous support for the car industry, undeterred by considerable spillovers that stabilized demand for its European neighbors to the east. These observations points us to a standard puzzle of comparative political economy: why did two center-right governments of similarly advanced capitalist democracies favor such different responses to a common shock?

Financial markets were liberalized around the time Peter Gourevitch published *Politics in Hard Times* (1986), which compares the responses in five advanced capitalist democracies to the international economic crisis then. The very first sentence states that "policy needs politics" because only political mobilization gives support and political power to those who can select among the many economic solutions available. This dominance of politics in the choice of economic policies is meant to hold generally but the argument is that we become aware of it only in times of crisis, when "patterns unravel, economic models come into conflict, and policy prescriptions diverge" (Gourevitch 1986, 17). The hypothesis that "politics dominates policy choice" has informed some of the most interesting work on the longer-term changes that led up to the recent crisis, most notably Peter Hall (2010) and Jonah Levy (2010), who show how reformed institutional pathways shape policies now. Mark Vail (2011), who covers the same ground as this contribution, namely crisis responses in France and Germany, emphasizes the constitutive role of political ideas for present crisis management. So what kind of politics can explain the dual difference—in political presentation and in effective policymaking—between two governments that are ideologically close and subject to the same constraints of EU institutions?

In its simplest form, the answer proposed here lies in a combination of electoral and interest group politics. Electoral politics tries to appeal to the majority or the median voter in each nation and thus projects a coherent as well as a reassuring, that is, expectable, narrative of crisis management. Interest group politics, by contrast, pushes policymakers to select among all the possible and feasible responses to the economic imperatives that different material interests represent. Tensions between these two arenas of public presentation and policy enactment will inevitably arise. It is the art of politics to make the narrative look sufficiently joined up with observable actions.

The speeches given and the measures taken for domestic political consumption and in EU crisis management provide evidence for the *dual politics* explanation of policymaking in hard times. The explanation both
supports and qualifies the thrust of Gourevitch's argument and his distinguished followers. Hard times, in the sense of an economic and intellectual crisis, are times of very visible politics, even when policymakers
choose to present themselves as merely responding to economic imperatives. The German example is illuminating in this respect. But economic
crises are also hard times for politics because policymakers are haunted by
market panic and the prerogative of political authority must be asserted.
This is not simply a matter of skillful managing of one's constituencies but
also of having adequate policies and instruments at hand, as the ongoing
European debt crisis shows.

Yet politics is a differentiated phenomenon and has many arenas in
modern society. Gourevitch (1986) privileges the politics of organized interests. Torben Iversen and David Soskice (chapter 2, this volume) follow
this line of argument closely, although the role for interest group coalitions
is predetermined by the institutional setting of liberal in contrast to coordinated market economies. My case study challenges the varieties of capitalism account at various levels. First, because they are both coordinated
market economies, France and Germany should show less stark variation
(see also chapter 10, this volume). The institutionally less tightly coordinated social partners in France should have made the government take
more decisive compensatory action, analogous to governments in liberal
market economies; yet it was Germany that manufactured a relatively
large stimulus on top of automatic stabilization. Finally, Iversen and Soskice do not sensitize us for the possible discrepancy in how policymaking
is presented and how it is realized, but instead focus strictly on the outcome. So the answer is incomplete. This criticism also applies to the ideational explanation of why France and Germany are coping with crisis so
differently (Vail 2011). It explains the rhetoric but not the action that liberalism in France means a state that claims to preserve equality before the
law and to care for aggregate welfare, whereas ordoliberalism in Germany
means a state as referee between groups with assured entitlements. This
chapter argues that both rhetoric and action is relevant for policymaking
in hard times.

Political economists also have to explore the counterhypothesis to
Gourevitch (1986), namely, that economic imperatives or functional needs
should dominate policy choice. Many economists and journalists take this
view implicitly or explicitly when they confidently explain how to stop the
crisis and then deplore that politicians, most notably Chancellor Merkel,
have failed to convince skeptical voters of their preferred solution, with

little regard for the political constraints that politicians face (see, for example, Paul Krugman, "A Continent Adrift," *New York Times*, March 16, 2009). If used for analysis rather than criticism, this view could explain the discrepancies between the French and the German actual responses with the asymmetry of the shock. But the presentation of the policies pursued must remain a mere ornament or distortion. Such discounting of electoral politics as short term can be found in institutional accounts as well (Levy 2010, 1). What casts doubt on the hypothesis and prescription of "economics dominates policy choice" is that many contradictory solutions have been proposed with equal confidence, and thus it takes more than identifying the most urgent economic problem to explain why Sarkozy favored different policies than Merkel. Yet different perceptions of how severely the economy would be affected could have played a role for the size and timing of policy measures. Evidence is scant for such an explanation.

The mismatch between what governments say they do and what they do is not hard to understand once we concede that capitalist democracy is a precarious political system (Caporaso and Levine 1992, 7; Iversen 2006, 601–2). The public presentation of policies must speak to constituencies and pivotal groups of voters, either by communicating a credible ideological stance or by conveying competence in solving their problems. Actual policies must accept that certain economic actors can make or break a policy, interest groups with veto power have to be satisfied, and redistributive effects of problem-solving may be undesirable. This discrepancy is a constant source of frustration for voters and has contributed to the popular cynicism that policymaking in democracies is inherently hypocritical. The delegation of many policies to the EU level has made this charge even more pertinent and the management of the two arenas more complicated, an interaction between the domestic and the supranational levels that resonates with chapter 3 in this volume. Governments often sign up to policies at the EU level that they present as off-limits at home, for instance, because they disadvantage privileged domestic actors in predictable ways. State aid rules are a case in point. EU politics tries to appeal to ideologically indifferent, mobile voters who prefer rational problem-solving to distributive conflict management. The practical EU agenda, by contrast, is driven and selected by supranational organized interests, often business but also social activists, supported by some state actors, and has non-negligible distributive consequences (Mabbett and Schelkle 2009). EU involvement tends to convey both a lack of political responsibility and a dominance of some economic interests under the veneer of technocratic problem-solving. But we will see that this normative tension played itself out differently in the financial crisis of 2008 to 2009 and the sovereign debt crisis of 2009 to 2010.

THE PRESENTATION OF
CRISIS MANAGEMENT

The early speeches and their reception in parliament and the wider public, as reported in the media, set the tone for how the government framed the crisis and proposed an obviously pertinent response. Domestic flagship measures tell us something of the revealed emphasis of strategies pursued. When interbank lending collapsed in the autumn of 2008, the two governments were in very different situations. France held the rotating EU presidency from July to December. Hence Sarkozy represented and spoke for the EU member states in many international fora, a task he took on with relish and to general acclaim. Merkel, by contrast, was at the start of a tight electoral race. It ended in September 2009 with a comfortable majority for a Conservative-Liberal coalition, though her own Christian Democratic party fared badly. This became a constant theme in the media during the first phase of the crisis: the French president stood in the limelight and therefore had to show command, and the German chancellor was the proverbial lame duck, leading a difficult-to-lead grand coalition in its dying days.

Early Speeches and Their Reception

The contrast in presentation is noticeable in the relevance of speeches for the public face of crisis management. Nicolas Sarkozy gave three speeches to a general audience that were referred to in the press, and in his own speeches, as the Toulon, the Argonay, and the Douai addresses; all of them can be downloaded from the Elysée website.[1] They were meant to be historical addresses to posterity, not shy of statements such as, "Destiny has thrown us into a situation where we have to reinvent the world" (2008a, 8, author's translation). Angela Merkel did not give any speech that can be called grand. In fact, those that the press considered to be significant and formally important—in parliament or to an annual party conference—were criticized as missed opportunities across the political spectrum. On her website, most speeches are merely summarized and cannot be downloaded.[2] An observer may be inclined to attribute this to a difference in style, easily explained by different political systems that select different personalities to represent a country—presidential here and proportional-representative there.

The political system does not determine the substance of what is presented, however. Timing, chosen audience, and content of these addresses could not have been more different. The first of Sarkozy's crisis speeches was given on September 25, 2008, ten days after the collapse of Lehman Brothers; Merkel gave her first significant address to the Bundestag on

October 7. The French president characterized the crisis as structural, to which one had to respond with structural policy (Sarkozy 2008a, 2; 2008b, 5–6). Thus, the pace of reform had to accelerate, for which he gave the specific examples of abolishing the thirty-five-hour week, less [sic] public employment, and more budget responsibility for hospitals. The message that the crisis must lead to more and faster reforms was reiterated in subsequent speeches (Sarkozy 2008a, 5–6; 2008c, 7).

Merkel refrained from giving a particular interpretation of the crisis. She emphasized that the present situation required two responses: classical crisis management, which she defined as very short term, and international financial reregulation in the medium to long term, a process, she reminded the audience, that she had promoted during her G8 presidency in 2007 (2008a, 1, 5). She also warned that reforms should not be postponed now, specifically fiscal consolidation, lowering nonwage costs of labor, increasing retirement age, and investing more in education (2008a, 8). Her message of reform continuity was considerably less emphatic than Sarkozy's, however. And she would qualify it. In her address to the party conference in December, she rejected calls for immediate tax cuts in a much quoted statement: "What we will not do is to replace directly effective, temporary stimulus measures by structural tax reforms" (Peter Ehrlich, Nikolai Fichtner, and Claudia Kade, "Alles wird gut," *Financial Times Deutschland*, December 2, 2008, p. 23). By that time, it had dawned on the chancellor and her finance minister, Steinbrück from the Social Democratic Party (SPD), that fiscal stimulus may be necessary and she thus conceded that costly reforms would have to wait.

In both parliaments, urgency and a somewhat battered opposition did not leave much room for debate and change (Elsa Freyssenet, "Parlement: après l'unité anticrise, des tensions avec l'Elysée," *Les Echos*, December 23, 2008, p. 2; Gunter Hofmann, "Schlucken und zustimmen; Erst die Grosse Koalition, jetzt die Grosse Überforderung: Der Bundestag traut sich wenig zu," *Die Zeit*, March 12, 2009, p. 4.). In France in particular, opposition parties feared that it would not go down well with the electorate if they held up the passing of emergency measures. Concessions to the opposition concerned minor issues, such as the "greening" of the stimulus, as the government pursued its reform of speeding up the process of infrastructure planning (Christophe Jakubyszyn, "Crise. Nicolas Sarkozy en visite dans une usine de Saint-Gobin," *Le Monde*, November 6, 2008, p. 16). Sarkozy also worked hard on the message "we're all in this together," namely that the management of the crisis should transcend party politics in parliament. Thus, he invited the social partners to a summit in the Elysée in February 2009, and subsequently announced a three-month consultation of civil society with his revamped government under premier Fillon (Cécile Cornudet, "Nicolas Sarkozy souhaite faire émerger un 'nouveau modèle de croissance'," *Les Echos*, June 23, 2009, p. 2). Sarkozy's popularity ratings soared when the crisis reached a climax.

By contrast, Merkel struggled with opposition in her own party early on. Back and front benchers in the Bundestag reminded her constantly that the party had promised to lower taxes and public debt, so as not to leave the manifesto of tax reduction to the Liberals (Jan Dams, "Merkels 'schwerste Entscheidung'; Regierung beschliesst neues Konjunkturpaket," *Die Welt*, January 28, 2009, p. 2; Stefan von Borstel, "Steinbrück verteidigt Konjunkturpaket: 'Es gab kein Drehbuch,'" *Die Welt*, January 31, 2009, p. 2). Yet, when she promised to reduce taxes after the election, the governors of the Länder, where the Christian Democratic Union of Germany (CDU) and the Christian Social Union of Bavaria (CSU) were in power, questioned this promise publicly, in view of their precarious public finances (Claudia Kade, "CDUler lehnen Merkels Wahlgeschenk ab, "*Financial Times Deutschland,* May 4, 2009, p. 9). The grand coalition was lucky that the opposition suffered from similar schizophrenia: both the Liberals and the Greens opposed stimulus plans in the Bundestag and voted for it in the Bundesrat as members of coalitions in the Länder (Dorothea Siems, "Im Zweifel für die Konjunktur; FDP hebt das 50-Milliarden-Paket über die letzte Hürde," *Die Welt*, February 21, 2009, p. 2). Consent by her backbenchers to the second stimulus in January 2009 had to be ensured by simultaneously introducing a constitutional debt brake (Dagmar Rosenfeld, "Herr Kampeter wirft seinen Zettel weg; Für den führenden Haushälter der Union stellt die Krise alle Werte auf den Kopf," *Die Zeit*, February 26, 2009, p. 4). The debt brake (Schuldenbremse) prohibits the federal government from raising any new public debt from 2020 onward, earlier for the Länder. It was embedded in the constitution with a two-thirds majority from the ruling parties in the Bundestag; the Greens and the Left voted against, the Liberals abstained but promised to help it through the Bundesrat. Germany later promoted the debt brake as a possible reform for EU fiscal governance, and was first rebuffed but succeeded at the end of 2011. Its radicalism is astounding. In any growing economy, this provision implies a debt to GDP ratio that converges asymptotically to zero and denies an ageing society the continuous supply of what is a relatively safe asset in most OECD countries. It is a prime example of electoral politics in hard times, magnified through EU crisis management.

Flagship Programs of Intervention

A stimulus package was decided upon in France at the end of 2008. A special ministerial job was created, for Patrick Devedjian to oversee its implementation and evaluation. On the official website[3] and in the president's speeches, the stimulus package was all about investment "because stimulating through investment allows us to support today's economic activities by boosting competitiveness for tomorrow" (Sarkozy 2008b, 6–7; 2008c, 1). The flagship of the program was a set of 1,000 projects that had to be identified by February 2009, 75 percent of which had to be implemented in 2009. It is safe to assume that these expenditures on a project basis were rather small scale and hardly of macroeconomic significance. Yet they projected decisiveness of the state in confronting the challenges and made the intervention visible in every part of the country. Other items show an emphasis on targeted intervention as well, to particular sectors (car industry and construction, of infrastructure and housing) and vulnerable groups (small and medium enterprises, low-income households). The protection for those threatened by unemployment, homelessness, and over-indebtedness had already been a theme in Sarkozy's Toulon address (2008b, 5). There he had announced that the financial sector would be taxed to spend more on social assistance; the stimulus contained a one-off payment of €200 to each adult on benefits.

Germany had two stimulus packages around 2008 and 2009, neither of which had a single authority. All pertinent ministries were involved—finance, employment, and economics in the lead. The official website on the stimulus measures put emphasis on "relief to citizens and firms" in the form of lower taxes and a sizeable reduction of social security contributions.[4] These measures targeted the middle classes, notably the core workforce and families. The flagship of the German stimulus package, initiated by the Social Democrats, became a short-term work program that was made more generous in terms of duration for workers—up to twenty-four months for 2009, eighteen months for 2010—and relief from social security contributions for employers—50 percent.[5] This could be done by an ordinance of the federal employment minister and did not require parliamentary approval, as the Social Democratic minister in charge noted publicly (Michael Kopp, "Scholz denkt über Verlängerung von Kurzarbeitergeld nach," Die Welt, February 20, 2009, p. 33). The Employment Agency paid 60 percent, 67 percent for parents, of the net wage lost due to short-term work. Participation exploded from about 50,000 in May 2008 to 1.5 million workers in May 2009 (Arpaia et al. 2010, 35). This maintained an estimated equivalent of 500,000 full-time jobs, keeping unemployment at a stable level of about 3.5 million.[6]

Both governments extended substantial support to the car industry, which was one of two sectors that the French president singled out in his Douai address; the other was housing. The French stimulus awarded €1,000 to every buyer of a car that did not exceed a certain CO_2 emission threshold and who scrapped a car that was at least ten years old. Moreover, the president stated in strong words that all support to firms, such as to develop an electric car, would be given only to those located in France, even though he must have been aware that such grandstanding would raise eyebrows in Brussels (Sarkozy 2008c, 3–4). Soon afterward, support for Peugeot and Renault was granted on condition that they would not close down any factory in France for at least five years. This provoked a storm of protest in central and eastern Europe because it raised the specter of plant closures there. The European Commission stepped in with state aid rules, backed by France's successor in the EU presidency, the Czech Republic, which had made the "coordinated support for the car industry" one of its priorities.[7] France withdrew the condition without further ado.

Germany extended support through an even more generous cash-for-clunkers program, after it had granted tax breaks for newly bought cars and subsidies to R&D even earlier. The car-scrapping scheme paid a so-called environmental premium of €2,500 for the acquisition of a new, cleaner car that replaced a car at least nine years old, no matter where produced. This stabilized production in other countries as well because the import share in the value of cars is considerably higher than for the average of consumer goods (Blum and Freye 2009, 9). The German government was aware of these spillovers or leakages, which should have strengthened the case for a coordinated stimulus as David Cameron rightly remarks (see chapter 4, this volume). The authorities lent instead a helping hand to German business so that it could benefit from stimulus packages elsewhere.[8] The government was equally tempted by protectionism for the car industry, except that it protested its innocence and would never admit to such blatant patriotic interference as the French president. The government allegedly conditioned credit guarantees for a third party's takeover of Opel from General Motors on the maintenance of national production capacities. Backed by Belgium, Spain, and the United Kingdom, member states that saw their Opel plants under threat, the European Commission reminded the German government that the stipulation of "a specific business plan . . . which defines the geographic distribution of restructuring measures" would not be allowed under state aid rules (2009). Subsequently, the then Competition Commissioner Neelie Kroes cajoled the German government into providing written assurance that any entity that promised to restructure Opel would get the credit guarantee. When the Germans duly complied, GM called off the protracted negotiations with an interested buyer and started negotiating the guarantee (Caroline de Gruyter, "'Steely Neelie' Just Wants to Finish the Job," *NRC Handelsblad*, November 19, 2009). Interest group politics was again foiled by EU state aid rules.

CRISIS MANAGEMENT AND ITS OUTCOME

An observer confined to watching public debates and noting the conspicuous crisis measures would have expected high and predominantly discretionary stabilization in France and little action in terms of both volume and discretion in Germany, as some media did (Nelson Schwartz, "France, Unlike U.S., Is Deep into Stimulus Projects," *New York Times*, July 6, 2009). Table 5.1 presents an overview of legislation that the two governments have labeled, sometimes retrospectively, as crisis measures that were taken in 2008 and 2009.

The most striking observation is that the German legislatures (Bundestag and Bundesrat) were much more activist than the supposedly hyperactive French administration. France had one stimulus package proposed and passed in December 2008, with an envelope of €26 billion for 2009 to 2010. If we include the emergency measure against youth unemployment in April 2008, we get to slightly more than €27 billion. Germany had three stimuli within thirteen months with an aggregate of about €70 billion. Similarly, the French Assemblée Nationale passed one act on stabilizing the financial system in October 2008, and the Germans had no less than five that tried to ensure the stability of the financial system, at least one of them targeted directly at a particular Landesbank (Hypo Real Estate). The activism is partly an outcome of a more legalistic approach in Germany compared with France: a debt brake has now been enshrined in the German constitution, whereas the French government makes fiscal consolidation the task of the annual budget negotiations, as usual.

Against this background, how much demand stabilization did the discretionary packages (stimulus) and the automatic stabilizers provide? The relative shares give us an additional clue to the role of political decision-making in state intervention. Moreover, how big overall is the state's contribution to aggregate demand likely to be over the duration of the stimulus packages? Table 5.2 summarizes the answers. The figures differ from those reported in chapter 4 of this volume (table 4.4) because Cameron uses EU data that record measures supporting banks (nationalization, recapitalization, and loans but not guarantees) as government expenditure and interprets such expenditure as demand stimulus. By contrast, both the OECD and the IMF take out bank support measures when calculating the stimulating effect of government expenditure because these measures provide liquidity and capital buffers held by banks that do not stimulate demand in the wider economy. The EU figures, provided in the context of fiscal surveillance, thus overstate the stimulating effect of government expenditure especially for countries with sizeable bank bailouts, such as the United States, the United Kingdom, and Ireland (see endnote 10 in Cameron).

Table 5.1   Legislative Measures Against the Crisis in 2008 and 2009

	France	Germany
2008		
April	Emergency plan for the Employment of the Young (€1.3 billion) proposed	
October	Stimulus Plan for the Financing of SMEs proposed; Support Plan for the Financing of the Economy passed (measures to stabilize financial system incl. deposit guarantee)	Stabilization of Financial Markets Act (defines conditions under which banks can get state aid) proposed and passed
November		First stimulus package proposed (Schutzschirm für Arbeitsplätze), later dubbed Konjunkturpaket 1
December	Stimulus package announced and passed (€26 billion)	First stimulus package passed (€11 billion)
2009		
January		Second stimulus package (Konjunkturpaket 2, €50 billion over two years) and car-scrapping scheme (Environmental Premium) passed
February	Pact for the Automobile Sector implemented; Social measures for the most vulnerable announced at Social Summit	Amendment of the Stabilization of Financial Markets Act proposed (creates temporary guarantee fund and possibility to nationalize banks)
March		Act to improve prudential supervision proposed; Federal Commission proposes debt brake (phasing in from 2011)
April	Fund for Social Investment introduced	
June		Bad Bank Act (provides basis for rescue of Landesbanken) proposed; Debt brake, including necessary change of Constitution, passes both Houses
July		Act on prudential supervision and Bad Bank Act passed

Table 5.1   (Continued)

	France	Germany
August		Act on the reorganization of systemically important banks proposed
December		Growth Acceleration Act (€8.5 billion, mostly tax relief for families and firms) passed

Source: Author's compilation based on Présidence de la République (2009)and Bundesministerium für Finanzen (2009).

We notice first that Germany stimulated much more than France even though the estimated shortfall in demand, as measured by output gaps (potential GDP minus actual GDP relative to potential GDP), were of comparable size over three years. However, public accounting conventions in France (accrual basis) and in Germany (cash basis) are likely to lead to an underestimation of the French effort and a corresponding overestimate of the German effort. The OECD breakdown shows only €12.7 billion (2009, 17), thus excluding French measures such as a suspension of taxes on new investment, prepayment for services from private firms, or promises to invest by state-owned enterprises. For all these measures, fiscal costs will accrue only after 2010.[9] Even so, the difference between the French and the German stimulus is considerable.

The bulk of the French government's stabilization effort relied on automatic stabilizers, that is, the administration hoped that reduced tax revenues and increased spending on unemployment benefits would do the trick. Christine Lagarde, then French finance minister, summed up this strategy with an aside on the United States: "The difference is that the French model provides shock absorbers that were already in place. We haven't had to reinvent our unemployment, health or welfare systems" ("The French Model: Vive la difference!" *The Economist*, May 7, 2009, p. 28) This introduces some dissonance in the president's presentation of policy measures and suggests that the economics minister and Prime Minister Fillon were not fully behind Sarkozy's strategy of "politics must dominate." The problem in the Great Recession was, however, that automatic stabilizers were deemed insufficient to avoid a collapse of economic activity. Moreover, more than half of the German effort relied on automatic stabilization. Fortunately for the administration, built-in stabilizers were more effective according to the most recent study with the best available dataset (Dolls, Fuest, and Peichl 2009).[10] Compared with France, German income taxes are more progressive and countercyclical variations of the

Table 5.2   Anatomy of Fiscal Stabilization in France and Germany

			France	Germany
Fiscal stimulus, net effect[a]			–0.6	–3.0
Tax measures		Total	–0.2	–1.6
	Individuals		–0.1	–0.6
	Business		–0.1	–0.3
	Consumption		0.0	0.0
	Social contributions		0.0	–0.7
Spending measures[b]		Total	0.4	1.4
	Investment		0.2	0.8
	Transfers to households		0.1	0.2
	Transfers to businesses		0.0	0.3
	Transfers to subnational governments		0.0	0.0
Automatic stabilization[c]			–3.4	–4.2
Budget elasticity for income shock[d]			0.37	0.48
Output gaps	2008		–0.6	0.9
	2009		–4.5	–5.2
	2010		–4.0	–4.4
Total fiscal stabilization[e]			–4.0	–7.2

Source: Author's calulations based on OECD (2009) and Dolls, Fuest, and Peichl (2009), table 2.

[a] Total over 3 years as percentage of GDP in 2008; figures for 2010 are forecasts.

[b] An increase in spending is a positive figure that adds to the (negative) fiscal stimulus, that is, the budget deficit.

[c] Sum of budget elasticity times output gaps (as share of GDP of that year) in fiscal year 2008–2010.

[d] A figure like 0.48 for Germany says that a 1 percent drop in every household's income leads to a lower budget balance by almost half a percent.

[e] Figures with different denominators (GDP figures for different years) have been added up here, so the total is only an approximation.

budget rest to a lesser extent on proportional social security contributions (Dolls, Fuest, and Peichl 2009, 15, 21, 26). Hence, despite a similar shortfall in demand over three years, overall stabilization by public finances was considerably higher in Germany than in France, and this difference is due to considerably more discretionary stabilization and somewhat more effective automatic stabilization.

Can this difference in actual stabilization efforts be explained by different economic needs as policymakers perceived them at the time when decisions had to be taken, as the "economics dominates" proponents

Table 5.3   Forecasts by the IMF and the EU

	Unemployment			Real Growth		
	2008	2009	2010	2008	2009	2010
France						
IMF Forecasts						
Fall 2007	8.6	8.0	n.a.	1.9	2.0	n.a.
Fall 2008	7.7	8.3	n.a.	0.8	0.2	n.a.
Spring 2009	7.8 [a]	9.6	10.3	0.7 [a]	–3.0	–0.2
EU Forecasts						
Fall 2007	8.2	8.1	n.a.	2.0	1.8	n.a.
Fall 2008	8.0	9.0	9.3	0.9	0.0	0.8
Spring 2009	7.8 [a]	9.6	10.7	0.7 [a]	–3.0	–0.2
Germany						
IMF Forecasts						
Fall 2007	6.5	6.3	n.a.	2.4	2.0	n.a.
Fall 2008	7.4	8.0	n.a.	1.8	—	n.a.
Spring 2009	7.3 [a]	9.0	10.8	1.3 [a]	–5.4	0.3
EU Forecasts						
Fall 2007	7.7	7.6	n.a.	2.1	2.2	n.a.
Fall 2008	7.3	7.5	7.4	1.7	0.0	1.0
Spring 2009	7.3 [a]	8.6	10.4	1.3 [a]	–5.4	0.3

Source: Author's compilation based on International Monetary Fund (2007, 2008, 2009) and DG Ecfin (2007, 2008, 2009).

[a] actual estimate, not forecast

suggest? To explore this, table 5.3 shows the short-term forecasts for unemployment and growth that the IMF and the EU issued at crucial stages, namely when the crisis was in full swing in the United States but not in Europe (the autumn of 2007), after the Lehman collapse in the fall of 2008 when the first stimulus programs were discussed, and when the crisis reached its climax, in the spring of 2009.

Between the autumn of 2007 and of 2008, the IMF revised the estimate for French unemployment in 2008 downward and upward for Germany. The revisions in forecasted growth were the same for both countries and became much more pessimistic for Germany in the spring of 2009 only. However, when the EU unemployment forecasts for 2009 and 2010 became rather pessimistic for France in the fall of 2008 but remained constant for Germany, the IMF revised up again, from an over-optimistic starting point. From then on, forecasts deteriorated rapidly for both but only Germany responded with a second and third stimulus package, possibly shocked by the correct forecast of an output fall of around 5 percent and of deteriorating unemployment in 2010. The size of the first stimulus programs in fall 2008, bigger in France than in Germany, is however at odds with the initial good news for France and the bad news for Germany, especially from the IMF. Subsequently, the case for another stimulus program became as strong for France as it was for Germany. The economics-dominates hypothesis thus gets only weak support from this exercise of matching perceptions of economic necessities with policy responses.

A look at the outcomes also gives no clear-cut evidence for or against an economic explanation of the difference between the two. Among euro area countries, France was one of the least affected by the downturn in 2009, output eventually dropping by 2.5 percent, and Germany was one of the worst hit with a contraction of 5 percent, against an average of 4 percent in the euro area as a whole (IMF 2010a, para 1).[11] The record on unemployment is almost the reverse: after a low of 7.2 percent in June 2008, unemployment in France rose to 9.8 percent in October 2010, according to Eurostat. Contrary to all forecasts, German unemployment rates were stable, rising ever so slightly from a low of 7.2 percent in the third quarter of 2008 to 7.5 percent in the fourth quarter of 2009. After that, rates kept falling, to 6.7 percent in October 2010. The IMF estimated that the short-term work program made the greatest contribution to this "labor market miracle," along with firms' efforts to keep skilled workers and labor market reforms (IMF 2010b, para 11). What looked like a largely statistical success in 2009 seems to have tided German firms effectively over the downturn.

CRISIS AND CRISIS MANAGEMENT OF THE EU

By 2010, a modest but assured recovery was under way in the Euro area, an average real growth estimated at 1.7 percent; figures for France were 1.6 percent and for Germany 3.7 percent (Eurostat data as of December 2010). But more testing times were in the offing for the monetary union, starting in markets for Greek government bonds in December 2009 and proceeding to Irish markets for sovereign debt in November 2010. The strategies and their perceived success at the EU level will be described at more length for the second crisis.[12] The French government favored a proactive political lead from the EU while the German administration projected its preference for conspicuous problem-solving to the EU level, namely, concerted stabilization only when proved necessary. This difference in political visions for a united Europe is long-standing and allows us to observe each government making the general case for its preferred way of dealing with the inherent tension between political and economic imperatives of policymaking. I argue that the two crises saw first the pre-

ferred German and then the preferred French strategy prevailing, with the
latter entering new territory.

Battling Through the First Crisis

The different visions for EU crisis management can be detected in the first
speeches analyzed earlier. In his Toulon address, Sarkozy suggests that the
union needs to question "its doctrine of competition, [think about] its capacity to raise resources, its economic policy instruments and the objectives of monetary policy" (2008b, 4). This was a bold attack on at least two
fundamental values of the Economic and Monetary Union (EMU), namely,
competition in the internal market and price stability as the lexicographic
goal of the European Central Bank (ECB). The speech also contained barely
veiled criticism of the EU's approach to supranational governance. First,
Sarkozy states emphatically that "self-regulation [of industry] as a solution to all problems, that's over" (2008b, 3). This is an outright rejection of
the so-called new method of harmonization, which has become a widely
used means of integration in the EU, especially in the financial sector
where it applied both to the Basel II framework and the Lamfalussy process of EU financial legislation. Sarkozy also stated categorically that he
would not engage in a policy of austerity because it would lead into recession (2008b, 6; compare 2008a, 8). He became even more outspoken later
and noted with satisfaction that there was movement in the criteria of the
Stability Pact (Sarkozy 2008c, 6). By December 2009, twenty of twenty-
seven member states had an excessive deficit procedure, Germany then
joining France, which had one since April. The Council of ministers followed the recommendations of the Commission in each excessive deficit
case even though the Stability Pact has an exemption clause for severe recessions. Obviously, no government feared that it would have to pay a fine.

Merkel, in her first crisis speech about two weeks later, was short and
specific on the subject of Europe, arguing that there are two ways in which
national and European crisis management should not be linked. First, she
criticized the Irish way of protecting only domestic enterprises and dis-
criminating against those from other member states.[13] Second, she dis-
tanced herself from proposals to join up crisis management fully—for example, by paying into a fund that organizes stabilization for all
twenty-seven member states (Merkel 2008a, 4). This was directed against
Sarkozy's proposal for a European sovereign wealth fund that would protect European firms against takeovers. It was never created because the
United Kingdom was also opposed and the European Commission was
skeptical of its protectionist air (Pierre Avril, "Sarkozy veut des fonds sou-
verains en Europe," *Le Figaro*, October 22, 2008, p. 7). Coherence of na-

tional action would be the term of art that Merkel used henceforth to describe what desirable coordinated stabilization meant to her, that is, a minimalist reconciliation of national measures so as to prevent negative side effects on each other.

The European Economic Recovery Plan (EERP), agreed on in December 2008, simply added what member states had declared to be their fiscal stimulus for 2009. The total was a respectable €200 billion, of which €30 billion came from the budget of the European Commission, amounting to about 1.5 percent of EU GDP. The EERP made Germany pass at least the first small stimulus so as to have something to show, against the declared wishes of then Finance Minister Steinbrück from the SPD. Though hardly a concerted initiative, it was certainly not a mean feat either to get twenty-seven member states with their national parliaments into line. For Europe, the Great Recession had only just begun, and the Bush administration, in a much more dire situation, had difficulties getting its stimulus plan through Congress. The praise for this achievement went to Sarkozy, while Merkel became Madame Non in the international press because she had vetoed any idea of a more coordinated stimulus, such as the general reduction of VAT, which the European Commission had supported (Cécile Cornudet, "Sarkozy se veut aussi énergique sur la scène française qu'à l'international," Les Echos, October 20, 2008, p. 3; "Bremser in Berlin," Financial Times Deutschland, November 27, 2008, p. 27).

In this first crisis, the German government arguably ended in its preferred equilibrium while France had to content itself with the praise for achieving it. As I argue in more detail elsewhere, the EU played a constructive, technocratic role in crisis management, which was achieved without any lasting institutional changes, and member states retained their (shared) sovereignty over stabilization measures (Schelkle 2012). This constrained role for the EU was, in all likelihood, economically costly in terms of foregone stabilization that more coordination could have achieved (see chapter 4, this volume). It was certainly not the EU that Sarkozy had envisaged in his Argonay address: "Technocratic Europe, the Europe where there is no politics anymore, the Europe that doesn't debate, the Europe that doesn't decide, the Europe that doesn't move anymore, this very Europe is about to make room for a political Europe, which decides, which moves, which thinks" (2008b, 3). His preferences did not prevent Sarkozy from enjoying his presidency of a technocratic Europe, however, stressing that what he proposes is closely coordinated with Merkel whenever possible (4). It became increasingly less possible, though, and there was real tension in Franco-German relations by the end of 2008.

Battling Through the Second Crisis

In the subsequent sovereign debt crisis, the French president was to get his political Europe, with a vengeance. The crisis started in December 2009, after Greek bonds were downgraded and the president of the European Central Bank announced that the bank intended to phase out lending against low-quality bonds. After yet another Eurostat report on what was an open secret, namely that the Greek administration had provided unreliable and outright fraudulent data, the Economic and Financial Affairs Council (EcoFin) overcompensated for its previous neglect. It imposed an impossibly stringent and intrusive budgetary adjustment program in February 2010. To ask the Greek government to do the democratically impossible did not exactly calm nervous markets. In March, the heads of state had to plan for the eventuality of a bailout, to the tune of €30 billion in bilateral loans at nonconcessional interest rates of about 5 percent. They were topped up by half of the EU contribution again from the IMF. The IMF's inclusion in the package was highly controversial, not only between France and Germany but also within the German government. German Finance Minister Schäuble closed ranks with his French colleague, Christine Lagarde, and President Sarkozy, arguing that the U.S. government would not call on the IMF if California were in dire straits (Bundesregierung 2010). But the Chancellery was in favor of IMF involvement, for fiscal reasons and because Merkel opposed the creation of yet another EU competency.

The first rescue package for Greece soon turned out to be too small and too short term, so by May 2, 2010, the members of the euro area pledged €80 billion, the IMF contributing another €30 billion. Euro area members guaranteed the loans according to their paid-up shares in the ECB. In an unprecedented display of urgency, ECB President Trichet and IMF President Strauss-Kahn descended on the German Bundestag at the end of April to get parliamentary approval of Germany's share in the package.[14] It was a strange coincidence that all these appeals for more action had a French accent, but the Bundestag was apparently impressed and passed the bill.

The role of and demands on the ECB were sources of controversy at the summit of heads of state, only five days after the Greek rescue package had been agreed upon. In a fascinating *Financial Times* account, Tony Barber tells the story of these negotiations ("Dinner on the Edge of the Abyss," October 11, 2010, p. 7). Sarkozy, deeply shocked by the presentation of the ECB president, shouted at Trichet that he should stop hesitating. By this, Sarkozy meant that the ECB should buy (and not only lend against) government bonds, following the example of the U.S. Fed and the Bank of England, a remarkable call for Anglo-Saxon financial management from this French president. Predictably, Merkel rushed to the defense of the ECB's independence.[15] France was backed by the southern fringe and the Dutch and Finnish governments expressed support for the German position. Trichet made it a point of not giving his consent, waiting for governments to agree on a European Financial Stability Facility (EFSF) before any ECB decision would be announced. The proudly independent central bank had already swallowed its pride by agreeing to lend against Greek bonds whatever their rating only a day after the package was agreed; this finally calmed Greek bond markets, although the strange decision to single out Greek bonds increased pressure in Irish, Portuguese, and Spanish bond markets. While resisting the pressure from governments, the ECB thus accepted the pressure from markets, which must have been infuriating for Sarkozy. Trichet did announce that the ECB would buy government bonds only after the temporary rescue mechanism had been agreed.

The conflict over the exact institutional set-up of this EFSF came to a head at an EcoFin meeting on May 8 and 9, 2010. The European Commission wanted a fund operating under EU authority that can sell a common euro bond backed by a collective government guarantee. But Merkel preferred an arrangement based on bilateral loans, analogous to the earlier Greek rescue package. She got support from the Commission legal services, which found that the creation of the Commission's fund would require treaty changes. During these negotiations between economics and finance ministers, Sarkozy and Merkel conferred over the phone. And a G7 conference call, as well as a phone conversation between President Obama and Chancellor Merkel, drove home the message that not only the European but world financial stability hung in the balance. The deadlock was apparently broken by a senior civil servant from the Dutch finance ministry who proposed a temporary Special Purpose Vehicle until mid-2013 (Tony Barber, "Dinner on the Edge of the Abyss," *Financial Times*, October 11, 2010, p. 7). It has the right to raise funds backed by identifiable, individually rated government guarantees to the tune of €440 billion. The commission may add €60 billion guaranteed by the EU budget, the IMF up to €250 billion. Merkel warmed to this complex arrangement based on somewhat dubious financial technology because this vehicle is not under European Commission control and does not issue a common euro bond. The price to pay for this intergovernmental, private law set-up is that a bilateral loan may not be forthcoming from all members. For instance, the then youngest euro area member Slovakia opted out of the Greek rescue package.[16]

Predictably, the establishment of the EFSF, fully operational since early

August, did not end the turmoil. After all, the entire arrangement signaled to bondholders that assistance had to be negotiated each time and this is likely to precipitate the need for assistance because bondholders may want to sell whenever they are unsure whether timely assistance is forthcoming. Interest rates on Irish bonds rose from September, and the crisis escalated in November 2010, when a doomed Irish government planned for a four-year austerity program against rising opposition in parliament. It had no plan B and refused EU assistance until the EcoFin Council officially requested the government to seek assistance on November 21. The Irish authorities preferred to bow to market pressures rather than to EU-IMF conditionality. The ECB president had earlier stated that he was not amused about the high money demand of Irish banks, accounting for about one-fifth of all ECB assistance to banks. Before that, Merkel had raised alarm in bond markets by proposing that in the future private bondholders must share the burden of rescue packages (Garrett FitzGerald, "Ireland Is Paying the Price of Three Follies," *Financial Times*, November 22, 2010). Together these comments contained a stark warning to the Irish government that it must stop abusing the ECB as its national printing press and Germany was not willing to back future rescues to the extent it was forced to do in the Greek package. Merkel's initiative was all the more remarkable for the fact that German (as well as French) banks are heavily exposed to debt of the peripheral countries; hence the emphasis on the future.[17]

Before 2007, Ireland's spectacular growth had made its fiscal situation the envy of all other euro area members, enjoying a budget surplus despite low taxes that attracted foreign investors and criticism of unfair tax competition, especially from France and Germany. With its fatal decision to guarantee or take over the debt of all banks without letting any of them fail, the government turned Ireland into one of the most indebted member states if contingent liabilities were taken into account: at the end of 2009, its bank rescue operations added 176 percent of GDP to a general government debt ratio of 65.5 percent (European Commission 2010b, 6). The government then proceeded to reinforce the procyclical tendency of markets and embarked on a severe austerity program that led the Irish economy into a vicious circle of recession, worsening public finances and rising interest rates.

In a rare display of unity, the French and the German government issued, on October 18, a joint declaration on necessary reforms of economic governance, nine days before an EU summit on exactly the same topic. The so-called Deauville declaration made two formal proposals that Merkel and Schäuble had ventured before.[18] First, budgetary surveillance and economic policy coordination should be strengthened by making "a wider range of sanctions . . . more automatic." Second, treaty changes should come into effect before 2013 that would ensure "adequate participation of private creditors" in crisis resolution and introduce a new form of sanction, namely, the suspension of voting rights for European Council members in severe breach of their membership obligations.

Each of these proposals was contentious: many member states opposed automatic sanctions and the withdrawal of voting rights; the ECB rejected standard haircuts for private bondholders; and European Commission President Barroso came out vehemently against a withdrawal of voting rights. At the summit at the end of October, the task force under van Rompuy was sent away to work out an acceptable reform proposal. It was finally agreed in mid-December. The possibility of withdrawing voting rights was dropped, not least because Ireland was certain to need another referendum for such a wide-ranging treaty change. The reduction of private bondholders' claims in any future debt restructuring will be decided on a case-by-case basis, but collective action clauses that allow a bail-in have to be included in all bond issues after 2013 and private claims are subordinated to the claims of the new European stability mechanism (European Council 2011). The automaticity of sanctions was qualified by the principle of a *reverse majority*. This means that a qualified majority is required to reject a commission recommendation of opening a procedure at the end of which a pecuniary sanction will be imposed; a qualified majority is no longer required for acceptance. The media were quick to issue their standard verdict on EU summits, namely, that proposals had been watered down. But this misses the point of how much more stringent and punitive the regime has become. More and tougher sanctions on more acts of disobedience are now more difficult to reject. The failure to undertake enough structural reform, which is the code term for labor market and pension reform, can be punished by withholding EU funding. Excessive imbalances in the current account can now be fined like excessive deficits. The wording should not detract from the fact that they will be imposed only on countries in deficit (Schelkle and Mabbett 2010).

Automaticity was to become the key word of the reform debate, used extensively in speeches of the ECB president, Commissioner of Economic and Financial Affairs Ollie Rehn, and the German finance minister. The position of the critics was summarized by the French economics minister early on: "A fully automatic system, a power fully in the hands of experts? No" (Raf Casert, "France Clashes with Germany, ECB over Automatic Budget Sanctions," *USA Today*, September 27, 2010). Governments should have the last word, not economists' prescriptions turned into rules. The

German counterposition was apparently not only backed by Austria and the Netherlands, but also the Nordic countries, EU members outside the euro area, and the majority of central and eastern European governments (Barysch 2010). The Deauville declaration showed the way to a compromise in its call for "*more* automaticity." The principle of reverse majority gave meaning to the *more* and also shifts political responsibility onto the European Commission if a contentious recommendation passes.

This is hardly a triumph of prudent economics dominating policy choice. The politics is arguably more about discipline than modernization, but politics it is in the sense of Sarkozy's "political Europe which decides, which moves, which thinks." Crisis management has become formalized and the EFSF, complemented by a permanent European Stability Mechanism (ESM) from 2012 onward, is the latest example of political institution-building. A further piece of evidence for a more political Europe is the introduction of what is called a European semester. It changes the timing of EU fiscal surveillance and national budgetary processes such that the EU and both the European Commission and the Eco-Fin Council scrutinize prebudget plans of governments before they go to national parliaments. In the following year, the commission will deliver a report on how well the legislature and the executive have followed the guidelines that will also be debated in the European Parliament (European Commission 2010a, 12). The European semester started in January 2011. It remains to be seen what happens if a national parliament is stroppy and insists on its sovereignty in budgetary matters.

The second crisis and the reforms it triggered have perverted the political strategy of letting economic needs conspicuously dominate the choice of policy. The policymaking style of problem-solving addressed Markel's political constraints rather well in a national context. But there it was underpinned by effective fiscal stabilization. No such capacity for macroeconomic stabilization has been created at the EU level. All that the ECB delivers is due to a tacit acceptance of its quasi-fiscal role. When this capacity is missing as political stakes are raised, such as in the EU, the strategy cannot protect particular governments and the political system of the EU against overstretch and overreach. Sarkozy, like French presidents before him, allowed the transformation to happen because he never fully grasped a rationale that is contrary to what meets his political constraints at home. But the reformed framework abdicates power, reinforces economic pressures, and lets market forces dictate policy choices, even though they are manifestly counterproductive and inconsistent: Irish bonds are shunned when investors find the austerity measures too lenient and when they find them too hard. At least there is some justice in that these Irish bonds end up with the ECB, the main promoter of reforms that politicize the EU without empowering it.

THE POLITICAL ECONOMY OF CRISIS MANAGEMENT

This chapter has explained the French and German responses to the two phases of the financial crisis in terms of political strategies that try to manage distinct and often conflicting political and socioeconomic requirements. The findings suggest that the presentation of interventions followed stereotypes that presumably appeal to the silent majority but actual policies defied these stereotypes. However, actual policies were also not simply dictated by economic necessity. On the contrary, had they been, Germany should have been more forthright in its first stimulus and France should have launched a second stimulus. German official response largely followed the logic of electoral politics mediated by party coalitions in a federal system, upholding the ever popular housewife maxim of fiscal belt-tightening in hard times. Similarly, Sarkozy projected the ever popular idea of statesmanship directly to his voters in order to pursue an existing reform agenda for which he had been elected. Interest group politics raised its head at times in both countries, most notably when it came to rescue packages for the car industry. Hence the conclusion that it is electoral politics for presentation and interest group politics for effective stabilization that characterizes the phenomenologically different responses of both countries.

The claim that institutions determined the politics—and through that the policies—in each case does not seem generally valid. Contrary to expectations in the varieties of capitalism literature, corporatist venues played no discernible role in Germany, whereas the Elysée staged a get-together of social partners. The federal set-up was a noticeable factor in German crisis management. But for once the coalition governments in the Länder acted as facilitators rather than as veto players, given the dire fiscal situation. Institutional pathways can explain the importance of particular measures: even though short-term work programs did exist in both countries, they represented more of an opportunity in Germany with its complex legislative procedures because an ordinance allowed the program to be extended. Yet, it still required a social democratic minister in office who spotted the opportunity for supporting his core constituencies in a big way.

The dual—cynics would say duplicitous—politics in hard times observed in the two countries has arguably wider significance for the political economy of crisis management in capitalist democracies, especially under conditions of European integration. Playing up the extent of intervention as the French government did can be understood as an attempt to demonstrate the sovereignty of political decision-making, a strategy that is borne by considerable trust in achieving economic outcomes as intended. Playing down the extent of proactive intervention, in the German way, can be seen as an attempt at damage control for the political system, guarding against the case in which the economic system does not respond as intended and exposes the weakness of the state. The Franco-German conflict over the appropriate response, national and European, was at its intellectual base a legitimate debate about how one can protect and possibly strengthen the realm of the political when a financial crisis threatened to reduce politics to "it's the economy, stupid." The European dimension made the dilemma of crisis management and economic intervention generally even more salient and public. A supranational response was desperately needed but the capacity for transnational policymaking was also uncertain.

The French position was that we need a visible "return of politics" (Sarkozy 2008a, 2) and the policy measures the government put up to stabilize the economy were appropriate to convey this message: 1,000 projects all over France, identified quickly and the money disbursed rapidly. The favorable ratings in the polls prove that Sarkozy had fulfilled expectations and addressed his political constraints. Ironically, a high-visibility strategy holds the state hostage to the economy's fortune, at least in advanced capitalist democracies where electoral loyalty is nontraditional and dependent on the perception that government works. The French case study provided an example. It is a well-known problem of macroeconomic stabilization that shovel-ready projects are hard to find in large enough volumes to make a well-timed impact. And it seems that the French government did not manage either, if we accept the disappointing employment performance as a relevant indicator. The political backlash came in March 2010 when Sarkozy's party experienced a devastating defeat in regional elections (Levy 2010, 23). Similar considerations apply to a political Europe. French presidents want to expand and pool overtly political decision-making in the European Union, so as to govern economic processes more forcefully. A Europe that is very visible and does not shy away from open conflict may make citizens interested in what arguably shapes their lives as much as national politics. Yet, the limited political and fiscal resources at the EU's disposal make this a high-risk strategy. It is easy to blame Brussels, and Brussels is blamed more easily, because nobody feels particular allegiance with this far-off place of decision-making.

The German position was that "the state will," in the sense of should, "retreat from direct intervention" as soon as trust returns to markets

(Merkel 2008b, 1). The lack of a grand narrative about the role of the political did indeed fit the government's strategy of responding to economic needs with a display of the popular politics of restraint. The German political elite instinctively favors a more cautious approach, possibly because the rhetoric of a strong state is taboo but also to avoid overstretching state capacities. So the government chose to be pushed into decisive state intervention rather than to engage in it proactively. This has worked out well in the first phase of the crisis. But even if it had not, Merkel could have responded, "We never pretended that we would save the market from itself." The problem with this strategy is that insisting on limited political responsibility means that policymakers are always behind the curve because they restrain their capacity for intervention and thus become driven by market forces. The fallout from the second crisis is a case in point. Merkel wanted EU political decision-making to manage and contain economic interdependence. But the disciplinarian approach of "economics alias fiscal rules should dominate" did not preserve a technocratic Europe as desired. It led to more interdependence in economic terms because markets remain unstable. The economic governance reforms have also increased interdependence in political terms; the corresponding reflex of responding to every economic imbalance with ever more intrusive intervention in national budgetary processes politicizes conflicts over economic adjustment in an unintended way. These interventions are perceived as a diktat on national democracy, by Irish, Greek, and German taxpayers, and others, of course, for which an EU democratic deficit is already blamed. It would be more pertinent to blame national democracies' imposition on each other for the diktat (see also chapter 6, this volume).

Both governments actually tried to stick to their political agenda and did not simply abandon their promises at the first opportunity, contrary to what a cynical view of modern politics suggests. The French president tried to instrumentalize the looming Great Recession for his reform politics. In fact, Sarkozy stuck to this so faithfully that he strained the lever, declaring opening hours on Sunday crucial for combating the crisis was never credible. But he had political space for making crisis management and his structural reforms complementary projects and was keen to use it. This was more difficult for the government in Germany. Fiscal consolidation and rolling back the state had been Merkel's electoral promises, yet these promises were directly crowded out by the Great Recession. Her response to this was to promise a return to virtue after the worst is over. The EU served as a platform to make this commitment credible. Hence, her government insisted on a frugal, self-restrained EU and only the most dramatic circumstances, such as the near collapse of euro markets, could get her off that track. Her stubbornness was counterproductive for the

European Union but indicates the tenacity of a politician holding on to an idea of limited state involvement.

Finally, the two government responses analyzed here are noteworthy against the background that European integration is often accused of being a homogenizing force and of eradicating political in favor of economic imperatives (Scharpf 1999). The two rather different political visions of European integration that France and Germany project shaped the crisis responses of the EU, arguably constraining a more decisive response one way or the other (see chapter 4, this volume; see also Krugman, "A Continent Adrift," *New York Times*, March 16, 2009). The tale of the two crises, however—namely that the EU policy framework remained intact in 2008 and 2009 while the sovereign debt crisis of 2009 led to fundamental changes—shows that EU economic governance is at a crossroads.

The politicization of the EU has not been accompanied by increasing the capacity for macroeconomic policymaking. Most economists doubt that this political Europe can deliver effective stabilization because it is denied the instruments for doing so (Forum 2010). This spells trouble for the future. After all, the taboo of a carefully manufactured separation between monetary and fiscal policy is broken. The ECB has been repeatedly degraded to a printing press, substituting for some form of joint public debt management required for this separation. The German-led reaction has been to do just more of the same, hoping that tougher fiscal surveillance will prevent a Greece or Ireland from happening again. Yet, markets ignored the reports from Eurostat about dodgy Greek statistics since 2002 when growth prospects looked good, and they abandoned the country when it entered recession, leaving Greece hopelessly over-indebted. Tougher fiscal surveillance would also not have prevented the Irish debacle or the looming Spanish crisis because private sector debt was the problem in each case. And by the end of 2011 it was still, to the extent that sovereign default would cause serious difficulties for European banks (Patrick Jenkins, Sharlene Goff, and Patrick Mathurin, "Bank Ties Across EU Carry Risk Concerns," *Financial Times*, December 2, 2010, p. 25). Not economics but market panic has dominated policy choices since late 2009, given the lack of appropriate instruments that would allow each problem case to be treated adequately and differently (see chapter 6, this volume).

The French and the German visions of a political Europe have become strangely aligned during the second crisis. The French government likes the new economic governance framework because it becomes an additional instrument for the executive, in form more overtly a fourth branch of government (Majone 1993). The German government hopes that, in substance, this strengthened branch can force all members on the path of economic virtue, lowering the potential for disturbances to its own national well-being. The problem is that the new politics lacks the ability for policymaking, in particular a fiscal backing of the joint monetary policy. The new framework makes the EU conspicuously political without adding capacity for delivering policies that can resist market forces pushing governments into procyclical tightening. The EU is thus learning the hard way that politics also needs effective policy.

I am indebted to the ANU project and in particular Natalie Windle (2009) for making me aware of this source for an analysis of responses to the crisis. For the reporting of the press, I have used LexisNexis Economics and chosen three quality newspapers in each country that represent the political spectrum (*Le Figaro* and *Le Monde* in France, *Die Welt* and *Die Zeit* in Germany) as well as a financial paper (*Les Echos* and *Financial Times Deutschland*); the key words I used were *crisis*, *stimulus*, and *parliament* in the respective language.

NOTES

1. The three speeches were all given in 2008, on September 25, October 23, and December 4 (see http://www.elysee.fr/president/les-actualites/discours/discours.18.html?cat_id=7; accessed April 12, 2012).
2. The addresses in 2008 that received some resonance in the media were a formal pronouncement (Regierungserklärung) on October 7, her presentation of the first stimulus in parliament on November 26, and her speech to the CDU party conference on December 2, 2008 (see http://www.bundeskanzlerin.de/Webs/BK/De/Aktuell/Archiv16/Artikel/artikel.html; accessed April 12, 2012).
3. Portail du Gouvernment, "Plan de relance de l'économie française," December 9, 2008, http://www.gouvernement.fr/gouvernement/plan-de-relance-de-l-economie-francaise (accessed April 12, 2012).
4. Die Bundesregierung, http://www.konjunkturpaket.de (accessed April 12, 2012).
5. France also had a short-term work program but limited duration to six weeks at a time and a maximum of 600 hours per year, about eighteen weeks (Arpaia et al. 2010, 28).
6. http://www.bundesregierung.de/Content/DE/Magazine/MagazinSoziales FamilieBildung/079/skurzarbeit-und-investitionspakete-zeigen-vor-ort-wir kung.html (accessed April 12, 2012).
7. See http://www.eu2009.cz/en/news-and-documents/news/czech-presi dency-calls-for-coordinated-support-for-car-indus-10653/index.html (accessed April 12, 2012).

8. On the Germany Trade & Invest website, the government's economic development agency, the Economics Ministry, maintains a link intended to help the German export industry to seize the opportunities created by stimulus packages around the world, in particular in the areas of infrastructure and green technology. This link was removed by the end of 2011 but could then still be found on websites of various industry and trade associations.

9. The accrual method can explain why in his announcement of the stimulus package of €26 billion, the French president could play down the budgetary impact to €15.5bn., with explicit reference to Maastricht (Sarkozy 2008c, 5).

10. The OECD shows the two tax-transfer systems as being equally responsive (Girouard and André 2005, table 9) but this is based on aggregate estimates of revenue and spending elasticities of the budget, not on the microsimulation of how a specified shock changes national taxes and transfers and thus disposable household income (as in Dolls, Fuest, and Peichl 2009).

11. This does not contradict the similarity of output gaps noted in table 5.2; it simply means that demand fell in each country along with the national output, less in France than in Germany. In fact, the positive output gap of 0.9 percent of GDP for 2008 in Germany tells us that demand collapsed earlier than output.

12. The financial crisis of 2008 and 2009 triggered a flurry of activity in financial reregulation, on which the two governments largely agreed. This is left out for reasons of space.

13. Merkel's critique referred to the Irish government's decision in early October 2008 to grant deposits of six Irish banks only. This raised the specter of a bank run all over Europe as British savers started to open savings accounts with Irish banks. The Irish government had to withdraw or extend its guarantee to all resident banks, in line with EU rules (for more details, see Schelkle 2012).

14. Chronologie der Krise, "Griechenland: Rettungspaket beschlossene Sache," April 28, 2010, http://hw71.wordpress.com/2010/04/28/griechenland -rettungspaket-beschlossene-sache/ (accessed April 12, 2012).

15. Merkel had earlier voiced unusually outspoken critique of the ECB's interventions which were too unorthodox for her taste (Bertrand Benoît and Ralph Atkins, "Merkel Mauls Central Banks," *Financial Times*, June 2, 2009).

16. Slovak prime minister Radicova explained in an interview that "it would have been politically impossible for her to explain to her voters why Slovakia is lending €816m to the Greeks while she was embarking on a fiscal reform programme aimed at reducing the Slovak deficit by €1.7bn" (Jan Cienski, "Popular Premier's Tough Choices," *Financial Times*, October 6, 2010, p. 8). Slovakia was later cajoled into taking part and the government fell over this decision.

17. As of June 2010, German banks are exposed to Irish debt to the tune of $138.6 billion, second only to U.K. banks. This is largely due to one German Landes-

bank, Depfa, which is now part of the nationalized Hypo Real Estate (Patrick Jenkins, Sharlene Goff, and Patrick Mathurin, "Bank Ties Across EU Carry Risk Concerns," *Financial Times*, December 2, 2010, p. 25).

18. The Franco-German declaration of October 18, 2010, is available online at *Élysée.fr* (see http://www.elysee.fr/president/root/bank_objects/Franco -german_declaration.pdf; accessed April 12, 2012).

REFERENCES

Arpaia, Alfonso, Nicola Curci, Eric Meyermans, Jörg Peschner, and Franco Pierini. 2010. "Short Time Working Arrangements as Response to Cyclical Fluctuations." *Occasional Papers* 64 (June). Brussels: European Commission, Directorate-General for Economic and Financial Affairs.

Barysch, Katinka. 2010. "Divisions Remain over Euro Reform." *Centre for European Reform*, October 8, 2010. Available at: http://centreforeuropeanreform.blogspot .com/2010/10/divisions-remain-over-euro-reform.html (accessed April 12, 2012).

Blum, Ulrich, and Sabine Freye. 2009. "Abwrackprämie—wer zahlt die Zeche?" Study commissioned for *Die Welt*, May 3, 2009. Available at: http://www .fh-brandenburg.de/~brasche/assets/lehre/intum/Mitnahmeeffekte _Abwrackpraemie.pdf (accessed April 12, 2012).

Bundesministerium für Finanzen. 2009. "Entwicklung der Finanzmarktkrise." Available at: http://www.bundesfinanzministerium.de/nn_69120/DE/Buer-gerinnen_und_Buerger/Gesellschaft_und_Zukunft/finanzkrise/076_Entwick-lung_Finanzmarktkrise.html?_nnn=true (accessed April 12, 2012).

Bundesregierung. 2010. "Griechenland muss sich selbst helfen." Reprint of interview with Wolfgang Schäuble by the *Frankfurter Rundschau*, February 13, 2010. Available at: http://www.bundesregierung.de/Content/DE/Interview/2010/ 02/2010-02-13-interview-schaeuble-fr,layoutVariant=Druckansicht.html (accessed April 12, 2012).

Caporaso, James A., and David P. Levine. 1992. *Theories of Political Economy*. Cambridge: Cambridge University Press.

DG Ecfin. 2007. "Economic Forecast Autumn 2007." European Economy No. 7/2007. Available at: http://ec.europa.eu/economy_finance/publications/ european_economy/forecasts_en.htm (accessed April 12, 2012).

———. 2008. "Economic Forecast Autumn 2008." European Economy No. 6/2008. Available at: http://ec.europa.eu/economy_finance/publications/european _economy/forecasts_en.htm (accessed April 12, 2012).

———. 2009. "Economic Forecast Spring 2009." European Economy No. 3/2009. Available at: http://ec.europa.eu/economy_finance/publications/european _economy/forecasts_en.htm (accessed April 12, 2012).

Dolls, Mathias, Clemens Fuest, and Andreas Peichl. 2009. "Automatic Stabilisers and the Economic Crisis: EU vs U.S." *IZA* discussion paper no. 4310. Bonn: Institute for the Study of Labor. Available at: http://ftp.iza.org/dp4310.pdf (accessed April 12, 2012).

Eichengreen, Barry. 2007. *The European Economy Since 1945: Coordinated Capitalism and Beyond*. Princeton, N.J.: Princeton University Press.

European Commission. 2009. "State Aid: Commission Statement on Aid for Opel Europe." *Europa.eu*, Memo 09/411, September 23, 2010. Available at: http://europa.eu/rapid/pressReleasesAction.do?reference=MEMO/09/411&format=HTML&aged=0&language=EN&guiLanguage=en (accessed April 12, 2012).

———. 2010a. "Enhancing Economic Policy Coordination for Stability, Growth, and Jobs: Tools for Stronger EU Economic Governance." *Europa.eu*, COM(2010), 367/2, June 30, 2010. Available at: http://ec.europa.eu/economy_finance/articles/euro/documents/com_2010_367_en.pdf (accessed April 12, 2012).

———. 2010b. "Eurostat Supplementary Table for the Financial Crisis." *Eurostat*, October 18, 2010. Available at: http://epp.eurostat.ec.europa.eu/portal/page/portal/ver-1/government_finance_statistics/documents/EDP_Oct_2010_supplementary_table_financial_crisis_pub.pdf (accessed April 12, 2012).

European Council. 2011. "Conclusions, December 16–17, 2010." *Europa.eu*, January 25. Available at: http://www.consilium.europa.eu/uedocs/cms_data/docs/pressdata/en/ec/118578.pdf (accessed April 12, 2012).

Forum. 2010. "Eight Months Later—Has the Eurozone Been Stabilised or Will EMU Fall Apart?" *Intereconomics* 45(6): 340–56.

Girouard, Nathalie, and Christophe André. 2005. "Measuring Cyclically-Adjusted Budget Balances for OECD Countries." *OECD Economics Department* working papers No. 434. Paris: Organisation for Economic Co-operation and Development.

Gourevitch, Peter A. 1986. *Politics in Hard Times: Comparative Responses to International Economic Crises*. Ithaca, N.Y.: Cornell University Press.

Hall, Peter A. 2010. "The Political Origins of Our Economic Discontents: Contemporary Adjustment Problems in Historical Perspective." Draft chapter for *Politics in the New Hard Times: The Great Recession in Comparative Perspective*, edited by Miles Kahler and David Lake.

International Monetary Fund. 2007. *World Economic Outlook: Globalization and Inequality*. October. Washington D.C.: International Monetary Fund.

———. 2008. *World Economic Outlook: Financial Stress, Downturns, and Recoveries*. October. Washington D.C.: International Monetary Fund.

———. 2009. *World Economic Outlook: Crisis and Recovery*. April. Washington D.C.: International Monetary Fund.

———. 2010a. "France: 2010 Article IV Consultation." *IMF* country report no. 10/240. Washington, D.C.: IMF.

————. 2010b. "Germany: 2010 Article IV Consultation." *IMF* country report no. 10/85. Washington, D.C.: IMF.

Iversen, Torben. 2006. "Capitalism and Democracy." In *Oxford Handbook of Political Economy*, edited by Donald Wittman and Barry R. Weingast. Oxford: Oxford University Press.

Levy, Jonah D. 2010. "The Return of the State? French Economic Policy Under Nicolas Sarkozy." Paper presented at the 106th Annual Meeting of the American Political Science Association. Washington, D.C. (September 2–5, 2010).

Mabbett, Deborah, and Waltraud Schelkle. 2009. "The Politics of Conflict Management in EU Regulatory Processes." *West European Politics* 32(4): 699–718.

Majone, Giandomenico. 1993. "The European Community: An Independent 'Fourth Branch of Government'?" *EUI* working paper SPS no. 93/9. Florence: European University Institute.

Merkel, Angela. 2008a. "Regierungserklärung von Bundeskanzlerin Dr. Angela Merkel." *Bulletin der Bundesregierung* Nr. 104–1. October 7, 2008. Available at: http://www.bundesregierung.de/nn_1514/%20Content/DE/Bulletin/2008/10/104-1-bkin-bt-regerkl.html (accessed April 12, 2012).

————. 2008b. "Rede von Bundeskanzlerin Angela Merkel auf dem Arbeitgebertag der Bundesvereinigung der Deutschen Arbeitgeberverbände e.V. (BDA)." November 4, 2008, Available at: http://www.bundeskanzlerin.de (accessed April 12, 2012).

Organisation for Economic Co-operation and Development (OECD). 2009. "Fiscal Packages Across OECD Countries: Overview and Country Details." *Economic Department* working paper. Paris: OECD.

Présidence de la République. 2009. "Bilan d'étape, 1er juillet 2009." Available at: http://www.elysee.fr/president/les-dossiers/economie/face-a-la-crise/sommets-sociaux/bilan-d-etape-1er-juillet-2009/bilan-d-etape-avec-les-partenaires-sociaux.6329.html (accessed April 12, 2012).

Sarkozy, Nicolas. 2008a. "Mesures de soutien à l'économie." *Élysée*, October 23, 2008. Available at: http://www.elysee.fr/president/les-actualites/discours/discours.18.html (accessed April 12, 2012).

————. 2008b. "Discours de M. le président de la République à Toulon." *Élysée*, September 25, 2008. Available at: http://www.elysee.fr/president/les-actualites/discours/discours.18.html (accessed April 12, 2012).

————. 2008c. "Plan de relance de l' économie française." *Élysée*, December 4, 2008. Available at: http://www.elysee.fr/president/les-actualites/discours/discours.18.html (accessed April 12, 2012).

Scharpf, Fritz W. 1999. *Governing in Europe: Effective and Democratic?* New York: Oxford University Press.

Schelkle, Waltraud. 2012. "Good Governance in Crisis or a Good Crisis for Governance? A Comparison of the EU and the U.S." *Review of International Political Economy* 19(1): 34–58.

Schelkle, Waltraud, and Deborah Mabbett. 2010. "The Van Rompuy Reforms: Type 1 and Type 2 Errors and One Small Bright Spot." *Intereconomics* 45(6): 350–53.

Vail, Mark. 2011. "Liberalism, Keynesianism, and French and German Responses to the 'Great Recession.'" Paper presented at the APSA 2011 Annual Meeting. Seattle, Wash. (September 1–4, 2011). Available at: http://ssrn.com/abstract =1899994 (accessed April 12, 2012).

Windle, Natalie. 2009. "France: Dominant Leadership." In *Framing the Global Economic Downturn: Crisis Rhetoric and the Politics of Recessions*, edited by Paul t'Hart and Karen Tindall. Canberra: The Australian National University. Available at: http://epress.anu.edu.au/wp-content/uploads/2011/05/whole_book8 .pdf (accessed April 12, 2012).

Chapter 6 | The Sorrows of Young Euro: The Sovereign Debt Crises of Ireland and Southern Europe

Klaus Armingeon and Lucio Baccaro

THIS CHAPTER EXAMINES the sovereign debt crisis of the so-called GIIPS countries—Greece, Ireland, Italy, Portugal, and Spain—focusing in particular on the interaction between national political economic conditions and membership in the eurozone. Ever since Peter Gourevitch's seminal *Politics in Hard Times* (1986), comparative political economy scholars have been accustomed to expecting different national responses to crises, and have generally explained such diversity by reference to different institutional arrangements. Thus, most comparative political economists today would anticipate that, faced with a common external shock, national actors would have multiple options from which to choose and that domestic politics ultimately determines which policy response is selected. Similarly, they would expect institutional differences at the country level, for example, different "varieties of capitalism" (Hall and Soskice 2001), to matter for the type of strategic response that gets selected, with countries closer to the coordinated market economy pole, such as Italy (at least as far as industrial relations are concerned, Thelen 2001) reacting differently from countries closer to the liberal market economy camp, such as Ireland, and from countries that cannot be clearly assigned to either type, such as Greece.

In contrast with these views, we argue that domestic institutions and politics matter very little for explaining responses to the sovereign debt crisis, and that external constraints are much more important. In this case, there is only one policy response and it is imposed from outside. All that is left for domestic actors to do is to find ways to blunt popular opposition to the imposed policy.

We do not wish to generalize this claim unduly. Policy discretion has not disappeared everywhere. As we explain later, the GIIPS predicament is still a special case. Core euro-area countries, particularly Germany, retain the ability to choose alternative policies (see chapter 5, this volume). Nonetheless, the sovereign debt crisis reveals two things: first, a dramatic shrinking of the policy space for peripheral countries as a result of monetary unification; and, second, the a built-in neoliberal bias of the euro project, forcing nonliberal countries such as Greece, Italy, Portugal, Spain, in addition to Ireland, to adjust in a neoliberal direction.

The common GIIPS response consists of an attempt to engineer an internal devaluation vis-à-vis core eurozone countries, especially Germany, through cuts in wages and public expenditures. This strategy has not been freely chosen by the countries in question, but has been forced on them either directly, through conditionality linked to bailout packages, or indirectly, through very high interest rates on sovereign debt. The strategy is by no means distributionally neutral, because it includes reforms aimed to (further) liberalize and deregulate key parts of the labor market and industrial relations systems, and to scale down the welfare state. It has so far been self-defeating, that is, it has worsened rather than ameliorated prospects for financial solvency and brought the eurozone to the brink of collapse. If fully implemented, it will profoundly change the social contract in the countries in question, and possibly in Europe as a whole.

ECONOMIC PROBLEMS IN PERIPHERAL COUNTRIES

The sovereign debt crisis exploded in 2010 when international financial markets' doubts about the ability of the Greek sovereign to repay its bonds led to the country losing access to the private bond market. The Greek government was forced to call in the so-called troika of the European Union, the European Central Bank, and the International Monetary Fund (EU-ECB-IMF) for a bailout package, which was agreed in May 2010. Similar concerns later spread to other weak currencies. This led to similar bailout packages for Ireland (November 2010) and Portugal (May 2011). At the time of writing (December 2011), Spain and Italy are still able to finance themselves in private bond markets at considerable risk premia, but both countries are major causes for concern.

The five countries have had competitiveness problems since 2000 (Scharpf 2011). Nominal unit labor costs—nominal wages divided by a volume measure of labor productivity—have been increasing faster than in Germany, where they have remained virtually stable, and they have even declined slightly in mid-decade. The pattern is rather uniform across sectors, with one exception. In Ireland, the competitiveness problems are entirely concentrated in the building and services sectors, that is, the non-exposed sectors, while the manufacturing sector has not been losing competitiveness with respect to Germany (see chapter 10, this volume). This implies that Ireland, among the countries being affected by the sovereign crisis, is probably the best placed to return to export-led growth.[1]

The phenomenon of competitiveness loss is usually blamed on union wage militancy. However, evidence of wage militancy at work is not plentiful.[2] In Greece, Italy, and Spain, the countries for which hourly wage data are available, wages continued to be much lower than in Germany. In the period in question, they simply rose in line with German wages, with no sign of convergence. On the other hand, productivity trends were quite different. Although productivity continued to grow in Germany at the same pace as before, it grew more slowly in Greece, was practically flat in Spain, and even declined in Italy. This signals problems with the pattern of sectoral specialization of these countries—problems that are unlikely to be solved simply by cutting wages.

The standard solution to a competitiveness problem is exchange-rate devaluation. This would allow countries to increase their exports, at least temporarily, and particularly in cases like Ireland and possibly Italy, in which the manufacturing sector has historically been strong. The need to engage in socially painful and politically costly reforms of employment protection, unemployment insurance, and industrial relations systems would not be as great, though some reforms, such as pension reform in Greece and Spain, would have to be done anyway to adapt to changing demographic conditions. In addition, an exchange-rate devaluation would probably be more effective in reducing real wage wages than nominal wage cuts, as wages tend to be sticky. Furthermore, devaluation would probably increase domestic inflation, and this in turn would alleviate the debt problem for reasons discussed shortly.

By ruling out exchange rate devaluation, membership in the eurozone severely limits the countries' policy discretion. International economic observers have drawn attention to the case of countries outside the eurozone, such as Iceland or the United Kingdom, with similar and sometimes even more serious fiscal problems than countries inside, such as Ireland and Spain, which have managed to eschew the pressing financial problems of the latter.

For example, Paul Krugman has contrasted the experiences of Ireland and Iceland after the crisis.[3] Both are small open economies. In both cases the crisis was due to deregulated national banks dramatically expanding their balance sheets—from 170 percent of GDP at the end of 2003 to 880 percent of GDP, an Organisation for Economic Co-operation and Development (OECD) record, at the end of 2007 in the Icelandic case (OECD 2009b,

20)—by borrowing in foreign markets to finance a domestic real estate boom. When interbank markets froze after the Lehman Brothers debacle, and creditors insisted on repayment and other banks were unwilling to issue new loans, these banks collapsed, precipitating their respective countries in a devastating crisis. The policy response was, however, very different between the two countries. As argued in the next section, the Irish response was fully orthodox: the sovereign guaranteed the debt held by foreign lenders, slashed public expenditures, increased taxes, and engaged in structural reforms involving inter alia public sector wage cuts, as well as cuts in the minimum wage and unemployment benefits. In Iceland, the government refused to guarantee the debt owned by non-foreign residents (which means that they had to take sizeable "haircuts" on their claims); introduced capital controls to stop capital flight, and let the national currency devalue markedly against other currencies. In January 2007, 1,000 Icelandic kronar could buy about €11; two years later it was less than €6.

Despite worse initial conditions, Iceland is currently faring no worse, and arguably better as far as employment outcomes are concerned, than Ireland. Krugman draws the conclusion that "heterodoxy is working a whole lot better than orthodoxy" (Paul Krugman, "Lands of Ice and Ire," *New York Times*, November 24, 2010). In December 2011 none other than the IMF praised Iceland's unorthodox policies and argued that they suggested an alternative approach to crisis response.[4] Such conclusions may be exaggerated: since events are still unfolding one cannot exclude that GDP and employment will deteriorate further in Iceland and pick up again in Ireland. Nonetheless, one solid fact is on heterodoxy's side: Iceland has recently regained access to international financial markets,[5] whereas Ireland is relying on a lifeline provided by the EU, ECB, and IMF. It seems paradoxical that a policy intervention like the Irish one, designed especially to reassure international bond markets, should be less reassuring than that of Iceland, which included the "original sin" of capital controls. Yet it is not the first time that this happens, as suggested by the experience of Malaysia during the Asian crisis of the late 1990s, whose response also included capital controls (Stiglitz 2002).

In a recent paper, Paul De Grauwe (2011) discusses a similar contrast between Spain and the United Kingdom. In 2009, Spain had a public deficit of 11.1 percent of GDP and the United Kingdom one of 11.4 percent. Public debt was 53.3 percent of GDP in Spain and 69.6 in the United Kingdom.[6] Thus it looked, based on economic fundamentals, as though Spain were in better shape than the United Kingdom. Yet one year later, the country that was perceived to be at risk of a sovereign debt default, as reflected in interest rate and Credit Default Swap (CDS) spreads, was the former and not the latter. De Grauwe argues that the reason is that Spain is in the euro and the United Kingdom is not. The United Kingdom devaluated massively: one sterling was worth €1.5 in January 2007; by January 2009 it had lost a third of its value. Spain could not do the same.

De Grauwe also compares the likely policy responses of two identical countries faced with an unfavorable shock that increases public deficit and debt (2011). One country controls its own currency, and the other is a member of a monetary union. In the former country, if investors become nervous about the solvency of the sovereign, they are likely to respond by selling government bonds and then the currency in which the bonds are denominated. However, the liquidity—denominated, say, in British pounds—is trapped in the country, where it might be used to purchase the outstanding government bond stock. Even if private investors are unwilling to do so, the national central bank may be persuaded to purchase them. In other words, international financial markets cannot cause a liquidity crisis in a country which, like the United Kingdom, controls its own currency. Also, the investors' selling the national currency sets in motion an equilibrating mechanism. The exchange rate tends to depreciate, which makes exports cheaper and imports more costly. This in turn both stimulates GDP growth and increases domestic inflation.

In the case of a member of a currency union, the situation is quite different. When the unfavorable shock hits, international investors sell government bonds just as in the previous case. However, the liquidity is denominated in the common currency, that is, is not bottled up in the country in question but migrates elsewhere and is used to purchase, for example, German bonds. The government of the country in question has no way to force the central bank to provide the needed liquidity because it has no control over it. It has to ask private financial markets to provide the needed liquidity. These may demand prohibitively high interest rates and in so doing may render the dreaded scenario—insolvency and eventually default—more likely. In these circumstances, the government may try to boost the markets' confidence in its solvency by engaging in austerity policies, that is, cutting public expenditures or increasing taxes, or both. The problem is that by doing so, the government risks setting in motion a vicious cycle of austerity worsening the recession, requiring even more austerity, and so on. What started off as a liquidity crisis may, through self-fulfilling expectations, become a solvency crisis. In other words, the government of a currency union finds itself in the same position as the government of an emerging market country issuing debt denominated in a foreign currency.

In brief, although a country that has its own currency has some equilibrating mechanism (essentially exchange rate devaluation), which brings it back to a "good" equilibrium, the other can only hope that if it inflicts enough pain on itself, international financial markets will start believing in its long-term solvency again and provide the needed liquidity at reasonable interest rates. One key difference between the two countries' experiences is inflation and, associated with it, nominal GDP growth. In fact, as De Grauwe explains, "a necessary condition for solvency is that the primary budget surplus . . . be at least as high as the difference between the nominal interest rate and the nominal growth rate times the debt ratio" (2011, 6–7):

$$S \geq (R - G)D$$

where S is the primary budget surplus, that is, current receipts minus current expenditures net of interest payments in percentage of GDP; R is the nominal interest rate the government pays on its debt; G is the nominal growth rate; and D is the stock of debt in percentage of GDP.

It follows that the more the nominal growth rate exceeds the nominal interest rate, the smaller the primary surplus needed for the government to maintain its solvency will have to be, that is, the less the need for austerity. In other words, more austerity is needed of countries that are unable to resume nominal growth at rates about the cost of capital facing them. This probably explains why Iceland, which managed to return to nominal wage growth relatively quickly,[7] was able to access international financial markets before Ireland, which did not, even though it was the poster-child of austerity policies. It also explains why the United Kingdom, where nominal growth has been five times as great as in Spain in 2010, and is expected to be twice and 1.6 times as great in 2011 and 2012, respectively, is perceived by international financial markets as less worrisome than Spain.[8]

These considerations suggest that the policy response of the European countries currently entangled in the sovereign debt crisis—Greece, Ireland, Italy, Portugal, and Spain—is made particularly difficult by the institutional constraints linked to their membership in the eurozone: they cannot devalue their currency and they are unlikely to pull themselves out of their debt problem through inflation, given the ECB's well-known aversion to inflation. Instead, they are being forced into a kind of highly procyclical fiscal policy (austerity at a time of recession), which may ultimately prove self-defeating in the sense that it may worsen rather than alleviate the liquidity problems these governments are experiencing. In other words, markets may become even more doubtful that, with time, the countries in question will grow out of their debt problem. Rising CDS spreads despite the bailout packages signal exactly this kind of market fear.

With exchange rate devaluation or tolerance of higher medium-term inflation out of the picture, the countries are being forced into an *internal devaluation*: they are being asked to engineer a recession strong enough to lower wages below productivity and thus make up for the lost competitiveness. This explains why, independent of the governments' political orientation, the policy response is very similar in these countries and why fiscal consolidation, involving cuts in public sector wages and reduction of public sector employment, is at the core of the policy package everywhere. In addition, structural measures aiming to increase the degree of competitiveness of the labor and product markets are being implemented. Industrial relations systems are being reformed to increase the ability of companies to opt out of higher level agreements, thus promoting bargaining decentralization. Reforms of the pension system are being introduced with a view to reducing public expenditure on the aged. Unemployment insurance systems are being reformed to make it easier for the unemployed to bid down the wage of the employed.

The only real choice left to national governments concerns the type of policy process through which the reform packages are to be implemented. All governments seek as much as possible to avoid a unilateral approach. Thus they either seek to co-opt the parliamentary opposition in a grand coalition or to use corporatist channels of policy formation whenever they have an opportunity to do so. The next section examines these dynamics at the country level.

CRISIS RESPONSE AT THE COUNTRY LEVEL

We analyze developments in Greece, Ireland, Spain, and Portugal. Because Italy was a late comer to the sovereign debt crisis—the crisis in Italy effectively started only in the summer of 2011—it is not included in this overview. The Italian situation is addressed in the conclusion. Country case studies cover developments until December 2011.

Greece

Compared with the other three countries, Greece faces the largest challenges both in economic and political terms. In strictly economic terms, a debt default seems inevitable. The only remaining question seems to be whether an uncontrolled default can be avoided, for example, through increased IMF and EU transfers and guarantees. In political terms, the main political actors find it very difficult to reach consensus on adjustment measures.

In contrast to Iceland and Ireland, the Greek crisis was not caused primarily by the financial sector running amok, but seems to be more appropriately characterized as an old-style story of government living beyond its means. The banks did not hold toxic assets or structured investment vehicles in large quantities (IMF 2009, 5). In June 2009, the OECD country report on Greece argued that the country had "initially held up better during the global economic crisis than many other OECD countries." The delayed impact of the international crisis in late 2008 was due to buoyant exports to the Balkans and strong wage increases, which supported consumption (OECD 2009a, 8–9).

The problems really started in January 2001, when Greece joined the eurozone on the basis of fake public account statistics. Judged by the criteria of the Treaty of Maastricht, Greece did not qualify to participate in the eurozone because of its excessive public debt and deficits. Greek statistics remained unreliable afterwards. However, even counterfeited data were bad enough to trigger a first excessive deficit procedure by the European Commission in 2004, which was dropped in 2007. A second excessive deficit procedure was launched in February 2009 (European Commission 2009).

The conservative New Democracy (ND) government was ousted by the socialist party (PASOK) in October 2009. The PASOK won the election on a program that included a fiscal stimulus and measures to promote "green development" (Mavrogordatos and Marantzidis 2010, 998). Immediately after the election, the new government accused its predecessor of concealing the gravity of the economic and fiscal situation. Because the public deficit was reaching 13 percent of GDP and debt was rising, the PASOK changed course and embraced austerity, and the ND took to criticizing PASOK for exactly the same restrictive policies the ND had pursued when in government.

In May 2010, the authorities requested a three-year assistance program from the IMF, the ECB, and the European Commission. The IMF contributed €30 billion with an initial disbursement of €5.5 billion. The eurozone partner countries committed €80 billion with a first disbursement of €14.5 billion. In return, the Greek government promised a number of reforms (see IMF 2010b, 3). The measures involved public-sector wage cuts, a pension freeze for the next three years, pension reform (including an increase in the women's retirement age to sixty-five and incentives to postpone retirement), increases in indirect taxes, exemptions from minimum wages, and easing of restrictions on collective dismissals.

Although these commitments were in principle respected, the situation of Greek public finances did not improve. From the end of 2010 on, the reform process lost momentum. The third review under the standby agreement with IMF and EU arrived at the conclusion that targets had not been fully met (IMF 2011a), and the fourth and fifth reviews came to even more alarming conclusions. In response to the fourth review, the Greek government committed to an even stronger austerity program on June 9, 2011, putting more emphasis on privatization than in previous programs. With the memorandum of understanding accompanying the fifth review, the Greek authorities promised to implement the agreed measures. However, the economic situation failed to improve. In fact, economic growth and fiscal adjustment have constantly been below expectations (IMF 2011c, 2011d).

It seems clear that Greece stands little chance of accessing private bond markets at reasonable interest rates soon, and that the rate of economic growth needed to stabilize, let alone reduce, sovereign debt is far above anything realistic. In a partial and belated realization of this untenable situation, Greece and its EU partners agreed in principle to a debt write-down by private creditors of 50 percent of the sovereign bonds' face value in October 2011. The details were agreed to in February 2012.

When the socialist government started the structural reform projects, the majority of the population supported the austerity measures.[9] By the spring of 2011, however, public opinion had turned against the government's austerity plan.[10] This change is not surprising, because wages fell by 12 percent from 2010 to 2011.[11] Wage cuts, dismissals, pension adjustments, and tax increases will have to be pursued even more rigorously in the future.

Although the employers supported the austerity policy, the unions vigorously opposed it, both before and after the EU-IMF intervention. This is despite the socialist government's commitment to "fairness in the distribution of the adjustment burden" and promise to "invite representatives of businesses and labor to sign a social pact for the duration of the program" (IMF 2010b, 5–6). Close to the Communist Party (7.5 percent of votes in 2009), which has a Marxist-Leninist orientation (Zervakis 2004, 638, 640) and garnered 7.5 percent of the votes in 2009 (Mavrogordatos and Marantzidis 2010, 993), the activist wing of the fragmented and decentralized union movement is hostile to both the conservative and the socialist party. Union density is about 18 percent in the private sector and 60 percent in the public sector, which was hit the hardest by the austerity measures. The communist union front, All Workers Militant Front (PAME), has been particularly active in organizing protests, but other unions have participated as well.[12] In particular, the unions representing workers in the public power corporation oppose privatization plans. A large and growing part of the opposition to the austerity plan consists of young and unemployed citizens who are not represented by the unions. This lost generation of young people regards all politicians as corrupt and the political system as illegitimate.

Given the circumstances, the government has very little to offer to the social partners. The social pact—announced in the memorandum—was never concluded, in contrast to Spain and Ireland. Only recently has something resembling a grand coalition appeared on the Greek political stage. PASOK and the conservative New Democracy have a very confrontational relationship. For example, in May 2011, ND did not support PASOK's austerity plans, which it had itself claimed to pursue until 2009, despite the fact that such plans were necessary to obtain another installment of the EU-IMF credits. In 2010 and 2011, the leadership of the socialist party fought on two fronts: on the one hand, against the EU and the IMF, which pushed for more comprehensive structural reforms, and, on the other hand, against the conservative party, large parts of the trade union movement, the electoral constituency of the socialist party, and a broad and sometimes violent grassroots protest movement, which opposed these reforms.

In the fall of 2011, the socialist government resigned because it could not get parliamentary support for the requested structural reforms. It was replaced by an interim government, supported by the two largest parties and a small right-wing populist party. The EU and the IMF made their payments conditional on the joint support of the reform program by both major political parties. In November 2011, the leader of the major opposition party ND gave his consent to the program. Had it refused to do so, the EU and the IMF would have withheld payments to Greece. However, even after the accession to power of a nonpartisan government in November 2011, politics continues to be highly conflictual as politicians engage in tactical skirmishes aimed to place them in the best starting position for the next election, which is scheduled for 2012.

Ireland

The Irish crisis was quite deep in comparative perspective: GDP declined by 17 percent in nominal terms and 11 percent in real terms between 2008 and 2010. Unemployment increased threefold, from 4.5 in 2007 to 13.5 percent in 2010 (European Commission 2011a, 10). Ireland's fiscal adjustment so far—€20.8 billion, the equivalent of 13 percent of GDP in 2010—is the largest ever recorded (Whelan 2011, 7).

At the origin of the crisis was the puncturing of a huge real estate bubble. In addition, the global recession had deeply negative consequences for a small open economy such as Ireland, which was heavily reliant on trade. The real estate bubble was caused by the rapid expansion of the bank's balance sheet to finance the real estate boom. When house prices started to decline in 2007, several national banks found themselves faced with what until the end of 2008 was presented and perceived simply as a liquidity problem, that is, a temporary difficulty in rolling over their loans. To avoid a financial paralysis similar to the one that had seized the United States after Lehman Brothers had been allowed to go bankrupt by the U.S. government, at the end of September, the Irish government provided a blanket guarantee of bank liabilities, €440 billion, initially limited to two years. Lucy Barnes and Anne Wren argue that this guarantee was necessary, because the precrisis growth model was based to a large extent on construction, which was financed by cheap credits for homeowners (see chapter 10, this volume). As of January 2011, the Irish state had spent €46 billion, 29 percent of GDP, on a failed attempt at redressing the banks' crisis (European Commission 2011a, 13). Not surprisingly, public deficit and debt skyrocketed (Kelly 2010; Whelan 2011).

The response to the crisis never included—as it did in Spain—a Keynesian moment, and retrenchment was always the name of the game. In early 2009, after making bank creditors whole, the government sought to improve its fiscal situation by reducing public-sector wages and cutting public expenditures. To mobilize consensus for its austerity solutions, initially it sought to rely on well-consolidated corporatist channels. Policymaking had been negotiated in tripartite fashion in Ireland since the late 1980s. However, private employers appealed to the "inability to pay" clause of the national agreement to either freeze wage increases or even implement nominal pay cuts. For the public sector, no such clause was available and the only choice for the government—a coalition between the centrist Fianna Fail and the Green Party—was to persuade the unions to agree to a 7.5 percent special pension levy, amounting to a unilateral pay cut of equivalent amount (Sheehan 2010). The unions dragged their feet and, rather than patiently negotiate in the social partnership tradition, the government decided to implement the cuts unilaterally.

Despite this decision, the unions continued to negotiate. They called for a social solidarity agreement in which they accepted the principle that government needed to reduce public expenditures by €13 billion, 1.3 billion per year from public-sector cuts, but proposed that rather than taking straight nominal wage cuts, public-sector workers would take instead an unpaid leave of twelve days (McDonough and Dundon 2010, 555). At some point in the process, it seemed that an agreement could be reached on this basis (Regan 2011). However, the government negotiators changed their minds unexpectedly at the last moment and, rather than signing the agreement with the unions, preferred to go for unilateral wage cuts of 15 percent on average. These cuts were included in the November 2009 budget.

The union proposal to exchange wage cuts for more holidays had angered many in the Irish public sphere: it was interpreted as an irresponsible demand by pampered public-sector workers to enjoy even more leisure at a time the country desperately needed public services. The unpopularity of such a proposal might explain the government's last-minute about-face. In fact, the unions' attempt to organize worker mobilization in protest was largely unsuccessful.

Because of the failure of centralized negotiations, it looked as though 2010 would be the first year since 1987 in which collective bargaining would be decentralized at the enterprise level. However, the unions, which really did not have any serious strategic alternative to engaging with government and employers at the national level, negotiated two peak-level agreements in the first half of the year. One applied to the private sector: the parties agreed to jointly issue centralized recommendation for decentralized collective bargaining, and in this way restored some form of wage coordination. The second pertained to the public sector. With what came to be known as the Croke Park agreement, the government committed to not have recourse to public-sector wage cuts in the future, and to reduce payroll through attrition only, and the unions guaranteed industrial peace for the next four years. Productivity would be increased by a workplace transformation agenda that the unions agreed to support and promote actively. Of the two sectoral agreements, the public-sector one was by far the most important: as a result of decades of erosion, the union density rate was only about 20 percent in the private sector, but around 80 percent in the public sector (D'Art and Turner 2011).

However, the Croke Park agreement did little to assuage Ireland's fiscal problems. The situation worsened considerably in late 2010, when the two-year government guarantee of banks' loans was approaching expiration, and the Irish banks found themselves unable to access interbank markets. The government was forced to knock at the doors of the EU, ECB, and IMF for financial assistance. A bailout package was put together in November for a total of €85 billion. This included measures to recapitalize and downsize the financial sector; a fiscal consolidation effort of €15 billion in four years (to be achieved through expenditure cuts and higher taxes), six of which were frontloaded in 2011; and broader structural measures concerning the labor market and the pension system. The retirement age would be progressively increased to sixty-eight years. The minimum wage would be cut by 12 percent (€1); the institutional mechanisms for minimum-wage determination in low-wage sectors would be relaxed; unemployment insurance benefits would be lowered and activation provision strengthened; finally, condition of access to some liberal professions would be liberalized (European Commission 2011a). The average interest rate on Ireland's bailout package was set at 5.5 percent, about 3 percent above the EU's cost of borrowing (European Commission 2011a, 40)—a rate that many in Ireland considered too high.

One of the most controversial aspects of the EU-IMF bailout plan was the insistence by EU and ECB negotiators, unlike their IMF counterparts, that bank creditors be made whole, a concession that they obtained from the Irish government. Although the numbers are unclear, most Irish bank creditors are, or were at the beginning of the crisis, foreign banks from core eurozone countries, especially Germany and France. Not surprisingly, the Irish public regarded such insistence—which the ECB justified by fear of contagion—with much suspicion.

After negotiating the bailout package, the Irish government resigned and new elections were held in February 2011. The electorate delivered an historic defeat for the Fianna Fail (FF) party, which it perceived to be largely responsible for the financial crisis debacle. FF declined from seventy-seven to twenty seats in the lower chamber, and became the third party in the country by electoral strength. The election was won by the Fine Gael and Labour parties, which formed a coalition government. One of the themes of the electoral campaign was the promise made by Fine Gael, and especially by the Labour Party, that the new government would renegotiate the financial package with the EU and ECB, and obtain less prohibitive interest rates or "haircuts" for bank creditors. After the election, the new government made a timid attempt to put the issue of loan renegotiation on the European agenda, but was immediately blocked by the German chancellor.

The outlook seems rather bleak for Ireland: the economic rationale behind the bailout plan was that through fiscal restructuring Ireland would quickly overcome its competitiveness gap and be able to return to export-led growth. Consistent with this plan, unit labor costs declined by 20 percent relative to 2008. Some respite came from the decision of European authorities in July 2011 to lower the interest rate paid on the EU-IMF bailout funds to about 3 percent. However, Ireland could not take full advantage of its improved competitiveness because of the weakening of the international economy (IMF 2011e). Consequently, the Croke Park agreement with the public sector unions began to be called into question. In December 2011, government members were divided about it. Some argued that it had helped Ireland navigate the crisis without major social disruptions and therefore its terms (no more wage cuts and redundancies) should be honored. Others retorted that as further cuts became necessary, a renegotiation was inevitable.[13] In brief, more austerity might be on its way.

Portugal

In Portugal, the development of the economic crisis and its impact on the country's fiscal position have much in common with Greece. As in Greece, the global crisis did not hit through the banking system. Rather, declining demand deepened the structural weakness of the Portuguese economy and led to soaring public deficit and debt. In addition, growing unit labor costs caused a deterioration of the trade balance: Portugal has lost 20 percent of its international market share since the mid-1990s. The difference with Greece is in the extent of the problems. Debts have been lower—88 percent in 2010. Growth has been stronger. Unit labor cost increases have been smaller (OECD 2010a).

The socialist government introduced three austerity programs beginning in February 2010. However, it failed to gain a parliamentary majority for a fourth program in March 2011 and had to step down. Acting as a caretaker government, it requested IMF and EU support in April 2011. The IMF and EU asked to discuss the recovery program with all major parties and social partners. In the general election of June 5, 2011, the major conservative party (the PSD) and another conservative party (the CDS-PP) obtained the majority of parliamentary seats.

The EU-IMF bailout package came with extensive conditionality attached. According to the Memorandum of Economic and Financial Policies (IMF 2011b), the Portuguese government pledged to freeze public wages and pensions through 2013 (this is in addition to the 5 percent average cut in public-sector wages introduced as part of the third austerity program); levy a special contribution on pensions above €1,500 in 2012; reduce the number of civil servants in central government by 2 percent by 2013; reduce the number of civil servants at the local and regional level by 2 percent annually; reduce spending on defense, state-owned enterprises, regional, and local government; and increase taxes.

When in power, the main strategy of the socialist government—which controlled only 42 percent of parliamentary seats (Magone 2010)—had been trying to reach an agreement with the conservative opposition. This worked reasonably well until the fourth austerity program. In fact, the first three austerity packages were supported by an uneasy "grand coalition." In April 2011, however, the situation changed as the conservative opposition saw a chance to oust the sitting socialist government by withdrawing support in parliament. Later on, the negotiation with the EU and the IMF, which insisted on having all potential winners of the election at the bargaining table (except those on the left of the political spectrum, who refused to participate), contributed to bringing the parties closer together.

After the election, the strategic situation reversed, as the conservative parties become the ones having to pursue a tough austerity policy. The memorandum of understanding with the EU and the IMF legitimizes the liberal policies envisaged by the new prime minister, who thus considers the memorandum as a support for his planned reforms. In addition, he has already hinted at the possibility that even more cuts in social and public spending may be needed. For cases in which parliamentary rules require two-thirds majorities, such as employment protection legislation and constitutional rules, the government depends on the support of the socialists.[14] Although the odds of Portugal's overcoming of its sovereign debt crisis are much better than those of Greece, it is far from clear that support for the austerity plan will pay off in economic or electoral terms. Hence it may make sense for the socialists to support moderate austerity plans but shy away from any radical plans—exactly as the conservatives have done when in opposition.

The process of policy formation has not involved the social partners, that is, unions and employers, except marginally. The employers' Confederation of Portuguese Industry has supported the austerity measures insofar as they have helped liberalize the labor market, particularly by reducing restrictions on hiring and firing. In addition, they have asked for state subsidies to lower the costs of dismissals, and pleaded for less and more effective state involvement in the economy.[15] However, the unions have been unwilling to sign onto a social pact. Although two main trade union organizations—a socialist union (UGT) and an organization that is closer to the Communist Party (CGTP)—have signed a largely declaratory agreement on employment and competitiveness, they have never been involved in a fully fledged tri- or bipartite adjustment plan. In particular, the UGT has repeatedly refused to strike an agreement because of its opposition to austerity measures. In March 2011, it seemed that a social pact was near, but in the end it failed to materialize. For the trade unions, it was not clear that they had anything to gain from a pact centering on austerity. Considering that the two main union confederations compete for membership, signing onto a concession agreement meant considerable organizational risks. The unions preferred not to share responsibility for austerity policies and to present themselves as the uncompromising voice of the working class.

In the fall of 2011, the support of citizens for austerity policies was lower than in other European countries: 50 percent were of the opinion that measures to reduce the public deficit and debt were not a priority (compared with 37 percent in EU27, 31 percent in West Germany, 27 percent in Greece, 34 percent in Ireland, and 39 percent in Spain). Older citizens were significantly less in favor of austerity measures than the rest of the population.[16]

Although the unions called a general strike in November 2010 for the first time in twenty years, mobilization against austerity policy has been less extensive than in Greece or Spain, but an *indignados* (indignant) movement similar to the Spanish one has seen the light of day. In March 2011, four young college graduates organized a rally using Facebook: 200,000 citizens in Lisbon and 80,000 in Porto protested against the lack of opportunities for the younger generation. Although trade unions and political parties joined these demonstrations, the core of the movement was clearly outside the established party and interest organizations.[17]

In December 2011, the IMF concluded its second review under the agreement between Portugal, the EU, and the IMF. The report stated that Portugal's structural reform program was broadly on track, but the deteriorating European economy made it difficult to reach macroeconomic targets. Consequently, the new government had been only partially successful in reducing public deficit (IMF 2011f). In the meantime, social conflict has intensified. In December 2011, the trade unions called for a general strike and various additional demonstrations. This general strike was considerably more successful in terms of participation and impact than previous strikes in 2010. There was also an increase in political violence. Tax offices were attacked with Molotov bombs and a demonstration organized by the *indignados* resulted in fights between police and protesters.[18]

Spain

Spain was severely hit by the global economic crisis that followed the collapse of the shadow banking sector in the United States. GDP declined by 3.9 percent in 2009 and 0.4 percent in 2010 (IMF 2010a, 41). The labor market impact of the crisis was the deepest in the OECD, and the unemployment rate increased from 11.3 percent in 2008 to 20 percent in 2010; youth and, to a lesser extent, women were the most affected categories (IMF 2010a, 8; OECD 2010b, 24). As in Ireland, the crisis was due to the bursting of a huge real-estate bubble, which in turn provoked a stark contraction of the construction sector, Spain's growth engine in the 2000s. In addition, just like other countries of the eurozone periphery, Spain encountered problems related to competitiveness—specifically, nominal prices and wages grew faster in Spain than in core countries. This contributed to a growing external debt problem between 2000 and 2010 (OECD 2010b, 23).

The government's initial response to the crisis was very different from that of Ireland or Greece. The socialist government engaged in expansionary fiscal policy to counter the adverse effects of the crisis on income and employment. One of the most important provisions was the extension of unemployment benefits, €426 per month, for the unemployed whose benefits had expired on January 1, 2009.[19] Discretionary spending, combined with the effect of automatic stabilizers, led to a dramatic increase in public deficit—11.2 percent of GDP in 2009 and 9.3 percent in 2010 (IMF 2010a, p. 41).

The other notable trait of Spain's initial response was the government's commitment to social dialogue. This had been one of the dominant characteristics of the Spanish political economy in the 2000s. In keeping with this recent tradition, on July 29, 2008, the tripartite social partners signed a declaration of principles outlining a shared policy response to the economic crisis, in which they committed to take joint action on employment policy, collective bargaining, and social protection.[20]

Notwithstanding the parties' stated commitment to social dialogue, important differences began to emerge. The employers began to demand more drastic measures, particularly in the domains of collective bargaining structure, employment protection, and social security. They were often supported by the main opposition party, the Partido Popular (PP). The first rupture occurred in 2009, when the social partners were, for the first time since 2002, unable to negotiate the yearly centralized agreement on wage guidelines.[21]

The socialist government's response to the crisis changed dramatically in late 2009 and, most clearly, in 2010, when growing doubts about the sustainability of the peripheral countries' fiscal positions began to affect the Spanish economy and to be reflected in growing prices on CDS on Spain's public debt (IMF 2010a, 6). In an attempt to regain the confidence of international financial markets, the government undid many of the expansionary measures of the previous two years, slashed public spending, and engaged in structural reforms of the labor market and the pension system. The policy process used was a mix of unilateralism and corporatism under the "shadow of hierarchy" (Visser and Hemerijck 1997). Essentially, the government would impose tight parameters and deadlines on social partner negotiations. If unions and employers were able to reach an agreement by the set date, the government would ratify it. Alternatively, it would regulate by decree. Unlike Portugal, the government was never able to build a grand coalition around its structural reform proposals, due to the staunch opposition of the PP.

In January 2010, as part of a broader fiscal adjustment program, the government issued proposals to increase from fifteen to twenty-five the number of reference years for the calculation of pension benefits and to increase the retirement age from sixty-five to sixty-seven. The unions responded very negatively to this proposal and organized strikes in all major Spanish cities against it.[22] Interestingly, in 2010 unions and employers were once again able to reach an agreement on national wage guidelines. This agreement included an opt-out clause for companies under duress.[23]

The government's turn-around toward fiscal adjustment proceeded with a partial freeze of public-sector hiring.[24] This was followed by more drastic measures, such as an on-average cut of 5 percent in public sector wages. The unions voiced their dissent by organizing a public sector strike in June 2010.[25] In the same month, following a failure of the social partners to reach an agreement on the issue, the government issued a unilateral reform of employment protection legislation. The reform reduced severance pay in the event of an unfair dismissal, eased the criteria for fair dismissals, and broadened the conditions under which companies could opt out from collective agreements.[26] It was saluted as a major step forward toward fiscal sustainability by both the OECD and the IMF (OECD 2010b; IMF 2010a). The unions responded by organizing a general strike at the end of September 2010. However, participation in the strike seems to have been unequal, with the industrial sectors responding more promptly and massively than the service sectors.[27] In any case, the union mobilization did not manage to alter the legislative reform.

In December 2010, a new set of governmental reforms of clearly neoliberal orientation was introduced, again with a view to convincing international financial markets that Spain was solvent. The package included the repeal of the extension of unemployment insurance for those who had exhausted their benefits on January 1, 2009 (€426 per month), as well as reductions in corporate tax rates and partial privatizations.[28] All of these were unilateral reforms. However, social dialogue was not dead. In February 2011, the parties signed a social pact on "growth, employment, and the guarantee of pensions." The highlight of the pact was a negotiated pension reform. With this, the unions accepted several provisions against which they had mobilized a year before. In exchange, they obtained some measures aimed to increase stability of employment, such as a reduction of social security contributions for companies hiring young workers and long-term unemployed, and €400 per month for the unemployed whose benefits had ceased.[29]

In the following months, the social partners were unable to reach an agreement on the reform of collective bargaining agreements and the government intervened by decree on June 10, 2011. The key point of this reform was the broadening of circumstances in which an enterprise contract could legally bypass a higher level contract. In addition, the reform introduced a maximum time for contract renewal (between eight and fourteen months) after which mediation and arbitration would intervene to resolve the dispute.[30] Unions and employers had been very close to reaching an agreement among themselves on these issues, but the negotiation then reached an impasse due to the changing attitudes of the employers. Apparently, these had thought that after the local election of May 2011, which had severely punished the Socialist Party, they would be able to obtain more favorable conditions if the government regulated the issue directly.

While the parties were still negotiating on collective bargaining reform, a new collective actor appeared on the horizon of Spanish politics, the Movement of 15 May or the *Indignatos* (Indignants). This is composed of young people who protest against their status as precarious workers by camping in public squares or demonstrating in front of public buildings. Initially, the movement seemed to express generic frustration against the elites in general, but then became progressively more political in its demands, although always very careful to present itself as being outside official party and union circles. The movement has articulated a broad transformative agenda that goes from the introduction of proportional representation—to weaken the stronghold of the two largest political parties, the Socialist Party and the Popular Party, whose policies are perceived to be very similar—to the right to a dwelling for everyone, to increases in taxation for high incomes, to the introduction of taxes on speculative financial transactions. In general, the movement seeks to assert the primacy of participatory democracy over the technical indictments of markets.

In September 2011, in an effort to strengthen the long-term credibility of its fiscal stance, Spain reformed its constitution to introduce a balanced-budget provision. In the early general elections of November 2011 the electorate delivered the Socialist Party its worst defeat since the establishment of democracy and granted the Partito Popular a majority of seats. The new conservative prime minister has made it clear that his government will continue the austerity policy of the previous government.

ARE THERE ALTERNATIVES TO AUSTERITY POLICY?

When the crisis hit, the fiscal positions of the GIIPS countries differed considerably. Greece had the worst initial conditions. By contrast, Spain and Ireland had comparably sound starting positions. Italy had a high and growing public debt. However, because it had kept the public deficit fundamentally in check during the recession of 2009, it was initially spared the onslaught of bond markets. In Portugal, the crisis was less the result of a sudden deterioration of public finances than of long-standing problems accumulated over the years.

The fiscal responses to the first stage of the crisis in 2008 and 2009 were also very different: strongly countercyclical in Spain, moderately counter-cyclical in Portugal, procyclical in Greece (although with limited implementation of announced austerity measures), and strongly procyclical in Ireland (see chapter 4, this volume). In Italy, the government was able to maintain public expenditures broadly in line with receipts by essentially forfeiting any stimulus package. The Keynesian approach in 2008 and 2009 certainly exacerbated fiscal problems in Spain, but it was not the main cause of these problems. Given the increase in unemployment and in particular in youth unemployment, fiscal passivity would have been hard to defend for a socialist government. Similarly, Ireland could have avoided the debt crisis had it not guaranteed the liabilities of most categories of bondholders. The actions of the Greek and Portuguese governments since the fall of 2007 did not dramatically worsen the fiscal situation of the two countries. They were already in trouble when the crisis hit.

In terms of political and institutional resources, Ireland, Italy, and Spain were in a more favorable position than Portugal and Greece. Although it controlled only 52 percent of all parliamentary votes, the Irish government was relatively strong due to the weakness and mutual infighting of the opposition parties (O'Malley 2009, 2010). In addition, it could rely on a long tradition of successful policy concertation between government and social partners (Hardiman 2002; Baccaro and Simoni 2007; Roche 2007). In Italy, the center-right coalition government of the Freedom People Party and the Northern League, elected in 2008, had solid majorities in both houses of parliament. It could also count on the potential support of at least two of the three major union confederations, with which it had struck agreements in the past (Baccaro and Pulignano 2010). After the national election of 2008, the majority supporting the Spanish socialist government was small (Delgado and Nieto 2009, 2010). However, well-functioning corporatist institutions were in place (Royo 2006). Thus the government could hope to strike agreements with the social partners.

In contrast, the socialist government of Portugal, elected in 2009, was a minority government (Magone 2010). Corporatist traditions were much less developed in this country than in Ireland and Spain (Molina 2011). In Greece, both major parties followed a populist strategy consisting of proposing solutions during periods in opposition that they did not try to implement when in government (Mavrogordatos and Marantzidis 2010, 1000). The relationships with interest organizations were clientelistic (Kritsantonis 1998; Lavdas 2001). There was little prospect of corporatist concertation.

Regardless of their very different starting positions, by 2011 all five countries found themselves entangled in very similar sovereign debt crises: international financial markets lost confidence in each country's ability to stabilize its public debts and repay its bonds, and began to demand higher and higher interest rates to roll over existing loans or issue new ones. Greece, Ireland, and Portugal, one after the other, lost access to private bond markets and had to be bailed out by the EU and the IMF between 2010 and 2011. Spain and Italy are for the time being still able to finance themselves on private markets, albeit at high interest rates.

Governments of different political orientations, of different political strength, and with different capabilities for concertation with the social partners found themselves implementing essentially the same structural adjustment program centered on public sector cuts, pension reform, easing of employment protection legislation, weakening of unemployment insurance, and flexibilization of collective bargaining. The most ironic case is that of socialist Spain, which entered the crisis in 2008 arguing that it would use the crisis as an opportunity to upgrade its growth model, shifting it from low value-added sectors, such as construction, to more knowledge and technology-intensive sectors,[31] and ended up doing pretty much the same things as anyone else. The socialist government was finally replaced by a conservative one that promised to pursue the same austerity policy, only more rigorously, exactly as it had happened five months before in Portugal.

The only type of choice left to governments was in the modalities used to mobilize popular consensus for, or at least blunt hostility against, austerity policies: a grand coalition in Portugal and later in Greece and Italy; a mix of unilateralism and concessionary corporatism in Ireland and Spain; and unilateralism by default, due to the failure of both the parliamentary and corporatist channels, in the early stages of the Greek response. Incumbent governments were unseated by the opposition in parliamentary elections in Greece in 2009, Ireland in 2011, Portugal in 2011, and Spain in 2011. Political parties at the opposite end of the political spectrum in Greece and Portugal took turns accusing the other party for policies they themselves had implemented, or tried to implement, when in power.

As illustrated by the formula discussed earlier, the parameters for public debt sustainability are the primary budget surplus, the difference between the nominal interest rate the country faces when trying to finance itself on the bond market and the nominal growth rate of GDP, and the debt to GDP ratio. The higher (lower) the difference and the higher (lower) the ratio, the greater (less) the need for a high primary budget surplus. Given the difficulty of lowering the debt to GDP in the short to medium term, it would seem that the best way to ensure debt sustainability would be to return to high nominal growth as quickly as possible, or to lower the country's borrowing rate, or, even better, doing both. Yet this is not the approach followed by the European policymaking elites. They have been focusing solely on the primary surplus to be obtained preferably through lower public expenditures and, as a second best, through increased taxes. The problem with this approach is that imposing restrictive fiscal policies to a country already in recession may unleash a vicious cycle of consolidation followed by contraction, which requires further consolidation, etc. One would think that after the Asian crisis of 1998 and 1999, in which the IMF was widely criticized for imposing austerity policies that ended up worsening the recession (Blustein 2001; Stiglitz 2002), this lesson would have been learned. Yet apparently it has not.

In the absence of the devaluation option, which would involve the return to national currencies and the end of the euro, returning to nominal growth as quickly as possible would imply a different monetary policy by the European Central Bank, one that would reconsider the anti-inflationary consensus prevailing among policymakers (Blanchard, Dell'Ariccia, and Mauro 2010), and realize that moderate inflation could contribute to solving the crisis. If the ECB were more tolerant of inflation than it is, it would continue with a policy of easy money for some time.

In normal circumstances this would raise inflation, and initially the rise would be higher in the core eurozone countries, especially Germany, where the economy was overheating in the first half of 2011, but modest in those, such as the GIIPS, that are stagnating. This would be equivalent to a real appreciation of the core economies with respect to the peripheral economies: the competitiveness gap would become smaller through this channel. In other words, the alternative to the internal devaluation of the GIIPS countries currently being pursued would be an internal reevaluation of the core euro countries.

However, a standard policy of easy money would be unlikely to go very far in current conditions because it would be limited by what Keynesian economists refer to as a liquidity trap, namely, nominal interest rates close to the zero lower bound (Krugman 1998; Eggertsson and Krugman 2011). The ECB's official interest rate is currently only 1 percent. Although it is higher than the American Fed's 0.25 percent, it could not go much lower. Also, a lower official interest rate would do little to address the most pressing problem: the GIIPS countries' inability to finance themselves at acceptable interest rates in private bond markets. In these circumstances, the ECB would have to engage in quantitative easing as well, namely, expand the bank's balance sheet by buying sovereign debt of the GIIPS countries. By doing so, it would boost the bonds' prices and lower their interest rates. Arguably, the simple announcement of such a policy would cause the interest rates on Italian and Spanish debt to fall. At the same time, such an activist policy would compromise the independence and reputation of the ECB and may lead to a higher inflation rate in the future. Thus, the export-oriented countries have good economic reasons to oppose it (see chapter 2, this volume). In addition, the German government would have serious domestic problems were it to give up one of its main compensations for accepting the euro in the Maastricht negotiations, that is, the assurance that the policy of the ECB would continue the policy of the German Bundesbank.

A more activist stance by the ECB is not the only option. An alternative option that has been floated would involve the introduction of Eurobonds, which would be jointly guaranteed by eurozone members, at least up to 60 percent of GDP for each member country. This proposal has been recently endorsed by the European Commission (2011b). However, the introduction of Eurobonds would increase the interest rates that Germany and other "virtuous" countries pay on their own debt.

Still another solution would involve financial guarantees voluntarily provided by euro area members. Although some steps have been taken in this latter direction, they have been utterly inadequate relative to the scale of the problem. In 2010, the European partners introduced the European Financial Stability Facility (EFSF) and provided it with a lending capacity of €440 billion, jointly guaranteed by the euro area countries in rough proportion to their GDP. Once operational, the EFSF will be able to lend to countries or banks in financial distress. It will be replaced by a permanent European stability mechanism (ESM) in 2012. In late 2011 lending capacity and corresponding government guarantees were increased to €780 billion, and then effectively to €1 trillion. Even this amount, however, is dwarfed by the magnitude of the GIIPS debt: the Italian public debt alone amounts to €1.9 trillion. It is therefore not surprising that the increase in the EFSF's firepower has done nothing to stem the sovereign debt crisis. Only a massive increase of financial guarantees would reassure international financial markets.

All proposals discussed would mutualize, and hence reduce, the risk associated with GIIPS sovereign debt, thus lowering the interest rates demanded by bond markets. However, not only would they impose costs to Germany and other core euro countries, they would also run into legal and political problems. The ECB-as-lender-of-last-resort proposal conflicts with Article 123 of the Treaty on the Functioning of the European Union (TFEU), which prevents the ECB from directly purchasing government bonds. The Eurobond proposal contradicts Article 125 of the TFEU, which establishes that member states shall not be liable for financial commitments assumed by other member states. Instead, financial guarantees voluntarily provided by governments are not incompatible with EU treaties per se: treaty modifications were negotiated in late 2010 especially to provide stability mechanisms with a legal basis. However, these guarantees have proven extremely controversial politically: the electorates of Germany, Finland, the Netherlands, Slovakia, and other countries are justifiably against what they perceive as transfers to the fiscally profligate governments of southern Europe, and they oppose further expansion of the various bailout programs.

As a consequence, the European response so far has been far from linear or effective, and can be characterized as muddling through. After announcing in 2010 that Greece would not default and that they would build a safety wall around it to prevent contagion, the European elites have seen country after country get embroiled in the crisis, and they have eventually had to acknowledge Greece's partial default. From a regulatory point of view, an important measure has been the negotiation in December 2011 of new rules imposing automatic sanctions, and the loss of fiscal sovereignty, to countries that violate the Stability and Growth Pact. These new rules go under the name of fiscal union, but they lack crucial elements of a fiscal union as it is known in federal states. In a fiscal union, if a region is hit by an asymmetric shock or has a structural competitiveness problem, the effects are buffered by transfers that are largely accepted by the nation. Instead, the new rules of the EU institutionalize a procyclical fiscal policy in the event of a negative shock without legitimizing a system of transfers to structurally weak economic regions in the EU.

In the absence of an appropriate policy response, almost against its own will, the European Central Bank has had to intervene in the sovereign bond market repeatedly to avoid the capitulation of Spain and Italy, but its interventions have been temporary, partial, and indirect. It has, on and off, bought Italian and Spanish debt on the secondary market. Recently, it has provided European banks with ample liquidity, in the hope that at least part of this liquidity would be used by banks to buy GIIPS sovereign debt.

The emphasis of the European policymaking authorities on austerity as the solution to the crisis—the IMF has taken a more flexible position (Stiglitz 2011)—seems to be explained by a combination of legal, institutional, and ideational factors, and by the interests of key players. With respect to the former, as argued, European treaties prevent the ECB from directly purchasing government debt, and rule out the governments' assumption of liability for other governments' debt. European law can in principle be changed. However, this requires such a high degree of consensus—unanimity—that change is unlikely.

With respect to economic ideas, European elites seem to have embraced the so-called expansionary fiscal contraction doctrine, that is, the idea that fiscal contraction has expansionary consequences through non-Keynesian channels (Giavazzi and Pagano 1990; Alesina and Perotti 1997; Alesina and Ardagna 1998, 2009).[32] The problem with this doctrine is that the evidence supporting it is weak at best. Unsurprisingly, recent work by the IMF concludes that fiscal contractions are typically contractionary (Guajardo, Leigh, and Pescatori 2010; see also Perotti 2011). By the end of 2011, the IMF had started to send clear warnings against an aggressive fiscal consolidation.[33] The idea that one can improve fiscal solvency through austerity policy seems to be based on shaky empirical, if not theoretical, foundations.

Finally, with regard to interests, the current policy approach—one in which the ECB does not compromise its independence and anti-inflationary stance by engaging in quantitative easing, restrictive fiscal policies are further institutionalized by tightening fiscal rules, and countries are left to fend for themselves, that is, to seek to regain market confidence through austerity policy—suits the interests of key euro players well, particularly Germany. The reasons are explained in chapter 2 of this volume: countries relying on exports as the main driver of growth have an interest in a macroeconomic regime in which monetary and fiscal policies remain credibly conservative. Export-led countries are especially wary of fiscal profligacy, which would lead to real exchange rate appreciation and would thus impair export competitiveness. The euro has been built around such a regime. It is no surprise that Germany and other export-oriented countries have so far blocked all attempts to respond to the sovereign crisis by altering its basic macroeconomic parameters—monetary and fiscal conservatism. It is instead more surprising that other countries, which do not have the particular institutional infrastructure necessary for export-oriented growth, have been willing to go along. For that, it would probably be necessary to invoke the institutional and ideational elements discussed.

So far austerity policy has proven unable to restore the fiscal solvency of the GIIPS countries. In addition, and perhaps more importantly, it has also led to the erosion of democratic legitimacy. A viable national democracy requires that the people have a say on policy (Held 1991). This ability to choose has been eroded by economic and political globalization in the past several years. As long as there is no compensating democratic process at a level above the nation state, democratic legitimacy is endangered (Kielmansegg 1996; Follesdal and Hix 2006; Schmidt 2008; Keohane, Macedo, and Moravcsik 2009). The four country cases show three clear signs of a deficit of democratic legitimacy.

First, a basic idea of democracy is that parties can make a difference. In the four countries under consideration, however, this seems no longer to be the case. Incoming governments such as the Greek socialist government in 2009, the Irish Fine Gael & Labour government in 2011, and the recent conservative governments in Portugal and Spain, had no choice but to continue the policy of the previous government. This became absolutely clear in May and June 2011 when the EU and the IMF insisted on settling the terms of the austerity memorandum with all major Portuguese parties that stood a chance to be elected into government in 2011. The same thing happened in Greece in November 2011.

Second, most European democracies depend on the support of organized interests. Both the corporatist (Lehmbruch 1979) and pluralist literatures (Truman 1962) started from the idea that citizens may establish and join interest organizations that make a difference in the political process. This happened either through lobbyism and pressure politics (pluralism) or through institutionalized participation in the process of policy formulation and implementation (corporatism). The country cases illustrated showed that interest groups can now choose between entering agreements where they agree to concessions (such as the Spanish pension agreement and the Irish Croke Park deal), or mobilizing members for fights that so far have not produced concrete results.

Third, in all four countries, trust in national governments, that is, the percentage of respondents saying that they tend to trust their national government, has dropped dramatically between spring 2007 and November 2010: from 39 to 12 percent in Ireland, from 46 to 22 percent in Greece, from 34 to 20 percent in Portugal, and from 54 to 22 percent in Spain.[34] Trust in other democratic institutions is at dramatically low levels, too. In particular, political parties were trusted by only 5 (Greece), 9 (Ireland), 14 (Portugal), and 11 percent (Spain) of citizens in the fall of 2010.[35] In addition, the quality of democratic participation in terms of knowledge and motivation is poor in Greece, Portugal, and Spain compared with other democratic nations (Bühlmann and Kriesi 2007). The democratic systems of the southern European countries are experiencing a major loss of legitimacy and active support by citizens.

The euro was never a purely economic project but was instead strongly motivated by political considerations. There were many doubts about the economic wisdom of creating a currency union within a region that was weakly politically integrated and was far from being an optimal currency area with labor mobility and price and wage flexibility across regions. For example in 1986, Fritz Scharpf argued that a common currency and interest rate in Europe would be a potentially explosive device (Sprengsatz) given the different industrial relation and wage-setting systems in Europe ("Ein Sprengsatz für die Gemeinschaft. Plädoyer gegen eine Europäische Wirtschafts- und Währungsunion," *Die Zeit*, December 12, 1986, p. 32). The main motivation behind the euro was always political: it was hoped that it would drive the integration project toward political integration. Some hoped that it would constitute an object of identification for Euro-

pean citizens, just like the German mark had once been an object of identification for the German nation. It would be deeply sad if, faced with its
first major crisis, the euro of all things would turn out to be a cause of
disenchantment and frustration not just toward European integration but
democracy in general.

CONCLUSION

We have argued that the sovereign debt crisis of the GIIPS countries represents a case in which domestic politics, either party- or interest group-
based, has no effect on the selection of the policy response. To be certain,
variation is significant at the country level in the way in which domestic
actors seek to blunt popular opposition—through concessionary corporatism in Ireland and Spain and grand coalitions in Portugal and Greece—
but the truth is that none of this variation makes any difference for the
type of policy response selected, austerity, which is imposed from outside.
At least so far, austerity policy has failed to provide a solution to the crisis.
On the contrary, it may have aggravated it.

In the summer of 2011, the sovereign debt crisis deepened further and
enmeshed the third economy of the eurozone—Italy. The unfolding of
events was similar to other GIIPS countries. Growing concerns about a
Greek default led financial markets to shun the bonds issued by other financially weak countries, including Italy.[36] The result was that interest
rates on the Italian treasury's ten-year bonds shot up and reached 7 percent on an annual basis, and the spread with corresponding German
bonds rose above 5 percent. Rising interest rates increase the costs of ser-
vicing the Italian public debt and worsen the Italian fiscal position, making it necessary to increase the primary surplus as suggested by the formula discussed earlier.

The speculative attacks on Italy confirm one of the points made earlier,
namely that financial markets evaluate a country's solvency by looking
first at its growth prospect rather than at its fiscal position at a particular
time. In fact, although the Italian public debt was 120 percent of GDP in
2011, that is, very high, it had been higher than 100 percent since the start
of the euro, actually since the early 1990s.[37] In contrast, Italy's public deficit, an estimated 4 percent in 2011, was lower than both the eurozone average, 4.3 percent, and France, 5.8.[38] Conscious of the country's weak fiscal
fundamentals, the Italian policymaking authorities had refrained from
passing any meaningful stimulus package during the recession of 2008
and 2009.

Italy's economic problems are similar to those of the other GIIPS countries: the country has been losing competitiveness with respect to Ger-

many and other core countries in the last ten years, not so much due to wage militancy as to stagnant productivity increases. Growth has been anemic and constantly below the OECD average. Despite frequent fiscal consolidation adjustments since the early 1990s, Italy has been unable to significantly reduce its public debt.

Faced with a speculative attack, the response of the Italian political class was similar to that of the other countries. Despite deep differences between the center-right coalition in power and the center-left coalition in opposition, the opposition decided to support the government's emergency austerity package in the summer of 2011.[39] Thus, the measures were swiftly approved. The opposition made it very clear that it acted out of a sense of responsibility and that it did not agree with the content of the package.[40] In fact, the austerity package was fiscally regressive in that it cut, by 5 percent, all tax deductions, proportionally more important for lower incomes, including those for dependent children.[41] Its stated goal was to bring the Italian public deficit to zero by 2014. Yet despite these efforts, the pressure on Italian bonds did not abate. Mounting tensions led to a change of government in the fall of 2011. The center-right government was replaced by a government of technocrats, supported by a three-way grand coalition among center-right, center, and center-left parties. The new government engaged in a thorough program of labor market and product market liberalization with the explicit support of European elites.

It can be argued that the need for neoliberal reforms was always implicit in the way the euro was designed, that is, as a currency union with no proper fiscal budget attached, and that the countries concerned knew what was in store. Academics anticipated that in the event of asymmetric shocks affecting some countries and not others, wages and prices in the adversely affected countries would have to fall relative to the other countries. Given less than perfectly competitive labor and product markets, this process of deflation would be slow and the countries in question would have to accept protracted periods of unemployment above the European average unless they decided to pass liberalizing reforms of the labor and product markets and reduced the size of the welfare state (Obstfeld 1997, 242; Alesina, Ardagna, and Galasso 2010). Thus reforms that should have been introduced at the beginning of the process for the euro to work have been postponed until now.

It seems ironic after the Lehman Brothers collapse and the global financial and economic crisis that ensued that a policy approach that assumes markets know best would still have so much purchase on policymakers (Stiglitz 2009; Schettkat 2010). The GIIPS countries have already relinquished exchange rate, monetary, and fiscal discretion by virtue of their membership in the euro. They are now being forced to hurriedly pass a series of deep-reaching structural reforms. The hope is that these reforms will increase the countries' long-term growth rate, and even have expansionary effects in the short term. Whether these effects will materialize remains to be seen. In the meantime, the reforms threaten to have momentous consequences for the future of European societies.

The authors would like to thank Sabina Avdagic, Nancy Bermeo, Jonas Pontusson, and Fritz Scharpf for helpful comments on a previous version.

NOTES

1. These statements are based on time series data on nominal wage costs by sector available in the Annual Macro-Economic (AMECO) database of the European Commission, http://ec.europa.eu/economy_finance/db_indicators/ameco/index_en.htm (accessed June 15, 2011).
2. The statements that follow are based on data from the OECD's Structural Analysis Database (STAN), http://stats.oecd.org (accessed June 13, 2012; subscription required).
3. Paul Krugman, "Lands of Ice and Ire," *New York Times*, November 24, 2010, http://krugman.blogs.nytimes.com/2010/11/24/lands-of-ice-and-ire/ (accessed June 10, 2011).
4. IMF Survey Magazine, "Iceland's Unorthodox Policies Suggest Alternative Way Out of Crisis," *Internal Monetary Fund*, November 3, 2011, http://www.imf.org/external/pubs/ft/survey/so/2011/car110311a.htm (accessed December 23, 2011).
5. "Iceland Makes Successful Return to Bond Markets," *Irish Times*, June 11, 2011, http://www.irishtimes.com/newspaper/finance/2011/0611/1224298736664.html (accessed July 27, 2011).
6. AMECO Database, variables UBLGE and UDGG.
7. This is based on data from the OECD Main Economic Indicators database.
8. AMECO Database, variable UVGD.
9. See Björn Hengst, "Fanal in den Flammen," *Spiegel Online*, May 5, 2010, http://www.spiegel.de/politik/ausland/0,1518,693221,00.html (accessed May 20, 2010).
10. This is based on Eurobarometer survey 74, November/December 2010.
11. European Industrial Relations Observatory Online, "2011 Report on Economy and Employment," http://www.eurofound.europa.eu/eiro/2011/10/articles/gr1110029i.htm (accessed April 4, 2012).
12. See PAME, "About PAME," *All Workers Militant Front*, May 17, 2010, http://

www.pamehellas.gr/content_fullstory.php?pg=1&lang=2 (accessed July 27, 2011).

13. See Mary Minihan, "Tanaiste Says No Changes to Croke Park Deal," *Irish Times*, December 13, 2011, http://www.irishtimes.com/newspaper/ireland/2011/1213/1224309001492.html (accessed December 27, 2011).

14. Manfred Bleskin, "Portugal: Vom Regen in die Traufe," *N-TV Kommentare*, June 6, 2011, http://www.n-tv.de/politik/politik_kommentare/Portugal-Vom-Regen-in-die-Traufe-article3510346.html (accessed July 27, 2011).

15. See Maria da Paz Campos Lima, "EC, ECB and IMF Meet with Social Partners before Setting Bailout Conditions," *EIRO online*, May 23, 2011, http://www.eurofound.europa.eu/eiro/2011/05/articles/pt1105019i.html (accessed July 27, 2011).

16. This is based on Eurobarometer survey 74, November/December 2010.

17. "Geração à rasca," *Wikipedia*, http://de.wikipedia.org/wiki/Geracao_a_rasca (accessed July 27, 2011).

18. See *Neue Zürcher Zeitung*, "Portugal im Bann des Streiks," November 25, 2011, http://www.nzz.ch/nachrichten/politik/international/portugal_im_bann_des_streiks_1.13410931.html (accessed April 20, 2012).

19. Esteban Villarejo, "Government Plan to Boost Economy and Protect Unemployed People," *EIRO online*, April 30, 2009, http://www.eurofound.europa.eu/eiro/2009/02/articles/es0902049i.htm (accessed July 27, 2011).

20. Juan Arasanz Díaz, "Social Dialogue Agenda Seeks to Address Economic Crisis," *EIRO online*, November 14, 2008, http://www.eurofound.europa.eu/eiro/2008/10/articles/es0810019i.htm (accessed July 27, 2011).

21. Juan Arasanz Díaz, "Social Dialogue at a Standstill Due to Recession," *EIRO online*, March 16, 2009, http://www.eurofound.europa.eu/eiro/2009/02/articles/es0902029i.htm (accessed July 27, 2011).

22. Pablo Sanz de Miguel, "Trade Unions Strike over Proposed Pension Reforms," *EIRO online*, March 31, 2010, http://www.eurofound.europa.eu/eiro/2010/02/articles/es1002029i.htm (accessed July 27, 2011).

23. Pablo Sanz de Miguel, "Agreement Reached on Employment and Collective Bargaining 2010–2012," *EIRO online*, March 31, 2010, http://www.eurofound.europa.eu/eiro/2010/02/articles/es1002019i.htm (accessed July 27, 2011).

24. Pablo Sanz de Miguel, "Government Cuts Back Job Offers in Public Sector," *EIRO online*, May 25, 2010, http://www.eurofound.europa.eu/eiro/2010/04/articles/es1004011i.htm (accessed July 27, 2011).

25. Pablo Sanz de Miguel, "Government Endorses Plan to Cut Public Deficit," *EIRO online*, July 28, 2007, http://www.eurofound.europa.eu/eiro/2010/06/articles/es1006011i.htm (accessed July 27, 2011).

26. Pablo Sanz de Miguel, "Government Approves Law Proposing Urgent Labour Market Reform," *EIRO online*, September 23, 2010, http://www.euro

found.europa.eu/eiro/2010/07/articles/es1007011i.htm (accessed July 27, 2011).

27.   Pablo Sanz, "Cause and Effect of General Strike," *EIRO online*, November 23, 2010, http://www.eurofound.europa.eu/eiro/2010/10/articles/es1010011i.htm (accessed July 27, 2011).

28.   Pablo Sanz de Miguel, "Government Endorses New Measures to Encourage Growth and Reduce Deficit," *EIRO online*, March 2, 2011, http://www.euro found.europa.eu/eiro/2010/12/articles/es1012021i.htm (accessed July 27, 2011.

29.   Pablo Sanz de Miguel, "Agreement Signed on Growth, Employment, and Guaranteed Pensions," *EIRO online*, May 11, 2011, http://www.eurofound.europa.eu/eiro/2011/02/articles/es1102031i.htm (accessed July 27, 2011).

30.   Ministerio de Empleo y Seguridad Social, "Aprobado por el Consejo de Ministros el Real Decreto-Ley," Gobierno de Espana, June 10, 2011, http://www.tt.mtin.es/periodico/Laboral/201106/LAB20110610_2.htm (accessed June 11, 2011).

31.   Juan Arasanz Díaz, "Social Dialogue Agenda Seeks to Address Economic Crisis," *EIRO online*, November 14, 2008, http://www.eurofound.europa.eu/eiro/2008/10/articles/es0810019i.htm (accessed July 27, 2011).

32.   Arguments about expansionary fiscal contraction come in two forms. One has to do with the role of expectations and *Ricardian equivalence*: adjustments based on increased taxes have no effects on present consumption as forward-looking consumers have already anticipated the need for future increases in taxation and adjusted their consumption patterns accordingly; adjustments based on public spending cuts signal (when credible) that future taxes will be lower than in the past and thus increase present consumption (Giavazzi and Pagano 1990). The other argument emphasizes increased competitiveness (Alesina and Perotti 1997). Cuts in public sector employment lower private sector wages by increasing labor supply and reducing the private sector workers' reservation wage. Similarly, cuts in income taxes reduce wage demands by the unions (Alesina et al. 2002, 573). Both channels reduce labor costs and increase profits. Higher profits, in turn, translate into greater investments (for textual evidence that the ECB subscribes to the expansionary fiscal contraction thesis, see Trichet 2010).

33.   IMF, "Transcript of the Updates to the World Economic Outlook/Global Stability Report/Fiscal Monitor Press Briefing," *International Monetary Fund*, January 24, 2012, http://www.imf.org/external/np/tr/2012/tr012412.htm (accessed January 29, 2011).

34.   Author's calculations from Eurobarometer 74, Fall 2010.

35.   Author's calculations based on Eurobarometer 67 and Eurobarometer 74.

36.   See Andrea Greco, "'Vendono perché non ci credono' e torna lo spauracchio

del '92," *la Repubblica*, July 12, 2011, http://www.repubblica.it/economia/2011/07/12/news/allarme_operatori-18999710/ (accessed July 27, 2011).

37. See Ameco database, variable UDGG (accessed July 27, 2011).
38. See Ameco database, variable UBLGE (accessed July 27, 2011).
39. See "L'opposizione raccoglie l'appello del Colle poche modifiche e tempi rapidi per la manovra," *la Repubblica*, July 11, 2011, http://www.repubblica.it/politica/2011/07/11/news/napolitano_coesione-18960725/ (accessed July 27, 2011).
40. See Alessandra Longo, "Bersani: 'Ora la svolta cambieremo un decreto che colpisce i deboli,'" *la Repubblica*, July 15, 2011, http://www.repubblica.it/dal-quotidiano/interviste/2011/07/15/news/bersani_ora_la_svolta_cambieremo_un_decreto_che_colpisce_i_deboli-19147772/ (accessed July 27, 2011).
41. See "Manovra, tagli a tutti i bonus fiscali stangata da 70 miliardi in due anni," *la Repubblica*, July 14, 2011, http://www.repubblica.it/economia/2011/07/14/news/manovr_le_nuove_misure-19116357/ (accessed July 27, 2011).

REFERENCES

Alesina, Alberto F., and Silvia Ardagna. 1998. "Tales of Fiscal Adjustments." *Economic Policy* 27(October): 489–545.

———. 2009. "Large Changes in Fiscal Policy: Taxes Versus Spending." *NBER* working paper no. 15438. Cambridge, Mass.: National Bureau of Economic Research.

Alesina, Alberto F., Silvia Ardagna, and V. Galasso. 2010. "The Euro, and Structural Reforms." In *Europe, and the Euro*, edited by Alberto Alesina and F. Giavazzi. Chicago: University of Chicago Press.

Alesina, Alberto F., Silvia Ardagna, Roberto Perotti, and Fabio Schiantarelli. 2002. "Fiscal Policy, Profits, and Investments." *American Econimic Review* 92(3): 571–89.

Alesina, Alberto F., and Roberto Perotti. 1997. "The Welfare State, and Competitiveness." *American Economic Review* 87: 921–39.

Baccaro, Lucio, and Valeria Pulignano. 2010. "Employment Relations in Italy." In *International and Comparative Employment Relations*, 5th ed., edited by Greg J. Bamber, Russell Lansbury, and Nick Wailes. Crows Nest, AU: Allen & Unwin.

Baccaro, Lucio, and Marco Simoni. 2007. "Centralized Wage Bargaining, and the 'Celtic Tiger' Phenomenon." *Industrial Relations: A Journal of Economy and Society* 46(3): 426–55.

Blanchard, Olivier, Giovanni Dell'Ariccia, and Paulo Mauro. 2010. "Rethinking Macroeconomic Policy." *IMF* staff position note SPN/10/03. Washington, D.C.: International Monetary Fund.

Blustein, Paul. 2001. *The Chastening: Inside the Crisis that Rocked the Global Financial System, and Humbled the IMF*. Cambridge, Mass.: PublicAffairs.

Bühlmann, Marc, and Hanspeter Kriesi. 2007. "Political Participation. Quantity Versus Quality." Unpublished manuscript, University of Zürich.

D'Art, Daryl, and Thomas Turner. 2011. "Irish Trade Unions under Social Partnership: A Faustian Bargain?" *Industrial Relations Journal* 42(2): 157–73.

De Grauwe, Paul. 2011. "The Governance of a Fragile Eurozone." Unpublished manuscript. University of Leuven.

Delgado, Irene, and Lourdes Lopez Nieto. 2009. "Spain." *European Journal of Political Research* 48(7–8): 1114–19.

———. 2010. "Spain." *European Journal of Political Research* 49(7–8): 1173–78.

Eggertsson, Gauti B., and Paul Krugman. 2011. "Debt, Deleveraging, and the Liquidity Trap: A Fisher-Minsky-Koo Approach." Unpublished manuscript.

European Commission. 2009. "Report from the Commission. Greece Report Prepared in Accordance with Article 104(3) of the Treaty (2009 02 18)." Brussels: European Commission.

———. 2011a. "The Economic Adjustment Programme for Ireland." *European Economy* occasional paper no. 76. Brussels: European Commission. http://ec.europa.eu/economy_finance/publications/occasional_paper/2011/pdf/ocp76_en.pdf (accessed June 13, 2012).

———. 2011b. "Green Paper on the Feasibility of Introducing Stability Bonds." Brussels: European Commission. http://ec.europa.eu/economy_finance/consultation/stability_bonds/pdf/green-pepr-stability-bonds_en.pdf (accessed June 13, 2012).

Follesdal, Andreas, and Simon Hix. 2006. "Why There Is a Democratic Deficit in the EU: A Response to Majone, and Moravcsik." *Journal of Common Market Studies* 44(3): 533–62.

Giavazzi, Francesco, and Marco Pagano. 1990. *Can Severe Fiscal Contractions Be Expansionary? Tales of Two Small European Countries*. Cambridge, Mass.: MIT Press.

Gourevitch, Peter A. 1986. *Politics in Hard Times*. Ithaca, N.Y.: Cornell University Press.

Guajardo, Jaime, Daniel Leigh, and Andrea Pescatori. 2010. "Will It Hurt? Macroeconomic Effects of Fiscal Consolidation." In *World Economic Outlook: Recovery, Risk, and Rebalancing*. Washington, D.C.: International Monetary Fund.

Hall, Peter A., and David Soskice. 2001. "An Introduction to Varieties of Capitalism." In *Varieties of Capitalism. The Institutional Foundations of Comparative Advantage*. Oxford: Oxford University Press.

Hardiman, Niamh. 2002. "From Conflict to Co-ordination: Economic Governance, and Political Innovation in Ireland." *West European Politics* 25(4): 1–24.

Held, David. 1991. "Democracy, the Nation-State, and the Global System." In *Political Theory Today*. Cambridge: Polity Press.

International Monetary Fund (IMF). 2009. *Staff Report for the 2009 Article IV Consul-*

tation: Greece. IMF Country Report no. 09/244. Washington, D.C.: International Monetary Fund.

———. 2010a. "Staff Report for the 2010 Article IV Consultation: Spain." Country Report no. 10/254. Washington, D.C.: International Monetary Fund.

———. 2010b. "Greece: Request for Stand-by Agreement." Country Report no. 10/111. Washington, D.C.: International Monetary Fund.

———. 2011a. "Greece: Third Review under the Stand-by Arrangement." Country Report no. 11/68. Washington, D.C.: International Monetary Fund.

———. 2011b. "Portugal: Letter of Intent, Memorandum of Economic, and Financial Policies, and Technical Memorandum of Understanding." May 17, 2011. Washington, D.C.: International Monetary Fund. http://www.imf.org/external/np/loi/2011/prt/051711.pdf (accessed June 13, 2012).

———. 2011c. "Greece: Fourth Review Under the Stand-By Arrangement and Request for Modification and Waiver of Applicability of Performance Criteria." Country Report no. 11/175. Washington, D.C.: International Monetary Fund.

———. 2011d. "Greece: Fifth Review Under the Stand-By Arrangement, Rephasing and Request for Waivers of Nonobservance of Performance Criteria; Press Release on the Executive Board Discussion; and Statement by the Executive Director for Greece." Country Report no. 11/351. Washington, D.C.: International Monetary Fund.

———. 2011e. "Ireland: Fourth Review Under the Extended Arrangement and Request for Rephasing of the Arrangement—Staff Report; Letter of Intent; Memorandum of Economic and Financial Policies; Technical Memorandum of Understanding; Letter of Intent and Memorandum of Understanding on Specific Economic Policy Conditionality (College of Commissioners); Staff Supplement; Press Release on the Executive Board Discussion." Country Report no. 11/356. Washington, D.C.: International Monetary Fund.

———. 2011f. "Portugal: Second Review Under the Extended Arrangement." Country Report no. 11/363. Washington, D.C.: International Monetary Fund.

Kelly, Morgan. 2010. "Whatever Happened to Ireland?" *CEPR* discussion paper no. 7811. London: Centre for Economic Policy Research.

Keohane, Robert O., Stephen Macedo, and Andrew Moravcsik. 2009. "Democracy-Enhancing Multilateralism." *International Organization* 63(1): 1–31.

Kielmansegg, Peter G. 1996. "Integration und Demokratie." In *Europäische Integration*, edited by Beate Kohler-Koch and Marcus Jachtenfuchs. Opladen, Germany: Leske + Budrich.

Kritsantonis, Nikos. D. 1998. "Greece: The Maturing of the System." In *Changing Industrial Relations in Europe*, edited by Anthony Ferner and Richard Hyman. Oxford: Blackwell.

Krugman, Paul R. 1998. "It's Baaack: Japan's Slump, and the Return of the Liquidity Trap." *Brookings Papers on Economic Activity* 29(2): 137–205.

Lavdas, Kostas A. 2001. "Griechenland. Verbände und Politik." In *Verbände und*

Verbandssysteme in Westeuropa, edited by Werner Reutter and Peter Rütters. Opladen, Germany: Leske + Budrich.

Lehmbruch, Gerhard. 1979. "Liberal Corporatism, and Party Government." In *Trends Toward Corporatist Intermediation*, edited by Philippe C. Schmitter and Gerhard Lehmbruch. Beverly Hills, Calif.: Sage Publications.

Magone, José M. 2010. "Portugal." *European Journal of Political Research* 49(7–8): 1130–38.

Mavrogordatos, George T., and Nikos Marantzidis. 2010. "Greece." *European Journal of Political Research* 49(708): 991–1000.

McDonough, Terrence, and Tony Dundon. 2010. "Thatcherism Delayed? The Irish Crisis, and the Paradox of Social Partnership." *Industrial Relations Journal* 41(6): 544–62.

Molina, Oscar. 2011. "Social Pacts, and Collective Bargaining Autonomy in Portugal, and Spain." Paper presented at the CES Conference. Barcelona (June 20–22, 2011).

O'Malley, Eoin. 2009. "Ireland." *European Journal of Political Research* 48(7–8): 986–91.

———. 2010. "Ireland." *European Journal of Political Research* 49(7-8): 1017–24.

Obstfeld, Maurice. 1997. "Europe's Gamble." *Brookings Papers on Economic Activity* 28(2): 241–317.

Organisation for Economic Co-operation and Development (OECD). 2009a. *Economic Surveys: Greece 2009*. Paris: OECD.

———. 2009b. *Economic Surveys: Iceland 2009*. Paris: OECD.

———. 2010a. *Economic Surveys: Portugal. September 2010*. Paris: OECD.

———. 2010b. *Economic Surveys: Spain 2010*. Paris: OECD.

Perotti, Roberto. 2011. "The 'Austerity Myth': Gain Without Pain?" Unpublished manuscript, Bocconi University.

Regan, Aidan. 2011. "The Rise, and Fall of Irish Social Partnership: Euro-Irish Trade Unionism in Crisis?" Unpublished manuscript, University College Dublin.

Roche, William K. 2007. "Social Partnership in Ireland and New Social Pacts." *Industrial Relations: A Journal of Economy, and Society* 46(3): 395–425.

Royo, Sebastián. 2006. "Beyond Confrontation. The Resurgence of Social Bargaining in Spain in the 1990s." *Comparative Political Studies* 39(8): 969–95.

Scharpf, Fritz W. 2011. "Monetary Union, Fiscal Crisis, and the Preemption of Democracy." Working paper. Koeln: Max-Planck Institute.

Schettkat, Ronald. 2010. "Will Only an Earthquake Shake Up Economics?" *International Labour Review* 149(2): 185–207.

Schmidt, Manfred G. 2008. *Demokratietheorien: Eine Einfuhrung*, 4th ed. Wiesbaden: Verlag für Sozialwissenschaften.

Sheehan, Brian. 2010. "Public Sector Unions Launch Action against Pay Cuts."

EIRO online, March 15, 2010. http://www.eurofound.europa.eu/eiro/2010/01/articles/ie1001039i.htm (accessed April 1, 2010).

Stiglitz, Joseph E. 2002. *Globalization and Its Discontents.* London: Penguin.

———. 2009. *Freefall: Free Markets, and the Sinking of the Global Economy.* London: Penguin

———. 2011. "The IMF's Switch in Time." *The Economists' Voice* 8(2): 1–2. DOI: 10.2202/1553-3832.1855.

Thelen, Kathleen A. 2001. "Varieties of Labor Politics in the Developed Democracies." In *Varieties of Capitalism: The Institutional Foundations of Comparative Advantage,* edited by Peter A. Hall and David Soskice. New York: Oxford University Press.

Trichet, Jean-Claude. 2010. "Central Banking in Uncertain Times: Conviction, and Responsibility." Presented at the symposium Macroeconomic Challenges: The Decade Ahead. Jackson Hole, Wy. (August 27, 2010).

Truman, David B. 1962. *The Governmental Process: Political Interests, and Public Opinion.* New York: Alfred A. Knopf.

Visser, Jelle, and Anton Hemerijck. 1997. *A Dutch Miracle: Job Growth, Welfare Reform, and Corporatism in the Netherlands.* Amsterdam: Amsterdam University Press.

Whelan, Karl. 2011. "Ireland's Sovereign Debt Crisis." *Centre for Economic Research* working paper 11/09. Dublin: University College Dublin.

Zervakis, Peter A. 2004. "Das politische System Zyperns." In *Die Politischen Systeme Osteuropas,* 2nd ed., edited by Wolfgang Ismayr. Opladen: Leske + Budrich.

PART II | Cases and Comparisons

Chapter 7 | The Politics of the Pop: The U.S. Response to the Financial Crisis and the Great Recession

Nolan McCarty

RECENT RESEARCH ON the American political economy has stressed the emergence of at least two salient features: The first is the increasing levels of political polarization, partisanship, and ideological rigidity (McCarty, Poole, and Rosenthal 2006; Theriault 2008). This polarization in turn has made policymaking more difficult and contributed to gridlock (McCarty 2007). The second is the increasing political salience of economic inequality. Not only has the party system divided more along income and class lines (McCarty, Poole, and Rosenthal 2006; Gelman et al. 2007), but politicians and policymaking have become more responsive to the interests of high-income voters relative to the poor (Bartels 2008; Gilens 2011). This responsiveness to high-income interests is not only true of the Republican Party, which is consistently antitax and regulation, but also the Democratic Party, which is divided internally on these issues (see Hacker and Pierson 2010).[1]

But how durable are these generalizations about American politics? Might they simply be the result of a political climate in which growth and prosperity were taken for granted and the government wasn't expected to do much? Would polarization continue in an environment where government action was necessary? Would economic decline produce a greater mobilization in policies that would address the problems of lower-income Americans?

There is no truer test of the nature of a politico-economic system than its performance in a crisis. Consequently, much is to be learned from how the

United States responded to the financial crisis and the Great Recession that it spawned. This chapter argues that the crisis did little to change these fundamental features of American politics. First, except perhaps at its very height, the crisis did not induce greater bipartisan cooperation and flexibility. If anything, the result has been greater partisan divisions on economic policies and priorities. Second, partisan polarization and the divisions within the Democratic Party combined to have a very constraining impact on the policy alternatives available to fight the crisis. In particular, proposals designed to ameliorate income inequality, whether by constraining incomes at the top or raising incomes at the bottom, fared poorly in the policy process.

In making the case that the configuration of ideology and economic interest underlying the party system shaped the policy response, I focus on four specific points. First, deep ideological divisions over economic policy did not disappear in the face of the crisis. If anything, polarization was enhanced in the long run. Second, polarization in combination with the supermajoritarian features of the U.S. policymaking system (especially the executive veto and Senate filibuster) placed hard constraints on the legislative response, especially in the area of fiscal policy and financial market reform. Third, the response was delayed by a combination of the ideological debates and short-run electoral calculations of a presidential election year. Fourth, even after the 2008 election handed power to the Democratic Party, the response was constrained by internal party divisions as well as by Republican opposition and obstruction. Although the focus of this chapter is on events through the end of 2010, the pitched battles over the debt ceiling and payroll taxes in 2011 show that the patterns identified have continued, if not intensified.

IDEOLOGY AND THE CRISIS

"There are no atheists in foxholes and no ideologues in financial crises." Ben Bernanke (New York Times, September 21, 2008).

For the purposes of this chapter, an ideology is a set of basic beliefs about how the world works and about what is right or wrong. Ideologies are distinguished from other beliefs in part based on their rigidity. Because they are deeply held and often based on basic principles, ideological beliefs are much less responsive to new information, persuasion, or context. Consequently, one can distinguish the ideologue from a pragmatist who would be more open to information and arguments. The pragmatist agrees with Lord Keynes' famous quip, "when the facts change I change my mind." Even if they are responsive to new information, the ways in which ideologues adjust their views will be tempered by their preexisting beliefs. In other words, ideologies are the framework in which individuals interpret new data. Consider a fairly striking example of this phenomenon. To ameliorate the recession brought on by the financial crisis, President Obama and the Democratic majorities in Congress passed a $787 billion stimulus plan with very little support from Republicans. The administration had forecast that the plan would prevent the unemployment rate from exceeding 8 percent. But by July 2009, it had risen to 9.5 percent and showed no signs of retreat. Democratic leaders and advisors interpreted the news as an indication that the stimulus plan had not been large enough. Laura Tyson, a member of Obama's Economic Recovery Advisory Board, said that the unemployment situation proved that the stimulus plan was "a bit too small" (Adam Shamin, "Obama Adviser Says U.S. Should Mull Second Stimulus," *Bloomberg*, July 7, 2009). Democratic majority leader Steny Hoyer declared that "we need to be open to whether we need additional action [on economic stimulus]" ("U.S. Should be Open to Second Stimulus—Congressional Leader," *Reuters*, July 7, 2009). The Republican response was quite different. Republican house leader John Boehner crowed that "[the stimulus plan] was supposed to be about jobs, jobs, and jobs. And the fact is it turned into nothing more than spending, spending, and more spending on a lot of big government bureaucracy" (Boehner 2009). So the new information revealed in the employment numbers led to far less, rather than more, consensus on the effects of the stimulus package.

Of course, all policymakers and citizens have to rely on ideology to some degree. Without an existing belief structure, it is very hard to make sense of the world. The former Federal Reserve chairman Alan Greenspan told a congressional panel that "ideology is a conceptual framework . . . the way people deal with reality. Everyone has one. You have to. To exist, you need an ideology." Clearly, Greenspan is correct. But so is the response to his comment by Betty McCollum (D-MN), "If we need an ideology, if we need a philosophy to govern, as Mr. Greenspan suggested, I would suggest we give pragmatism a try, we give common sense a try" (U.S. Congress 2008). Ideologies and doctrines are a poor substitute for intelligence, reason, and evidence. Beliefs in socialism and Marxism impeded economic development in much of the world for most of the twentieth century. But more recently, doctrinal beliefs in deregulation and the infallibility of markets abetted the crisis of 2008. I call these doctrines "free-market" conservatism (FMC). Like most ideologies, FMC is based on a core set of principles. Markets are always better at allocating resources than bureaucracies. Consequently, government should be extremely limited. Government should only engage in the basic protections of life and property, specifically only those that cannot be provided by the market place, but even free-market conservatives disagree about what these are. Because markets allocate resources best, taxes and regulations should be as low as possible.

Before the crisis of 2008, FMC had plenty of support from Democrats as well as Republicans. Bill Clinton twice reappointed Alan Greenspan as Fed chair and signed, with the endorsements of Larry Summers and Robert Rubin, the Gramm-Leach-Bliley bill that repealed Glass-Steagall. Only eighty-six representatives opposed passage of the bill in the House, although a large majority of Democrats did oppose it in the Senate. Only a handful of the most liberal Democrats voted against Greenspan's reappointments.

FMC, though, was far from the only set of ideological doctrines that contributed to the 2008 crisis. Egalitarianism fueled some of the excess in the mortgage market. Subprime and prime mortgage lending, especially to racial and ethnic minorities, was seen by many as an effective tool for redistributing income and wealth. Both the Clinton and Bush administrations (though for rather different reasons) pushed the idea of maximizing home ownership. In doing so, each promoted policies that further distorted the incentives away from renting and toward owning. One of the major pushes during the Clinton administration was to require that Fannie Mae and Freddie Mac increase the share of their loan portfolios dedicated to mortgages for low- and middle-income families.

These policies were continued during the administration of George W. Bush, but with different ideological objectives. For President Bush, increasing home ownership rates was a key component of his "ownership society," the philosophical thrust of which was that homeownership and asset accumulation promoted less reliance on the government (for cross-national evidence on the political effects of homeownership and appreciation, see chapter 11, this volume). The more government policy could be used to promote investing and homeownership now, the less demand there would be for government in the future.[2] Barney Frank has recently conceded that ideological blinders were behind his opposition to reforming Fannie Mae and Freddie Mac earlier (Donovan Slack, "Stance on Fannie and Freddie Dogs Frank," *Boston Globe*, October 14, 2010).[3]

So, although it is clear that the origins of crisis lay in the combination of beliefs that supported deregulation of financial markets and government intervention into housing markets, wouldn't information about the disastrous effects of this combination undermine these beliefs?

To make the case that these beliefs were rigid and inflexible in light of the crisis, I make heavy use of DW-NOMINATE estimates of legislator ideal points (see McCarty, Poole, and Rosenthal 1997). These measures are derived from roll call votes under the assumption that legislators make their choices in accordance with the spatial model of voting. Previous work on Congress has shown that for much of American history, a single liberal-conservative dimension can account for a very large proportion of congressional roll call voting (Poole and Rosenthal 1997; McCarty, Poole, and Rosenthal 2006). From time to time, a second dimension captures distinct patterns on regional, racial, religious, or social issues.

Data about legislative behavior before the crisis are very consistent with an emphasis on ideological consistency. For example, in recent years, the explanatory power of the ideological model has increased dramatically. Nolan McCarty, Keith Poole, and Howard Rosenthal report that the explanatory power of a single ideological dimension model grew appreciably from the 1960s to the current period (2006, fig. 2.1). The first dimension now correctly predicts more than 90 percent of the votes cast in the House and Senate. [4] Moreover, this is not merely a consequence of the size of an increased winning coalition. Over the past two decades, the number of legislators voting on the winning side has declined and the classification success of the spatial model has increased. In a nutshell, Congress has witnessed less consensus and more ideology.

An important question, however, is the extent to which one can characterize these positions as reflecting ideology. As discussed, if the positions reflected ideological commitments, we would expect them to be quite stable across issues and over time. Consistency across issues is clear. Despite the fact that the congressional agenda contains hundreds of issues spanning economic, social, and environmental policy domains, a single left-right dimension can account for the vast majority of the roll call votes cast. This is precisely because positions on taxes are good predictors of preferences over regulation, which are good predictors of views on welfare, and so on. A related question is which of the many issues confronting Congress is most closely related to the left-right continuum. Although many observers might stress the importance of racial attitudes and social issues as the defining cleavages of American politics, my research with Poole and Rosenthal has documented that it is economic issues and debates about the role and scope of the federal government that have mapped most closely onto our continuum (see Poole and Rosenthal 1997, 2007; McCarty, Poole, and Rosenthal 1997, 2006).[5]

Ideological positions are also quite stable for politicians throughout their career. Of course, a few prominent examples of politicians whose positions do change can readily be pointed out. But for the most part, legislators' positions on the scale move significantly only if they switch parties. Even a member whose constituency changes quite dramatically either by elevation to the Senate or through major redistricting rarely changes positions in a significant way. In a very careful study, Poole and

Rosenthal (2007) show that a model in which legislators maintain the same ideological position throughout their careers performs just as well statistically as one where legislators are able to change positions in each biennial term.

Moreover, the behavior of legislators deviates in large and systematic ways from the preferences of their average or median constituent. This finding persists even when we do not worry about the mismeasurement of constituency interests or preferences. For example, senators from the same state do not vote identically. Most obviously, senators from the same state but different parties pursue very different policy goals. The difference is picked up in their polarized ideology scores. If the two senators are from the same party, they are, of course, more similar.[6]

Of course, NOMINATE scores do pick up many factors other than ideology, including some constituency effects, interest group influence, and pressure from party leaders and activists. Moreover, the ideological scores are not perfect predictors of behavior on a given decision so these other factors may be especially important in some contexts.

This consistency of ideological behavior has importance consequences for understanding the timing of policy changes over time. Because the individual behavior of legislators is so stable, political shifts in ideology occur mainly through the replacement process of elections. This feature of American politics has had important ramifications in previous financial and economic crises. During the Panic of 1907, the American financial system was saved primarily because J. Pierpont Morgan had the power and influence to act as a de facto central banker. But, in the aftermath, ideological opposition to central banking precluded its establishment. Congress passed only the modest Aldrich-Vreeland Act, the only substantive reform of which was to allow groups of national banks to issue emergency currency.[7] It was only after the Democrats picked up a net of 118 seats in the House, 19 Senate seats, and the presidency in the elections of 1910 and 1912 that they gained enough of a majority to pass the Federal Reserve Act. Similarly, the market-oriented ideologies of Hoover and the Republican Party limited the use of federal authority in response to the stock market crash in October 1929. Consequently, the most significant policy changes occurred only after Roosevelt took office more than three years later, in March 1933. The current crises were no different, because without the electoral shifts of the 2008 election, the government's fiscal stimulus and financial reform programs would have been much different in size and emphasis.

As I highlight in the case studies, ideologically driven politics continues to shape responses to financial crises. But first let me provide an important piece of quantitative evidence for ideological stability. Figure 7.1 compares estimated ideal points using votes of the 110th Congress from

Figure 7.1   Before Lehman Versus After Lehman

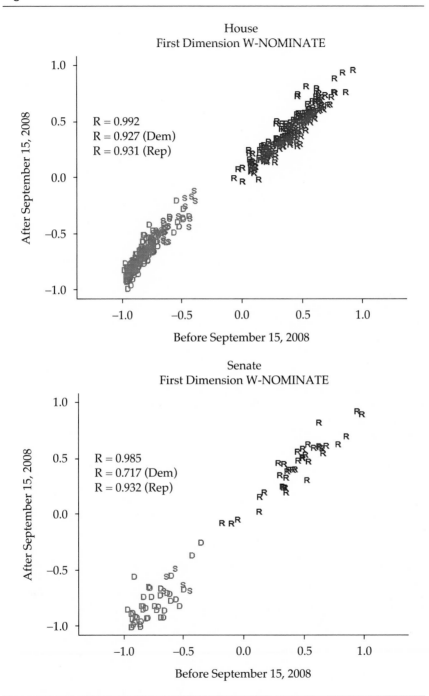

House
First Dimension W-NOMINATE

After September 15, 2008

R = 0.992
R = 0.927 (Dem)
R = 0.931 (Rep)

Before September 15, 2008

Senate
First Dimension W-NOMINATE

After September 15, 2008

R = 0.985
R = 0.717 (Dem)
R = 0.932 (Rep)

Before September 15, 2008

Source: Author's compilation based on Voteview.com (2010).

its start in January 2007 through September 15, 2008, when Lehmann crashed, with separate ideal points estimated on the remaining roll calls in the 110th House and those in the 111th through July 31, 2010. In the House, there is no indication of important ideological change, with correlations greater than 0.9, even within party. In the Senate, the story is the same, except for a somewhat lower correlation among Democrats.

Perhaps foxholes convert atheists, but financial crises do not seem to have the same effect.

POLARIZATION

Not only has politics become more ideological over the past few decades, but the ideological gap between the political parties has widened as well. Based on the average distance between Republican and Democratic legislators on the NOMINATE scale, McCarty, Poole, and Rosenthal (2006) show that party polarization in Congress is currently higher than any other time since Reconstruction. The previous high corresponded to the original Gilded Age of the 1890s.[8]

It is not mere coincidence that the patterns of ideological polarization of our own Gilded Age look like those of the 1890s. Both were periods of little regulation, booming economies, and increasing concentrations of income and wealth. In both eras, the Republican Party was the defender of the free-market gospel and was largely successful in preventing the government regulation of markets. It was also an era of frequent financial crises and panics with major crises in 1893 and 1907.

My collaborators and I argue that economic inequalities and political polarization are strongly linked (McCarty, Poole, and Rosenthal 2006). At least two mechanisms are at work. The first is a causal effect of economic inequality on political polarization. As we have argued, the primary ideological dimension of American politics is the role of the state in regulating the economy. So in periods when economic rewards to unfettered markets are huge, support for free-market conservatism increases, especially among those individuals and groups who benefit the most. Of course, the losers will attempt to use the power of the state to capture some of those economic rewards outside the market. This effect has been reflected in the solidifying of Republican support in the middle to upper-middle classes (McCarty, Poole, and Rosenthal 2006, chap. 3; Gelman et al. 2007) and the increased relationship between legislative behavior and the median income of her constituents (McCarty, Poole, and Rosenthal 2006, chap. 2).

The second mechanism is embedded in the supermajoritarian structure of American political institutions. If policymaking in the United States were purely majoritarian, the current majority would implement its preferred policy. So polarization would tend to produce policy oscillations as majorities shift, but have no clear effect on the average policy. But institutions such as the presidential veto and the Senate filibuster also inhibit majority rule and allow the policymaking process to gridlock (Krehbiel 1998; Brady and Volden 2005). Polarization exacerbates these propensities because it is considerably harder to reach agreements with opposite party presidents or get sixty votes for cloture when the parties are farther apart.[9] So political polarization leads to policy gridlock that makes economic reforms difficult to implement. Not only can the economic losers not form a coalition to redirect the allocation of resources, but the government cannot effectively respond to those economic shocks and crises that increase polarization. This polarization-induced gridlock has especially large effects on policies where the status quo drifts, due either to inflation such as the minimum wage or to technological or economic shifts such as the case with certain regulatory policies.

Although our argument did not directly address financial policies and regulations, plenty of evidence supports linkages between political polarization and the concentration of wealth and resources in the financial sector. Recently, the economists Thomas Philippon and Ariell Reshef (2009) have estimated the wage rate of employees of the financial sector relative to wages of equally skilled workers in other sectors of the economy from 1908 to 2006. These wage ratios ranged from a low in the 1970s of 1.05, indicating that financial workers enjoyed a 5 percent premium, to 1.7 in 2006 when financial workers made 70 percent more than comparable workers in other parts of the economy.[10] In their statistical analysis, they find that the main determinants of the financial sector wage premium are financial deregulation and corporate activities related to initial public offerings and credit risk.

Consistent with the previous arguments about polarization and inequality, the cycles in financial sector wages closely match our measure of polarization over the past century. Figure 7.2 plots the ratio of finance wages to average wages against polarization in the House, measured as the difference between the mean Democratic and Republican NOMINATE scores.

Both polarization and wages in finance are high at the beginning and end of the twentieth century. But both indicators are at a low for much of the middle of the century following financial market reforms and the middle-class political economy created by the New Deal. Financial innovation and deregulation that increased wages in the financial sector relative to other sectors increased later inequality. These shifts aided politicians who espoused free market principles, which helped sustain the Republican move to the right and polarization.

Figure 7.2   Polarization and Relative Wage

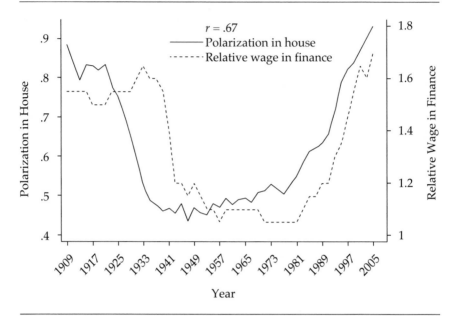

Source: Author's compilation based on McCarty, Poole, and Rosenthal (2006) and Philippon and Reshef (2009).

Differences in the timing of the wage and polarization series are important, however. In particular, political polarization begins to increase before the onset of rising wages in the financial sector.[11] This suggests that polarization may have had a causal impact on the financialization of the economy. Clearly, two channels are at work. The first is Republican movement toward FMC and Democratic acceptance of these arguments when applied to finance (see the following section). The second is the effects of regulatory drift produced by polarization and gridlock. That Congress did pass some important pieces of financial deregulation, and occasionally on a bipartisan basis, might seem to undermine the emphasis on polarization-induced gridlock. But, in many cases, such as the repeal of Glass-Steagall, the old regulatory regime was so weathered by years of neglect that final repeal was not very controversial or consequential.[12]

FINANCE AND THE DEMOCRATIC PARTY

Despite the important roles that ideology and polarization played in the lead up to and aftermath of the crisis, it would be foolish to dismiss the role of the financial sector as an interest group that has substantial influence over politicians from both parties. But because its commitment to FMC naturally aligns the Republicans with the financial sector, I focus primarily on the impact the financial lobby has had on the Democratic Party in its approach to the crisis.

One of the most important effects of the political activities of the financial sector has been to create significant divisions within the Democratic Party over financial market regulation and economic policy more generally. As argued in *Polarized America*, voting behavior and partisan identification in the United States have become much more structured by income over the past forty years, the Republican Party faring somewhat better among the middle class and above and the Democratic Party getting a majority of the votes from the middle class and down (see also Bartels 2008; Gelman et al. 2007). But as the Democratic Party began to depend more heavily on the votes of lower-income voters, the party became more dependent on the resources of wealthier supporters and interest groups, especially as the financial and political muscle of organized labor waned. Consequently, the Democratic Party now has two distinct wings—votes and money. The financial services industry is one of the primary constituents of the money wing. From the party's perspective, the financial sector makes an almost ideal constituency, almost as good as Hollywood. That, unlike many other industries, hedge funds do not pollute the environment, at least not directly, and do not have especially tendentious labor relations, makes for much less conflict with other Democratic constituencies like environmentalists and labor unions.

Data provided by the Center for Responsive Politics (CPR) allow me to examine in some detail the increasing financial dependence of the Democratic Party on the financial services industry. [13] Figure 7.3 reveals that campaign contributions from the financial sector increased almost threefold between 1992 and 2008, even after adjusting for inflation. This growth exceeds that of all of the industrial sectors tracked by CPR with the exception of the legal profession.

The current magnitude of financial sector giving is also astonishing. Four subsectors of the industry are in the top ten of all industry contributors: securities and investments, real estate, insurance, and miscellaneous finance. Combined, the industry contributions swamp the otherwise top industry—the legal profession.[14] Figure 7.3 also reveals that the growth in financial industry contributions has been concentrated in two sectors: securities and investments, and real estate. It is certainly no coincidence that these are exactly the sectors that played such a big role in the 2008 financial crisis.

Of course, it is not simply the magnitude of the contributions that mat-

Figure 7.3   Campaign Contributions from Financial Sector

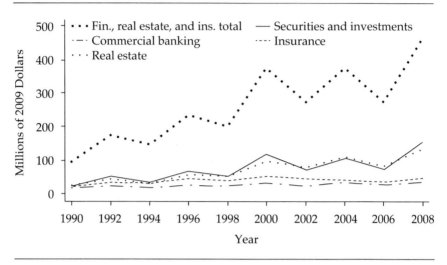

ters, but the way they are allocated. Figure 7.4 demonstrates how different financial sectors have allocated their money across the two political parties since 1990. Two features stand out. The first is the importance of majority party control in Congress. The financial industry tends to shift its contributions based on which party controls Congress. Before 1994, a majority of the money went to the Democratic Party, which controlled the House and the Senate. Following the 1994 elections, contributions shifted heavily toward the newly empowered Republicans, especially among insurers and commercial banks. Following the Democratic takeover in 2006, the money switched back to about where it was in the early 1990s.

The second important point is how well the Democratic Party has done with the securities and real estate industries even when it had little power in Washington. Although it may seem inconsistent with the Democratic Party's ideological orientation on economics, the financial sector has become a very important constituency for the party.

It's not just about the campaign money, of course. As Torben Iverson and David Soskice point out in chapter 2 of this volume, the U.S. comparative intuitional advantages in financial services lead politicians of all parties to support deregulation of the industry. As a result of these policies, finance has obtained a structural position in the U.S. economy that commands respect of politicians of all stripes.[15] This political deference to finance is especially prominent in boom years, when the sector is able to tie its good fortunes to a general prosperity. The financial sector has also

Figure 7.4   Democratic Share of Contributions

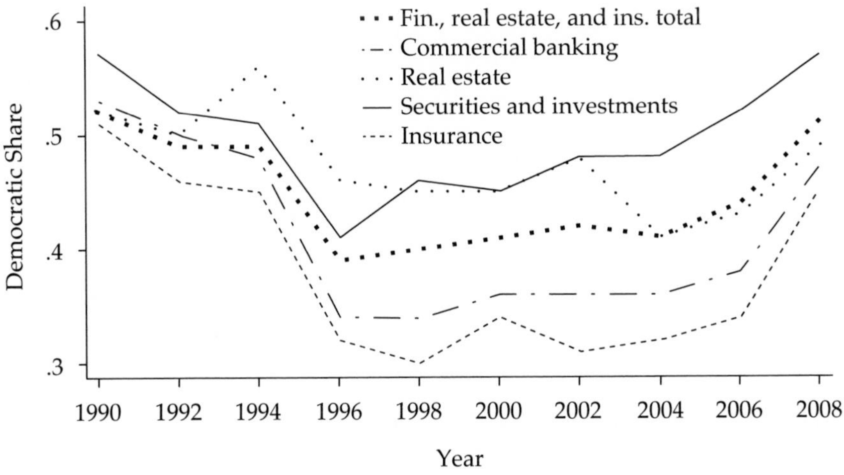

Source: Author's compilation based on Opensecrets (2009).

obtained a high social and cultural status from which the Democratic Party benefits by association. So as more of the country's intellectual and human capital is drawn into the financial services, Democratic administrations have become very dependent on the financial sector for expertise about financial and economic policy. Whereas George W. Bush hired Treasury secretaries from manufacturing (Paul O'Neill) and transportation (John Snow), the Treasury secretaries under Clinton and Obama have been notable for their ties to Wall Street. Finally, the revolving doors that exist in both parties between government, academia, and Wall Street have not only aligned material incentives, but have also become a conveyor belt for FMC ideas about the benefits of unregulated financial markets.

THE POPS

The roles of ideology, institutions, and interests in regulating (or not) the financial sector now outlined, the discussion now turns to how these factors shaped the fiscal and regulatory response to the financial crisis.[16]

The Politics of Fiscal Stimulus

Following a noticeable slowdown in the economy at the end of 2007, the Bush administration proposed an economic stimulus package in January of 2008. The centerpieces of his proposal were one-time income tax rebate checks and business tax breaks. Although discretionary fiscal policy had long fallen out of favor among conservatives, the focus on tax cutting minimized the break with ideological orthodoxy.

Although Democrats also supported an expansionary fiscal program, they did not support the Bush plan's sole reliance on tax relief. Democratic legislators argued strongly that the package should include increased spending, especially on unemployment insurance, aid to states, and public works. Leading Democratic presidential candidate Hilary Clinton put forward a plan for $70 billion in spending for housing, heating subsidies, and state aid and for $40 billion in tax rebates if conditions worsened. Another point of ideological conflict was the refusal of the administration and Republicans to support rebate checks for those workers who did not pay federal income tax, essentially arguing that rebates for non-income taxpayers constituted welfare.

In formulating their response to the president's plan, Democratic leaders faced two problems. First, the 2006 elections that had provided them with their legislative majority also added a large number of fiscal conservatives to their caucus who were more likely to oppose expansions of social spending to stimulate the economy. Second, the leadership was concerned with the party's fiscal image. The party had used the spiraling deficits of the Bush years to put itself forward as a party of fiscal responsibility. This new reputation solidified support, not just of independent voters, but also with the money wing. Consequently, Democratic leaders were wary of getting too far in front of the president in such a way that they might once again be branded as big spenders. Complicating matters even more was that any stimulus plan would involve the Democratic Congress waiving the pay-as-you-go budget rules that they reinstituted when they regained control of Congress (Steven Weisman and David Herszenhorn, "Bush and Congress Seen Pushing for Stimulus Plan," *New York Times*, January 12, 2008).[17]

So, despite important partisan and ideological differences with the structure of a stimulus plan, the House of Representatives quickly passed a $164 billion package that more or less hewed to the administration priorities. But the Democratic leadership of the Senate pushed for a much more extensive plan costing $204 billion, which included extensions of unemployment insurance, subsidies for home heating, and subsidies for the coal industry. Although the larger measure earned the support of eight Republican senators, including several in tough reelection situations, Democratic leaders failed to obtain cloture, and the measure failed (David Herzenhorn, "Senate G.O.P. Blocks Additions to Stimulus Bill," *New York Times*, February 7, 2008).[18] The Senate then passed a measure that tacked on payments to Social Security recipients and disabled veterans to the House bill and passed the measure 81 to 16. The House then adopted the Senate version 380 to 34 (Herszenhorn, "Congress Votes for a Stimulus of $168 Billion," *New York Times*, February 7, 2008). President Bush then signed the final $168 billion package.

Although an unusual level of bipartisanship (especially for the House) led to very quick passage of the first stimulus bill, the necessary political expedients may have minimized its effectiveness. The insistence on rebate checks rather than adjusted tax withholding meant that it was still several months before the money hit the economy.[19] Moreover, that the rebates came in the form of income tax credits rather than offsets to payroll taxes meant that many low-income Americans, and those most likely to spend the refunds, did not receive assistance. The lack of aid to states and support for unemployment extensions also allowed the financial situation of states and the unemployed to deteriorate. Moreover, the specter that the bill might be used to make the Bush tax cuts permanent meant that durable changes in tax law that might have had strong economic effects were off the table (Steven Weisman and Edmund Andrews, "Economists Debate the Quickest Cure," *New York Times*, January 19, 2008).

The bill heralded the end of bipartisan cooperation on fiscal stimulus. As the elections of 2008 approached, Democrats increasingly called for a second round of stimulus, and Republicans were just as adamant in their resistance. The shape of the next fiscal program would be determined by the presidential and congressional elections of the fall. The partisan debate followed the traditional ideological pattern. John McCain and the Republicans argued that any future stimulus ought to focus on personal and business income tax cuts by making the Bush era tax cuts permanent, and Barack Obama and the Democrats argued for more spending targeted to the low-income, the unemployed, and struggling homeowners. The Democrats also stressed the need to boost infrastructure spending by funding *shovel-ready projects*.

After Barack Obama won the election in November, many thought that he might encourage a lame duck congressional session to take up debate on stimulus measures. But it was determined that any such measures might be limited by opposition from President Bush. Consequently, stimulus legislation was not taken up until the new Congress reconvened in January, and the expectation was that passage would not occur until after inauguration.[20]

Although President Obama campaigned on behalf of a $175 billion stimulus plan, spiraling job losses and cuts in production suggested that a much more expensive package would be necessary. By the end of November, Democratic leaders were pushing for a package closer to $300 billion.

By December, the target number had reached $600 billion, and some economists, both Democrat and Republican, argued that the package should be twice that large.

Several factors complicated the formulation of the American Economic Recovery and Investment Act. The first is that the urgency of the situation and the exigencies of a presidential transition—much of the economic team was not yet in place—made it impossible to formulate an administration proposal—Congress would have to write the proposal itself. This would open the door to funding many congressional pet projects that were hard to justify on purely macroeconomic grounds. But in some sense, the loading up of pork was unavoidable. Most economists were pushing for a very large number, and the money had to be spent on something. This outcome, however, helped foster an image of the new administration as fiscally undisciplined.

The congressionally led process also undermined any hopes that the Obama administration had for a bipartisan pact with the Republicans. Such cooperation was considered important both because Obama had promised to foster a "postpartisan" environment in Washington and because it would have better insulated him against charges of pursuing a left-wing agenda.

By January, the size of the proposed package had reached $775 billion and grew to $825 billion by the end of the month. But it remained much smaller than what even some Republican economists were advocating. This advocacy seems to have had little effect on Republican politicians, however. Moreover, fissures within the Democratic Party emerged over the size of the tax cut provisions relative to social spending and investment on infrastructure (Peter Baker and David Herszenhorn, "Senate Allies Fault Obama on Stimulus," *New York Times*, January 8, 2009). For their part, the Republicans began to attack the program as too large and too light on tax cuts. Concerns about deficits and debt began to be expressed openly by Republicans and some moderate Democrats.

The largest hurdle that the stimulus bill had to overcome was the sixty vote cloture requirement in the Senate. Any successful bill would require the support of all the Democrats, independent Joe Lieberman, and at least two Republican senators. The most obvious candidates for crossing over were the moderate Republicans Olympia Snow (Maine), Susan Collins (Maine), and Arlen Specter (Pennsylvania). These three were lobbied intensively by the administration as well as the Republican leadership. The major stumbling block became the overall size of the package. The moderate Republicans and Lieberman supported cloture on an $838 billion Senate package, but insisted that they would support no final bill with a price tag greater than $800 billion. To get the bill under this cap, House and

Senate negotiators agreed to slash $25 billion from a proposed state fiscal stabilization fund, eliminate a $16 billion line item for school construction, and reduce money for health insurance for the unemployed (David Herszenhorn and Carl Hulse, "Deal Reached in Congress on $789 Billion Stimulus Plan," *New York Times*, February 11, 2009).

The roll call voting divisions on stimulus exactly mirror the ideological conflicts that prevailed before the crisis. In the final passage vote in the House, the package was opposed by all of the Republicans and six Democrats. Five of the six Democratic defectors were among the Democrats with the most conservative ideal points. In the Senate, all the Democrats and the three moderate Republicans made up the filibuster-proof majority.

On signing the $787 billion package, Obama did not rule out a second stimulus package (Sheryl Gay Stolberg, "Signing Stimulus, Obama Doesn't Rule Out More," *New York Times*, February 17, 2009). But public support for the package was never very strong. At the time of passage, a bare majority supported its passage.[21] But strong majorities felt that tax cuts rather than spending increases were the most effective part of the package.[22]

When joblessness failed to decline, the Recovery Act not only fell in popularity, but voters increasingly split on partisan lines. But, most important, independent voters who had been crucial to Obama's election began to accept the Republican narrative that the stimulus package had harmed the economy. Table 7.1 provides partisan breakdowns for two questions asked in July of 2009:

So far, do you think the government's stimulus package has made the economy better, made the economy worse, or has it had no impact on the economy so far?

In the long run, do you think the government's stimulus package will make the economy better, will make the economy worse, or will it have no impact on the economy in the long run?

The polls also found that 65 percent of the public opposed a new stimulus package, and strong majorities prioritized deficit reduction.[23] As public opinion turned against further stimulus, the difficulty of selling a new package to moderate Democrats, especially those facing tough reelections in 2010, increased (Sewall Chan, "Democrats Are at Odds on Relevance of Keynes," *New York Times*, October 18, 2010). Consequently, the administration rejected calls from the left for a second round of fiscal expansion.

But some individual elements of the stimulus package were modestly popular with voters, especially the extension of unemployment benefits.

Table 7.1   Public Opinion on the Effects of the Stimulus Plan

July 24–28, 2009	Better	Worse	No Impact
Overall – so far	24.7	12.5	57.3
Overall – future	44.3	21.9	28.1
Republican – so far	15.1	26.2	51.6
Democrat – so far	35.6	3.7	55.5
Independent – so far	22.0	12.4	61.0
Republican – long run	22.7	37.4	33.7
Democrat – long run	59.7	10.2	25.6
Independent – long run	44.1	22.2	6.6

Source: Author's compilation based on CBS News/New York Times (2009).

So the administration strategy shifted from a focus on macroeconomic stimulus to targeted social and infrastructure spending as well as tax breaks designed to subsidize job creation.[24] But even these more modest approaches were contentious. A bill to extend unemployment benefits was filibustered in the Senate for several weeks. The bill passed only when newly elected Republican Scott Brown switched his vote in favor.

Assessing the extent to which ideology and polarization inhibited the U.S. fiscal response is somewhat complicated. The United States did have one of the largest discretionary stimulus bills among developed economies (see chapter 11, this volume). But a conclusion that this implies that its highly polarized political environment did not impede its response is premature. First, because the financial crisis that precipitated the worldwide recession was focused on the United States, one would expect the need for a compensatory fiscal response to be higher, ceterus paribus. Second, although political constraints were important in the United States, economic and financial ones were less so. The status of the dollar as the international reserve currency and the flight to the security of U.S. treasuries make deficit spending much cheaper in the United States. Moreover, unlike Europe, the United States is unencumbered by a commitment to a common currency. Third, the $787 billion price tag vastly overstates the stimulative effect of the bill. Much of the package was used to offset declines in state and local spending.[25] Many provisions in the package would have passed as standalone legislation. For example, 10 percent of the package was an adjustment to the Alternative Minimum Tax that Congress has repeatedly made over the past decade. As even the president now admits, the infrastructure spending was very delayed in getting into the economy.[26] Finally, the size of the U.S. package needed to be larger because it was delayed for several months because of the presidential election and transition. By comparison, most of the other stimulus packages in the OECD were passed in November 2008. Ultimately, the size, delay, and composition of the stimulus bill limited its impact. Robert Hall (2010) estimates that the stimulus package reduced GDP shortfall during the recession by 2 percent from 10.2 percent to 8.2 percent.[27]

In summary, the U.S. fiscal response to the crisis was affected in very important ways by the ideological and constituency structure of the party system. Modest bipartisanship was possible at the beginning of the recession, but the window for cooperation closed quickly as the crisis deepened and the election neared. A quick and coherent response was undermined both by the divergent ideological commitments across the parties and divisions within the Democratic Party.

U.S. Financial Market Reform

The financial reform effort began in earnest in June 2009 when the administration released an eighty-nine-page outline of its reform priorities. The plan focused on four major areas: the creation of a Financial Services Oversight Council that would help coordinate regulatory agencies and provide macroprudential oversight, a modest revamping of the structure of banking regulation, enhancement of the government's ability to take over and unwind failed financial firms, and the creation of a new regulatory structure for consumer and investor protection. The proposal was immediately attacked from the left and right ends of the ideological spectrum.

The criticism from the left focused on what was missing. In particular, the administration had not proposed doing enough to rein in the executive compensation practices that many felt were responsible for excessive risk taking. Moreover, the administration's proposal was seen as taking a light touch in terms of regulating derivative and securitization markets. The proposal also did little to reform credit rating agencies whose AAA certifications of subprime securitizations helped trigger the crisis.

Conservatives focused on two aspects. The first was just a general opposition to more regulation especially in the area of consumer and investor protection. The second was the fear that the creation of a resolution pool for unwinding failed financial firms would perpetuate moral hazard and lead to more government bailouts. One area where left and right converged was in the criticism of the expanded role of the Federal Reserve, which the left blamed for ignoring the crisis and the right blamed for being too quick with bailouts.

House and Senate committees began work on legislation in the autumn of 2009. Despite concerns that progressives in the House would try to pull the bill to the left, the bill that emerged from the House Financial Services committee hewed very closely to the administration's blueprint. When the bill came to the floor, the two most substantial amendments came from Bark Stupak (D-MI) to tighten rules for central clearing of derivative contracts and for securitization. These amendments were supported overwhelmingly by the left wing of the Democratic Party and allowed those members to go on the record as supporting much more stringent regulation of Wall Street. Ultimately, House Bill 4173 passed on December 11 by a vote of 223 to 203. All Republicans voted against the bill, as did twenty-seven Democrats. Not surprisingly, the Democratic defectors were much more heavily concentrated in the moderate wing, as measured by NOMINATE scores. Some liberal members did oppose the bill, however, for not going far enough.

The main Senate proposal was unveiled in November 2009. Senate Banking Chairman Christopher Dodd proposed sweeping changes in the power of the Federal Reserve to regulate banks. The Fed would be left with very little role in consumer protection and systemic risk regulation. Consequently, the Dodd proposal was seen as considerably more ambitious than the administration proposal or the House bill. Presumably, Dodd and his staff may have felt, however, that the bill would appeal to the populist, anti-Fed Republicans.[28]

But Republican opposition to Dodd's original plan was substantial. Following Scott Brown's victory in the special Senate election in Massachusetts, it became clear that some Republican support would be necessary to secure the sixty votes needed for cloture. Consequently, Senator Chris Dodd spent several weeks trying to negotiate with some of the panel's Republican members in hopes of securing some level of bipartisanship. After negotiations with the ranking minority member Richard Shelby (AL) collapsed, Senator Dodd engaged Senator Robert Corker of Tennessee. The primary sticking point in these negotiations was the structure of the proposed Consumer Financial Protection Agency (CFPA). Backers of the CFPA insisted that for the agency to be effective, it must be fully independent and have full rulemaking and enforcement power. Republican opponents wanted any new powers vested in an existing agency, preferably the Federal Reserve. But these negotiations also collapsed.

Senator Dodd unveiled his final plan on March 15. In many ways, the plan moved much closer to the House bill and scaled back many of its earlier provisions. It adopted some Republican demands in the hopes of ultimately attracting GOP support but it did include the so-called Volcker Rule banning proprietary trading by deposit-taking banks (Brady Dennis, "Sen. Dodd to Introduce Plan to Overhaul Financial Regulatory System," *Washington Post*, March 15, 2010; Sewall Chan, "Reform Bill Adds Layers of Oversight," *New York Times*, March 16, 2010; Binyamin Applebaum, "Six Key Points of the Financial Regulation Legislation," *Washing-*

ton Post, March 16, 2010). Such a prescription had been pushed by former Federal Reserve chair Paul Volcker, but it was not endorsed by the administration until earlier 2010. It appears that this endorsement was at least in part due to criticism from the left that the administration's proposals were toothless.

The Senate version moved in a considerably pro-regulation direction when a measure backed by Arkansas Democrat Blanche Lincoln was added to the bill. Lincoln's provision called for the largest commercial banks to spin off their lucrative derivatives trading operations (Brady Dennis, "Sen. Blanche Lincoln's Derivatives-Spinoff Plan Gains Support in Congress," *Washington Post*, June 15, 2010; Binyamin Applebaum, "Lawmakers at Impasse on Trading," *New York Times*, June 23, 2010; Edward Wyatt, "Veto Threat Raised Over Derivatives," *New York Times*, April 16, 2010). Initially, the proposal engendered opposition not only among Republicans but also the administration and Democrats from New York.

Passage of the Senate Bill occurred on May 20. To obtain cloture, three Republican senators, Susan Collins and Olympia Snowe of Maine and Scott Brown of Massachusetts, supported the bill to offset the opposition of Democrats Russ Feingold and Maria Cantwell, who opposed the bill for not going far enough. Charles Grassley opposed cloture but voted for the final bill.

House and Senate conferees worked over the next month to iron out the differences between the two versions of the bill. Negotiations focused on three key areas. The first was whether automobile dealerships would be covered by the new consumer protection agency as called for by the Senate. Senate Democrats yielded to moderate Democrats in the House and agreed to exclude auto dealers from the authority of the new consumer protection agency. The second concerned the Volcker Rule. Here it was agreed that that banks would be barred from making some kinds of investment, but still could invest up to 3 percent of their equity in hedge and private equity funds. Finally, negotiators watered down Senator Lincoln's derivative provisions by allowing banks to trade some common and relatively safe derivatives. It required, however, that speculative trading must be done through a separately funded subsidiary.

Almost all of the key decisions moved the reforms in a more conservative direction from the Senate version. Because cloture had been obtained on the Senate version the previous month, it is likely that many of these concessions were unnecessary to obtain passage of the conference report. Rather, the changes in conference reflected disagreements among Democrats about how aggressively to reform the financial sector.

The pattern of voting on the Dodd-Frank conference report in the House very much mirrors the vote on the original House plan except that two Republicans supported the bill on final passage. But the patterns of Democratic opposition remained the same: some moderate Democrats defected because the bill went too far and some liberal-populists attacked it for not going far enough. But the effects of Democratic defections in the House were minor.

The same cannot be said of Democratic defections in the Senate. The vote on the Senate conference report reflected an almost perfect liberal-conservative split. The NOMINATE model makes only two errors: predicting that Scott Brown (R-MA) would oppose and that Russ Feingold (D-WI) would support the bill. Feingold's defection had important consequences for the shape of the bill. Because of his opposition and refusal to vote for cloture, a third Republican vote, in the person of Scott Brown, was needed.

Promoting Brown into this pivotal position occasioned a significant change to the bill. One of the provisions to come out of the House-Senate conference was a levy on large financial firms to pay for the costs of financial regulation. This provision was quickly dubbed a bank tax. As a result, Brown, who had supported the earlier Senate version, began to waver. The provision not only ran counter to his ideological opposition to anything resembling a tax increase, but would have been costly to large financial firms in Brown's home state (David Herzenhorn, "Bank Tax Is Dropped in Overhaul of Industry," *New York Times*, June 30, 2010).

In the aftermath of the death of Senator Robert Byrd, a defection by Brown would necessitate picking up both Democrats who had opposed the original Senate bill, Feingold and Washington's Maria Cantwell. Cantwell came around, Feingold did not, and the bank tax was removed to get Brown's vote. As a result, $19 billion in costs were shifted from the banks to the taxpayer. Feingold performed the legislative equivalent of voting for Nader in Florida in the 2000 presidential election: standing on principle only to get an outcome he could not possibly have wanted (Nolan McCarty, Keith Poole, Thomas Romer, and Howard Rosenthal, "The Price of Principle," *Huffington Post*, July 20, 2010). The bill was signed by President Obama on July 21, 2010.

Again cross-national comparisons are of limited value in assessing the constraining effect of ideology, institutions, and interests in financial reform. In some areas, the regulatory responses of Europe and Japan were similar or a bit less extensive than those of the United States. Consider the regulation of over-the-counter (OTC) derivatives. The Dodd-Frank bill requires central clearance and exchange trading for almost all derivatives contracts but provides exemptions to nonfinancial firms who use derivatives for hedging purposes. The European Commission's rules unveiled in mid-September 2010 followed almost exactly the same blueprint, generally requiring central clearance or exchange trading but subject to exemptions very similar to those in Dodd-Frank. At this point, however, it is difficult to say whether the similar outcomes were driven by similar political pressures or whether the EC simply succumbed to the need to eliminate opportunities for regulatory arbitrage.

In other areas, outcomes diverged. France, Germany, and Britain have instituted or are considering instituting taxes on financial transactions and institutions designed to curtail risk taking behavior (Dealbook, "France, Germany, Britain Support Bank Tax," *New York Times*, June 22, 2010; Patrick Jenkins, " New Taxes to Slash European Bank Profits," *Financial Times*, January 11, 2011). In the United States, similar proposals made little headway and, as discussed, even a modest bank tax was killed, by Feingold and Brown. Other countries, most notably Britain, made much more significant reforms to their regulatory structures than the United States did. Dodd-Frank also left compensation practices in the financial sector relatively intact as other nations moved more aggressively to tax or regulate bankers' bonuses.

Although the international comparisons are not particularly informative, a historical one might be. Franklin Roosevelt took office in 1933 in the midst of both a depression and a financial crisis. His House majority was considerably larger than Obama's (313 to 257) and he had the same Senate majority, but the cloture requirement was two-thirds rather than the current provision of three-fifths. Despite these similarities in context, Roosevelt was more successful in reforming the financial sector during his first two years in office. The achievements include:

- the Emergency Banking Act
- the joint resolution nullifying gold clauses in bond contracts
- the Glass-Steagall Act, which separated commercial and investment banking and created deposit insurance
- the Securities Act of 1933
- the Securities Exchange Act of 1934, which created the SEC

So what explains the differences in outcome? A first explanation might be that the financial sector was much more politically influential in 2009 than in 1933. After all the reforms in 1933 came in year four of a financial slump rather than year two. The prolonged crisis may have weakened the clout of the financial industry whereas U.S. banks were earning record profits by the time the ink dried on Dodd-Frank. The public image of the industry was harmed by evidence of malfeasance produced by the Pecora

Commission.[29] But other indicators suggest that the financial industry was still a political force. Philippon and Reshef's data on financial wages suggest that the premium to finance did not peak until 1936. So the industry's relative economic position seems not to have deteriorated before the New Deal reforms were enacted. Moreover, the influence of finance on the Democratic Party seems to be roughly similar. The Obama administration has been criticized for close ties to Wall Street, and FDR relied heavily on financiers such as Bernard Baruch, Joseph Kennedy, and Herbert Lehman. Campaign finance records from the pre-disclosure era are sketchy, but evidence suggests that Roosevelt and the Democratic Party raised large sums from the financial sector in the 1932 election.[30]

The effects of the political clout of finance are unclear, but differences in polarization appear to be an important part of the story. By 1933, polarization had fallen to relatively low levels in both the House and the Senate (McCarty, Poole, and Rosenthal 2006). Consequently, much of the financial reform agenda passed with substantial bipartisan support. In the Senate, only five Republicans opposed the Emergency Banking Act and Republican senators voted 15 to 13 in favor of creating the Securities and Exchange Commission. Despite the party's long-held commitment to hard money, ten Republican senators supported the Gold Reserve Act. Despite vociferous lobbying against it by the banks, the Glass-Steagall Banking Act passed the House 191 to 6 and the Senate on a voice vote.

To the extent that there were disputes about financial reform, they tended to revolve around cleavages within the financial sector. Consider Glass-Steagall. By the time it passed, its most controversial provision was not the separation of commercial and investment banking, but provisions for deposit insurance. The original exclusion of state chartered banks led Huey Long to filibuster the bill for twenty-one days—the pre–Strom Thurmond record.[31] At the same time, conservative Republican Arthur Vanderberg successfully amended the bill to speed up the creation of the insurance fund, provoking a veto threat from FDR whose Republican Treasury Secretary William Woodin opposed deposit insurance ("Roosevelt Warns Against Bank Bill," *New York Times*, June 5, 1933; FDIC 1984). So, unlike the divisions over Dodd-Frank, the conflicts were not structured so heavily around party and ideology. This lack of structure facilitated the compromises necessary to move the legislation forward. Such opportunities were limited in 2010.

THE LAME DUCK SESSION

In the elections of November 2010, the Democrats lost sixty-three House seats along with their majority and narrowly maintained control of the

Senate after losing six seats. These losses have been attributed in part to the adverse reaction of voters, especially independents, to the party's response to the crisis. In districts where John McCain received more than 45 percent of the vote in 2008, 75 percent of Democratic House members who voted for the stimulus bill lost reelection (46 of 61). But of those five who voted against, three were reelected.[32]

Even with the healthy partisan majorities it held through 2009 and 2010, the Obama administration had been unable to expand upon its 2009 efforts at stimulus or to provide an extension of unemployment benefits. After the election, it found itself in a much more difficult bargaining situation. The pending loss of House control and trimming of its Senate majority meant that these agenda items would have to be taken up in a lame duck session. Thus Democratic legislators would be called upon to move on many of the same policies that the voters had appeared to repudiate. There was also of course pressure to avoid the across-the-board tax increases that would result from the expiration of the Bush-era tax cuts on December 31. The administration had pledged to keep the tax cuts for families making less than $250,000 and let the rest expire. This approach, they argued, balanced the need to avoid tax increases in a recession with the goal of adding progressivity to the tax structure to offset growing economic inequality.

The Republicans also faced a difficult situation. The party has a long-standing commitment to making the Bush cuts permanent at all income levels. If they let the tax cuts expire, they would have little hope of restoring them in the upcoming congressional term. So the lame duck became a game of chicken.

But rather than push the dispute to the brink, the Obama administration reached out to Republican leaders to fashion a compromise. But given the polarized environment, finding a middle ground on each of the issues—tax cuts, unemployment insurance, and other stimulus—would be impossible. So the underlying principle of the compromise was to trade on differences in issue salience so that each side could get what it most valued and give on other issues.[33] The Republicans procured an extension of all of the tax cuts, albeit for only two years. The Republicans also received a favorable deal on the provisions for the estate tax with a higher exemption and lower rate than would have prevailed without the legislation.[34] The Democrats got fiscal stimulus and relief measures targeted at low-income and unemployed workers. The employee contribution to Social Security was reduced from 6.2 percent to 4.2 percent for a year and $57 billion was appropriated for extended unemployment benefits (David Herszenhorn, "Congress Sends $801 Billion Tax Cut Bill to Obama," *New York Times*, December 17, 2010).

Reflecting the nature of a compromise of this sort, the opposition to the plan came from the ideological extremes of both parties. Progressives were particularly upset with the extension of tax cuts for high-income families and the estate tax provisions. Some even expressed concern that the payroll tax deductions would undermine the Social Security system. Conservatives were similarly dismayed to not get a more permanent extension of the tax cuts and that the extension of unemployment benefits would contribute to the deficit.[35]

Ultimately, polarization did not lead to gridlock—but it may have led to something far worse. Instead of a compromise that provided targeted stimulus and a transition to a more efficient, fair, and certain tax code, the bill increased the deficit by almost $900 billion while pushing off the date of reckoning to the shadows of the 2012 election.

CONCLUSIONS

Rather than restructure the American political economy, the financial crisis highlighted its dominant features. First, the crisis appeared to do little to change the distribution of beliefs among elected leaders about free markets and the role of government intervention. Although some leading figures like Alan Greenspan and Barney Frank may now have regrets about the positions that their ideologies led, various camps in the economic policy debates are as entrenched as much as before.

Ideological rigidity and polarization limited the policy response in many important ways. On fiscal policy, the government response became quickly ensnared in age-old partisan divisions over tax cuts, social spending, public investment, and deficits. To borrow a phrase from the former White House Chief of Staff Rahm Emanuel, neither side wanted to let a crisis go to waste. In 2008, Republicans sought to use the incipient recession to make the Bush tax cuts permanent. In 2009, Democrats wanted to use the crisis to make big investments in infrastructure and alternative energy. In the end, despite polarization, both sides got some of what they wanted—sort of. Although some have heralded the compromise as a triumph of bipartisanship, it is not the kind of bipartisanship likely to produce comprehensive solutions that balance the short run need to increase employment with the long-term imperative to control deficits.[36]

On financial regulation, ideology and polarization in combination with internal debates within the Democratic Party had a profound impact on the final outcome. At every stage, the scale and scope of the reform depended on the exact degree of intervention that the sixtieth senator would tolerate. But even if it were not for the filibuster, the pro-finance tendencies of moderate Democrats and the administration itself meant that many more fundamental reforms were never considered. The Dodd-Frank bill regulates the finance industry more or less as it existed before the crisis. None of the reforms designed to shrink the size of individual financial firms or the industry itself, such as a new firewall between commercial and investment banking, was ever on the agenda. Reforms that might have modestly reshaped the industry, such as the Volcker Rule or the ban on derivative dealing by banks, were vastly watered down or left to future regulatory rulemaking where they might be eviscerated by the finance industry lobbyists.

Finally, those who thought the crisis might fundamentally alter the social contract or patterns of economic power must be sorely disappointed. As might be predicted by Larry Bartels (2008) or Martin Gilens (2011), the modicum of policy responsiveness during the crisis was responsiveness to the interests of middle and higher-income citizens. The only major provision that may materially benefit lower-income and poor Americans is the new Consumer Financial Protection Agency. Of course, even that benefit is not a given. Once the politics of rulemaking at the CFPA begins, a revitalized financial services industry will be a formidable player. But even if the CFPA is not undercut by finance lobbyists, new rules and regulations may dry up credit to the poor. Financial reform is also unlikely to have any major impact on incomes at the top. CEO compensation is very closely related to firm size, and Dodd-Frank did little to shrink the size of financial firms. It is doubtful that nonbinding shareholder resolutions on executive compensation, the so-called say-on-pay provisions, will have much of an impact on compensation practices.

NOTES

1. This chapter is based on ongoing collaborations with Keith Poole, Howard Rosenthal, and Tom Romer.

2. In the current era of polarization some aspects of housing policy were bipartisan exceptions. It is important, however, to remember that the objectives each party brought to the issue were quite polarized. Had a centrist position prevailed on each of these objectives, housing policy would have been quite different.

3. Many analysts agree that ultimately the GSEs in the subprime market played only a limited direct role in the housing and credit crises. Yet the GSEs participation in that market may well have added legitimacy to the huge expansion of this market and the unsavory practices of mortgage lenders. This debate is well documented in the majority report and dissent of the Financial Crisis Inquiry Commission (*The Financial Crisis Inquiry Report*, January 2011, http://www.fcic.gov/report).

4. McCarty, Poole, and Rosenthal (2006) report these measures only through

2005, but unreported calculations by the author indicate that predictive success of the ideological model continued to grow through the end of 2010.

5. The explanatory power of the ideological model has increased in part because positions on racial and social issues have become more like the divisions on economic issues, not the other way around (but see Carmines and Stimson 1989; Mendelberg 2001).

6. Even here, however, there are differences. Consider California Democrats Diane Feinstein and Barbara Boxer. They not only represent the same state but were first elected by exactly the same electorate on the same day in 1992. In the most recent senate term, Boxer has an ideology score of −0.601 making her the third most liberal member of the U.S. Senate. Conversely, Dianne Feinstein's ideal point is just −0.384, making her the thirty-seventh most liberal (for evidence of the wide ideological latitude House members have in representing their districts, see Poole and Romer 1993).

7. The act also created the National Monetary Commission whose reports became the basis of the Federal Reserve Act.

8. The large swings in polarization over the course of the past 140 years might appear to contradict the previous discussion about ideological rigidity. Most of the changes in polarization, however, are generated by electoral turnover and replacement, rather than by the repositioning of incumbent politicians. In other words, polarization has been increasing because each entering cohort of legislators is more polarized than the departing cohort. These cohort changes reflect changes in voter beliefs and interests as well as changing in the mobilization of ideological and interest groups.

9. A standard measure for the propensity for legislative gridlock is the distance between the ideal point of a Senator pivotal for overriding veto and the ideal point of the senator pivotal for invoking cloture (see Krehbiel 1998). McCarty (2007) shows that 75 percent of the variance in this measure is attributable to changes in party polarization.

10. This financial wage premium is also a major determinant of the overall level of income inequality in the United States.

11. The correlation of financial wages and polarization ten years prior is 0.90.

12. Clearly, polarization is not the only factor that produced gridlock on financial market reform. Informational asymmetries between the regulators and the industry also made it difficult for policies to keep up with innovations (for more discussion on this point, see McCarty, Poole, Romer, and Rosenthal 2010).

13. *Openscrets*, http://www.opensecrets.org (accessed April 23, 2012).

14. Lawyers and law firms contributed $126 million in 2008. A big chunk of these contributors may also have had interests in financial industry regulation.

15. Iverson and Soskice's argument and its varieties of capitalism logic do have

limitations, however. First, substantial financial liberalization occurred in both liberal market and coordinated market economies. So a dominant financial sector does not appear to be a necessary condition for financial liberalization or deregulation. Second, within the United States, financial deregulation took place alongside the deregulation of many sectors such as transportation and energy. In many of these instances, deregulation occurred not because the regulated sector was dominant but because it was being strongly challenged by unregulated competitors within the same industry, such as when bank account interest rates were deregulated in the 1980s to level the playing field between commercial banks and money market mutual funds. So the comparative institutional logic does not do a good job of accounting for the specifics of deregulation in the United States.

16. Ideally, one would like to be able to assign weights to the explanatory power of each of these factors. Unfortunately, this really is not possible in this episode. I would argue that each of these factors played a crucial role at some critical juncture in the response to the financial crisis.

17. Pay-as-you-go rules allow for points of order against spending proposals that are not funded by increased tax revenues or offsetting spending cuts.

18. Some observers suggested that Senate Majority Leader Harry Reid's main rationale for pushing the bigger program was to put Republican senators on record for opposing specific provisions in an election year.

19. By contrast, the personal tax cuts in the 2009 stimulus package were implemented through changes in the withholding schedule. But this mechanism seems to have denied President Obama political credit for the cuts (Michael Cooper, "From Obama, the Tax Cut Nobody Heard of," *New York Times*, October 18, 2010).

20. This resulted in the United States implementing a stimulus program several months after most other nations had done so.

21. CBS News/*New York Times* Poll, February 2–4, 2009. Available at: http://webapps.ropercenter.uconn.edu/CFIDE/cf/action/ipoll/abstract.cfm?keyword=&keywordoptions=1&exclude=&excludeoptions=1&topic=Any&organization=CBS+News&fromdate=02%2F01%2F2009&todate=02%2F28%2F2009&sortby=DESC&label=&archno=USCBS2009-02A&start=summary&abstract.x=19&abstract.y=10&abstract=abstract (accessed April 23, 2012).

22. CBS News/*New York Times* Poll, February 2–4, 2009. In response to "In your opinion which will do more to get the U.S. out of the current recession: increasing government spending, or reducing taxes?" only 16 percent said increase spending while 63 percent favored lower taxes.

23. CBS News/*New York Times* Poll, July 24–28, 2009. Available at: http://webapps.ropercenter.uconn.edu/CFIDE/cf/action/ipoll/abstract.cfm?keyword=&keywordoptions=1&exclude=&excludeoptions=1&topic=Any&organiza

tion=CBS+News&fromdate=07%2F24%2F2009&todate=07%2F31%2F2009
&sortby=DESC&label=&archno=USCBSNYT2009-07B&start=summary
&abstract.x=10&abstract.y=12&abstract=abstract (accessed April 23, 2012).

24. Sheryl Gay Stolberg, "Obama Calls Jobs Bill a First Step," *New York Times*, March 18, 2010; Jackie Calmes, "Obama to Propose Tax Write-off for Business," *New York Times*, September 6, 2010; "Obama Pushes Transportation Spending," *New York Times*, October 11, 2010.

25. Hall calculates that by the first quarter of 2010, total purchases by federal, state, and local governments had fallen around $25 billion below its trend level (2010).

26. Of course, other countries' packages may be overstated in a variety of ways as well. But it is beyond the scope of this chapter to sort out.

27. Estimates by the Congressional Budget Office are in the same ball park (2010).

28. Seventeen such Republicans voted against the reconfirmation of Chairman Bernanke in January 2010.

29. Of course, there were no shortage of damaging allegations against the industry in 2009 and 2010; the most politically important was the SEC case against Goldman Sachs over its Abacus mortgage-backed CDOs.

30. In the 1928 and 1932 elections, the Democratic National Committee received nearly 25 percent of its funds from "bankers and brokers." The Republican National Committee received approximately the same share from these sources (Overacker 1932). In retaliation against the New Deal reforms of their industry, this percentage fell to 3.3 percent in 1936 (Overacker 1937).

31. Senator Glass charged, however, that Long was doing the bidding of the New York bankers ("Glass Links Banks to Attack by Long," *New York Times*, December 6, 1933).

32. Because so few Democrats voted against the stimulus bill, caution is warranted in making comparisons with votes on other aspects of the Democratic agenda. But despite its salience, the vote on health care reform seems to have had a much more modest impact. Of Democratic health care supporters in the 45+ percent McCain districts, nineteen of thirty won reelection whereas thirty of thirty-six opponents did—a differential of only 20 percent. The relationship between the vote on Dodd-Frank and reelection in these districts is of a similar magnitude.

33. This is not unlike the structure of the unfortunate logroll over housing policy that aided the crisis.

34. Technically, the estate tax had been repealed in 2010, so establishing any estate tax was a departure from the Republican goal of extending all the tax cuts and not raising taxes in a recession. Nevertheless, liberal Democrats were especially incensed about the high exemption and low rates. Consequently, they forced a vote on an amendment to strike the estate tax provisions, which,

had it been successful, might have unraveled the compromise (see Paul Sullivan, "Estate Tax Will Return Next Year, but Few Will Pay It," *New York Times*, December 17, 2010).

35. The progressive opposition was somewhat more pronounced than that of the conservatives. Of the House members in the most liberal quartile, 71 percent opposed the compromise but only 25 percent of the most conservative quartile opposed it. Support was highest among moderate Republicans in the third quartile, 88 percent of whom supported the bill.

36. The lame duck achievements of the repeal of the Don't Ask, Don't Tell policy toward gay military service and the ratification of the Strategic Arms Reduction treaty are more clearly bipartisan achievements.

REFERENCES

Bartels, Larry. 2008. *Unequal Democracy: The Political Economy of the New Gilded Age.* Princeton, N.J.: Princeton University Press.

Boehner, John. 2009. "Comments on Fox News Sunday, July 5, 2009." Available at: http://mediamatters.org/mobile/research/200907050004 (accessed July 3, 2011).

Brady, David W., and Craig Volden. 2005. *Revolving Gridlock: Politics and Policy from Jimmy Carter to George W. Bush,* 2nd ed. Boulder, Colo.: Westview Press.

Carmines, Edward G., and James A. Stimson. 1989. *Issue Evolution: Race and the Transformation of American Politics* Princeton, N.J.: Princeton University Press.

CBS News/*New York Times*. 2009. "CBS News/*New York Times* Poll: Economy/ Health Care Reform, July 24–28, 2009." Available at: http://webapps.roper center.uconn.edu/CFIDE/cf/action/ipoll/abstract.cfm?keyword=&keyword options=1&exclude=&excludeoptions=1&topic=Any&organization=CBS+News &fromdate=07%2F24%2F2009&todate=07%2F31%2F2009&sortby=DESC&label =&archno=USCBSNYT2009-07B&start=summary&abstract.x=10&abstract .y=12&abstract=abstract (accessed April 23, 2012).

Congressional Budget Office. 2010. "Estimated Impact of the American Recovery and Reinvestment Act on Employment and Economic Output from April 2010 Through June 2010." Washington, D.C.: Government Printing Office. Available at: http://www.cbo.gov/publication/21671 (accessed June 14, 2012).

Federal Deposit Insurance Corporation (FDIC). 1984. *The First Fifty: A History of the FDIC 1933–1983.* Available at: http://www.fdic.gov/bank/analytical/first fifty/ (accessed January 27, 2011).

Gelman, Andrew, Boris Shor, Joseph Bafumi, and David Park. 2007. "Rich State, Poor State, Red State, Blue State: What's the Matter with Connecticut?" *Quarterly Journal of Political Science* 2(4): 345–67.

Gilens, Martin. 2011. *Paying the Piper: Economic Inequality and Democratic Responsiveness in the United States.* Unpublished manuscript, Princeton University.

Hacker, Jacob, and Paul Pierson. 2010. *The Winner-Take-All Politics: How Washington Made the Rich Richer—and Turned Its Back on the Middle Class*. New York: Simon & Schuster.

Hall, Robert E. 2010. "Fiscal Stimulus." *Daedalus* 139(4): 83–94.

Krehbiel, Keith. 1998. *Pivotal Politics: A Theory of U.S. Lawmaking*. Chicago: University of Chicago Press.

McCarty, Nolan. 2007. "The Policy Consequences of Political Polarization." In *Transformations of American Politics: Activist Government and the Rise of Conservatism*, edited by Theda Skocpol and Paul Pierson. Princeton, N.J.: Princeton University Press.

McCarty, Nolan, Keith T. Poole, Thomas Romer, and Howard Rosenthal. 2010. "Political Fortunes: Of Finance and Its Regulation." *Daedelus* 139(4): 61–73.

McCarty, Nolan, Keith T. Poole, and Howard Rosenthal. 1997. *Income Redistribution and the Realignment of American Politics*. Washington, D.C.: American Enterprise Institute.

McCarty, Nolan, Keith T. Poole, and Howard Rosenthal. 2006. *Polarized America: The Dance of Ideology and Unequal Riches*. Cambridge, Mass.: MIT Press.

Mendelberg, Tali. 2001. *The Race Card: Campaign Strategy, Implicit Messages, and the Norm of Equality*. Princeton, N.J.: Princeton University Press.

Opensecrets. 2009. "Finance/Insurance/Real Estate." Available at: http://www.opensecrets.org/industries/indus.php?Ind=F (accessed April 23, 2012).

Overacker, Louise. 1932. *Money in Elections*. New York: Macmillan Press.

———. 1937. "Campaign Funds in the Presidential Election of 1936." *American Political Science Review* 31(3): 473–98.

Philippon, Thomas, and Ariell Reshef. 2009. "Wages and Human Capital in the U.S. Financial Industry: 1909–2006." *NBER* working paper 14644. Cambridge, Mass.: National Bureau of Economic Research.

Poole, Keith T., and Thomas Romer 1993. "Ideology, Shirking, and Representation." *Public Choice* 77(1): 185–96.

Poole, Keith T., and Howard Rosenthal. 1997. *Congress: A Political-Economic History of Roll Call Voting*. New York: Oxford University Press.

———. 2007. *Ideology & Congress*. New Brunswick, N.J.: Transaction Publishers.

Theriault, Sean M. 2008. *Party Polarization in Congress*. New York: Cambridge University Press.

U.S. Congress. House. 2008. "The Financial Crisis and the Role of Regulators: Hearing Before the Committee on Oversight and Government Reform." 111th Congress, 2nd sess., October 23.

Voteview.com. 2010. "Roll Call Data" [database]. Available at: http://voteview.com/downloads.asp#PARTYSPLITSDWNL (accessed April 23, 2012).

Chapter 8 | Politics and Policies in Two Economic Crises: The Nordic Countries

Johannes Lindvall

IN THE GREAT Recession, the deep economic downturn of 2008 to 2009, European governments adopted expansionary fiscal policies quickly, and with little apparent controversy. In December 2008, the member states of the European Union agreed on a European Economic Recovery Program, which included discretionary stimulus measures amounting to 1.5 percent of GDP. The program was implemented by national parliaments in the beginning of 2009. In February of that year—when the U.S. Congress passed the American Recovery and Reinvestment Act, containing $787 billion in tax cuts and spending increases over three years—the Bundestag approved a stimulus plan for Europe's largest economy, Germany. In April 2009, at a summit in London, the leaders of the G20 countries announced that they were undertaking an "unprecedented and concerted fiscal expansion" in order to avert an impending employment crisis (Corsetti et al. 2010, 7; compare chapters 4 and 5, this volume).

Eighty years earlier, in the Great Depression, democratic governments adopted expansionary fiscal policies gradually and hesitantly, if at all. Many political scientists, notably Peter Gourevitch (1984) and Margaret Weir and Theda Skocpol (1985), have sought to explain why only a few countries "broke with orthodoxy" in the Great Depression, to use Gourevitch's phrase, and why those that did did so little, relative to what one might have expected. The Great Recession offers us a new opportunity to examine national responses to a global economic shock, and, by comparing the Great Recession with the Great Depression, to identify some of the circumstances specific to each event.

One possible explanation for the differences between the 2000s and the 1930s is that governments learn from the past. Twenty-first-century politicians could look back to the Great Depression and apply the economic theories that it inspired, such as John Maynard Keynes's *General Theory* (1936). Christina Romer—the first chair of the Council of Economic Advisers under President Obama and a scholar of the Great Depression—said in 2009 that the economic downturn of 2008 and 2009 was directly comparable to the crisis of the 1930s, and that policymakers were able to avoid another depression because the lessons had been learned: "the shocks we have faced have been similar in the two episodes," Romer noted, "but the policy responses have been vastly different" (2009, 1).

My own analysis of macroeconomic policymaking in the 2000s and 1930s centers on the role of underlying conflicts over political-economic institutions. The main argument of this chapter is that politicians care more about the indirect political effects of economic policies than about the direct economic effects, which means that the adoption of expansionary programs requires broad agreement among pivotal decision-makers about important political-economic institutions, especially the labor market and the welfare state. To control, as far as possible, for confounding factors such as the influence of economic ideas and the magnitude of economic shocks, I concentrate on the Nordic countries, particularly Sweden, where Keynesian ideas were already established, *avant la lettre*, in the early 1930s, and where the Great Depression did not have the catastrophic effects on output and employment that it had in countries such as Germany and the United States.

The timeframe of the analysis is 1929 to 1933 and 2008 to 2010. In the early 1930s, politicians in Sweden and the other Nordic countries had strong reasons to believe that new programs for fiscal stimulus would have far-reaching political effects, which complicated interparty bargaining. In the 2000s, by contrast, fiscal policies were not discussed in those terms: political parties disagreed on the size and composition of stimulus packages, but they were not concerned about their indirect effects on institutions. This explains the willingness of the center-right governments that were in power in most of the Nordic countries at the time to adopt expansionary fiscal policies in the Great Recession.

POLITICAL CONFLICTS OVER ECONOMIC POLICIES

The explanation just outlined is informed by a general argument about the decision situations that politicians find themselves in when they consider which policies to adopt in economic downturns. The argument is primarily relevant to political systems with more than one veto player, such as multiparty systems and systems with constitutional power-sharing mechanisms that allow for divided government, because it is concerned with the potential for disagreement among political parties with some measure of influence over government policy. Moreover, the argument is mainly concerned with fiscal policy, especially with the adoption (or nonadoption) of countercyclical fiscal policies. This policy option was first "worked out" in the 1930s (Gourevitch 1986, 48), and was quickly recommended as a response to the 2008 to 2009 downturn by international economic organizations such as the International Monetary Fund (Spilimbergo et al. 2008; IMF 2009).

Consider four possible sources of disagreement on the adoption of expansionary fiscal policies in an economic downturn. The first type of disagreement originates in different beliefs about the effects of economic policies. This is the subject matter of a vast literature on the role of economic ideas (that is, collectively held beliefs about how the economy works) and the manner in which such ideas are developed, advocated, and institutionalized in different political systems (see, for example, Weir and Skocpol 1985; Hall 1989; Blyth 2002; Lindvall 2009; Mandelkern and Shalev 2010).

The second type of disagreement involves different preferences over macroeconomic outcomes. Many models of economic policymaking assume that political parties assign different priorities to goals such as employment, growth, and inflation. Douglas Hibbs's classic study of macroeconomic policy in advanced democracies, for example, is based on the idea that left- and right-wing parties have different preferences over these sorts of economic outcomes (1977, 1468–71). Similarly, the influential institutionalist literature that emerged in the 1980s and 1990s was based on the premise that wage bargaining systems and central banks matter to political outcomes since they influence the ability of governments to actually achieve low unemployment, high growth, and low inflation, which are what parties mainly care about (see especially Scharpf 1991; but see also Iversen 1999, part II, which suggests that parties are also motivated by preferences over institutions).

The third type of disagreement emerges from different preferences over the distributional profiles of stimulus packages. The stabilization, allocation, and redistribution functions of fiscal policy cannot be neatly separated in practical decision-making. By definition, expansionary fiscal policies involve either tax cuts or spending increases, or both, which introduces a distributional dimension in any fiscal policy decision, because taxing and spending decisions benefit particular groups of voters. When they wish to make fiscal policy more expansionary, parties on the left typically propose increased benefits to individuals or increased spending on public services, whereas parties on the right typically favor tax cuts, turning economic policy discourse into a familiar ideological struggle.

The fourth type of disagreement is based on different preferences over political-economic institutions. When governments seek to stimulate the economy by setting up new policy programs or making significant changes to existing programs, the adoption of expansionary fiscal policies shapes core institutions in the labor market or the social welfare system. Because many labor market programs and social policy programs are highly path dependent, such changes potentially contribute to the reallocation of income, wealth, and political power far beyond the next election.

One of the main conclusions that emerge from a comparison between the Great Recession and the Great Depression is how sensitive economic policymaking is to the fourth type of conflict described here. There are good reasons to expect both beliefs, preferences over economic outcomes, and short-term distributional politics to influence political conflicts over economic policies, but politicians are arguably more concerned with the long-term institutional effects of the policies they pursue than with any of these other things, and political parties are likely to have strong and diverging preferences over long-term institutional trajectories (Lindvall 2010, 11). Moreover, political conflicts that emerge from disagreements over institutions are particularly difficult to resolve, because institutional effects are difficult to predict, which means that risk-averse parties may prefer to maintain the status quo rather than agreeing to change institutional equilibria in ways that might do damage to their long-term political interests.

This argument suggests that expansionary fiscal policies should be most controversial, and hence most difficult for political parties to agree on, where basic political-economic institutions are contested and economic policies are expected to have indirect effects on how these institutions operate. I show that at least in Sweden and the other Nordic countries, these conditions were met in the early 1930s, but not in the late 2000s, explaining the nature of political debates in these two periods, and the choices that governments made.

THE GREAT DEPRESSION AND THE GREAT RECESSION

Comparing the 1930s and the 2000s is a risky enterprise. In the eighty years that passed between the Great Depression and the Great Recession, the world changed. Large welfare states were established. The relationship between financial markets and the real economy changed, and changed

Table 8.1 Total Fall in Output

	Great Depression	Great Recession
Sweden	−9.2	−5.8
Denmark	−2.6	−6.6
Finland	−6.5	−8.2
Norway	−7.8	−1.7
United States	−29.4	−3.9

Source: Author's compilation based on Maddison (1982, table A7) and OECD (2012).
Notes: The table, which is based on yearly GDP data, shows the total fall in output from the peak year before the crisis to the worst year of the crisis. The data from the 1930s and the data from the 2000s are not directly comparable since they are based on different GDP definitions.

again. The United States became the world's supreme economic and military power. In western Europe, representative democracy, far from a foregone conclusion in the 1930s, was institutionalized and consolidated. Finally, the increasing density of international economic institutions and organizations allowed governments in the Great Recession to overcome some of the collective action problems that typically plague the coordination of fiscal policies across borders (see chapter 3, this volume).

Yet the root causes of the Great Depression and the Great Recession were remarkably similar, which makes it very tempting for scholars of comparative political economy to compare the political responses to these two events (compare Gourevitch 1986, 221): in both periods, the crisis emerged in the United States, beginning as a financial crisis but turning into a full-blown macroeconomic crisis that involved a sharp fall in aggregate demand and output.

Economic Circumstances

Sweden has featured in many influential studies of the 1930s, making it especially interesting to compare the Swedish responses to Great Depression and the Great Recession (see, for example, Weir and Skocpol 1985; Gourevitch 1986). But Sweden and the other Nordic countries are also important test cases for another reason: economic and intellectual conditions in the 1930s and 2000s were relatively similar in these countries, and the variation in policy responses cannot be explained by party politics because the center-right governments of the 2000s were more willing to engage in stimulus than the center-left governments of the 1930s.

The figures in table 8.1 show that, with the exception of Denmark in the 1930s and Norway in the 2000s, where the effects were even smaller, the

Table 8.2   Peak Level of Unemployment

Country	Great Depression	Great Recession
Sweden	7.3	8.4
Denmark	16.0	7.5
Finland	6.2	8.4
Norway	10.2	3.5
United States	22.3	9.6

Source: Author's calculations based on Maddison (1982, table C6); OECD (2011, harmonized unemployment rates).

Notes: The table, which is based on yearly unemployment data, shows the highest level of unemployment (as a percentage of the labor force) during the two crises. The Danish figure for the Great Recession is based on the average of the first three quarters of 2011. It is difficult to estimate overall unemployment in the 1930s. Niels-Henrik Topp (2008) presents unemployment figures for Denmark that are significantly lower than those reported here. On the other hand, figures based on data from unemployment insurance funds suggest that unemployment among union members was higher than reported here.

total decline in economic output between the peak year before the crisis and the worst year of the crisis was in the range of 5 to 10 percent in the Nordic countries in both the 1930s and 2000s. This sets the Nordic countries apart from the United States, which is included for comparison and where, as table 8.1 shows, the Great Depression was an altogether different sort of event.

A similar pattern can be observed in the unemployment data in table 8.2, although the comparison is complicated by the difficulty of estimating unemployment rates in the 1930s. Judging from the figures in the table, rates in the 1930s were much higher in the United States than in northern Europe, where the Great Depression and the Great Recession were more similar. The increase in unemployment in the early 1930s was perhaps a more significant political event, but this was probably a result of the little social protection the unemployed had during the Great Depression, which meant that the human costs of unemployment were higher.

Economic Ideas

In both the Great Recession and the Great Depression, leading macroeconomists in Sweden and the other Nordic countries argued that the government should adopt expansionary fiscal policies, which means that the intellectual differences between the 2000s and 1930s were smaller in the Nordic countries than in most other advanced economies.

In the Great Recession, the chair of the Swedish Fiscal Policy Advisory Council, Lars Calmfors, began to advocate more expansionary fiscal policies already in the autumn of 2008 ("Orimligt med tystnadsplikt," *Affärsvärlden*, November 11, 2008), and in the spring of 2009, the council's annual report proposed a more expansionary policy than the government was then pursuing (Finanspolitiska rådet 2009). Nothing about this was unique: leading macroeconomists in most European countries—including Germany's traditionally conservative Sachverständigenrat—were also in favor of a fiscal stimulus in the 2008 to 2009 recession. Danish economists, for example, played a role similar to that of their Swedish colleagues in the first year of the crisis (Det økonomiske Råd 2009; Sørensen et al. 2009).

What is interesting about the Nordic countries, however, is that in the 1930s so many economists already advocated countercyclical fiscal policies, particularly through public works. In Sweden, this was the view of many members of the Stockholm School (Jonung 1991), such as the future Liberal Party leader Bertil Ohlin (Carlson and Jonung 2002) and Erik Lundberg, who noted some two decades after the depression that deficit spending and demand-oriented policies had long been accepted by Swedish economists (1953, 266–71). These ideas were not limited to academic circles. In their comparative study of economic policies in the 1930s, Margaret Weir and Theda Skocpol point out that the Swedish state was open to the influence of new economic ideas, as a result of "long-established mechanisms for bringing experts, bureaucrats, and political representatives together for sustained planning of public policies" (1985, 129). Gunnar Myrdal, a social democratic economist, famously wrote a supplement to the 1933 government budget, where he presented the case for expansionary fiscal policies (1933). Economists in the other Nordic countries also advocated countercyclical policies in the 1930s. Niels-Henrik Topp shows that support for the idea of expansionary fiscal policies was strong among prominent Danish economists (1988, 513–15; see also Garside and Topp 2001, 725). Jukka Pekkarinen (1989, 322–23, 334) argues that the ideas that we now associate with the Keynesian revolution were well known in Finnish economic circles as early as 1930, although these ideas had not yet influenced the policy debate. In Norway, economists such as Ragnar Frisch played a role very similar to that of the Stockholm School in neighboring Sweden (Hanisch, Søilen, and Ecklund 1999).

Party Politics

Another curious fact about Sweden—and Denmark—is that the center-right government in power in the 2000s pursued a more expansionary fiscal policy than center-left governments did in the Great Depression, which is surprising, given that most models of macroeconomic policy-making assume that left-of-center governments are more concerned with employment promotion than right-wing governments are.

When the financial crisis that began in 2007 developed into a full-blown macroeconomic crisis in the autumn of 2008, Sweden, Denmark, and Finland had center-right coalition governments. In Sweden, a four-party majority coalition, led by the Conservative Party (Moderaterna), had been in power since the autumn of 2006. In Denmark, a minority coalition between the Liberal Party and the Conservative Party had been in power since 2001 on the basis of semiformalized cooperation with the right-wing populist Danish People's Party (Dansk Folkeparti). In Finland, a coalition of the Center Party, the National Coalition Party, the Swedish People's Party, and the Greens had, by the time of the 2008 to 2009 recession, been in power since 2007. The only exception was Norway, which had been governed by a social democratic-led center-left coalition government since 2005.

In the 1930s, by contrast, the Center Left had the upper hand. In Sweden, a Social Democratic minority government was formed in 1932, and in the following year, it secured its position through the parliamentary cooperation with the Farmers' Party (Bondefòrbundet). In 1936, the two parties established a formal coalition. Denmark was governed by the Social Democrats and the Social Liberal Party (Radikale Venstre) from 1929 to the German invasion in 1940, although the two other major Danish parties, the Conservatives and the Liberals, commanded a majority in the upper house, Landstinget, until 1936 (Topp 1987, 170–71). In Norway, the Social Liberal Party and the Farmers' Party formed a series of minority governments in the first half of the 1930s, until a social democratic government won power with the support of the Farmers' Party in 1935. The exception was Finland, which was dominated by conservative parties in the interwar years.

FISCAL POLICIES IN THE GREAT RECESSION

As several other contributions to this volume show (see especially chapters 4, 5, and 11), the sizes of stimulus packages, and their composition, varied among European countries in 2008 and 2009. On the basis of this evidence, some scholars, notably David Cameron (2010), have argued that European fiscal policies in the aftermath of the Great Recession were relatively unremarkable, at least in comparison with the stimulus policies that the U.S. Congress adopted in February 2009, a few weeks after the inauguration of President Obama.

Compared with the conservative fiscal policies that most European states had pursued in the 1980s, 1990s, and 2000s, however—and the orthodox ideas that were predominant then—that EU member states agreed on, and nonmember states such as Norway followed, a coordinated stimulus program in the 2008 to 2009 downturn remains a significant political event. European macroeconomic thinking before the crisis was based on the premise that independent central banks would be able to achieve optimal levels of output and employment through inflation targeting and the judicious use of monetary policy instruments, particularly the short-term lending rate. Fiscal policy was oriented toward medium- and long-term objectives, not short-term macroeconomic goals (compare Lindvall 2010, chapter 3).

In any event, there is no doubt that Sweden and the other Nordic states pursued expansionary fiscal policies in 2009 and 2010. Denmark and Sweden have the largest automatic stabilizers in the European Union, and yet, as I will show, Denmark, Finland, Norway, and Sweden enacted large discretionary packages. Klaus Armingeon (forthcoming) ranks all four countries covered in this chapter as "slightly" countercyclical, but he counts the Danish and Finnish policy responses among the more expansionary of the "moderately expansionary" governments. According to data from the European Commission (2010, 20), discretionary stimulus measures in 2009 and 2010 in Sweden, Denmark, and Finland were in the range of 0.7 to 2.7 percent of GDP. The maximum was Sweden in 2010. The Norwegian government's stimulus program was also large in both comparative and historical perspective (St. prp. 37, 2008–2009, 5).

Policies

When the budget for 2009 was prepared within the Swedish Finance Ministry in the summer of 2008, Fredrik Reinfeldt's center-right coalition government expected only a small downturn, so the stimulus measures were limited (Nationalekonomiska föreningens förhandlingar 2009, 80), and most of the measures presented as stimulus measures in the final document (Prop. 2008/09:1, 4, 20) were in fact permanent policy changes that the government had originally adopted for reasons that had little to do with the economic crisis.

In late 2008 and early 2009, however, when it was clear that the downturn would be deeper than expected, the government developed a stimulus program that was sent to parliament in January 2009 (Prop. 2008/09:97). It included infrastructure investments, increased spending on education and active labor market programs, support for the automobile sector, and a special form of tax credits for home repairs, which was meant to maintain economic activity and employment in the construction sector (Prop. 2008/09:100, 43–48).

Two months before the government sent its first stimulus bill to parliament, the main opposition party—the Social Democrats—had already proposed its own stimulus plan (Mot. 2008/09:Fi7), which was rejected by the parliament's standing committee on economic policy (Bet. 2008/09:FiU12), and by the center-right majority in parliament, in anticipation of the government's own plan.

The government followed up its first stimulus package with further stimulus measures in the revised budget for 2009 (Prop. 2008/09:100, 29), which included a large increase in state funding for municipal governments, and in the budget for 2010 (Prop. 2009/10:1), which included a reduction of income taxes—the fourth in a succession of such cuts that the center-right government had adopted since it was formed in 2006. The Social Democrats were strongly in favor of the increase in funding for municipal governments; they had made a similar proposal already in the autumn of 2008, but they opposed the tax cuts. There were two additional differences between the stimulus packages that the center-right government and the social democratic opposition proposed between November 2008 and September 2009. First, the Social Democrats opted for a fiscal stimulus sooner, in November 2008 rather than January 2009, and would initially have preferred a slightly larger package (Mot. 2008/09:Fi15, 4–5). Second, they included some increased transfers to households in order to increase private demand (Mot. 2008/09:Fi7, 3), something that the government did not do.

According to Susanne Ackum, who headed the Finance Ministry's Economic Policy Department during the 2008 and 2009 downturn, the government's philosophy was that macroeconomic stabilization in a "normal" downturn should be left to monetary policy, and to automatic stabilizers (Interview, Stockholm, November 29, 2010). When it became clear that the downturn was exceptionally deep, however, the government considered other options. The first step was to increase spending on labor market policy in order to support the unemployed. The government then looked into the possibility of immediately implementing reforms that the government had originally planned to propose later, such as the new tax credits for home repairs. These two types of measures were included in the first stimulus bill (Prop. 2008/09:97). Discretionary fiscal measures, such as the extra funding for municipalities that followed later in the spring of 2009, was the last step.

The government resisted some of the discretionary measures that the opposition proposed, such as increased transfers to households, because they were not "cost-effective," Susanne Ackum says. Torbjörn Hållö, a social democratic economic adviser, maintains that the Social Democrats and the government simply disagreed on the effects of supporting households. "We argued that it was best to target groups with little [financial] room for maneuver," Hållö explains. "We therefore concluded that it was best to improve housing benefits for pensioners and benefits for families with small children" (Interview, Stockholm, November 30, 2010). The Social Democrats argued that the method of boosting private demand that the government later opted for—tax cuts (Prop. 2009/10:1, 24–25)—was misguided, because the relatively well-off individuals who benefited from this policy had a higher propensity to save. The government, on the other hand, believed that cutting income taxes on labor, through the earned income tax credit reform, was a "structurally sound" policy that would increase labor supply in the medium and long term while at the same time increasing aggregate demand in the short run (Susanne Ackum, interview).

As the government increased the volume of stimulus spending in the course of 2009, including many proposals that the Social Democrats had included in their own parliamentary bills, some of the differences between the government's and the main opposition party's fiscal policies disappeared. The remaining difference, from the autumn of 2009 onward, was that the opposition opposed the government's income tax cuts. In other words, the political debate settled into a familiar left-right pattern. Overall, the stimulus plans that parties presented when the crisis was deepest, in early 2009, were relatively similar. Both the government and the Social Democrats wanted to support the automobile industry, increase spending on active labor market programs, increase infrastructure investments, subsidize home repairs, and eventually—from April 2009 onward—both the government and the opposition were in favor of large transfers from the central government to municipal governments in order to maintain employment in the public sector. All these measures are noteworthy for their low political salience. Concerning the transfers to municipal governments, one factor to keep in mind is that municipal governments in Sweden are directly elected, which means that the center-left opposition parties controlled many of the municipalities that stood to receive additional funding.

In comparison with parliamentary debates in the 1930s, what is most striking about the parliamentary debates over Swedish fiscal policy from 2008 to 2010 is that they were almost exclusively concerned with the economic effects of various proposals, and not with their long-term political and institutional effects (Prot. 2008/09:82, 7 §; Prot. 2008/09:134, 9 §). One of the main messages of the social democratic economic spokesman, Thomas Östros, in the spring of 2009 was that it was irresponsible of the government to cut taxes when the deficit was already very large, which was at least partly a political objection, in addition to an economic one, but Östros did not refer to the specific measures that the government had proposed during the crisis, but to the policy of tax cuts that the government had pursued for several years before the crisis. Matters were different in the 1930s: the parliamentary debates then were concerned with the likely political repercussions of the government's stimulus program itself.

The governing parties presented a united front, and it is difficult to establish whether the internal negotiations between the governing parties before the bills were sent to parliament involved disagreements over long-term political effects. However, that the government and the opposition presented similar stimulus plans strongly suggests that the underlying political disagreements, concerning the implications of these specific policies, were relatively insignificant.

Politics

Why was the center-right government in power during the 2008 to 2009 downturn so willing to engage in fiscal stimulus—more so, in fact, than the then social democratic government was in the 1930s? And why was the adoption of expansionary fiscal policies so uncontroversial? A plausible answer to both questions is that basic political-economic institutions were not strongly contested in Sweden in the late 2000s—neither in the labor market, nor in the domain of social policy—which meant that at least in the short term, political parties could judge fiscal policies on their economic merits, without concerning themselves with how stimulus policies would influence any underlying conflicts over institutions. The comparison with the 1930s in the following section will show that matters were different during the Great Depression.

When the crisis of the 2000s occurred, the Swedish industrial relations regime was relatively stable, as a result of major settlements in the 1990s. The Industrial Agreement of 1997 had created a new set of norms and institutions for wage bargaining at the sectoral level that proved to be resilient, establishing a new labor market regime after twenty years of conflict and uncertainty concerning Sweden's wage bargaining regime (Elvander 1997, 2002). Meanwhile, the policy of inflation-targeting that the central bank had pursued since the early 1990s had won the confidence of both unions and employers (Lindvall 2008).

The absence of polarizing conflicts over institutions in the Great Recession is apparent not only in the domain of industrial relations, but also in that of social policy. The ideological conflicts over the size of the public sector and the role of the state in the economy that characterized the 1930s—and the 1970s and 1980s—had subsided by the 2000s. The center-

Figure 8.1   Public and Mandatory Private Social Expenditures in
Sweden, 1980 to 2007

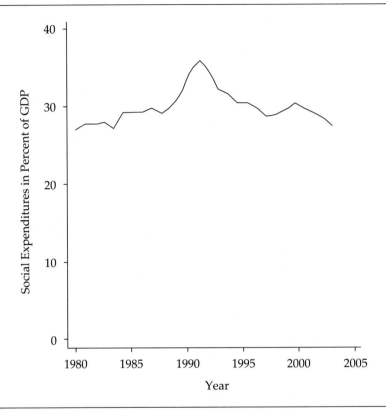

Source: Author's compiliation based on Armingeon et al. (2011).
Note: Public social expenditures as a percentage of GDP.

right parties won the general election of 2006 by pursuing an electoral
strategy that was based on accepting many policies that were previously
associated with the Social Democrats. Before this, the Social Democrats,
who were in government from 1994 to 2006, had already moved toward
the center. Most important, the main Swedish political parties had converged when it came to the size of the public sector: social expenditure as
a percentage of GDP had been more or less constant in Sweden since 1980
(see figure 8.1). The fluctuations in figure 8.1 around the mean are best
explained by changes in the denominator, GDP, rather than changes in the
party composition of the government.

As a result of these underlying political trends, political debate about what the long-term political effects of the government's or the opposition's initiatives during the crisis might be was minimal. Neither the increased spending on infrastructure (roads, railroads, public buildings, green energy), the extra spending on welfare services that enjoyed broad bipartisan support, nor the additional funds for active labor market policies were criticized by opposition parties, or, as far as we know, by any of the junior parties in the Conservative-led government. The government simply introduced programs that were tangential to policies it was already pursuing. All additional, discretionary measures had broad political support.

Another factor that should be considered in this context is that Sweden had experienced a deep financial and economic crisis from 1991 to 1993, and all political parties wanted to avoid another prolonged period of negative growth and mass unemployment. Sweden is in some ways similar to Japan, which also experienced a deep and prolonged crisis in the early 1990s, shaping its institutions and policy responses (see chapter 9, this volume). However, the legacy of the 1990s is perhaps more obvious in the domain of financial regulation and with respect to support for ailing banks and financial institutions, not in the domain of fiscal policy.

FISCAL POLICIES IN SWEDEN IN THE GREAT DEPRESSION

The main objective of the Social Democratic minority government formed in Sweden in 1932 was to adopt new labor market policies. The party's labor market reform agenda dated back to 1930, before Sweden was much affected by the Great Depression (Lundberg 1985, 6). In March 1933, the new government sent four bills to parliament concerning the issue of unemployment, requesting approximately 195 million Swedish kronor to fund public works, increasing government borrowing in order to pursue a countercyclical fiscal policy. In addition, the government wanted to introduce a public unemployment insurance system and make a series of important changes in the administration of labor market programs.

A special committee, Särskilda utskottet, was formed to negotiate the government's proposals. Cross-party agreement was soon reached on 160 million kronor in funding for new labor market programs (Nyman 1944, 40). Three other issues proved to be much more controversial: a proposed increase in compensation for participants in public works programs (the most controversial issue), administrative reforms (the abolition of the labor market authority that had been established during World War I), a ban on the practice of allocating relief workers to plants, firms, and establishments that were involved in industrial conflict, and the introduction of unemployment insurance. As Nils Unga (1976) has documented, these measures, and not the principle of deficit spending as such, were the main sources of conflict between the government and the opposition.

Following a major compromise with the Farmers' Party on May 26 and 27, 1933—the so-called Cow Trade—the Social Democrats were eventually able to implement most of their policies: approximately 180 million kronor were allocated to public works, wages for the participants were set at market rates, and the "conflict directives" concerning public workers and industrial conflicts were altered. But the government also had to make important concessions. The old labor market authority remained in place, unemployment insurance was not included in the agreement and was introduced only the following year, and the government had to support the Farmers' Party's protectionist agricultural policies, abandoning its traditional policy of free trade (Nyman 1944, 60–64).

When it comes to the implications of the new labor market policies for fiscal policy, the scope of the government's program was more limited than one might have expected, given the attention that this policy compromise has received in the literature. Many economists regard the programs as small given the depth of the recession (Jonung 1977, 55–57; Lindbeck 1991, 453), and furthermore, the government loans were paid back quickly and the approved funds were not fully used, limiting the macroeconomic impact of the new programs (Helmersson 1972).

The total allocation of funding to public works when the May 1933 compromise was adopted amounts to approximately 2 percent of GDP, of which only 98 million kronor—about 1.2 percent of GDP—were actually used (calculation based on Johansson 1967; Edvinsson 2004). However, the previous year's budget also included spending on employment policy, and the total allocation of funding to all unemployment policy measures increased by only some 130 million kronor (about 1.6 percent of GDP) between fiscal years 1932–1933 and 1933–1934 (see Helmersson 1972, 16). These numbers are similar to the allocation to Sweden's stimulus program for 2009 (1.7 percent of GDP), and clearly lower than the allocation for 2010 (2.7 percent of GDP), even if the 1933 compromise was adopted three years after the beginning of the recession.

Most economists and economic historians consequently believe that fiscal policy had a relatively minor impact on Sweden's economic recovery in the mid- to late 1930s. According to Erik Lundberg, the undervalued currency from 1931 onward, when Sweden went off gold standard, was the main factor behind the recovery (1985, 9), which was led by an increase in international demand for Swedish raw materials, forestry products, and semimanufactured goods (Lindbeck 1991, 453).

Politics

Why were the stimulus programs in Sweden in the early to mid-1930s so small, relative to what one might have expected? Why was the government more concerned with institutional changes—such as administrative reforms, wage-setting for relief workers, and the introduction of comprehensive unemployment insurance—than with the fiscal stimulus as such, considering that the allocated funds were not fully used? And why were the Conservatives, the Liberals, and parts of the Farmers' Party caucus so strongly opposed to the government's plan? One plausible answer to all these questions is that the basic political-economic institutions were strongly contested in Sweden in the early 1930s, which meant that political parties were primarily concerned with how the new stimulus policies would influence latent political conflicts.

During the Great Depression, the relatively harmonious labor market model that Sweden would become famous for in the postwar period (Shonfield 1965) had yet to materialize. The 1938 Saltsjöbaden Agreement, which would establish peace on the Swedish labor market, still lay in the future. Political parties were acutely sensitive to any influence that new legislation and new public spending might have on the balance of power between employers and trade unions.

The most comprehensive study of Swedish labor market policy in the 1920s and 1930s investigates the implications of one of the main issues in the parliamentary debates in 1933—the level of pay for participants in public works programs (Unga 1976). The Social Democrats argued that the wages paid to those who were allocated to public works programs should be equal to the lowest wages offered to manual laborers in the same geographical area. The Conservatives and the Liberals, on the other hand, wanted wages to be lower for those who were offered public works. The center-right opposition, including the Farmers' Party, was concerned with the economic and political power that the government's policy would give to the trade unions, which were then, as now, closely affiliated with Sweden's Social Democratic Party.

Unga shows that the issue of market wages for public works was raised within the trade union movement already in the late 1920s, before the Social Democrats introduced their new labor market program in 1930. For the unions, existing relief programs represented low-wage competition (Unga 1976, 125), which was particularly problematic for the unions and the Social Democrats because it pitted the two wings of the labor movement against one another: municipal governments controlled by the Social Democrats often had to administer the very public works programs that the unions objected to (Unga 1976, 138).

As Bo Rothstein (1992, 129) observes, the existing system of relief works, established in the 1920s, undermined the trade unions in three ways. First, the existing labor market agency—the Unemployment Commission—could assign relief workers to firms where regular workers were on strike. Second, since relief workers were paid less than workers employed on the open market, the system led to a downward pressure on wages. Third, only about half of the unemployed received unemployment compensation, which again led to a downward pressure on wages. Solving these problems was the main objective of the Social Democrats, and concerns with the same set of issues motivated the center-right parties in their opposition to Social Democratic initiatives.

Another reason political debates about economic policies were so divisive in the Great Depression was the significant partisan disagreement concerning the scope of government. In Sweden, government spending in the 1920s had increased only moderately, and even fell in certain periods, including years when the Social Democrats were in power (Landgren 1960, 13–14). In the 1930s, however, government expenditures increased significantly under the Social Democrats (see Lundberg 1985, 10), which is what the right-wing parties anticipated in the parliamentary debates over the social democratic government's crisis program in 1933.

The role of general ideological disagreements over the size of the public sector in the 1930s is well known: several scholars of the 1930s have argued that one of the underlying aims of the right-wing opposition, in its efforts to block the Social Democratic labor market policy initiatives, was to avoid an expansion of the role of the state. This is the main theme of Leif Lewin's study of the period (1967, 97), and the economist Erik Lundberg, himself a participant in policy debates in the 1930s, later noted that "it was not only, or not even mainly, the actual policies carried out that aroused a strong political reaction from the Conservative Party as well as from the business community. Their fears centered mainly on the trends toward socialism" (1985, 11). The leading Conservative opponents of the government's plan in the Swedish parliament—Arvid Lindman in the Second Chamber and Ernst Trygger in the First Chamber—devoted large proportions of their speeches when the results of the deal between the Social Democrats and the Farmers' Party were debated to this specific issue. A comparison between the 1930s and the 2000s demonstrates that this factor made a big difference, especially to the manner in which right-of-center parties responded to demands for fiscal stimulus.

DENMARK, FINLAND, AND NORWAY

Now let us turn to Denmark, Finland, and Norway to see how they handled the Great Depression and the Great Recession.

The Great Depression

Most scholars of interwar economic policies in the Nordic countries agree that whereas Sweden did pursue fiscal policies that had some expansionary elements—although the stimulus program was small and appears to have had minor effects—the other Nordic countries did not pursue expansionary fiscal policies at all. In Denmark, Jukka Pekkarinen notes, economic policies were "predominantly conservative and orthodox" (1989, 340), and to the extent that economic policy contributed to the Danish recovery in the 1930s, this was a result of exchange-rate policy—a deliberate policy of currency depreciation—and not fiscal policy (see also Topp 1987).

Finnish economic policies in the late 1920s and early 1930s were even more conservative: public works programs were far less developed than in neighboring Sweden, and the size of the public sector—as a percentage of GDP—even declined in comparison with the 1920s (Pekkarinen and Vartiainen 2001, 77). However, Pekkarinen and Juhana Vartiainen also note that exchange rate policy was an exception to the rule: exchange rate policy was not conservative but "pragmatic," seeking to maintain profitability in export industries (2001, 79–80).

In Norway, finally, certain groups within the Labour Party converted to Keynesian policy ideas in the early 1930s, but the Labour Party did not win power until 1935, and when it did, it pursued more traditional fiscal policies, balancing the budget. The upswing had already begun in 1933 and 1934, before the Social Democratic rise to power, and it was driven, most likely, by the devaluation of the krone in 1931 (Hanisch, Søilen, and Ecklund 1999, 112–15).

On the basis of this brief overview, and the evidence on Sweden presented earlier, it is possible to make two observations.

First, for these four small, open economies, exchange rate policy appears to have played a more important role than fiscal policy in the 1930s. The Nordic countries abandoned the gold standard early (sometimes unwillingly, as in the Swedish case), let their currencies depreciate with the British pound, and in some cases—such as the Danish devaluation of 1933—governments and central banks made additional devaluations to support export-dependent sectors. Monetary policy played an important role in the Great Recession as well. That central banks reduced interest rates so quickly in the autumn of 2008 was an important step in the global response to the crisis. It is possible that the macroeconomic policy autonomy Norway and Sweden enjoyed by virtue of their floating exchange rates—Finland adopted the euro from the start and the Danish krone is pegged to the euro—is one part of the explanation for GDP falling less sharply in these two countries during the crisis.

Second, not only in Sweden (May 1933) but also in Denmark (January 1933) and Norway (1935), social democratic parties and parties representing farmers formed "red-green coalitions" in the 1930s. Yet only the Swedish government introduced expansionary fiscal policies, and even the Swedish program had limited scope, as discussed earlier. This suggests that the association between red-green coalitions and new forms of fiscal policies that Gourevitch (1986, chapter 4) identified in his influential study of the 1930s is less strong than he supposes. Consider, for example, the Danish Kanslergade Agreement (Kanslergadeforliget) on January 30, 1933, when the social democratic leader Thorvald Stauning's center-left government made a deal with the Liberal Party, which represented agricultural interests. The agreement included new labor market programs, an effective devaluation of the Danish krone—setting the exchange rate at 22.50 kroner against the British pound after one and a half years with a floating exchange rate—increasing the competitiveness of agricultural exports, the main export products in Denmark until the middle of the twentieth century—and a social policy reform that had been in preparation since the 1920s (Christensen 2005; Svendsen and Hoffmeyer 1968). It did not, however, include any expansionary fiscal policies, although the Danish Social Democrats had proposed deficit-financed public works in the autumn of 1932 (see "Regeringen vil optage Laan til store offentlige Arbejder," *Berlingske Tidende*, December 3, 1932, p. 6; "Regeringens kamp mot arbejdsløsheden." *Politiken*, December 3, 1932, p. 3). One interpretation of these events is that the primary purpose of the Nordic red-green coalitions was to resolve underlying political conflicts through institutional reform. The expansionary programs introduced in Sweden sustained the political compromise, not the other way around.

Industrial relations were more prone to conflict in the Nordic countries in the early 1930s than they were in the 2000s. In Norway, as in Sweden, trade unions and employer organizations had yet to sign a comprehensive agreement on how to conduct wage negotiations—such an agreement was signed only in 1935 (Hanisch, Søilen, and Ecklund 1999, 114)—and there were widespread strikes in the early 1930s. In Denmark, trade unions and employers had already concluded a comprehensive agreement on industrial relations that dated back to 1899. However, the relationship between employers and unions was a major issue in Denmark in the early 1930s. As Jesper Due, Jørgen Madsen, and Carsten Jensen show, the Danish wage bargaining system emerged, historically, from a series of decisions and compromises around the year 1900, but the consolidation of this system occurred in the course of the 1930s (1993, 111). Most important, the 1930s were a decade when the role of the state in wage bargaining was enhanced, through both the establishment of a national mediator and direct government intervention in wage bargaining negotiations. The first such intervention was, in fact, one important element of the 1933 Kanslergade Agreement. The government averted a major labor market conflict brewing at the time by adopting new legislation that forced employers and unions to extend existing collective agreements. In Finland, finally, the political situation at the time of the Great Depression was even more intense: a far-right, anticommunist group called the Lapua movement, active from 1929 to 1932, even sought to overthrow the government in 1932 (Stubbergaard 1996).

The Great Recession

The Nordic policy trajectories were similar in 2008 and 2009. In Denmark, the center-right government announced some discretionary stimulus measures already in 2008 (Finansministeriet 2008, 9), but, as in Sweden, the main stimulus measures were introduced in the course of 2009. The center-right government and the far-right Danish People's Party, on which the government depended for parliamentary support, adopted a significant piece of discretionary legislation in the spring of that year: a tax reform that was fully financed in the long term but was redesigned in order to produce a short-term expansionary effect (Finansministeriet 2009a, 7). In the budget for 2010, which was sent to parliament in August 2009, the government then announced new initiatives that were expected to support domestic demand and lead to higher growth and employment in 2009 and 2010—notably a large increase in public infrastructure investments (Finansministeriet 2009b). The Social Democratic opposition was highly critical of the government's emphasis on tax cuts, especially in light of the large tax cuts the government had implemented in 2007. As in Sweden, however, the party differences over stimulus policies diminished over time, and from mid-2010 onward, again as in Sweden, the main focus of economic policy in Denmark was the reduction of the budget deficit and the consolidation of public finances (Finansministeriet 2010).

In Norway, the center-left coalition government that had been in power since 2005 sent its first stimulus bill to parliament in January 2009 (St. prp. 37, 2008–2009). The Norwegian government prioritized raised government spending over tax cuts, increasing the transfers to municipal governments and the resources devoted to infrastructure investments (St. prp. 37, 2008–2009, 8), which reflected the government's general political orientation. Rather than taking up loans, the Norwegian government simply chose to devote a higher percentage than the normal 4 percent of the revenue from the oil-rich Norwegian state's sovereign wealth funds to current spending (Prime Minister's Office 2010, 118). Since the government was concerned that the economic situation was still uncertain in the autumn of 2009, it chose to devote a higher percentage to current spending in the fiscal year 2010 as well. In the Revised National Budget for 2010, however, the government declared that since the economic situation had improved since the budget bill was passed in the autumn, it was time to start reducing the deficit (Meld. St. 2, 2009–2010, 5–6).

The Finnish discretionary stimulus measures were similar in size to the expansionary packages adopted in the other Nordic countries—according to the Finance Ministry's calculations, they amounted to 1.8 percent of GDP in 2009 and 1.6 percent of GDP in 2010 (Ministry of Finance 2010). They had a different composition, however—40 percent of the measures represented tax cuts and the abolition of employers' national insurance contributions, and approximately 20 percent were categorized as "construction and renovation" and "civil engineering." Only 2 percent went to labor policy and education, and only 3 percent went to benefit increases. These priorities are consistent with the agenda of the center-right government, and arguably also with the economic model that Finnish governments have built after the deep recession of the early 1990s. In the budget for 2011, the government announced that there would be a transition from expansionary to restrictive (contractive) fiscal policies, and the temporary stimulus measures would be phased out gradually, just as in the other Nordic countries (Statsrådets kommunikationsenhet 2010).

POLITICS AND POLICIES IN ECONOMIC CRISES

A comparison of the Swedish policy responses to the crises of the 2000s and the 1930s suggests that concerns with the indirect, institutional effects of economic policy initiatives matter greatly to macroeconomic policy-making in economic downturns, at least in political systems where the adoption of expansionary policies requires agreement among several political parties. In the early 1930s, politics in Sweden—and in the other Nordic countries—was defined by profound conflicts, both in the domain of industrial relations and in the domain of party politics. In the late 2000s, on the other hand, Sweden—and arguably also the other Nordic countries—had experienced a relatively long period of stable labor market institutions and a basic political consensus concerning the size of the public sector and, more generally, the role of the state in the economy.

I conclude by discussing whether the argument developed here applies beyond the 1930s and 2000s, and beyond the countries studied here.

The 1970s

If this analysis of the relationship between distributive politics and macro-economic policymaking is accurate, it may help shed light on the way governments responded to the prolonged crisis of the 1970s, a period when class conflict had recently resurged in western Europe (Crouch and Pizzorno 1978). As I have argued elsewhere, political factors help explain why western European governments adopted different macroeconomic policies in response to the economic disturbances of the late 1960s and early 1970s (Lindvall 2010, chapters 2–3). Where the political arrangements that supported the postwar settlement were still stable, as in Austria and Sweden, governments used macroeconomic policy in an attempt to maintain growth and employment well into the 1980s. Where political arrangements had changed and new types of conflicts emerged, however, governments soon opted for "sound money" and "sound finance."

One possible counterargument to this interpretation concerns Sweden, where governments continued to use fiscal policy in an attempt to maintain low unemployment even as distributional and ideological conflicts intensified in the 1970s. Most controversially, Sweden's main trade union confederation proposed the introduction of "wage earner funds" that were designed to transfer power over large firms to the trade union movement (Pontusson 1987; Anthonsen, Lindvall, and Schmidt-Hansen 2009, 11). However, even if distributional and ideological conflicts became more intense in the 1970s, support was still widespread for the basic institutions and norms of the Swedish political economy, including the corporatist institutions that were first established in the course of the 1930s and the assumption that governments should deepen social reforms and defend the welfare state. When the center-right won the election of 1976, it actually ran on a platform of preserving the Swedish model from the excesses of the left (Petersson 1977), not on a platform of change.

Later on, beginning in the early 1980s, the political conflicts that had begun in the 1970s led some political parties, and the employer organizations, to adopt more radical policies with respect to the institutions that were associated with the Swedish model. A major labor market conflict in the spring of 1980 contributed to this change in strategy. In 1980–1981, the government introduced the first government bills since the Second World War that proposed significant cuts in public spending, changing the dynamics of political competition in Sweden. Economic policies also changed: the center-right governments that were in power between 1976 and 1982 pursued expansionary fiscal policies only in the period that led up to the second oil crisis; from 1979 to 1982, after the oil crisis, they did not (Lindvall 2004, chapters 2–3). As argued throughout this chapter, underlying political conflicts influenced the economic policy choices that governments made.

The Great Recession in the United States

The analysis presented here also has implications for how we should understand cross-country differences in the Great Recession. One country where the government appears to have struggled to find support for stimulus measures is the United States. In February 2009, Congress adopted a large discretionary fiscal stimulus program, the American Recovery and Reinvestment Act, but as Nolan McCarty shows in chapter 7, this volume, the Obama administration's economic team would have liked a bigger stimulus package, and no further stimulus packages passed through Congress in 2008 through 2010.

With hindsight, the political circumstances appear to have been unusually beneficial when the American Recovery and Reinvestment Act was passed. Only a few weeks had passed since the inauguration of the new president; the Democratic Party controlled both the presidency and the two Houses of Congress; most important, the political debate in the United States had not yet begun to revolve around basic political-economic arrangements, which became a major theme in the following years, when Congress deliberated over a major health-care reform. That political conflicts changed in this manner, as the Republican Party increased its representation in the Senate and the ideological heterogeneity within the Democratic Party became more apparent, led to a political situation where the argument presented here would lead us to expect the adoption of expansionary fiscal policies to be very difficult.

After the Great Recession

Finally, the arguments in this chapter have implications for how we should understand the political situation after the Great Recession. By 2010, many European governments—including those in Sweden and the other Nordic countries—had opted for more austere policies, though unemployment rates remained high. The economist Paul Krugman criticized the economic policies of European governments, suggesting that their policies represented "the victory of an orthodoxy that has little to do with rational analysis, whose main tenet is that imposing suffering on other people is how you show leadership in tough times" ("The Third Depression," *New York Times*, June 27, 2010). My analysis suggests a more straightforward, political explanation: as a short-term measure, to counter the immediate threat of a macroeconomic collapse, expansionary fiscal policy had few second-order political effects in 2008 and 2009. But it is likely that a more comprehensive, prolonged program of government intervention in the economy—what Margaret Weir (1992) calls social Keynesianism—would have had such effects.

I am grateful to the political advisers and civil servants who agreed to let me interview them about Danish and Swedish economic policies in the Great Recession: Susanne Ackum, state secretary in the Swedish Ministry of Finance (Stockholm, November 29, 2010); Morten Bødskov, deputy chairman of the Danish Social Democratic Party (Copenhagen, October 27, 2010); Sebastian de Toro and Torbjörn Hållö, advisers to the parliamentary caucus of the Swedish Social Democratic Party (Stockholm, November 30, 2010); and Jakob Hald, head of the Economic Policy Department in the Danish Ministry of Finance (Copenhagen, February 10, 2011). I am also grateful to the editors and to the other contributors to this volume for their helpful comments and advice. Moreover, I have benefited greatly from discussions of previous drafts at the University of Gothenburg, Lund University, Uppsala University, and Trinity College Dublin (Victor Lapuente, Anders Uhlin, Kåre Vernby, and Helen Callaghan were all very good discussants), and from discussions with Niels-Henrik Topp and Donald Winch about the differences between the Great Recession and the Great Depression. Finally, I would like to thank Alvina Erman for excellent research assistance.

REFERENCES

Anthonsen, Mette, Johannes Lindvall, and Ulrich Schmidt-Hansen. 2009. "Social Democrats, Unions, and Corporatism: Denmark and Sweden Compared." *Party Politics* 17(1): 118–34.

Armingeon, Klaus. Forthcoming. "The Politics of Fiscal Responses to the Crisis of 2008–2009." *Governance*.

Armingeon, Klaus, David Weisstanner, Sarah Engler, Panajotis Potolidis, Marlène Gerber, and Phillip Leimgruber. 2011. "Comparative Political Data Set I 1960–2009." Institute of Political Science, University of Berne, Switzerland. Database accessed on May 9, 2012.

Bet. 2008/09:FiU12. "Åtgärder mot konjunkturförsvagningen." Stockholm: Regeringskansliet.

Blyth, Mark. 2002. *Great Transformations*. Cambridge: Cambridge University Press.

Cameron, David R. 2010. "European Responses to the Economic Crisis." Paper presented at the Annual Meeting of the American Political Science Association. Washington, D.C. (September 2–5, 2010).

Carlson, Benny, and Lars Jonung. 2002. "Ohlin on the Great Depression." In *Bertil Ohlin: A Centennial Celebration*, edited by Ronald Findlay, Lars Jonung, and Mats Lundahl. Cambridge, Mass.: MIT Press.

Christensen, Jacob. 2005. "Socialreformen af 1933." In *13 reformer af den danske velfærdsstat*, edited by Jørn Henrik Petersen and Klaus Petersen. Odense: Syddansk Universitetsforlag.

Corsetti, Giancarlo, Michael P. Devereux, Luigi Guiso, John Hassler, Gilles Saint-Paul, Hans-Werner Sinn, Jan-Egbert Sturm, and Xavier Vives. 2010. *The EEAG Report on the European Economy 2010*. Munich: CES-Ifo.

Crouch, Colin, and Alessandro Pizzorno, eds. 1978. *The Resurgence of Class Conflict in Western Europe Since 1968*, vols. 1 and 2. Basingstoke: Macmillan.

Det økonomiske Råd. 2009. *Dansk økonomi, forår 2009*. Copenhagen: Det økonomiske Råd.

Due, Jesper, Jørgen Steen Madsen, and Carsten Strøby Jensen. 1993. *Den danske model*. Copenhagen: Jurist- og Økonomforbundets Forlag.

Edvinsson, Rodney. 2004. "Historical National Accounts for Sweden, 1800–2000." *Portal for Historical Statistics*, http://www.historia.org (accessed August 10, 2011).

Elvander, Nils. 1997. "The Swedish Bargaining System in the Melting Pot." In *The Swedish Bargaining System in the Melting Pot*, edited by Nils Elvander and Bertil Holmlund. Solna: Arbetslivsinstitutet.

———. 2002. "The New Swedish Regime for Collective Bargaining and Conflict Resolution." *European Journal of Industrial Relations* 8(2): 197–216.

European Commission. 2010. *Public Finances in EMU 2010*. Brussels: Directorate General of Economic and Financial Affairs.

Finansministeriet. 2008. *Økonomisk Redegørelse*. Copenhagen: Government of Denmark.

———. 2009a. "Aftale mellem regeringen og Dansk Folkeparti om forårspakke 2.0." Copenhagen: Government of Denmark.

———. 2009b. "Investeringer, velfærd og ansvarlighed: Finanslovforslaget 2010." Copenhagen: Government of Denmark.

———. 2010. "Aftale mellem regeringen og Dansk Folkeparti om genopretning af dansk økonomi." Copenhagen: Government of Denmark.

Finanspolitiska rådet. 2009. "Svensk finanspolitik: Finanspolitiska rådets rapport 2009." Stockholm: Government of Sweden.

Garside, W. R., and Niels-Henrik Topp. 2001. "Nascent Keynesianism? Denmark in the 1930s." *History of Political Economy* 33(4): 717–41.

Gourevitch, Peter. 1984. "Breaking with Orthodoxy." *International Organization* 38(1): 95–129.

———. 1986. *Politics in Hard Times*. Ithaca, N.Y.: Cornell University Press.

Hall, Peter A., ed. 1989. *The Political Power of Economic Ideas*. Princeton, N.J.: Princeton University Press.

Hanisch, Tore Jørgen, Espen Søilen, and Gunhild Ecklund. 1999. *Norsk økonomisk politikk i det 20. århundre*. Kristiansand: Høyskoleforlaget.

Helmersson, Eskil. 1972. "Svensk krispolitik under 1930-talet." Unpublished manuscript, Department of Economic History, Uppsala University.

Hibbs, Douglas A. 1977. "Political Parties and Macroeconomic Policy." *American Political Science Review* 71(4): 1467–87.

International Monetary Fund (IMF). 2009. *World Economic Outlook April 2009*. Washington, D.C.: International Monetary Fund.

Iversen, Torben. 1999. *Contested Economic Institutions*. New York: Cambridge University Press.

Johansson, Östen. 1967. *The Gross Domestic Product of Sweden and Its Composition, 1861–1955*. Stockholm: Almqvist & Wiksell.

Jonung, Lars. 1977. "Knut Wicksells prisstabiliseringsnorm och penningpolitiken på 1930-talet." In *Ekonomisk debatt och ekonomisk politik*, edited by Jan Herin and Lars Werin. Stockholm: Norstedts.

———, ed. 1991. *The Stockholm School of Economics Revisited*. Cambridge: Cambridge University Press.

Keynes, John Mayard. 1964/1936. *The General Theory of Employment, Interest, and Money*. New York: Harcourt Brace.

Landgren, Karl-Gustaf. 1960. *Den "nya" ekonomien i Sverige*. Stockholm: Almqvist & Wiksell.

Lewin, Leif. 1967. *Planhush ållningsdebatten*. Stockholm: Almqvist & Wiksell.

Lindbeck, Assar. 1991. "Comment." In *The Stockholm School of Economics Revisited*, edited by Lars Jonung. Cambridge: Cambridge University Press.

Lindvall, Johannes. 2004. "The Politics of Purpose." Ph.D. thesis, University of Gothenburg.

———. 2008. "Sweden: Stability Without Europe." In *The Euro at Ten*, edited by Kenneth Dyson. Oxford: Oxford University Press.

———. 2009. "The Real But Limited Influence of Experts." *World Politics* 61(4): 703–30.

———. 2010. *Mass Unemployment and the State*. Oxford: Oxford University Press.

Lundberg, Erik. 1953. *Konjunkturer och ekonomisk politik*. Stockholm: Konjunkturinstitutet, Studieförbundet Näringsliv och Samhälle.

———. 1985. "The Rise and Fall of the Swedish Model." *Journal of Economic Literature* 23(1): 1–36.

Maddison, Angus. 1982. *Phases of Capitalist Development*. Oxford: Oxford University Press.

Mandelkern, Ronen, and Michael Shalev. 2010. "Power and the Ascendance of New Economic Policy Ideas: Lessons from the 1980s Crisis in Israel." *World Politics* 62(3): 459–95.

Meld. St. 2. 2009–2010. "Revidert nasjonalbudsjett 2010." Oslo: Government of Norway.

Ministry of Finance. 2010. "Stimulus Measures of Finnish Central Government." Memorandum dated August 16, 2010. Helsinki: Government of Finland.

Mot. 2008/09:Fi15. "Åtgärder för jobb och omställning." Stockholm: Regeringskansliet.

—. 2008/09:Fi7. "Stimulanspaket mot jobbkrisen." Stockholm: Regeringskansliet.

Myrdal, Gunnar. 1933. "PM ang. verkningarna på den ekonomiska konjunkturutvecklingen i Sverige av olika åtgärder inom den offentliga hushållningens område." Appendix III in the Swedish government's budget bill (*statsverksproposition*).

Nationalekonomiska föreningens förhandlingar. 2009. "Finanspolitiska rådets rapport 2009." *Ekonomisk Debatt* 37(7): 67–96.

Nyman, Olle. 1944. *Krisuppgörelsen mellan Socialdemokraterna och Bondeförbundet 1933.* Stockholm: Almqvist & Wiksell.

Organisation for Economic Co-operation and Development (OECD). 2009. "Social Expenditure Database." Paris: OECD.

—. 2011. "Main Economic Indicators." Paris: OECD.

—. 2012. "National Accounts." Paris: OECD.

Pekkarinen, Jukka. 1989. "Keynesianism and the Scandinavian Models of Economic Policy." In *The Political Power of Economic Ideas*, edited by Peter A. Hall. Princeton, N.J.: Princeton University Press.

Pekkarinen, Jukka, and Juhana Vartiainen. 2001. *Finlands ekonomiska politik.* Stockholm: FIEF.

Petersson, Olof. 1977. *Väljarna och valet 1976.* Stockholm: SCB.

Pontusson, Jonas. 1987. "Radicalization and Retreat in Swedish Social Democracy." *New Left Review* 165(1): 5–33.

Prime Minister's Office. 2010. *Flertallsregjeringens statusrapport Politisk regnskap Stoltenberg II-regjeringen 2005–2010.* Oslo: Statsministerens kontor.

Prop. 2008/09:1. "Budgetpropositionen för 2009." Stockholm: Regeringskansliet.

—. 2008/09:97. "Åtgärder för jobb och omställning." Stockholm: Regeringskansliet.

—. 2008/09:100. "2009 års ekonomiska vårproposition." Stockholm: Regeringskansliet.

—. 2009/10:1. "Budgetpropositionen för 2010." Stockholm: Regeringskansliet.

Prot. Various years. "Records of the Proceedings in the Chamber of the Swedish Parliament." Prot. 2008/09:82, 7 §; Prot. 2008/09:134, 9 §. Available online at www.riksdagen.se (accessed May 7, 2012).

Romer, Christina D. 2009. "Back from the Brink." Speech at the Federal Reserve Bank of Chicago (September 24, 2009).

Rothstein, Bo. 1992. *Den korporativa staten.* Stockholm: Norstedts.

Scharpf, Fritz W. 1991. *Crisis and Choice in European Social Democracy.* Ithaca, N.Y.: Cornell University Press.

Shonfield, Andrew. 1965. *Modern Capitalism*. London: Oxford University Press.

Sørensen, Peter Birch, Michael Rosholm, Hans Jørgen Whitta-Jacobsen, and Eirik Schrøder Amundsen. 2009. "Finanslovsaftalen er kun et lille skridt i den rigtige retning." *Information*, December 3, 2009.

Spilimbergo, Antonio, Steve Symansky, Olivier Blanchard, and Carlo Cottarelli. 2008. "Fiscal Policy for the Crisis." IMF staff position note, December 29 (SPN/08/01). Washington, D.C.: International Monetary Fund.

Statsrådets kommunikationsenhet. 2010. "Gradvis övergång från stimulansåtgärder till åtstramande finanspolitik." Press release 251/2010. Helskinki: Prime Minister's Office.

St. prp. 37. 2008–2009. "Om endringer i statsbudsjettet 2009 med tiltak for arbeid." Oslo: Government of Norway.

Stubbergaard, Ylva. 1996. *Stat, kris och demokrati*. Lund: Arkiv.

Svendsen, Knud Erik, and Erik Hoffmeyer. 1968. *Dansk Pengehistorie 2: 1914–1960*. Copenhagen: Danmarks Nationalbank.

Topp, Niels-Henrik. 1987. *Udviklingen i de finanspolitiske ideer i Danmark 1930–1945*. Copenhagen: Jurist-og Økonomforbundets Forlag.

———. 1988. "Fiscal Policy in Denmark 1930–1945." *European Economic Review* 32(2–3): 512–18.

———. 2008. "Unemployment and Economic Policy in Denmark in the 1930s." *Scandinavian Economic History Review* 56(1): 71–90.

Unga, Nils. 1976. *Socialdemokratin och arbetslöshetsfrågan 1912–34*. Stockholm: Arkiv.

Weir, Margaret. 1992. *Politics and Jobs*. Princeton, N.J.: Princeton University Press.

Weir, Margaret, and Theda Skocpol. 1985. "State Structures and the Possibilities for 'Keynesian' Responses to the Great Depression in Sweden, Britain, and the United States." In *Bringing the State Back In*, edited by Theda Skocpol, Peter B. Evans, and Dietrich Rueschemeyer. Cambridge: Cambridge University Press.

Chapter 9 | The Global Economic Crisis and the Politics of Regime Change in Japan

Yves Tiberghien

UNLIKE IN THE United States or Europe, the 2008 to 2009 crisis did not hit Japan through the banking sector. Rather, it unfolded mainly through the contraction of global trade and the collapse of its key export engine, which led to a 6.3 percentage point GDP contraction in 2009 and forced the government to rely further on fiscal stimulus and increase its overall public debt, reaching 200 percent of GDP by 2010. In large part because the banks had barely recovered from the protracted financial crisis that followed the collapse of the great Japanese bubble in 1990, they had not loaded their balance sheets with large stakes in U.S. subprime mortgage–related securities, unlike European banks, nor had they been directly involved—this time—in large-scale subprime lending themselves. There was no evidence of a significant increase in bad loans on bank balance sheets. However, the global crisis of 2008 to 2009 came as a sequel to the collapse of the great financial bubble in 1990 and nearly two decades of near stagnation and slow, protracted structural change. Its impact on the Japanese system can only be understood in the context of this earlier crisis and the ensuing long and partial transformation.

The Great Recession coincided with a historic regime shift in Tokyo. In the election of August 30, 2009, the Democratic Party of Japan (DPJ) decisively defeated the conservative Liberal Democratic Party (LDP), which had ruled Japan continuously since 1955 save for ten months in 1993 and 1994. There can be no doubt that the economic crisis played a role in decreasing confidence in the government of Prime Minister Aso, but the outcome of the historic election of 2009 was overdetermined and expected independently of the global financial crisis, given a deep structural crisis of the LDP regime and a strong yearning for change among voters. The 2009 landslide was heralded by the LDP defeat in the Upper House elections of July 2007.

The DPJ did use the global crisis, as well as the public backlash against the process of gradual liberal reforms led by the LDP between 1996 and 2006, to promise a new direction in economic policy, one that would focus on strengthening public welfare provisions and shoring up Japan's social system. I call this new direction—announced by the DPJ in the summer of 2009—social-democratic because of its dual renunciation of neoliberal reforms and the old-style particularistic welfare politics of the LDP, rooted in the support of particularistic interest groups such as the construction industry and small and medium enterprises. As part of this new direction, the DPJ promised a child support allowance for all families, generous unemployment benefits, and a reduction of inequalities between permanent and irregular workers.

This historically new thrust hit not one but two bumps on the road in the summer of 2010. By June, it became apparent that the fiscal scope for a major expansion of universal welfare was not there, unless new resources could be found, such as an increase in the consumption tax, now among the lowest in the Organisation for Economic Co-operation and Development (OECD), at 5 percent. In addition, the DPJ government was beset by incompetence, internal tension, and corruption charges swirling around its secretary general. This led to a change of prime minister in May 2010 and a bitter loss in the Upper House election of July 2010. Thus, by the summer of 2010, the great social-democratic revolution of 2009 had lost both its fiscal capacity and its legislative capacity, given the strong bicameral system of Japan. Intense party bickering in parliament and the nuclear disaster of March 11, 2011, have further hamstrung the DPJ, leading to the downfall of Prime Minister Naoto Kan and his replacement by Yoshihiko Noda in September 2011. Although its original mandate remains and corresponds to genuine popular feelings, the DPJ government under Noda has moved further toward disaster relief, fiscal reconstruction (aiming at raising the consumption tax), and free trade.

One crucial theme emerging from the 2008 to 2009 crisis is the commitment by the victorious DPJ to a partially social-democratic agenda and to the rebuilding of the core strengths of the Japanese political economy, such as its training system and the provision of lifetime employment. To use the language of *Varieties of Capitalism* (Hall and Soskice 2001), after ten years of effort to liberalize a rigid coordinated market economy model (CME), in 2009 Japan made the choice to undo liberal reforms and tilt back toward strengthening the CME core. This chapter focuses on the following puzzle: why has Japan chosen to strengthen its CME institutions, seeking to reverse ten years of liberalizing structural reforms despite a very limited shock in 2008?

The analysis of Japan's attempt to move away from and back to its CME core provides crucial insights into the interactions between the CME model and increasingly intrusive global financial forces. It can also shed light on the process of change within some dimensions of the CME model in the face of a theoretical framework that emphasizes systemic linkages and institutional complementarities. In turn, the Japanese case may hint at internal political feedback mechanisms leading to the partial rejection of corrosive reforms.

I argue that the social-democratic and pro-CME turn in 2009 is the result of voter backlash against both the corruption of the LDP and the process of structural reforms pursued in the name of competitive adaptation to globalization. In particular, voters were dissatisfied with the rising inequality and social woes that came as a by-product of structural reforms. The extant economic system had been transformed, but the underlying values and political institutions had not, leading to a deep tension. The Japanese case illustrates the great challenges encountered by CME or stakeholder capitalist systems that seek partial reform in response to external incentives but find themselves in relatively unstable hybridized stages, reminiscent of Peter Hall's and Daniel Gingerich's bottom of the U-curve depiction (2009).

This chapter sees the Japanese pathway between 1980 and 2010 as a protracted effort to reconcile global finance with the tight ship of the CME. Japan partially deregulated its constrained financial system and opened up its capital account from the early 1980s, but without setting up the right supervisory institutions to match the new reality. This ill-supervised partial deregulation played a major role in inflating the great bubble of 1985 to 1990 (for a fuller account of Japan's experience with financial deregulation, see Tiberghien 2005). After years of dithering on the correct response to financial collapse, Japan finally recapitalized its banks in 1998 and mostly solved the bad loan problem between 2004 and 2006. From 1997 to 2006, it also initiated a structural reform process that sought to balance the preservation of the traditional institutional sources of comparative advantage and the underlying social contract with neoliberal reforms that responded to global signals and to lobbying by globally exposed actors (for a full account of post-1997 structural reforms, see Tiberghien 2007). This process of financial reforms, corporate governance reforms, labor reforms, and general deregulation facilitated corporate restructuring by large firms and helped their competitiveness. However, it came at the high cost of both large side-payments through deficit spending and rising inequality. It led the Japanese model to a relative unstable mixed system and generated partial backlash.

Japan in 2009 and 2010 found itself in the midst of a three-way tug of war involving traditional vested interests, new globalized actors, and voters who were all looking for a new stable system of political economy that could deliver both competitiveness and equity in the global economy. It was and remains, as of this writing, an intensely unstable situation. Clearly, Japan has reached a political impasse that has not yet been solved by the rise to power of the DPJ. Although many Japanese agree that some restructuring of the postwar system in the face of economic globalization and technological transformation is good, there may be a threshold of how much resulting inequality is politically sustainable. The landslide against the LDP in August 2009 may be related to reaching this threshold.

THE IMPACT OF THE GLOBAL SHOCK

The 2008 to 2009 crisis hit Japan through an old-style export collapse coupled with a stock market collapse that closely correlated with the U.S. stock market, and not a high-tech financial contagion. Manufacturing firms responded to this collapse by cutting back production. In the first two months of 2009, industrial production in Japan declined by 50 percent over the previous three months' average (IMF 2009, 8). This export-induced shock pushed Japan into recession in both 2008 and 2009, with growth rates of –1.2 percent and –5.2 percent respectively, compared with OECD averages of 0.2 percent in 2008 and –3.2 percent in 2009 (IMF 2010, 2). This recession was the final contributing factor for the political shift of August 2009.

At first glance, it is clear that the global crisis of 2008 and 2009 hit Japan hard. The Japanese GDP experienced a 3.3 percent (12.7 percent annualized) drop in the third quarter of 2008.[1] The collapse of exports, mainly to the United States, by over 20 percent explains the bulk of this shock, 3 percent of the 3.3 percent. The trend in the first quarter of 2009 continued at the same level, a 13 percent annualized drop. By March 2009, GDP was back to the level of five years before.[2] Recovery in the second half of 2009 has meant that the final number for 2009 growth was not –7 percent as feared in the spring, but "only" a loss of –6.3 percent for the year 2009 (IMF 2011). In 2010, Japan experienced a rebound with growth at 4.3 percent, associated with increased dependence on the Chinese market.

Between December 2008 and February 2009, exports plummeted to the level of 1995.[3] Given that nearly 60 percent of manufactured goods produced by Japan are exported, manufacturing output was hit extremely hard. In part due to concurrent reduction of stock, manufacturing output in the first quarter of 2009 was down to the level of 1983.[4] This collapse translated into a rise in unemployment, as it did in other countries. Unemployment went up from 3.8 percent in October 2008 to 5.6 percent, the postwar peak, in July 2009. Subsequent stimulus packages and recovery in exports in 2009 did have a strong effect afterward. By January 2010, unemployment was back down to 4.9 percent.[5] The rise of unemployment primarily affected nonregular workers, 207,000 of whom lost their jobs between October 2008 and June 2009 (Yoshinobu 2009, 11). Additionally, foreign financial institutions cut 11 percent of their total workforce between the summer of 2007 and December 2008.[6]

The Japanese stock market was hit even harder than its U.S. counterpart, even though U.S. and other foreign investors were the key actors involved. The Nikkei 225 index dropped from 14,000 in July 2008 to almost 7,000 in March 2009. By late 2009, it was also clear that deflation had returned in Japan.

On the other hand, as the dust settled, it became clear that the 2008 and 2009 crisis proved only a temporary shock in Japan, mostly through the channels of export collapse, and not a fundamental structural one. Most critical is that Japanese banks were not deeply involved in the global binge in financial instruments built on subprime mortgages. One estimate places subprime losses in Japanese banks at around $8 billion, in relation to global losses of at least $1 trillion.[7] Nonperforming loans (NPLs) held by Japanese banks barely inched up.[8] Even unemployment peaked extremely rapidly and quickly fell back to under 5 percent, still the lowest of any OECD country.

Japan's response to the crisis was relatively limited. It consisted mostly of traditional fiscal packages, principally in the fall of 2008 under Prime Minister Aso and again in the fall of 2009. The IMF estimates that these discretionary fiscal measures related to the crisis in 2009 and 2010 amounted to about 1.9 percent of GDP, just above the G20 average (IMF 2009, 24). These packages, combined with a rebound in exports, led to a relatively healthy recovery in 2010, the growth rate estimated at 4.3 percent for the year, compared with 3.0 percent for the OECD as a whole (IMF 2011). Like China and Korea, Japan seems to have come out of the worst of the export crisis around the middle of 2009. With a likely rollback of fiscal measures and strengthening yen, growth is predicted to slow down to 1.6 percent in 2011, versus 2.5 percent for the OECD as a whole, and 1.7 percent in 2012. In sum, Japan appears to have weathered the 2008 to 2009 crisis through a traditional combination of deficit spending and export rebound, but without major structural reforms.

With respect to public finance, Japan has emerged with diminished capacity for further action (IMF 2009, 26), given a fiscal balance of −8.2 percent of GDP in 2010 and at least −10 percent in 2011, given the additional shock of the March 11 tsunami, and the highest debt-to-GDP ratio in the OECD—197 percent in 2010 and 204 percent in 2011 (Cecchetti, Mohanty, and Zampolli 2010, 3). Yet, despite a sense of relative alarm in the government during the Greek crisis around May 2010, government bond yields have remained stubbornly low, oscillating between 1.5 percent and 1 percent over 2008 through 2010, pegged at 1 percent in September 2010 (IMF 2010, 10). Indeed, around 94 percent of that debt is in the hands of domestic actors, namely the Central Bank, government-run funds, and domestic financial institutions, which are content, so far, with a low interest rate. This creates a sense of stability, unlike in Greece or other similar countries with high shares of foreign holders. Even after the additional shock of the March 11 disaster and the worsening euro crisis, the Japanese bond market remains stable in early 2012. In sum, the 2008 to 2009 crisis was only one more bump on an already rocky road. To understand how it played out in the political process, we have to place the crisis in the longer sequence of the adjustment of the Japanese political economic model to its global environment.

JAPAN'S DISEQUILIBRIUM: FROM FINANCIAL DEREGULATION TO FINANCIAL CRISIS

Japan has long been seen as a key example of a nonliberal market economy or coordinated market economy, alongside Germany. The theoretical model offered by the varieties of capitalism (VOC) approach emphasizes that varieties of capitalism are defined by a set of interlocking and interdependent institutions spanning industrial relations, welfare, and finance. These institutions have arisen over time as original responses to coordination problems within national economies and are resistant to change (Hall and Soskice 2001). Across various systems, variations in corporate governance patterns, as well as finance, labor, and welfare, are stable and resilient. They are rooted in larger social and political institutions. These institutions were historically determined and are fundamental to each national approach to the organization of society and politics. Thus they cannot change rapidly.

Beginning in the mid-1980s, after most OECD countries deregulated finance and opened up their capital account, capital flows of various sorts —FDI, bank loans, as well as equity and bond portfolio flows—increased rapidly. This major change had a particularly large impact on CME systems, given the central role played by controlled finance in these systems. Among the various types of capital flows that came to interact with national systems after financial deregulation, equity inflows tended to have the most systemic effect, that is, the most serious pressures on government, because they had a direct impact on the general level of the stock market, with all its cascading effects, such as bank capital adequacy ratios and credit ratings throughout the economy.

The Interaction Between Portfolio Flows and Stakeholder Systems

Why are global portfolio flows particularly challenging to nonliberal systems? The primary answer is that global financial flows and deregulated finance are more compatible with liberal than with nonliberal systems. Capital markets form the cornerstone of a liberal system, but have long been the poor parents to their nonliberal counterparts. As Ronald Dore points out, financial deregulation and the rise in equity inflows in nonliberal systems generate tensions between stakeholder concerns stemming from the traditional set-up and newly introduced shareholder concerns (1999). Furthermore, the process of financial deregulation and capital control liberalization involves much greater challenges for nonliberal than for liberal systems, given that corporate financing is the core institution sustaining the whole system. Financial deregulation must thus be accompanied by a host of other legal moves, including the setup of supervisory institutions, as well as corporate and labor reforms. In the absence of these accompanying moves, the system risks remaining stuck in a transitional and dysfunctional stage. The initial complementarity and interlocking characteristics of the various components of a nonliberal system may become problematic as financial deregulation occurs and expectations about the system change (on institutional complementarity and institutional crisis, see Aoki 2002).[9] In an ideal world, prudential regulation and other structural reforms should be precursors to financial liberalization, rather than the other way around (for a review of the literature on sequencing and an application to financial liberalization in East Asia, see Walter 2002). However, sequencing almost always gets thrown off course, because liberalization is politically much easier to implement than re-regulation and structural reforms.

Japanese Deregulation and the Bubble of 1985 to 1990

This Japanese model started being transformed with internal and external deregulation, a process that began in 1979, but was critical in 1984 and 1985, and eventually played a key role in the inflating of a huge financial bubble from 1985 to 1990. The culprit was domestic financial liberalization, not capital account liberalization. In the early 1980s, Japan's financial authorities gradually deregulated domestic banking and allowed major corporations to access global bond markets for corporate financing. In response, banks engaged in increasingly risky lending operations, both to recoup the loss of their best customers and to take advantage of new opportunities. Because bank loans were used to buy real estate and real estate served as collateral for bank loans, bank lending was at the core of the bubble. Yet although financial liberalization began in 1984, the critical accompanying step of building up a Financial Services Agency (FSA) only came in 1998.[10]

I have argued elsewhere that such ill-supervised financial deregulation represented the "path of least political resistance for a government that had to maneuver between strong global pressures to liberalize and strong domestic interests opposed to the establishment of new financial regulations" (Tiberghien 2005, 431). Pushed by large corporations seeking to take advantage of a nascent financial globalization and by a U.S. government seeking to resolve bilateral trade conflicts indirectly through financial deregulation in Japan, the Japanese government also found itself restrained by domestic interest groups with strong ties to the LDP and banks, which are important contributors of campaign funds to the LDP. In the end, the government gave large corporations the freedom to borrow abroad, and compensated banks by allowing them to tap new markets and use new instruments, including the lucrative government bond market. Securities firms were compensated through more freedom in equity markets. Meanwhile, the Ministry of Finance (MOF) was denied the means to monitor banks and securities companies in this new environment and the no-failure guarantee was maintained. Given that financial globalization and financial deregulation were novel and relatively technical phenomena, political leaders were unable to forecast that the choices made between 1979 and 1986 would contribute both to the financial bubble and its subsequent collapse. In sum, this process of interactive navigation through points of political resistance led to a suboptimal equilibrium: discrete choices in response to different groups had compounding effects.

Ineffective and Delayed Response to the Collapse of the Asset Bubble

The sequence of nonresponse and dithering in response to the collapse of the real estate and equity prices is well known. From 1990 to 1995, a protracted political battle over electoral reforms and political realignment led to a total absence of political leadership at a time when the banking crisis turned into a massive credit crisis and deflation. The Ministry of Finance was mostly left in charge of the response and focused on defending its interests and networks rather than devising an effective course of action (Amyx 2004; Amyx and Drysdale 2003). Not until the fall of 1998 did an effective regulatory response materialize. At last, the Diet passed two bills provided for capital injections into banks to the tune of $80 billion and the nationalization of two major banks, LTCB and Nippon Credit Bank. Even then, the reduction of bad loans on bank balance sheets to a level low enough to alleviate the credit crunch did not happen until the 2004–2005 fiscal year, when Prime Minister Koizumi attempted a resolution through new accounting rules and tougher enforcement. Part of the solution came on the corporate side through a speeding of restructuring and bankrupt-cies, thus taking care of the bad customers themselves.

As analyzed by Jennifer Amyx, this sequence of policy initiatives sug-gests several conclusions that are relevant to the 2008 crisis. First, delay in dealing with bad loans and bad assets on bank balance sheets hurt the economy tremendously. Monetary and fiscal solutions are not enough, even though the conservatism of Japanese monetary policy played a role in the continuation of the deflation trap and the depth of the output gap (see Krugman 1999 and Werner 2003). Second, capital injections into banks at a level high enough to kick-start lending again are critical. Nationaliza-tion may be necessary when the situation is bad enough, as a way to dis-miss management and turn operations around. Capital injections must be combined with conditions, benchmarks, and a turnaround in manage-ment. They must be accompanied by accounting rules and credible super-visory authorities with the ability to monitor results. Finally, bank bailouts often prove to be a disaster with voters. The 1998 bailout, for example, was extremely unpopular, leaving voters aghast by the implied moral hazard and the injustice involved in using taxpayers' money to save a handful of bankers who had gambled too big.

This part of the Japanese sequence is not controversial. Loose monetary policy, combined with ill-supervised deregulation, led to the largest asset bubble the world had yet seen. Politicians played with the fire of financial deregulation as a cheap fix for other problems and without an understand-ing of the likely consequences. Once the bubble popped and the banking system froze, a concurrent process of political realignment robbed Japan of any political leadership until 1997. The MOF kept basic control of the pro-cess, but without the regulatory tools to take vigorous action, without the legitimacy to demand capital injection, and without the interest to attract attention to its past weaknesses. Leadership came back with two relatively strong prime ministers from 1997 to 2000: Ryutaro Hashimoto and Keizo Obuchi, followed by Junichiro Koizumi from 2001 to 2006. These leaders eventually resolved the banking crisis, eviscerated the MOF's previous power, and set up new supervisory authorities under the Financial Services Agency (FSA). However, kick-starting the Japanese economy seemed to require more than banking regulations and bank bailouts. A consensus emerged by 1997 that structural reforms of corporate governance, labor relations, and other key components of the CME system were necessary to fully solve the banking crisis and recover competitiveness. The newly active foreign equity investors, who proved to be the critical market makers on the Japanese stock market, also demanded such changes.

JAPAN'S PARTIAL STRUCTURAL RESPONSE FROM 1997 TO 2008

After 1997, a major shift in discourse and in the path of economic reforms took place in Japan. The government itself shifted its position from a support for the status quo to the active promotion of painful systemic restructuring. The significance of these structural reforms is considerable because they aimed at undoing the very features of the Japanese political economy that were once recognized as the foundations of the three-decade long economic miracle. These include links between manufacturers and suppliers, cross-shareholding ties, the lifetime employment system, the main bank system (Amyx 2004; Aoki and Dore 1994; Calder 1997; Meyer 1996), and a quasi-state guarantee against bankruptcy. These reforms were the most fundamental change to the Japanese economic system since 1945.

At the same time, for all the simplicity of the concept of improving the efficiency of capital utilization in the economy, systemic corporate restructuring posed fundamental economic, social, and political dilemmas. As demonstrated by Masahiko Aoki (1988), Jennifer Amyx (2004), and scholars of the varieties of capitalism approach (Hall and Soskice 2001; Thelen and Kume 2003; Thelen 2004), the entire setup of Japan's political economy relied on institutional complementarities among the various components. Firm organization, labor management, cross-firm networks, main bank relations, and interactions with the government all formed a coordinated whole that arose and linked firms to other actors and provided the basis for Japanese economic competitiveness. If large manufacturing firms moved forward under external competitive pressures and new pressures from foreign shareholders, cutting ties to inefficient banks, small companies, and inefficient labor, what would happen to their capacity to innovate, their social legitimacy, and to the Japanese system as a whole? Could key components of the system, such as corporate governance, be over-hauled without jettisoning other components, such as labor policy and in-company training? The dilemma for firms and policymakers became how to enable a smoother process of creative destruction and effect a higher degree of capital allocation, yet preserve the key linkages that lie at the core of Japan's comparative advantage.

Causality Behind Post-1997 Structural Reforms

A critical feature in the Japanese process of structural reforms has been the role played by political entrepreneurs in response to global incentives from equity markets. Scholars seeking to explain the limited structural reforms in Japan have emphasized several domestic variables, such as public opinion and political leadership (Amyx 2003), electoral reforms (Rosenbluth and Ross 2003), or bureaucratic leadership in response to a legitimacy crisis (Toya 2000). In my own work, I have argued that the po-litical economy of corporate reforms involves active political entrepre-neurs, such as Yosano Kaoru, Obuchi Keizō, Takenaka Heizo, and Koi-zumi Junichirō spending political capital and taking advantage of zones of political autonomy in pushing reforms over the resistance of interest groups and their own political parties (Tiberghien 2007). Political entre-preneurs are the key agents pushing corporate reforms forward in the face of divided interest group coalitions and political parties. The success of corporate reforms depends on the degree of political autonomy enjoyed by these leaders and the opportunities available to them to delegate part of the reform process to a dependable and unified bureaucracy.

The critical valve that sets the pace and mix of corporate reform is the degree of strategic political autonomy that political leaders enjoy in a given national setting at a given time. When government leaders can rely on a centralized party, have considerable control over a governing coali-tion, or have the ability to decrease political salience through delegation, they are more likely to take on the global investor compact and engage in broad-based reforms. When their autonomy is weakened, reforms are likely to be partial and to include costly bargains with the key constituents.

The space available to political entrepreneurs is much more limited and constrained in Japan than in many advanced democracies. Furthermore, political autonomy has ebbed and flowed dramatically under various prime ministers, from nearly nil under Murayama (1994 to 1996) and Mori (2000 to 2001) to relatively high under Hashimoto (1996 to 1998) and Obu-chi (1999 to 2000). Meanwhile, the unity and dependability of the bureau-cracy has steadily decreased between 1994 and 2005 as internal disagreements, conflicts between bureaucrats and politicians, and institutional change have fragmented and weakened the bureaucracy.

The Outcome of Reforms

In the late 2000s, as the dust cleared from a decade of corporate and government reform, what can be observed? Although partial, significant corporate change did take place. Firms across the board unveiled large restructuring plans, closing some factories, and reorganizing supply chains. Some traditional firms, such as Nissan and Sony, took more drastic steps, including severing ties with long-term *keiretsu* suppliers (Nissan). Large firms avoided direct layoffs, but they reduced their labor force through attrition and a relative increase in part-time and temporary staff. They also induced layoffs in subsidiaries and suppliers by removing financial support and ensuing bankruptcies. As a whole, the total manufacturing workforce reached a postwar peak of 11.9 million in the second quarter of 1999, up from 9.8 in the first quarter of 1990, the time of the bubble collapse. By the second quarter of 2005, the manufacturing workforce was down to 9.6, though it came back up to 9.9 million in the first quarter of 2006.[11] From the 1999 peak to the 2005 trough, the manufacturing workforce dropped by 18 percent. Meanwhile, the nonmanufacturing workforce showed no drop and increased gradually from 15.3 million in the first quarter of 1990 to 24.6 million in the second quarter of 1999 and 27.6 million in the first quarter of 2006. The structure of employment indicates one further change. The nonpermanent workforce increased from 20 percent in 1994 to nearly 33 percent in 2005 (David Piling, "Cash in the Kaisha: How an Overhaul Is Producing a Resurgent Corporate Japan," *Financial Times*, March 23, 2006, p. 9). Other indicators of active restructuring include new corporate structures, new shareholding structures in large firms, a budding market for corporate control, with active mergers and acquisitions, and an active use of new bankruptcy laws.

The net outcome of reforms is one of a stronger impetus for change, but enduring divergence in the actual laws and practices. Japan's political economic system is evolving and incorporating new elements but retaining traditional features. On the ground, the Japanese model may actually be in the midst of fragmentation, certain laws encouraging U.S.-style corporate restructuring, but other traditional regulations enduring. Some corporations, such as Nissan, are radically transforming their management mode, but others, such as Toyota, are maintaining traditional management practices. Thus, during the process of structural liberal reforms, the Japanese model has become hybridized, a trend that echoes the findings in chapter 10 of this volume.

Period of Stasis before the Storm

The period from September 2006 to August 2009 is strangely dysfunctional one of policy-making in Japan. Under three successive and increasingly ineffective LDP prime ministers—Shinzo Abe, Yasuo Fukuda, and Taro Aso—the structural reform process mostly stopped and policymaking became divided, especially after the opposition DPJ took control of the Upper House of parliament in July 2007. The debate on inequality started raging in early 2007 and opinion seemed to waver on the continuation of structural reforms, yet the economy seemed to emerge from its long doldrums and the crisis mood dissipated. This is when the 2008 financial crisis hit.

THE UNPLANNED EXTERNALITY: THE RISE OF INEQUALITY AND ITS POLITICAL CONSEQUENCES

Structural reforms of the Japanese model and systemic restructuring played a role in the rise of inequality and its ensuing impact on political legitimacy.[12] Although there is a vast amount of diverging evidence, the OECD 2006 survey of Japan provides an authoritative review of existing data in its chapter dedicated to inequality and poverty (OECD 2006, chap. 4; for some of the best work on inequalities in Japan, see Tachibanaki 1998, 2004, 2005, 2006b). According to the OECD, "income inequality and relative poverty among the working-age population in Japan have risen to levels above the OECD average" (97). The Gini coefficient for market income of the working-age population increased from 30.9 in the mid-1980s to 33.8 in the mid-1990s and 36.2 in 2000 (99). The jump in the second half of the 1990s contrasts to a stable situation for the OECD average—35.2 in the mid-1980s, 39.3 in the mid-1990s, and 39.3 around 2000. For the total population, the Gini coefficient moved up from 31.7 in the mid-1980s to 36.9 in the mid-1990s and jumped to 41.0 by 2000. With these figures, Japan finds itself right in the middle of the OECD, more unequal than Nordic and Continental countries, but more equal than Canada, Spain, the United States, and most eastern European countries.

When analyzing the aggregate Gini coefficient on disposable income, factoring in tax and social spending, the OECD finds lower figures, but rising figures nonetheless. The Gini coefficient rose from 27.8 in the mid-1980s to 29.5 in the mid-1990s and jumped as much in half the time by 2000 to 31.4. The jump from 1995 to 2000 is particularly striking relative to other OECD countries. No other OECD country except Sweden has experienced a similar rise in that period. Further international comparative data from the OECD confirm that Japan saw only a modest rise in income inequality in the period 1985 to 1995, but that inequality has risen more sharply, in contrast to other countries, since 1995 (Burniaux et al. 1998; Foerster and Mira d'Ercole 2005).

Causality Behind the Rise of Inequality

What is driving this rise in inequality and its acceleration since 1995 in Japan? Economists have emphasized a nexus of concomitant variables, but the key driving force is the aggregate corporate restructuring and increased dualism in the labor market. In his important work, Tachibanaki (2006a) identifies seven factors, some of which are broad proximate factors: recession-induced cost-cutting; technological change; demographic change, particularly aging; and a less redistributive tax policy.

However, the 2006 OECD Survey of Japan identifies one key factor: labor market dualism or, in other words, "the increasing proportion of non-regular workers, who are paid significantly less than regular workers" (OECD 2006, 97). These part-time and temporary workers increased their share of total employment from 18.5 percent in 1990 and 19 percent in 1996 to 30 percent in 2004 (101) and nearly 34 percent in 2008. This trend is the result of both a reduction in long-term stable employment and an increase in more flexible part-time labor.

Data from the Ministry of Health, Labor, and Welfare (MHLW) show that the proportion of nonregular staff in the economy was relatively stable at 20 percent until 1995. It gradually increases to 23 percent in 1998 and to 25 percent in 1999. But the big jump, from 25 percent to 33 percent, takes place between 1999 and 2006.[13] The trend has stabilized at 33.5 percent between 2006 and 2010. In December 2008, an OECD working paper focused specifically on the impact of this increase in nonregular workers (Jones 2008). The report finds a strong link between the increase in nonregular workers and inequality. On average, nonregular workers earn only 40 percent as much as regular workers on an hourly basis (11). The correlation between the increase in part-time workers and wage growth is strongly negative (15).

Roots of Increased Labor Dualism

The trend was driven by both economic realities and by new legal tools. The two key legal and political steps taken as part of the larger structural reforms happened in 1999 and 2004. In December 1999, under Obuchi, the law on dispatch[14] of nonregular workers was amended to liberalize the practice to a large array of sectors (see Tiberghien 2007). In 2004, under

Koizumi, the law was further revised to enable general dispatch of such workers to the manufacturing sector. The OECD report refers to those legal steps as key enabling factors.

Political Salience of Inequality and Growing Backlash Against Structural Reforms

Just as the accumulation of reforms passed since 1997 seemed to have resulted in a modicum of economic revival in 2006 and 2007, political leaders found themselves on the defensive in response to an unexpected growing social uproar about the rising inequality that accompanied the structural reform program. This uproar opened a new front in the battle over the future of Japan's political economy. Until 2006, the battle pitted reformist politicians against traditional politicians, who wanted to continue interest group politics centered on iron triangles. The linkages between interest groups and politicians served both in a narrow sense but could be sold to the public as a quasi-social policy, given the large number of beneficiaries. Reformists from Hashimoto to Koizumi fought against their conservative opponents, culminating into the 2005 general election, in which Koizumi soundly defeated his opponents over postal privatization. This victory seemed to hand Koizumi and his successor Abe a free mandate for further structural reforms.

It is in this context that the great debate over inequality has arisen. The rise of social discontent over inequality put the Abe administration in a bind, as it tried to balance continued pro-market structural reforms with minimal tools to address inequality. Inequality became a wedge issue and DPJ leaders made the strategic choice in 2007 to use it as a way to exploit the gaps between traditionalists and reformists within the LDP. DPJ leaders such as Ichiro Ozawa also saw the inequality issue as a great way to gain popular support.

Public Opinion Data on Inequality

How has Japanese public opinion reacted to rising inequality? The overall finding is that a great majority of Japanese, about 70 percent, are sensitive to inequality and that perceptions of inequality are on the rise over recent years. Data from the International Social Survey Program (ISSP) show a strong perception of inequality.[15] The proportion of respondents who agree with the statement "income differences are too large" is not only extremely high in 2009 results, 74 percent, it also shows a marked increase from 1999 levels, 64 percent (62). A similar survey published by Mainichi

Shinbun on January 6, 2006, found that 64 percent of Japanese believed that Japan had become an "unequal society"[16] and 71 percent believed that things would get worse in the future.

Surveys also clearly show that voters are both linking rising inequality to government policy and expect the government to play a role in the reduction of these inequalities. For example, the August 2006 Asahi survey asked the 73 percent of respondents who thought that inequality had increased whether "the gap increase was related to the policies implemented by the PM Koizumi." A surprisingly high proportion, 62 percent, responded that it was.

Links to the 2009 Election Results

Although exit polls in the 2009 election highlighted other more immediate issues than inequality such as employment concerns, pensions, and corruption, the backlash against structural reforms and broad economic concerns constituted dominant factors behind the landslide victory of the DPJ. The DPJ harnessed this general backlash and focused several components of its manifesto on the inequality problem.

DPJ Leader Yukio Hatoyama supported these targeted promises with broad statements against "U.S.-led market fundamentalism" and against reforms such as Koizumi's postal reforms that destroyed local communities, committing to a new approach that would include an increase in the welfare system and more wealth redistribution.[17] The Nikkei Shimbun quoted Hatoyama as saying that "it's no exaggeration to say that [the post-Cold War period] was a process in which the globalized economy destroyed the Japanese economy and market fundamentalism ruined Japanese society."[18] The Nikkei quickly proceeded to criticize such statements as dangerous and out of touch with reality. However, the LDP leader himself took on the issue of inequality and anti-structural reform backlash. He argued that structural reforms had gone too far and that some should be reversed. In a pre-campaign speech, he said, "It has come to a point where we can no longer ignore the effects of social distortions caused by the set of deregulations and structural reforms."[19]

Among the public at large, a small-scale Kyodo survey showed that 68 percent of voters who voted for the LDP in 2005 supported a change of government in 2009.[20] Among the factors cited for discontent, a top mention is the worsening of the income gap among workers and the increased proportion of temporary workers: 48 percent reported that they were worse off due to lower income or job insecurity.

On August 30, two sorts of income disparities seemed to have an impact on the vote outcome: urban job insecurity and growing rural-urban disparities in the wake of some of the Koizumi reforms. Commenting on the loss of key LDP strongholds in Yamagata, Gunma, Fukushima, Iwate, Yamanashi, Niigata, and other prefectures, the Nikkei noted, "One reason the LDP lost its grip on these areas is that they have been on the losing side of economic disparities that widened as the result of spending cuts initiated by Junichiro Koizumi, one of the party's most popular prime ministers. The ongoing recession has worsened their situation. Key LDP support groups may have migrated further from the party in this election."[21]

REGIME CHANGE IN AUGUST 2009: THE GREAT SOCIAL-DEMOCRATIC SHIFT

The DPJ's response to the economic crisis and to the inequality problem has been strong, both in terms of wording and attempted action. The clearest statement of a coherent response comes with the elaboration of a "third way" concept by Prime Minister Kan in his manifesto for the Upper House election of 2010. Although the concept is broader than just a response to inequality, it clearly fits with a set of coherent responses to rising inequality.

The 2009 Manifesto

The DPJ tried to harness the feeling with direct promises in its manifesto, centering its entire platform upon leader Hatoyama's core concept of fraternity (Democratic Party of Japan 2009). Promise number 38 in the detailed list of measures commits the new government to "extend employment insurance coverage to all workers in order to "provide people with a greater sense of security" (21). The core promise, however, is promise number 39, which promises to "rectify the excessive deregulation of employment and stabilize workers' livelihood" (21). Using language supportive of the core interdependencies in CMEs, the DPJ also aims at "promoting continuity in the transmission of technology and skills" (22). To achieve these goals, the DPJ committed to "ban, in principle, the dispatch of temporary workers to manufacturing jobs" and to ban "temporary employment contracts of two months and less" (22). It further commits to establishing the principle of "equal treatment for dispatched workers and other workers at the same workplace" (22). This constituted one of the major concrete promises made by the DPJ in fighting the election.

Additionally, promise number 40 commits the DPJ to raising minimum wages, establishing a national minimum wage of ¥800 and seeking an annual average of ¥1,000, and to target the growing population of working poor. Promise number 41 further concludes with a sweeping commitment "to realize equal treatment such that people doing the same work at the same workplace can receive the same wage, regardless of gender or regular or irregular status" (Democratic Party of Japan 2009, 23).

The 2010 Manifesto and Kan's Third Way Concept

The 2010 manifesto opens with Kan's strategic Third Way positioning (Democratic Party of Japan 2010). Contrasting with what he calls the First Way ("economic policy centering on public works") and the Second Way ("excessive market fundamentalism"), Kan's Third Way "represents a package of economic policies that address the issue of the economy, public finance, and social security in an integrated manner." It advocates a "stronger social security system." The manifesto includes a strong section in inequality, asserting that "we will work hard to eliminate economic disparities and to achieve a better work-life balance in Japan's labor force" (13).

The two key pledges remain similar to those made in 2009. The manifesto includes a promise to "promote the harmonization of lifestyles and work by ensuring equal and balanced treatment of persons performing the same work at the same work place." (Democratic Party of Japan 2010, 14) The second pledge is to complete the passage of the bill initiated by the cabinet on the dispatch of temporary workers. Under the work done in the first year of the DPJ, the manifesto lists item 46: "Review of System for the Dispatch of Temporary Workers." The manifesto indicates that "a bill has been submitted to ban, in principle, the dispatch of temporary workers to manufacturing jobs, a practice that has been a major factor in destabilizing employment" (24).

Early Budgetary Moves

In government after September 2009, the DPJ initiated two significant steps on the inequality front. The first consisted of lessening the employment insurance inequality. The 2010 manifesto lists this as a significant achievement under item 43: "standards for the application of employment insurance were eased to allow the system to cover all workers. The portion of employment insurance funded by the national treasury was increased to strengthen the finances of the employment insurance system" (Democratic Party of Japan 2010, 24).

Then Prime Minister Hatoyama introduced the change to the employment insurance (as part of the budget-related bills) in his cabinet email no.

24 dated March 26, 2010: "In the area of employment, we will drastically shorten the eligibility criteria for employment insurance, from a prospect of over six months of employment to over 31 days, in order to relieve the employment insecurity of people who work. We will also increase the resources for employment adjustment subsidies by a factor of more than 10 compared to the amount budgeted for the current fiscal year with the aim to alleviate the burden of business operators working hard to maintain employment" (Hatoyama 2010).

A second initial step consisted in increasing the minimum wage from ¥800 to ¥1,000, a measure committed in the manifesto of 2009 and only partially achieved by 2010. The manifesto of 2010 lists this item under result number 44: "an agreement has been reached among the business community, labor organizations and the government to raise the national minimum wage level to 800 yen as soon as possible, and to aim to achieve a national minimum wage level of 1,000 yen, while taking economic conditions into consideration." These are small steps, but they show a willingness of the DPJ to act on the wage inequality front. It is important to note, however, that this agenda stopped after the loss of the majority in the Upper House in July 2010. Neither Kan nor Noda have been able to take further steps toward these goals after that loss.

The Bigger Battle: The Revision of the Dispatch Law

As promised in its 2009 manifesto and targeting one of the major mechanisms identified by the OECD and MHLW behind the rise in wage inequality, the DPJ initiated a legal revision to ban, in principle, the dispatch of temporary workers to the manufacturing industry. Officially titled "Act for Securing the Proper Operation of Worker Dispatching Undertakings and Improved Working Conditions for Dispatched Workers," the government's bill aims to prohibit three kinds of dispatching: registered temporary staffing with daily jobs, temporary staffing in the manufacturing industry, and daily-based temporary staffing under two months. The bill represents a significant re-regulation of temporary labor, and thus a major reversal of the structural reform process, involving significant political maneuvering, coalition politics, and tensions between the DPJ and Keidanren.

Although the cabinet introduced the bill on April 6, 2010, and Diet committee debates took place on May 28, 2010, the legislative process was interrupted by the resignation of Prime Minister Hatoyama on June 1 and the breakdown of the coalition with the SDP. By the time of the Upper House election in July, the bill was not completed. It further languished in the divided Diet throughout the fall of 2010 and during all of 2011. By 2012, it was clear that the loss of control in the Upper House prevented further legislative action.

Impact of DPJ's actions on DPJ's Support Base

How can we evaluate the early steps taken by the DPJ since coming to power on the heels of the Great Recession? Although more systematic data are necessary to evaluate the contribution of the DPJ's actions against inequality to voters' reactions, it is safe to say that the initial DPJ actions fitted well with the wishes of the majority of voters, as expressed in public opinion polls. The DPJ agenda on inequality seemed to follow the position of the median voter on these issues closely and could be seen as a positive contributor to electoral support. At the same time, it was not enough to counterbalance major unrelated political weaknesses during the 2010 Upper House election. After loss in that election, however, the DPJ's social democratic agenda stalled, and the fiscal hawks of the Ministry of Finance gained a dominant influence over both the Kan and Noda administrations. Caught between a growing awareness of fiscal constraints, possibly intensified by MOF, and a vindictive opposition-controlled Upper House, the DPJ could not pursue its 2009 promises any further. That, in turn, disappointed many DPJ supporters.

CONCLUSION

This chapter has put the shock of 2008 in Japan into the larger context of a protracted adaptation of the CME model to the new reality of global and deregulated finance. The 2008 financial crisis hit Japan primarily through the traditional export channel rather than through financial channels. The Japanese CME model was put off balance by a process of ill-supervised and ill-sequenced financial deregulation in the 1980s. After hesitating for years at the cost of a great output gap, Japan engaged in a twin process of banking reforms and partial restructuring of the key tenets of its CME system after 1997. This led Japan into a transitory stage, a public backlash against the externality of rising inequality, and eventual regime change in August 2009. The 2008 financial crisis was in essence one last shock in a long process that reflected the difficult adaptation of CME systems to global finance.

On the political side, entrepreneurial reform processes as a response to global incentives have played a major role in facilitating structural reforms. In turn, the emerging backlash against inequality has played an important role in the anti-LDP backlash in both the 2007 Upper House election and the 2009 Lower House election. Beyond the rise to power of the DPJ, the backlash against inequality is leading to a possible political transition that may see the rise of a new party or coalition of actors in defense of the vanishing middle class.

In sum, the strategy pursued by entrepreneurial reformers such as Obuchi and Yosano, and later more brashly Koizumi, reached its electoral limit. These reformers sought to solve the growing problem of declining support among urban floating voters by pursuing reforms that targeted the urban middle class. By moving the LDP toward the center, they risked losing some long-standing conservative supporters but were likely to gain more at the center. The strategy seemed to achieve a resounding success in the 2005 Lower House election, when the LDP swept through urban districts for the first time in decades, while holding up its core rural constituencies. With hindsight, 2005 was a blip, as the cost of structural reforms had not yet sunk down. It may have happened at the top of an early W-curve. By 2009, a reverse double-whammy happened: traditional rural supporters lashed out at the LDP for the costs from Koizumi structural reforms, and urban voters punished the LDP for stopping reforms after creating large social costs. As it turned out, Abe, Fukuda, and Aso pursued transitional economics, neither reversing the Koizumi structural reforms, nor taking them forward.

The situation also created an interesting dilemma for the DPJ after the election. On the one hand, the inequality backlash gave space for the DPJ to shift its platform away from a sole focus on liberal reforms and toward the issue of labor market and welfare protection. The DPJ moved to take advantage of this new wedge issue and gained some policy coherence in the process. At the same time, the DPJ retained enough of its traditional reform image and also became a home for traditional anti-Koizumi LDP conservatives through the coalition with leaders such as Kamei Shizuka. This created a difficult equation to square. How could the DPJ seek to revive the economy and continue the reform of the traditional Japanese system, but also move toward closing the inequality gap and consolidating welfare? By 2012, it became clear that the DPJ was able to do neither, and its attention became fully consumed by the twin urgencies of disaster relief and fiscal reconstruction in the wake of the March 2011 earthquake and tsunami.

This discussion thus places the shock of the global crisis of 2008 and 2009 within the prism of the protracted adaptation of a CME system, sustained by public support, to changing global finance. I have argued, in contrast to chapter 2 of this volume, that global financial markets did create tensions for the Japanese model and incentives for political entrepreneurs to reform components of the Japanese system. The Japanese system hybridized under the process of partial reforms and partial corporate adaptation, leading to an outcome similar to that observed in Ireland (see chapter 10, this volume). At the same time, the voter backlash against inequality and some of the other externalities of liberalizing reforms, plus the ensuing effort by the DPJ to roll back some of the reforms could lend support to the chapter 2 argument. Whether due to a dysfunctional transitional stage engendered by reforms or to voters rallying behind the earlier national system, the CME does show more resilience than expected.

Another theme arising from Japan's experience is the salience of rising inequality as an important variable that conditions the government's responses. Other systems—such as the United States, the United Kingdom, France, Korea, Taiwan, and of course China—are in the throes of an intensifying debate about inequality that affects the continuing response to the global crisis. Once inequality becomes politically salient, it generates incentives for political parties and government leaders to slow down programs of structural reforms. Inequality increases the costs of pursuing any further neoliberal reforms or deregulation, as they may worsen the situation. Politically salient inequality also creates incentives for politicians to devise remedies, but the Japanese case contains a cautionary tale: structural remedies with real costs for business are hard to implement without a robust governing coalition, and budgetary remedies are simply unrealistic without budgetary flexibility. By 2012, it is clear that the DPJ has not succeeded in passing its social-democratic legislative program, due to coalition fragmentation, poor leadership, and budget constraints.

By late 2011 into early 2012, despite its great power and autonomy, Japan's situation partially echoes that of the hybrid southern European countries analyzed in chapter 4 of this volume: because policymaking is unable to meet the expectations of voters and as fiscal retrenchment is eroding pillars of the social contract, trust in the government and in democracy is on the wane. Although the results are skewed in part by the additional shock of the Fukushima nuclear crisis, a recent survey on government trust by Edelman (Edelman Trust Barometer), presented at the 2012 Davos meeting, showed that Japan saw the largest drop between 2011 and 2012: from 50 percent to 25 percent.[22] Opinion polls in early 2012 likewise indicate low support for both the DPJ government and the LDP opposition. In this volatile political context, several new parties are being created and regional leaders are claiming higher legitimacy and clamoring for more power. Given the disappointment of voters and the inability of policymaking to address their preferences, Japanese democracy could go through a rough and uncertain period.

The author acknowledges support from the Hampton Fund at UBC and competent research assistance from Go Murakami.

NOTES

1. "Japan's Growth Path at Crossroads," *Nikkei Weekly*, February 23, 2009.
2. *The Oriental Economist*, March 2009, 77:3, p. 2.
3. *The Oriental Economist*, April 2009, 77:4, p. 2.
4. *The Oriental Economist*, February 2009, 77:2, p. 2.
5. Statistics Bureau, "Monthly Results," Ministry of Internal Affairs and Communications, http://www.stat.go.jp/english/data/roudou/154.htm (accessed March 28, 2012).
6. "Financiers Fear Firings from Afar," *Nikkei Weekly*, February 2, 2009.
7. Martin Fackle, "In Japan, Financial Crisis Is Just a Ripple," *New York Times*, September 19, 2008.
8. *The Oriental Economist*, March 2009.
9. Aoki, however, does not put the emphasis solely on financial deregulation as the agent of perturbation in the initial system.
10. This section incorporates past work by the author on the Japanese bubble (Tiberghien 2005).
11. Ministry of Finance Japan, "Quarterly Financial Statements Statistics of Corporation by Industry," http://www.mof.go.jp/english/pri/reference/ssc/historical.htm (accessed March 28, 2012).
12. This section summarizes and includes elements previously published in a longer research article in Japan (see Tiberghien 2011).
13. Statistics Bureau, "Historical Data of Employee by Type of Employment (Regular Staff, Non-regular Staff)," Ministry of Internal Affairs and Communications, http://www.stat.go.jp/english/data/roudou/lngindex.htm (accessed March 28, 2012).
14. Although the term *contracted workers* would be more correct by international standards, the Japanese texts continue to refer to *dispatched workers* in their English translation. This chapter uses the Japanese terms.
15. "Prevailing Sense of Disparity: From the ISSP Survey on 'Social Inequality,'" *NHK Monthly Report on Broadcast Research* 60(5): 56–76.
16. The exact phrasing of Mainichi Yoron Chosa is, "Some people point out that Japan is becoming an 'unequal society' in which children's future occupation and income are determined by the family background, such as their parents' income. Do you think that Japan is becoming an equal society?"
17. Mure Dickie, "DPJ Chief Hits at 'U.S.-Led' Globalism," *Financial Times*, August 10, 2009.

18. "Dispatches: Hatoyama's Anti-globalism Disquieting," *The Nikkei*, August 19, 2009, morning edition.
19. "Aso Says Departure from Koizumi's Structural Reforms Necessary," *The Nikkei*, July 31, 2009.
20. "68 of 100 Who Voted LDP in '05 Have Seen Enough," *Japan Times (Kyodo News)*, August 8, 2009.
21. "Wins in Cities, LDP Territory Sealed DPJ's Triumph," *The Nikkei*, August 31, 2009, morning edition.
22. Andrew Edgecliffe-Johnson, "Faith In Government Plummets, Research Says," *Financial Times*, January 23, 2012, p. 2.

REFERENCES

Amyx, Jennifer Ann. 2003. "A New Face for Japanese Finance? Assessing the Impact of Recent Reforms." In *Challenges for Japan: Political Leadership, US-China-Japan Triangle, Financial Reform, and Gender Issues*, edited by Gil Latz. Tokyo: Tokyo International House of Japan.

———. 2004. *Japan's Financial Crisis: Institutional Rigidity and Reluctant Change*. Princeton, N.J.: Princeton University Press.

Amyx, Jennifer Ann, and Peter Drysdale. 2003. *Japanese Governance: Beyond Japan Inc.* New York: RoutledgeCurzon.

Aoki, Masahiko. 1988. *Information, Incentives, and Bargaining in the Japanese Economy*. Cambridge: Cambridge University Press.

———. 2002. "Japan in the Process of Institutional Change." *Miyakodayori* 31 (January 25, 2002). Available at: http://www.rieti.go.jp/en/miyakodayori/031.html (accessed April 25, 2012).

Aoki, Masahiko, and Ronald Dore. 1994. *The Japanese Firm: Sources of Competitive Strength*. Oxford: Oxford University Press.

Aoki, Masahiko, Bo Gustafsson, and Oliver E. Williamson. 1990. *The Firm as a Nexus of Treaties*. Newbury Park, Calif.: Sage Publications.

Burniaux, Jean-Marc, Thai-Thanh Dang, Douglas Fore, Michael Foerster, Marco Mira d'Ercole, and Howard Oxley. 1998. "Income Distribution and Poverty in Selected OECD Countries." *Economics Department* working paper. Paris: OECD Publishing.

Calder, Kent. 1997. "Assault on the Bankers' Kingdom: Politics, Markets, and the Liberalization of Japanese Industrial Finance." In *Capital Ungoverned: Liberalizing Finance in Interventionist States*, edited by Michael Loriaux, Meredith Woo-Cumings, Kent Calder, Sylvia Maxfield, and Sofia A. Perez. Ithaca, N.Y.: Cornell University Press.

Cecchetti, Stephen G., Madhusudan Mohanty, and Fabrizio Zampolli. 2010. "The Future of Public Debt: Prospects and Implications." *BIS* working paper no. 300. Basel: Bank for International Settlements.

Democratic Party of Japan. 2009. "2009 Change of Government: The Democratic Party of Japan's Platform for Government—Putting People's Lives First." Tokyo: Democratic Party of Japan.

———. 2010. "Restoring Vitality to Japan: The Democratic Party of Japan's Policy Platform for Government—Putting People's Lives First." Tokyo: Democratic Party of Japan.

Dore, Ronald. 1999. "The Reform Debate in Japan: Patriotic Concern or Class Interest? Or Both?" *Journal of Japanese Studies* 25(1): 65–89.

Foerster, Michael, and Marco Mira d'Ercole. 2005. "Income Distribution and Poverty in OECD Countries in the Second Half of the 1990s." *Social Employment and Migration* working paper. Paris: OECD Publishing.

Hall, Peter A., and Daniel W. Gingerich. 2009. "Varieties of Capitalism and Institutional Complementarities in the Political Economy: An Empirical Analysis." *British Journal of Political Science* 39(3): 449–82.

Hall, Peter A., and David W. Soskice. 2001. *Varieties of Capitalism: The Institutional Foundations of Comparative Advantage.* Oxford: Oxford University Press.

Hatoyama, Yukio. 2010. "No. 24." *Hatoyama Cabinet E-Mail Magazine.* March 26, 2010.

International Monetary Fund (IMF). 2009. "Regional Economic Outlook, May 2009." Washington, D.C.: International Monetary Fund.

———. 2010. "World Economic Outlook: Recovery, Risk, and Rebalancing." Washington, D.C.: International Monetary Fund.

———. 2011. "World Economic Outlook Update, January 25, 2011." Washington, D.C.: International Monetary Fund.

Jones, Randall S. 2008. "Reforming the Labour Market in Japan to Cope with Increasing Dualism and Population Ageing." *Economics Department* working paper 652. Paris: Organisation for Economic Co-operation and Development.

Krugman, Paul. 1999. *The Return of Depression Economics.* New York: Norton and Company.

Meyer, Claude. 1996. *La puissance financiere du Japon.* Paris: Economica.

Organisation for Economic Co-operation and Development (OECD). 2006. *OECD Economic Surveys: Japan.* Paris: OECD.

Rosenbluth, Frances, and Schaap Ross. 2003. "The Domestic Politics of Banking Regulation." *International Organization* 57(2): 307–36.

Tachibanaki, Toshiaki. 1998. *Nihon No Keizai Kakusa: Shotoku to Shisan Kara Kangaeru.* Tokyo: Iwanami Shoten.

———. 2004. *The Economics of Social Security in Japan.* Northhampton, Mass.: Edward Elgar.

———. 2005. *Confronting Income Inequality in Japan: A Comparative Analysis of Causes, Consequences, and Reform.* Cambridge, Mass.: MIT Press.

———. 2006a. "Inequality and Poverty in Japan." *Japanese Economic Review* 57(1): 1–26.

——. 2006b. *Kakusa Shakai: Nani Ga Mondai Nano Ka.* Tokyo: Iwanami Shoten.

Thelen, Kathleen Ann. 2004. *How Institutions Evolve: The Political Economy of Skills in Germany, Britain, the United States, and Japan.* New York: Cambridge University Press.

Thelen, Kathleen Ann, and Ikuo Kume. 2003. "The Future of Nationally Embedded Capitalism: Industrial Relations in Germany and Japan." In *The End of Diversity? Prospects for German and Japanese Capitalism*, edited by Kozo Yamamura and Wolfgang Streeck. Ithaca, N.Y.: Cornell University Press.

Tiberghien, Yves. 2005. "Navigating the Path of Least Resistance: Financial Deregulation and the Origins of the Japanese Crisis." *Journal of East Asian Studies* 5(3): 427–64.

——. 2007. *Entrepreneurial States: Reforming Corporate Governance in France, Japan, and Korea.* Ithaca, N.Y.: Cornell University Press.

——. 2011. "The Political Consequences of Inequality in Japan." *Journal of Social Science* 62(1)(February): 77–99.

Toya, Tetsuro. 2000. "The Political Economy of the Japanese Financial Big Bang: Institutional Change in Finance and Public Policy-Making." Ph.D. diss., Stanford University.

Walter, Andrew. 2002. "Financial Liberalization and Prudential Regulation in East Asia: Still Perverse?" Working paper. Singapore: Institute of Defence and Strategic Studies.

Werner, Richard. 2003. *Princes of the Yen: Japan's Central Bankers and the Transformation of the Economy.* Armonk, N.Y.: M. E. Sharpe.

Yoshinobu, Kobayashi. 2009. "Revising the Worker Dispatching Act." *Social Science Japan* 41(September): 11–14.

Chapter 10 | The Liberal Model in (the) Crisis: Continuity and Change in Great Britain and Ireland

Lucy Barnes and Anne Wren

THE CURRENT CRISIS is a global one, but variation has been considerable across countries in the nature and scale of the economic downturn, in policy responses, and in the political impact. Why were some countries affected more than others, and what explains the varied policies implemented in response? The financial crisis has been characterized as a crisis of the Liberal variant of advanced capitalism, whose defining characteristics include light regulation, financial innovation, and credit expansion. We argue that the literature on varieties of capitalism provides an analytical framework for understanding divergence between the fates of the two varieties in the crisis, but, more important, that within these broad categories, considerable variation remains.

The crisis has thrown the significance of political-institutional variations within these regimes into sharp relief and made clear that intramodel variation can have important implications for economic development and for patterns of economic performance. Our argument focuses on cross-national variation within the Liberal model, and specifically on a comparison of the Irish and U.K. cases. To some degree, this is an exercise in trying to understand Ireland's particular vulnerability in the financial crisis in a comparative context: the extreme nature of the crisis in Ireland makes it important to understand its political economy, but it also risks making the Irish case sui generis with few generalizable explanations or lessons. The British comparison provides an analogue to Ireland in which much—though not all—of the political and economic context is shared.

This allows an analysis of the particular features in Ireland that led to its singularly problematic crisis as well as its divergent policy response.

We focus on the initial period of financial crisis, from the fall of 2008 to the spring of 2011, and in particular the divergent responses of the Fianna Faíl-Green and Labour governments incumbent in Ireland and the United Kingdom respectively when the crisis hit.[1] We do not deal with the subsequent sovereign debt crisis, which is covered instead in chapter 6 of this volume. Responses to the sovereign debt crisis display little variation in the countries concerned (indeed, Klaus Armingeon and Lucio Baccaro argue in chapter 6 that for the countries involved only one possible policy response effectively exists—internal devaluation—and it is imposed from outside the national political economy). Responses are also less well analyzed through the varieties of capitalism lens.

The policy responses of governments in the wake of the financial crisis then can be broadly categorized into two types, which we label *fiscal* and *financial*. The first refers to policy packages designed to stimulate the economy—the U.S. archetype here being the American Recovery and Reinvestment Act of 2009 (ARRA). Financial responses refer to policies oriented toward resolving difficulties in the banks specifically, the U.S. example being the Emergency Economic Stabilization Act of 2008, which created the Troubled Asset Relief Program. In the wake of the crisis, the Irish policy response differed significantly from that in the United Kingdom on both of these dimensions.

On the former dimension, Ireland implemented austerity responses at a time when most other governments were engaging in fiscal stimulus; and on the latter, the Irish bank bailout was more generous to creditors, left the state on the hook for larger liabilities than elsewhere, and led to the decline in the perceived creditworthiness of the Irish state and its need to access EU-IMF funds for liquidity. This variation is outlined in more detail in the following section. However, the short answer as to why the Irish government pursued policies so different from those enacted elsewhere, and particularly in the United Kingdom, is that it was left with little choice given the severity with which the financial crisis manifested itself. We argue that once the crisis hit, countries' capacity to respond was strongly shaped by their experience of the crisis. The interesting question from a political economy perspective, then, is how this experience was shaped by long-term political-economic and institutional structures.

VARIATIONS IN RESPONSES

The responses to the financial and economic crisis in the United Kingdom and Ireland diverged significantly, despite similarities in their economic models. In this section we describe this variation in policy responses and show how it can be traced to differences in the precise nature of the crisis in the two countries. The extreme severity of the crisis in Ireland and greater spillover of the financial crisis to the broader economy and government's fiscal position meant that the Irish government did not have the same policy tools available as the United Kingdom did. Our primary argument, however, is that this variation in the extent of the crisis in each country was itself the result of differences in the underlying political economic models in the precrisis period. It is this variation in political economic models, therefore, that explains both the nature of the economic shocks experienced in the two countries, and the policy responses to those shocks.

Fiscal Responses

The economic impact of problems in the financial sector became apparent over the course of 2008, and by the end of that year governments had adopted a variety of strategies to weather the crisis. In the United Kingdom, the November 2008 prebudget report introduced a number of stimulus measures. The most important of these in terms of size were an increase in the basic income tax allowance as well as a temporary 2.5 percent reduction in value-added tax (VAT). The package also delayed planned business tax increases, accelerated investment spending, and expanded guaranteed loans to small businesses (HM Revenue and Customs 2008).

By contrast, the Irish government at the time was announcing its budget for 2009, which included measures to increase tax revenues by approximately 1 percent of GDP (IMF 2009). These tax increases came from a 0.5 percent increase in VAT, and an income levy of 1 percent on gross incomes up to €100, 000 and 2 percent above that (Department of Finance 2009). The Irish government was to follow the 2009 budget with further austerity measures throughout 2009: a public sector pension levy introduced in February 2009 was estimated to reduce expenditures by a further percentage point of GDP (IMF 2009). A supplementary budget in April 2009 further consolidated the government's fiscal position, as did the annual budgets and four-year 2011 to 2014 National Recovery Plan announced in 2010. Overall, Ireland's fiscal adjustment will amount to €30 billion, of which €21 billion will have been implemented by the end of 2011 (Department of Finance 2011).

Thus the difference in demand management—fiscal policy—responses to the crisis between the United Kingdom and Ireland was considerable. The British government, along with most of the OECD, chose to introduce short-term stimulus packages designed to compensate for the decline in

Figure 10.1   Net Effect of Discretionary Stimulus on Fiscal Balance, 2008 to 2010

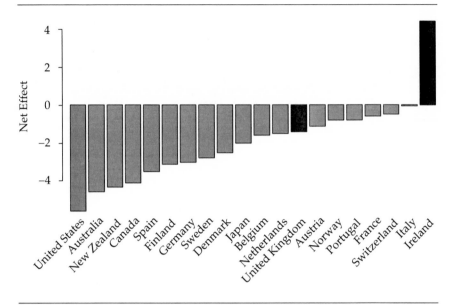

Source: Authors' calculations based on Lane and Milesi-Ferritti (2010).

world and domestic demand. In Ireland, however, the policies pursued were sharply contractionary (for broader cross-national comparisons on this, see chapter 4, this volume). Figure 10.1 shows data from the Organisation for Economic Co-operation and Development (OECD) on the net effect of discretionary policies on fiscal balance in the advanced industrial OECD countries between 2008 and 2010 (2009). Ireland is the only country in this group to have pursued austerity in its discretionary response, though similar responses were seen in Hungary, Bulgaria, Iceland, and the Baltic States (see Armingeon 2010).

Although the extent of the divergence of the Irish fiscal response is striking, it is not necessarily particularly puzzling. Rather, it can be seen as reflecting the extent of the economic constraints within which the Irish government was operating in this period, and the limitations that these constraints placed on policy choice. In the first place, the shock to output and employment when the crisis hit was considerably greater in the Irish case than in the United Kingdom. The Liberal growth models pursued both in Ireland and the United Kingdom in this period relied heavily on a credit-fueled expansion of domestic demand, increasing their vulnerability to contracting credit supply. In Ireland, however, greater dependence on the construction sector for jobs and output exacerbated these effects once the housing bubble burst.

Second, due to the strongly procyclical fiscal stance adopted in the boom years—especially the heavy reliance of tax revenues on stamp duties and other activity tied to housing, corporate tax, and VAT—the automatic impact of the downturn on the deficit in Ireland was much larger than in other countries, including the United Kingdom (IMF 2009; Lane 2011). The fiscal burden was further increased by the extent of financial support to the banks (Armingeon 2010), which weighed heavy as the result of both the nature of the financial policy response and the importance of the banks compared with the size of the economy. Bank recapitalization also had an important impact on the British government's fiscal position, but its relative size was much smaller.

All of these factors combined to place considerably greater constraints on the Irish government than its U.K. counterpart in crafting a fiscal response to the crisis. The immediate cause of Ireland's contractionary policy response, then, was the extreme depth of the economic and fiscal crisis; this feature, though, was the outcome of the political economy of Irish economic growth and development during the boom. This important difference between the United Kingdom and Ireland is outlined later in the chapter.

Financial Response

In most countries, policies aimed at resolving the banking crisis have included three core components. The first has been the extension of government-backed guarantees on the liabilities of the banks. The extent of these guarantees has varied considerably across countries and the Irish case is extreme. On September 30, 2008, the Irish government announced an unlimited guarantee on the liabilities of Irish banks. The analogous U.K. decision was to extend the level of deposit guarantees to $74,000 from around $50,000, which pales into insignificance in comparison (Beck et al. 2010; Carmassi, Luchetti, and Micossi 2010). The second component of the response has been the recapitalization of the banks, undertaken to various degrees as the extent of the liquidity crisis within the banks became clear. In Ireland, the extent of these injections has been massive, estimated at around 30 percent of GDP by the end of September 2010 (European Commission 2011), and at least 55 percent of GDP counting the state-backed bonds used to pay for the assets transferred to the newly established National Asset Management Agency (NAMA), the so-called bad bank. In the United Kingdom, the equivalent estimate is a much smaller 6 percent of GDP arising from the nationalizations of the Royal Bank of Scotland,

Lloyds, and Northern Rock.[2] The final component of policy aimed at resolving the crisis in the banking sector is regulatory reform, primarily increasing oversight and raising capital requirements. This last element of policy is being coordinated at the international level to a much greater extent, so we leave it aside for the present discussion. On the other two elements, bank guarantees and recapitalization, however, the difference between the U.K. and Irish cases, at least in the short run, was large. European Commission estimates placed the size of the Irish bailout at 229 percent of GDP in June 2009, compared with 27 percent of GDP in the United Kingdom,[3] and the size of the liability assumed by the Irish state led to a reduction in its perceived creditworthiness, increasing its borrowing costs on international bond markets and necessitating access to EU-IMF bailout funds in November 2010.

The proximate cause of this variation is again the difference in the scale of the crisis experienced in the financial sectors of the two countries. As we describe in the next section, the considerable expansion of the banking sector relative to GDP, and the comparatively more rapid expansion of credit, and the heavy concentration of bank lending in the domestic property sector, meant that the crisis posed a particularly grave threat to the stability of the Irish banking sector and, by extension, to the Irish economy (Honohan 2010; Regling and Watson 2010; European Commission 2011). This set of conditions lends credibility to the argument that the scale of the bank bailout was appropriate, given the risks of systemic failure plausible in the Irish case. However, the roots of the crisis in the Irish financial sector grew out of institutional characteristics of the growth model pursued in Ireland in the precrisis period. Some of these were shared with other Liberal economies, such as the United Kingdom: others were more distinct features of the Irish case. All were supported by a tight coalition of interests in the financial, banking, and construction sectors.

DECLINING TRADITIONAL SECTORS, DEBT, AND DOMESTIC DEMAND

The advanced industrial economies face significant challenges in responding to the current economic crisis. It is important to recognize, however, that the crisis occurred in the context of massive structural economic change in these countries, rooted in long-term processes of economic development. Deindustrialization has seen large-scale transfers of output and employment from traditional industrial and agricultural sectors to service sectors over the past thirty to forty years. We argue that the coincidence of these two crises is not accidental—the roots of the current financial crisis are tied to the responses of advanced industrial economies to the challenge of deindustrialization—and that the depth of the crisis that countries currently face is equally tied to these development paths. Liberal economies, like Ireland, the United Kingdom, and the United States, pursued growth based on the expansion of domestic demand, enabled by the expansion of private credit. The resulting shift in economic activity into nontraded service and construction sectors and reliance on credit made these economies particularly vulnerable in the crisis.

Deindustrialization has many causes and implications we do not discuss here. The key difference for us is the different responses to this common challenge in Liberal versus export-oriented countries (for more on the distinction between these two regime types, see chapter 2, this volume). Coordinated European regimes have reacted by maintaining relatively high levels of international competitiveness and continued strong export performance in manufacturing sectors, albeit with costs elsewhere. In contrast, the Liberal economies—with educational systems that create strong general, transferable skills; flexible labor markets, and decentralized wage-setting arrangements—have facilitated radical innovation in high-end knowledge-based service sectors. However, they have been less effective in maintaining export competitiveness, and are associated with higher levels of output and employment in nontraded sectors (Iversen and Soskice 2010). Another effect of this institutional combination, in particular of its incentives for radical innovation combined with risk-taking, was to facilitate the development and spread of high-risk financial activities.

In the Liberal economies, nontraded private sectors have replaced traditional traded sectors as the chief engine of employment growth. A large part of this expansion has occurred in nontraded private service sectors characterized by a low capacity for productivity growth, low levels of international trade and relatively high price and income elasticities of demand: personal services, wholesale and retail trade, and restaurants (Wren 2012). In Ireland over the past ten years the domestic construction sector has also accounted for an increasingly large share of employment growth.

Two sets of policies in particular facilitated the expansion in nontraded service sectors in the Liberal cases. First, flexible wage-setting institutions decoupled the wages of workers in less productive sectors, such as personal services, from their more productive counterparts, such as manufacturing. This allowed relative prices in these sectors to fall, which had the effect of increasing demand and employment, given high price elasticities of demand for these products (see Iversen and Wren 1998; Wren, Fodor, and Theodoropoulou 2012).

Demand for these types of services is also highly income-elastic, however (Kongsrud and Wanner 2005; Kalwij and Machin 2007). Many services—personal services in particular—are luxury items that tend to be

Figure 10.2   Nontraded Private Service Sector Employment Versus
Private-Sector Indebtedness

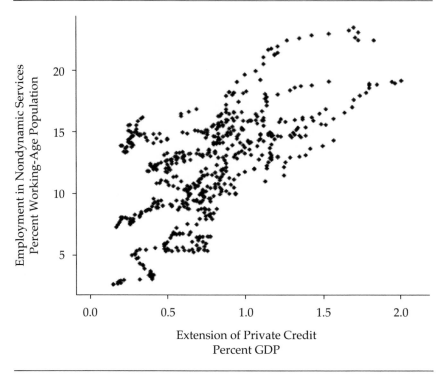

Source: Authors' figure. Private credit data from Beck et al. (2010); Employment data result of authors' calculations based on data from EU-KLEMS Growth and Productivity Accounts Database (2009).

consumed more as incomes rise (Fisher 1935; Clark 1940). As Mary Gregory, Wiemer Salverda, and Ronald Schettkat (2007) point out, the gap in rates of employment creation in nontraded service sectors between Liberal and continental European economies over this period is closely correlated with levels of consumer demand per head of population. A critical factor explaining patterns of consumer demand is savings behavior—or perhaps more pertinently its inverse, personal indebtedness (Soskice 2007). The link between the expansion of credit to the private sector and the expansion of employment in private service sectors is clear from figure 10.2, which plots employment (measured as employment as a percentage of the working age population) in low productivity, sheltered, service sectors (hotels and restaurants, wholesale and retail trade, and other community social and personal services) against a measure of private sector indebtedness (see also Wren 2012).[4] The dataset covers a set of seventeen OECD countries from 1970 to 2000.

The link between private credit and service expansion is unsurprising. Expanding cheap credit to households over this period created the impression of consumer wealth—directly, in providing credit lines for personal spending, and indirectly, in contributing to asset, especially house, price inflation. This increase in perceived wealth generated corresponding increases in output and employment for services with high elasticities of demand.[5] The availability of large quantities of cheap credit to households also led to increases in output and employment in the construction sector itself, particularly in the Irish case.

The combination of policies and institutions that underpinned the significant increases in private-sector indebtedness over this period has been much discussed elsewhere. First, a prolonged period of historically low real interest rates across the OECD area substantially lowered the cost of borrowing, which had important implications for the housing market in particular (Taylor 2009; Ahrend, Cournede, and Price 2008). Second, policies in the Liberal market economies promoted both radical innovation and risk-taking in the financial sector. The key institutional features of the system in the context of the crisis were light regulation and oversight and flexible wage-setting institutions, the latter allowing extensive use of profit-related bonuses for high-end workers. On the positive side, these institutions facilitated radical innovation in communications and information technology and in complex, knowledge-based services (Hall and Soskice 2001) and thus contributed greatly to the rapid increases in productivity, output, and trade in high-end services, and in areas of manufacturing in the last decades of the twentieth century (see Wren 2012).[6] More negatively, however, they also contributed to spreading the effects of the U.S. subprime mortgage crisis with innovation in securitization and facilitated reckless lending policies in the banking sector. In expanding credit, they underpinned employment creation focused on low-end nontraded service sectors—and in the Irish case, construction.

Figure 10.3 illustrates the expansion of private credit in the United Kingdom and Ireland and shows how these countries diverged from their export-oriented counterparts Germany and Sweden from the start of this century, and mirrored the rapid rates of credit expansion in the United States. The figure also makes clear that though all of these Liberal economies followed the same trajectory in this period, the rates at which private sector indebtedness accumulated differed. Ireland exhibited considerably higher growth rates in indebtedness from the early 2000s on. We return to this point in the next section.

Figure 10.3   Expansion of Credit to Firms and Households

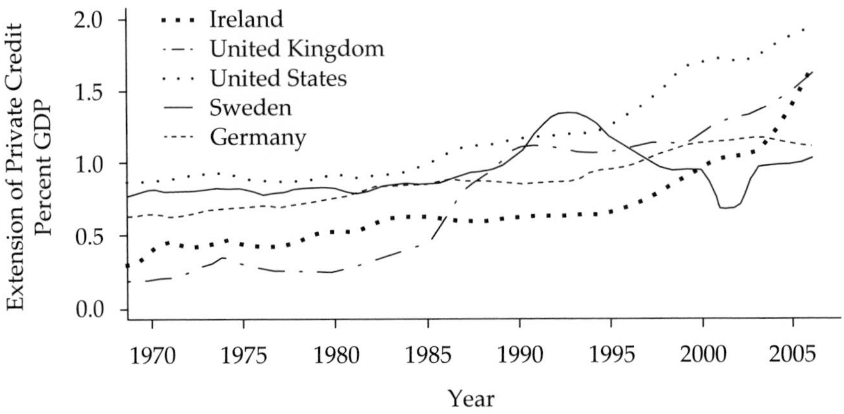

Source: Authors' calculations based on Beck et al. (2010).

Thus, in the period preceding the crisis, the Liberal economies relied increasingly on the expansion of credit to the private sector to create growth and employment, given declining traditional sectors. The empirical evidence so far suggests an important link between this characteristic of the Liberal model and the impact of the crisis itself. Philip Lane and his colleagues show that the level of private sector indebtedness precrisis is one of the best predictors of variation in the extent of the output shock impact of the current crisis and the resulting fiscal imbalance (Lane and Benetrix 2010; Lane and Milesi-Feretti 2010). Reliance on debt-financed private demand expansion made the Liberal economies particularly vulnerable to tighter credit conditions. Where export-oriented growth has remained a more important component of the economic model, as in Germany and Japan, the initial downturn stemmed more from the shock to world trade. As trade recovered, so did growth and employment in these economies. An important question for the Liberal model going forward, therefore, is whether it is feasible to maintain the same levels of employment in nontraded sectors under more restrictive long-term credit conditions.

These commonalities within the liberal variety of capitalism have been framed in the varieties of capitalism literature in terms of the complementarities among different types of economic institutions. Although we do not stress it here, we believe that these complementarities, and the political coalitions supporting them, are important in explaining differences in policy response between liberal markets and their coordinated counterparts.

However, in thinking about these questions, it is also important to recognize that the Liberal group of countries is far from homogeneous in economic and institutional terms and that intragroup variations have important implications for economic and political outcomes. We illustrate this point in the rest of this chapter through a comparison of the U.K. and Irish cases. Theoretically, this analysis is very much of a piece with the varieties of capitalism school, in that the interaction between political and economic institutions across different spheres underpins the variation between countries. This analytical toolbox, though, is more complex than simply the dichotomous division between two varieties, as is clear when considering intragroup variation between the United Kingdom and Ireland.

Variations Between the U.K. and Irish Models

Although the categorization of Ireland and the United Kingdom as Liberal economic regimes is useful, important differences in economic structure and institutions between the two countries led to differences in their growth trajectories in the precrisis period and, ultimately, to differences in their experiences of, and capacity to respond to, the crisis itself.

Pre-Bubble Boom: Ireland in the 1990s   Comparing the two countries' growth trajectories in the pre–bubble period, it is important to note that during the 1990s Ireland did experience a real economic boom, based on strong export performance and catch-up economic growth. Irish growth rates through the 1990s were higher than those of the United KIngdom: Irish GDP in 2000 was 2.37 times its 1990 level, whereas the U.K. economy grew to 1.6 times its 1990 size over the same period. This transition, however, also led to pressures on the housing market giving initial impetus to the property bubble. Ireland's rapid GDP growth was accompanied by an 18 percent growth in the working-age population in Ireland, as historically high levels of emigration slowed and reversed. This compares with only a 3 percent increase in the size of the U.K. population. Over the 1990s there was thus a greater real increase in the need for residential construction and development in Ireland, causing the initial increase in housing prices.

The second difference consequential here is that although both economies were making a transition into service sectors via successful job creation, their starting points were different. The United Kingdom's trajectory involved deindustrialization and a decline in manufacturing. Ireland's service expansion, by contrast, provided employment largely for those who would previously have not been part of the paid labor force, particularly women, and a shift out of agriculture. Service employment in Ireland was associated with higher participation rates and lower emigration far more than with a decline of manufacturing. This qualitative difference put further upward pressure on demand for housing, as a result of a concomitant social change, a shift toward smaller household sizes. In 1991, the average household size in Ireland was 4.45 people, and in the United Kingdom 3.22; by 2001, the respective figures were 3.85 and 3.09. In Ireland, the average household in 2001 was 13 percent smaller than it had been in 1991. Combined with the increase in population, this put significant upward pressure on the demand for housing at the end of the 1990s (Williams, Hughes, and Shiels 2003). Ireland's relatively late transition from a predominantly agricultural economy thus left an impression on its economic structure during the boom, as well as yielding a subtly different set of political underpinnings to the Liberal model in the Ireland, as we shall see later in the chapter.

Important institutional differences also existed between the two regimes. In particular, several features of the Irish case distinguished it from the more textbook Liberal institutional configuration in the United Kingdom and gave it something of a hybrid character. The first was Ireland's membership, since its inception in 1999, of the EMU, entailing the formal delegation of authority for Irish monetary policy to the European Central Bank (ECB) and, on the fiscal front, committing Irish policymakers to attempt to abide by the terms of the Stability and Growth Pact. Theoretically, this decision implied the creation of an institutional commitment to a conservative monetary regime. In practice, however, given the heterogeneity of economic conditions within the eurozone, it was to lead to the pursuit of relatively expansionary monetary policies in Ireland during the boom period, a point to which we will return.

The second was the centralization of wage bargaining at the national level in 1987. In contrast to the Liberal archetype, the social partnership process in Ireland resulted in seven centralized agreements in the twenty years up to 2008. Designed as a response to the inflation, unemployment and debt crises of the 1980s, the early agreements exchanged moderate wage increases for promised reductions in income taxes. They are generally agreed to have boosted competitiveness, contributing to the Irish economy's strong export performance and period of catch-up growth throughout the 1990s, and to attracting the foreign direct investment on which much of Irish exporting is based (Lane 1998; McGuinness, Kelly, and O'Connell 2008).

As we shall see, neither of these features prevented Ireland from suffering a particularly extreme form of the maladies of the Liberal model in the bubble period of the 2000s. In fact, the Irish experience raises broader issues about institutional compatibility—and in particular about the effectiveness of centralized wage negotiations in an essentially Liberal institutional environment. The social partnership model may not have caused the Irish crisis, but it certainly worked to exacerbate it during the bubble period, as we describe. On the other hand, in the context of current postcrisis debates about the capacity for reform of the Liberal model more generally, it could be argued that Ireland's institutional configuration creates a wider range of options for reform in the Irish case and, in particular, reduces the political costs associated with switching toward a more export-oriented model. The different elements of the Irish political economy may or may not lead to good, or sustainable outcomes, but the interactions have implications for outcomes that a variety of capitalism perspective can help us understand. However, this implies a theoretical approach somewhat different from the simple categorization of liberal and coordinated economies that sometimes characterizes analyses of varieties of capitalism. We return to this point in our conclusions.

Ireland and the United Kingdom in the Bubble Period

Both Ireland and the United Kingdom relied on private debt-based expansion in sheltered domestic sectors as the chief engines of employment expansion in the precrisis period. In spite of the strong export performance of the Irish economy from the end of the 1980s on, the share of employment in traded sectors declined even in the 1990s. From the end of the 1990s, employment became increasingly concentrated in nontraded private sectors and the expansion of private-sector debt in Ireland in this period was even more rapid than that in the United Kingdom, as previously discussed (see figure 10.3).

The particularly rapid expansion in private sector indebtedness in Ireland can be ascribed in part to differences in degree in some of the more problematic institutional features of the Liberal model. Thus, although light regulation and oversight was a common feature of the Liberal cases,[7] failures of oversight in the Irish case were extreme. In addition, they centered less on complex financial products than in the area of basic bank lending. In combination, these features led to an overextended banking sector with a portfolio over-reliant on the inflated domestic housing market (Honohan 2010; Regling and Watson 2010).

Ireland's regulatory lightness of touch may have contributed to its success in attracting foreign direct investment during the export lead growth of the 1990s, but it also allowed the bubble to develop largely unchecked. The establishment of the Irish Financial Services Regulatory Agency in

2003 did little to increase levels of regulatory oversight: substantial institutional independence from the Central Bank combined with a shortage of skilled staff led to information asymmetries in the regulatory structure, and allowed reckless lending behavior to continue unchecked (Honohan 2010; Regling and Watson 2010).[8] Within the banks, incentives for excessive risk-taking stemmed from remuneration schemes with large bonus components, not just among the upper echelons of financial sector employees, but also at lower staffing levels (Regling and Watson 2010).

In addition, these developments took place in the context of an increasingly loose monetary policy environment in Ireland. As discussed, Irish monetary policy changed significantly with EMU membership in 1999. Instead of the tightening of policy that might have been expected to accompany an institutional commitment to a relatively conservative monetary regime, the heterogeneity of economic conditions within the eurozone meant that EMU membership was associated with a significant loosening of monetary policy in Ireland. Interest rates, which had been set at levels significantly above Taylor rates throughout the 1980s and 1990s, switched to levels well below from 1999 on, as inflation conditions in the booming Irish economy moved increasingly out of line with their more sluggish European partners.

Arguably, when it comes to explaining the extent of the shock associated with the crisis, and the variations in crisis response across Ireland and the United Kingdom, however, the most important difference in patterns of economic performance in this precrisis period was not the rate of debt accumulation associated with the expansion of employment in sheltered domestic sectors, but rather the composition of that employment. Critically, in Ireland a large component of this expansion occurred in construction, whereas in the United Kingdom it was spread across the nontraded private sectors. Figure 10.4 shows that although employment in construction expanded rapidly in Ireland during the boom years, the United Kingdom—like Sweden and Germany—experienced no significant expansion in housing activity over the period, in spite of its boom in house prices. This difference in economic concentration had important consequences, as we have seen. But what accounts for the contrast?

Certainly it is accounted for in part by the variations in degree of the institutional weaknesses of the Liberal model: the relatively extreme version of the light regulation–loose monetary policy combination that existed in Ireland in this period. Because these features were endemic to the Liberal model more generally, however, they are not enough to fully explain the Irish construction boom; additional factors were also at play.

Part of the explanation is, in fact, structural, centering on the increased demand for construction in the period of catch-up growth in the late 1980s

Figure 10.4   Employment in the Construction Sector

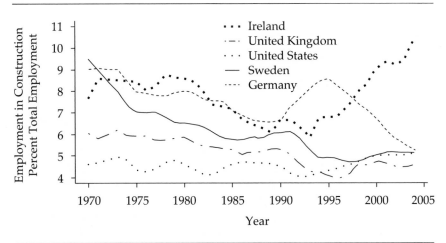

Source: Authors' calculations based on EU-KLEMS (2009).

and 1990s. In addition though, government policy played a direct role, contributing to house-price inflation itself, and facilitating the output and employment response. Both the tax system and the nature of the planning system provided institutional incentives for development and construction. In the United Kingdom, however, this set of institutional incentives for the expansion of construction was largely absent. We explore this important variation in more detail later.

Finally, from the late 1990s onward, weaknesses of the social partnership model in Ireland also became apparent. The exchange of wage restraint for income tax concessions had helped drive the export-oriented model in the 1980s and 1990s. In the absence of important institutional features typically associated with centralized wage bargaining in coordinated or export-oriented regimes, however (a credible commitment to a conservative monetary policy regime, and, ideally, a lead role played by export sectors concerned with international competitiveness), the Irish model failed increasingly to deliver wage restraint—and in particular to restrain the demands of sheltered public sector workers—in the general inflationary context of the 2000s (Kelly, McGuiness, and O'Connell 2008; Hardiman and Dellepiane 2011). The growing public sector wage bill formed an important component of the procyclical spending policies the Irish government pursued during the boom. Meanwhile, low income tax revenues meant that spending was financed by taxes strongly tied to the housing and construction boom: stamp duties on housing transactions, capital taxation, and VAT (Lane 2011; Honohan 2010). The IMF estimates that revenues from these sources represented over a third of total revenues in Ireland by 2007, compared with a figure of around one-fifth in the United Kingdom (IMF 2010).

A combination of exogenous factors and policy choices thus led Ireland to an over-reliance on the construction sector in terms of output, employment, and revenue in the precrisis period. The dependence of this sector on credit meant that during the crisis Ireland experienced a greater shock to output, employment, and revenue—and to government fiscal balance—than the United Kingdom. Combined with the constraints imposed by EMU membership—the requirement to attempt to abide by the terms of the Stability and Growth Pact—this difference largely accounts for the two countries' fiscal responses to the crisis: the Irish government simply had less latitude. Meanwhile, the extent of the crisis in the Irish banking system, which stemmed from its concentrated investment in property—and in domestic property in particular—added weight to the argument that the extensive Irish bank guarantee was necessary, given the risks of systemic failure. The root of the decision to support the banks thus lay in the precrisis development model. In the next section, we explore the political underpinnings of this model in the United Kingdom and Ireland—emphasizing commonalities and differences between the two.

THE POLITICAL FOUNDATIONS OF THE LIBERAL MODEL

The economic model outlined relied on a distinctive pattern of political support and political competition. Within the Anglophone countries, the Liberal growth model was fairly uncontested in the boom years. Coalitions based on the support of financial, real estate, construction, and development interests provided the elite political impetus, advocating light taxation and regulation, labor market flexibility, and employment growth in the service sector. Meanwhile, popular political support for this regime was ensured by high employment rates, rising asset (particularly housing) prices, easy access to the equity this provided, and debt-financed consumption facilitated by the extension of both mortgage credit and consumer credit more generally. Here we examine these common features of the politics of the Liberal model in the two countries, but also highlight variation in the composition of the coalitions supporting the model in the United Kingdom and Ireland. These variations affected the functioning of the Liberal model in the precrisis period and, as a result, the shock experienced, and the crisis response.

Political Coalitions in the Liberal Model

Traditional accounts of the coalitions underpinning different economic strategies often emphasize tensions rooted in the conflict of interests between internationally exposed and sheltered economic sectors (see, for example, Gourevitch 1986; Swenson 1991; Iversen 1999). This divide facilitates alliances between employers and workers in export-oriented sectors, united by a concern for maintaining international competitiveness. In the Liberal regimes in the precrisis period, the interests of export sectors were trumped in favor of a model with a strong emphasis on credit-fueled domestic consumption. A coalition representing the interests of the financial sector and sheltered domestic economic sectors, most notably construction and the public sector, came to dominate the interests of traditional export sectors in both countries, resulting in very different outcomes from those observed in export-oriented economies. Differences in their historical development trajectories, particularly Ireland's relatively late transition from agriculture, led to different weights within this sheltered coalition, which shaped the divergence in the experience of Ireland and the United Kingdom.

Common Elite Politics

A common feature of elite politics across the Liberal countries in the precrisis period was the growing influence of the financial sector. Nolan McCarty, in chapter 7 of this volume, effectively documents the growing significance of financial sector contributions to the campaign finances of both of the major parties in the United States. In the United Kingdom and Ireland, direct measures of political influence of this type are less readily available. Nevertheless, in the United Kingdom at least, the rise of a new elite politics that incorporated the interests of the City on both sides of the traditional left-right divide is apparent. Reflecting on the political economic model of New Labour, Simon Lee notes that the party under Blair and Brown emerged "as champion of the City rather than of manufacturing, and of predominantly consumer rather than producer interests" (2008, 20). Further, this strategy was explicitly stated in public addresses by Labour leaders (Coates and Hay 2000).

An indication of the importance of this support can be seen from considering donations to the Labour Party during the period.[9] Although the lion's share of donations to the Labour Party in the 2000s still came from trade unions and individual contributions, the profile of business donors to the party gives us an idea of whose interests are likely to have been heard within government. Table 10.1 shows the amount of money received

Table 10.1   Financial and Development Industry Company Donations to the Labour Party, 2005–2006

	National Labour Party Company Donations 2005 to 2006		Labour Party (including Constituency parties) Company Donations 2005 to 2006	
	Amount (£)	Share of company donations (%)	Amount (£)	Share of company donations (%)
Financial-development	103,416.00	13.2	157,218.50	16.1
Peripheral	209,515.00	26.8	227,877.00	23.4
Not financial-development	468,629.00	60	589,314.50	60.5
Total	781,560.00	100	974,410.00	100

Source: Authors' compilation of Electoral Commission (2011) data.

from companies by the Labour Party in 2005 and 2006. The left-hand panel shows statistics for donations to the national party, and the right-hand column includes donations to the local constituency Labour parties. We categorized every company for which we could find information, which was all but two companies, accounting for all but £8,402 of the donations, into three groups: those whose business activity was directly related to finance, property, development and real estate (for example, property developers and financial advisers); those whose activity was partially related, or for whom the extent of their reliance on financial and development activities was hard to gauge (for example, legal offices or lobby groups); and those whose activities were unrelated to financial and development activities (two examples are an antigenocide campaign and rail-freight companies).[10] In this period, donations from businesses either directly or indirectly linked to finance and development were contributing 40 percent of Labour's company donations.

Unsurprisingly, the financial sector accounts for an even greater share of the campaign contributions of the Conservative Party. Table 10.2 shows the share of Conservative Party cash donations coming from the financial services and property and development sectors between 2005 and 2010. Although the increase over this period may reflect the changing probabilities of a Conservative government, it is the overall level that is striking: by 2010 over half of the party's cash donations came from financial-sector interests.

Table 10.2   Financial Services Industry Donation to the Conservative Party

Year	Total Financial Services Industry Cash Contributions to CPCO	Yearly Total Cash Donations to CPCO (All Donors)	Financial Service Industry Contribution as Percentage of Total Cash Donations
2005	£2,748,527	£11,142,090	24.67%
2006	6,196,999	16,395,889	37.8
2007	6,175,695	16,728,005	36.91
2008	5,364,319	13,691,446	39.17
2009	10,849,884	20,813,184	52.12
2010	11,420,974	22,482,411	50.79

Source: Authors' compilation based on Mathiason and Bessaoud (2011).

Although the role of financial contributions in influencing policy choices is debated, money allows access to policymakers that may be more directly influential. For example, Conservative Party policy entitles donors giving more than £50,000 a year to "join David Cameron and other senior figures from the Conservative Party at dinners, post-PMQ lunches, drinks receptions, election result events and important campaign launches."[11] Given fifty-seven such donors (Mathiason and Bassaoud 2011), financial interests have ample opportunity to make their policy preferences and concerns known to senior political figures.

In Ireland, accurate data on political contributions are not available, but the channel of informal influence is at least as important. In addition to a much-publicized golf meeting with the former Anglo Irish Bank chairman Sean FitzPatrick in the summer of 2008, Brian Cowen's appointment diaries show that as minister for finance he met with Fintan Drury, an Anglo director and friend, at least ten times between September 2005 and May 2008. In contrast, he met officials from the financial regulator's office only eight times during his entire period of office (Lyons and Carey 2011, 136).

The increased economic weight of these groups is also likely to have increased their political weight. Thus policy reflected these interests—particularly with light regulation and easy monetary policy. Financial companies' competitive concerns centered more on flexibility and incentivizing innovation than on traditional wage restraint (Hall and Soskice 2001),[12] nor was inflation a particular concern to industries that, if anything, prefer an overvalued to an undervalued exchange rate (Frieden 1991, 446). This is in contrast to traditional business interests in agriculture and manufacturing, particularly those oriented toward export markets, for whom these

concerns are paramount. The decline of these traditional business interests thus reduced elite political barriers to the Liberal growth model, removing constraints on the inflationary demands of sheltered domestic
sectors.

In both Ireland and the United Kingdom, the public sector gained from
the growth model pursued in the Liberal economies, and public sector
unions occupied a privileged position. In the United Kingdom, the Blair
government reversed more than a decade of Thatcherite cuts in public
employment. Thus although public employment declined by nearly 14
percent in the United Kingdom between 1991 and 1999, it expanded by 17
percent between 1998 and 2009. In Ireland, the expansion of the public sector was even more marked: public employment increased by 7 percent
between 1991 and 1999, and by a staggering 27 percent between 1998 and
2009 (Department of Finance 2009; Hicks et al. 2005; Matthews 2010).
These figures underscore the increasing significance of the public sector in
Ireland. The lead role played by public sector unions in the Irish Congress
of Trades Unions, and thus within the social partnership process, gave
public sector unions a large stake in the procyclical pie, exacerbating the
fiscal vulnerabilities of the Irish model.

The critical difference between Ireland and the United Kingdom in this
period, however, was the greater role of development, including construction, interests in the finance, banking, and development coalition in Ireland. The key distinction for banking was the concentration of Irish investment in development, residential housing construction more specifically,
and in the hands of a small number of developers (Honohan 2010). The
distinction for the broader economy was the concentration of output and
employment in this sector. In the construction industry, the differences are
most pronounced: Ireland saw a far greater concentration of employment
than did the United Kingdom. As shown in figure 10.4, by 2004, more than
10 percent of employment in Ireland was in construction. By 2007, construction accounted for 20 percent of Irish GDP (IMF 2009). Employment
in finance in Ireland had also outpaced that in the United Kingdom by
around 2000, despite the latter's reputation as a global financial center
(Inklaar and Timmer 2008).

Although some of this expansion in construction in Ireland stemmed
from specific economic characteristics, it was also fed by the planning and
development context, and by explicit political decisions. The institutional
features of planning and development policy in the United Kingdom and
Ireland are similar: the formal rules on planning and development in Ireland were modeled on the British system (Evans and Hartwich 2005b).
The stringency with which the formal rules are applied in the two cases,

however, varies. This interacted with very different incentives for, and attitudes toward, development.

The Irish government pursued pro-development policies aggressively in the bubble period, with numerous tax incentives for development. Tax relief for construction, refurbishment, and conversion was available to owner-occupiers and residential investors under the Urban Renewal Schemes in place between 1986 and 2008. These included town renewal schemes covering 100 towns in Ireland, fifteen seaside resort schemes, and incentives for Living Over the Shop (LOTS) redevelopment, as well as other specific schemes. In 1998, these incentives were extended with the rural renewal scheme. The two noteworthy characteristics of these schemes are first, their generosity—in some cases, 100 percent of construction costs could be set against income for tax purposes—and their origination in the need for catch-up development in the 1980s, when they had beneficial effects.

Specific policy proposals aimed at putting a brake on house-price inflation were also routinely overturned or ignored under pressure from interests in the property sector. For example, a requirement in the Planning and Development Act of 2000 that all local authorities allocate up to 20 percent of all new residential developments for affordable social housing was amended under pressure from developers and construction interests to allow developers to substitute contributions of land or money in lieu of affordable housing. In March 2007, Fianna Fail chose to address issues of access by eliminating stamp duty for first-time buyers, a policy that would cost the state rather than the developers, and not dampen price increases. Similarly, the recommendations of the 1974 Kenny report that owners of agricultural land should be paid no more than the agricultural market value of their land, plus a supplement, designed to reduce the capacity of local authorities to confer windfall profits to landowners by rezoning agricultural land were never implemented.[13] Political support for this came from rural interests with very different preferences from their British counterparts.

The Role of Rural Interests

Agricultural interests in development wax and wane with the alternative potential uses of their land, in particular with agricultural or conservation subsidies. As the value of such subsidies decline, farmers and land owners become more favorable about releasing land for development (Pennington 2000). Thus, in the context of declining EU support for farmers in Ireland, agricultural owners were looking for alternative sources of income, including the sale of land for development. This had occurred in the United Kingdom with declining Common Agricultural Policy (CAP) payments in the late 1980s driving agricultural support of the 1987 Alternative Land Use and Rural Economy proposals. But the smaller size of agriculture in the economy in the United Kingdom by the 2000s makes this coalition partner a less important one than in Ireland, and the threat to farm incomes from the removal of subsidies was less pronounced in the United Kingdom.

In Ireland, the political relevance of agricultural interests is highlighted by rural support for both the major Irish political parties. Michael Laver (2005) estimates, for example, that Fianna Fail and Fine Gael attracted 76 percent of the vote in "open country" areas in 2002, compared with less than 55 percent in Dublin. In addition, although large farmers have typically supported Fine Gael, the role of small farmers in Fianna Fail's support base in the boom years (Marsh et al. 2008) is significant: the sale of agricultural land around urban centers for development, and the reinvestment of this income in more remote locations helped raise agricultural land prices and thus the wealth of agricultural interests during the boom years (Kitchin et al. 2010).

By contrast, the earlier decline of agriculture in the United Kingdom and the resulting land use profile created a large and electorally important group exerting countervailing pressure on moves toward development. The organizational manifestation of these interests is the Council for the Protection of Rural England. The bulk of its membership is driven by local amenity NIMBY interests, such as maintaining existing house prices by preserving a good view (Pennington 2000). Thus "conservative homeowners in Conservative shires could block or divert development which might otherwise occur near them" (Evans and Hartwich 2005a). In both Ireland and the United Kingdom, development came to reflect the interests of electorally important groups, but the nature of these interests differed. In Ireland, because of their greater size, influence, and threat to incomes, agricultural landowners could benefit from development. In the United Kingdom, their smaller electoral weight compared with NIMBY local interests put a brake on construction and development.

The political support of many organized economic interests in the Liberal economies is in line with complementarities between different aspects—particularly the reinforcing victories of sheltered interests—of the political economy. Here we have highlighted some of the dominant organized forces focusing on the ways these interests may constrain economic development and crisis response. Differences in organized interests between our two Liberal cases prove significant: the politics of development and land use go a long way to explaining the differences between the Irish and U.K. boom economics.

The Electoral Politics of the Liberal Model

In the Liberal model, interests that benefit from Liberal policy and light regulation understandably support the status-quo economic strategies. Positive impetus for Liberal growth comes from financial and development interests, which have channels of influence on the political system, as outlined earlier. How do these political economies maintain the support of voters and taxpayers who, apart from those at the top of the income-skill distribution, might have an interest in greater economic coordination? The answer is that asset-price (house-price) inflation and high employment led to greater satisfaction with the economy among middle-income voters than their stagnating wage levels would imply. The political importance of the asset-wealth effect is in buying the support of less well-paid workers in the context of the increased inequality associated with private service sector employment expansion under the Liberal model (on the three-way choice between the potential policy goals of employment creation, equality, and budgetary restraint associated with the service transition and the pursuit of a high employment–high inequality path in the Liberal cases, see Iversen and Wren 1998).

Data from the national election studies over the 2000s in both Ireland and, to a lesser extent, the United Kingdom show voters giving favorable assessments of their national economic situations. In Ireland, almost 75 percent of the population gave positive responses when asked how the general economic situation of the country compares with what it was twelve months ago. Although this figure is lower in Britain, when "same" responses are included, approximately 65 percent of British respondents gave a weakly positive response. These positive numbers are not completely surprising given that this was a period of economic growth and stability. Yet the distribution of income growth even in the boom was highly unequal. Two other key features, we argue, underpinned popular support of the Liberal model. Specifically, both employment and home-ownership in an era of rising house prices led individuals to support the growth model, and given the high rates of both of these, little controversy followed the Liberal growth agenda.

Credit expansion to individuals in the middle and lower end of the income distribution helped provide the means for middle- and low-income earners in the Liberal countries to continue to increase their levels of consumption as average wages have not kept pace with growth at the top end

(Montgomerie 2007; Warren and Tyagi 2004). The final step in the logic is then that the economic conditions have an impact on attitudes toward whole economic regimes as well as particular parties (Clarke, Dutt, and Kornberg 1993). Homeownership provides an economic resource, particularly in the context of asset-price inflation, that translates into greater support for the economic model. Thus, whereas other work on the politics of housing highlights its substitutability for welfare spending (Castles 1998; Kemeny 1980, 2005) or the partisan dynamics of housing policy (Schwartz and Seabrooke 2008; Watson 2008; chapter 11, this volume), the important aspect for political support for the Liberal model is that in the context of broad homeownership, rising house prices can deliver satisfaction with economic performance in the eyes of voters, even in the context of stagnant wage growth and increasing inequality. In the Liberal economies this is a large constituency: homeowners make up at least 65 percent of the population (The Economist 2002). Even among lower-income groups in the United Kingdom and Ireland, "half the poor" own their own home (Burrows and Wilcox 2000).

The critical losers from the Liberal growth model are current and future first-time buyers. Many of these future first-time buyers are too young to vote, and others have yet even to be born: thus politicians have little incentive to attend to them, and the political dynamics of house-price increases are analogous to those of deficit spending (Weale 2006). The likely outcome of the house-price element of the Liberal growth model is a severe dualism—the majority of the population benefitting from inflating asset prices at the expense of an excluded small minority and of future generations. The wealth effects of the property boom and consumption-led economic expansion itself can generate support from large swathes of voters.

Second, the Liberal growth model delivers employment growth, sustained by strong consumer demand. Large income increases at the top of the distribution and flexible labor markets create employment for the low-skilled, albeit at low wages. To the extent that maintaining low unemployment stems dissatisfaction with economic performance, political support for the model is also sustained. We can test the role of these Liberal models' goods—homeownership and employment—in generating satisfaction with the model.

Economic Satisfaction in the Liberal Model

The argument about the dynamics of the Liberal model yields the predictions that homeowners should express greater satisfaction with the economic circumstances (in the boom period), and that those who are employed should express greater satisfaction. These are the two independent variables of primary interest. For the former, we also differentiate between outright homeownership and owners who have a mortgage. A priori, outright ownership should yield greater security and thus contribute to more positive assessments of economic performance. However, since the extension of mortgage credit to new borrowers and to allow the release of equity from houses increasing in value, it could be that these mortgage-holders saw greater improvements to their economic situation. To gauge the impact of employment, we compare the employed to the unemployed and those not in the labor force. Because of their particular situation with regard to both home ownership and income, retirees are excluded from the analysis.[14]

We also include controls for income. Here we present results with three income groups constructed from the larger number of categories in the data so as to create roughly equal-sized groups (bottom third, middle third, top third) to make the categories comparable across countries and across time. In addition, controls for age and gender are included because they are both associated with economic position and standard in the literature.

The outcome we are interested in, public support for national growth models, is unsurprisingly not contained as a question in any surveys of public opinion. However, we can get an impression of how different types of voters are affected by the growth model by asking about their general assessment of the national economic situation. Specifically, we use the British Election Study and Irish National Election Study, which both ask respondents how the general economic situation of the country compares with what it was twelve months ago. The possible responses are as follows: got a lot better, got a little better, stayed the same, got a little worse, got a lot worse.

Because the dependent variable is an ordered scale whose levels do not necessarily correspond to equal intervals, we run ordered logit models to estimate the impact of the different characteristics on economic assessments.

Because we are interested in the commonalities of the Liberal model in the boom period, in the first instance, model 1 in table 10.3 shows the results from the boom years (Ireland 2002 and 2007; Britain 2005).

The regression results indicate that over the boom years, public opinion across individuals is consistent with the political dynamics of the Liberal model. Those who rent their homes were more likely to give a negative assessment of the national economic situation. The point estimate of the effect of having a mortgage is positive, indicating less-satisfied responses, but is very small and statistically indistinguishable from zero. The employed give more enthusiastic responses than those who are out of work.

Table 10.3   Determinants of Economic Evaluations During the Boom

	United Kingdom 2005, Ireland 2002 and 2007 (1)	United Kingdom 2005 (2)	Ireland 2002 and 2007 (3)	United Kingdom 2005 (4)	Ireland 2002 and 2007 (5)
Mortgage	0.04	–0.01	–0.16	0.1	–0.06
(SE)	(0.07)	(0.10)	(0.08)	(0.11)	(0.09)
t	0.51	–0.09	–1.92	0.9	–0.68
Renter	0.19	0.23	0.4	0.06	0.48
	(0.09)	(0.13)	(0.12)	(0.14)	(0.13)
	2.09	1.79	3.4	0.44	3.77
Employed	–0.21	–0.26	–0.5	–0.03	–0.33
	(0.08)	(0.14)	(0.09)	(0.16)	(0.1)
	–2.48	–1.93	–5.44	–0.19	–3.16
Middle income	–0.27			–0.37	–0.32
	(0.08)			(0.13)	(0.11)
	–3.37			–2.91	–2.83
High income	–0.6			–0.78	–0.59
	(0.09)			(0.14)	(0.12)
	–6.91			–5.72	–5.09
Age	–0.003	0.01	–0.01	0.01	–0.01
	(0.002)	(0.003)	(0.003)	(0.002)	(0.003)
	–1.5	2.31	–4.27	1.92	–4.07
Female	–0.16	–0.01	–0.25	–0.01	–0.26
	(0.06)	(0.08)	(0.08)	(0.08)	(0.09)
	–2.86	–0.14	–3.17	–0.08	–3.02
Residual deviance	11180.35	6551.88	6172.49	5893.87	5136.92
AIC	11206.35	6569.88	6192.49	5915.87	5160.92

Source: Authors' compilation based on British Election Study (2005) and the Irish National Election Study (2002–2007).

Note: Determinants of economic evaluations during the boom (INES 2002–2007; BES 2005). Ordinal logit models; low values of dependent variable indicate assessments that the economy has got better, high values indicate assessment that economy has got worse. Models 1, 3, and 5 include fixed effects for election-year and all models estimate four cut points for the latent variable (not shown).

These coefficients indicate the impact of changes on the underlying latent predictor. For a substantive interpretation, renters are five percentage points less likely than those who own their homes outright to respond that the economy has got a lot better. They are more likely to say that it has got a little better (two percentage points), stayed the same (one percentage point), or got a little worse (one percentage point). Unemployment has a similarly sized effect, a five percentage point reduction in the likelihood of the "best" response. For the sake of comparison, these are somewhat smaller effects than those of income: those in the lowest third of income are seven percentage points less likely to choose the most positive assessment than those in the middle-income group. Thus individual-level data from the two countries in the boom years are consistent with employment and homeownership underpinning support for the Liberal model among the population.

In this context, though, we might also expect to see differences between the U.K. and Irish cases. Just as the economic and elite political situation in Ireland were more extreme in the boom years, were popular responses to the elements of the growth model also more pronounced? Table 10.3 indicates that they were. Although the impact of employment and homeownership is evident in the U.K. case in model 2, the estimated effect size is smaller when compared with that in Ireland (model 3). The difference between the U.K. and Ireland models in the first two columns is that the point estimates for the effects in the United Kingdom are smaller than in the Irish cases: they are estimated with about the same precision. The important difference, though, is that in the United Kingdom, introducing income as a control variable (model 4) reduces the estimated effect size of the key Liberal model variables on economic assessments. In the Irish case (model 5), by contrast, the effects of homeownership and employment are robust to the inclusion of the income controls. Thus we can draw two conclusions. First, the more extreme incarnation of the Liberal model in the Irish case did lead to starker effects at the level of public opinion. Second, in Ireland the distribution of these benefits was more of an alternative to income in generating economic satisfaction than it was in the United Kingdom.

The final implication of the model for mass public support is that in the context of the crisis, when both asset-price growth and the employment performance of the Liberal model no longer prevail, we should see assessments of the economy decline to reflect actual economic circumstances. There is some evidence from the British Election Study in 2010 that this is the case: homeownership is no longer associated with more favorable assessments (not shown here for reasons of space). Yet in the United Kingdom, even in the aftermath of the crisis, the difference between the main political parties did not call the growth model itself into question. The, political reaction has been different in Ireland, where the major parties have advocated a shift to more export-oriented growth, and public support for the political party most closely associated with the Liberal expansion, Fianna Fail, completely collapsed in the 2011 election.

CONCLUSION

We have argued that variation in the policy responses in the U.K. and Irish cases in the immediate aftermath of the crisis are closely linked to differences in the underlying political economic model in the two countries. In terms of the first dimension of policy we consider—the fiscal response—greater reliance on the construction sector in Ireland, both for revenue and employment, meant that the shock to the fiscal balances in that country was considerably greater than in the United Kingdom. Although the immediate response to the crisis in the United Kingdom, like most other countries, was the implementation of a discretionary stimulus package, the budgetary constraints the crisis created in Ireland effectively ruled out this option, and led instead to sharp discretionary fiscal contraction. In terms of the second dimension—the size of the public subsidy to the banking sector—the massive scale of the response in Ireland in comparative terms stemmed from the depth of the crisis the Irish banking sector faced and the perceived risk of systemic failure. As we have argued, however, the economic and political weight of the construction sector during the boom provides an important explanation for the scale of the banking crisis.

Our discussion has highlighted political and institutional characteristics shared by both of these countries—and all Liberal economies—in the precrisis period that rendered them more vulnerable to the financial crisis in economic terms. We also identify the critical variations in these characteristics between the Irish and U.K. cases that account for the more severe shock experienced in Ireland—and the associated extreme response. In institutional terms, the key features of the model were light regulation and flexibility in wage-setting procedures, including the ability to offer extremely high profit-related bonuses. These features facilitated the radical innovation on which expansion in high-end knowledge-based services was based, contributing to an expansion in productivity, output, and employment in these sectors in the closing decades of the twentieth century (Hall and Soskice 2001; Wren 2012). Simultaneously, however, they encouraged risk-seeking lending practices that, combined with loose monetary policy, contributed to the credit boom and the asset-price bubble. The latter effect became the more important as credit expansion developed into a primary engine of employment and output growth in the first decade of the new century. When the crisis curtailed the supply of credit, the shock to the underlying growth model in these countries was profound.

In political terms, the model attracted the support of a powerful coalition of interests in exposed and sheltered sectors whose interests were fundamentally aligned as far as growth and regulatory policies were concerned. The increased economic and political sway of the financial sector is of paramount importance here. The overwhelming concern of traditional export-oriented manufacturing sectors was, and remains, the preservation of competitiveness and wage restraint. In contrast, the production profile of financial sectors led them to emphasize instead flexibility in wage-setting processes and light regulation as a means to enhance competitiveness. This sector had far less reason to be concerned with the effects of domestic inflation. The conditions therefore existed for the development of a powerful consensus between financial sectors and sheltered domestic interests in the public sector and in construction in support of a model based on light regulation, flexibility in wage-setting, and expansionary fiscal and monetary policy. Critically, the preference profile of the financial sector meant that, in contrast with traditional export-oriented manufacturing sectors, it had no particular interest in attempting to constrain inflationary demands from the sheltered sectors.

This broad set of economic and political characteristics was common to both the Irish and U.K. models in this period. In this chapter, however, we identify two critical differences between these cases that contributed to the variations in the size of the shock, and in turn to the policy response to the shock each experienced when the crisis hit.

The first stemmed from differences in the long-run development trajectories in the two countries. In contrast to the United Kingdom, industrialization occurred late in Ireland, and to some extent the industrial stage of development was bypassed in that the transition from agriculture to services was direct; that is, the industrial sector has always remained small in Ireland in relative terms. This variation had significant implications for the composition of the coalition supporting the Liberal model in each country. First, Ireland's period of catch-up growth in the 1980s created demographic conditions that jumpstarted the Irish property bubble, putting additional upward pressure on prices and creating demands for an output response. On its own, this set of factors increased the economic and political weight of the construction sector.

Second, the structure and influence of rural interests was different in Ireland than in the United Kingdom. The continued political relevance of the rural support bases of the two major political parties—Fianna Fail and Fine Gael—rendered both parties sensitive to the demands of the agricultural sector. Policies that facilitated the rezoning of agricultural land for development provided an income transfer to farmers, which fed the construction boom in Ireland and shored up the government's rural electoral support base. By contrast, in the United Kingdom, although the Conservative party benefits from a large amount of electoral support in rural areas, the structure of land use—which is associated with that country's earlier industrialization—creates a different set of interests more likely to be opposed to development than to favor it. In combination, this set of factors led to the implementation of a range of policies that were more favorable to development in Ireland, increasing the economic and political weight of the construction sector in the government's support coalition, and creating an alliance between development and agricultural interests.

Institutional differences were also important. In contrast to the decentralized bargaining common to most Liberal countries, Ireland centralized wage bargaining in a series of national wage agreements from the late 1980s on. The social partnership model was relatively effective in generating wage restraint, facilitating Ireland's export-led expansion during the 1990s. Components of the model would prove problematic in the 2000s, however. Offering income tax reductions in return for wage restraint led to an over-reliance on other more cyclical taxes, which exacerbated the fiscal impact of the economic crisis. Moreover, during the 2000s, national wage agreements became an effective channel for the transmission of inflationary wage demands from the public sector. These outcomes illustrate the problems involved in instituting an effective model of social partnership in the context of what was, in almost all other characteristics—light regulation, increasing role of the financial sector, Liberal monetary policy—a more typical Liberal model in this period.

From a theoretical perspective, the crisis presents an interesting challenge for the varieties of capitalism framework. On the one hand, this approach is premised on the idea that different countries are in economically successful equilibria in terms of their institutional configurations. The economic underperformance of the crisis is not easy to reconcile with this view because the development of the crisis was arguably endogenous to the evolution of the Liberal model in particular. On the other hand, the varieties of capitalism framework, and in particular its emphasis on the interaction of institutions across the political economy, are still very important in understanding variation in the extent of the impact the crisis had, and in the dynamics of government responses.

Applying this analytical framework to Ireland, for example, allows us to highlight the potential dysfunction associated with a hybrid model—in particular, the pursuit of centralized wage bargaining in the absence of an institutional commitment to tight monetary policy, and in an environment in which the influence of sheltered sectors in the wage bargaining process is too strong. Our analysis does suggest also, however, that the effects of institutional interactions cannot be separated from underlying structural economic conditions within the political economy. That the U.K. and Irish economies approached the transition to services in the last decades of the twentieth century from very different starting points—and in particular the continued economic and political weight of the agricultural sector in Ireland during the period—had important implications for the way in which the institutional model functioned, and hence for its economic effects.

A critical question is whether the Liberal economic growth model can be sustained in an era of stronger regulation and more constrained credit. Can the Liberal model be fixed? If not, is it politically and economically feasible to adopt a more export-oriented path? In the United Kingdom, the institutional and political preconditions do not exist to undertake this kind of radical reform. In institutional terms, wage-setting is well established at the decentralized level and is more appropriately designed to underpin expansion in sectors where comparative advantage is based on radical innovation—such as financial and business services—than traditional export-oriented sectors in which wage restraint is a more important determinant of the ability to compete. The task for the United Kingdom, therefore, is to compete more effectively in global markets to allow for the generation of higher levels of value added and of employment in these sectors, so that levels of reliance on domestic consumption-led expansion are reduced (see also Wren 2012). In political terms also, commitment to the Liberal model in the United Kingdom was reaffirmed by all of the major parties in the wake of the crisis, and appears to have been re-endorsed with the election of the Conservatives to office in 2010.

In Ireland, we would suggest that the political and economic capacity for a more radical model switch is arguably greater. First, the Irish economy already shares at least one important institutional characteristic with its export-oriented counterparts—that is, a twenty-year history of centralized wage agreements negotiated at the national level. Thus the costs of a move toward, or perhaps more accurately a return to, a more export-oriented model are perhaps less daunting than in the United Kingdom. Any future model of social partnership, or of coordinated bargaining more generally, however, will need to operate more effectively to deliver wage restraint if Ireland is to take a more sustainable export-oriented path. It remains unclear whether this is possible in an institutional environment in which monetary policy decisions by the ECB are seen as unrelated to domestic inflationary conditions, given the degree of economic heterogeneity within the eurozone.

Second, an implication of the varieties of capitalism approach is that it is precisely in those cases in which the institutional configuration of an economy is out of equilibrium that the capacity for reform is greatest.

Where mismatched institutions are associated with poor enough economic performance, the appetite for reform should be sufficiently high as to reduce the political costs of institutional change. Certainly the economic cost of the crisis—made clear to the public by the terms of the EU-IMF bailout and the associated finance bill of January 2011—is so high in Ireland that it has arguably created a greater appetite for reform. The perception of the Fianna Fail government's responsibility for the crisis itself and for the economic costs of the policy response led to that party's decimation in the 2011 election after seventy years of electoral dominance. On the other hand, despite strong electoral results for parties from the left of the political spectrum—Sinn Fein and the more centrist Labour Party—there is little indication as yet that a more fundamental reorientation in the Irish political-economic landscape has taken place. The Labour Party has gained a place in government, but only as the minority party in a coalition with Centrist Fine Gael. In other words, the outcome of the crisis has simply been the replacement of one centrist party (Fianna Fail) with another (Fine Gael) as the dominant governing party. Nevertheless, in the lead-up to the February 2011 election, parties across the economic spectrum in Ireland were calling, as they were not in the United Kingdom, for a return to a more export-oriented growth model.

The choice for Ireland at this point, therefore, is whether to engage in the institution-building required to switch to a more coordinated and effective export-oriented model. Or alternatively, whether to join its Liberal counterparts in pursuing a reformed Liberal strategy—with a greater emphasis on developing and exploiting skills-based comparative advantage in knowledge-based services, in particular, and reducing reliance on debt-based expansion in low productivity service sectors to generate employment.

NOTES

1. The Green party were minor coalition partners in the Fianna Faíl–led government during this period.
2. These estimates are a rapidly moving target. The source of these estimates—most recent at time of writing—is Robert Preston, Business Editor, BBC.
3. Although the size of the Irish bailout has almost certainly increased since then as the scale of the bad debts in the Irish banking sector has become more clear over time.
4. "Claims on the private sector by deposit money banks and other institutions" as a percentage of GDP are taken from Thorsten Beck and colleagues' database on financial development and structure (2010).
5. This effect is strengthened because these sectors are essentially nontraded

internationally so that the domestic component of demand is particularly important.

6. We believe it is critical that the benevolent functions of this institutional structure not be overlooked in assessing the implications of the current crisis for the Liberal model. We return to this point in our conclusion.

7. The exceptions were Australia and Canada, which opted for a more intrusive regulatory model in this period.

8. Regling and Watson's observation that the Consumer director set on the board of the Regulator during while the Prudential director did not reflects the initial mandate of this authority to facilitate increased competition in the banking sector in response to the consumer complaints about banking charges and underscores the emphasis on consumer interests within the Liberal model.

9. Unfortunately, comparisons with earlier periods are impossible as data on campaign contributions only began to be collected in the United Kingdom in 2000.

10. The full list of companies and their codings is available from the authors on request.

11. Conservative Party website, http://www.conservatives.com/Donate/Donor_Clubs.aspx (accessed February 23, 2011).

12. In support of this contention, some evidence indicates that flexibility in wage setting at the upper end of the earnings is an important determinant of employment creation in knowledge-intensive service sectors, like finance, but not in traditional sectors (Wren, Fodor, and Theodoropoulou 2012). In addition, evidence suggests that though foreign direct investment (FDI) in manufacturing sectors may be driven by the lower wages associated with weaker real exchange rates, FDI in service sectors is more likely to be associated with higher relative wages and profits (Walsh and Yu 2010).

13. "Committee on the Price of Building Land, Report to the Minister for Local Government Robert Molloy, Chairman Mr. Justice J. Kenny," *IrishLeftReview.org*, June 10, 2009, http://www.irishleftreview.org/2009/06/10/kenny-report-1974/ (accessed March 30, 2012).

14. Except where, in the British case, they are so poor as to be in receipt of the pension credit, which we were unable to distinguish in the data from the working-age poor.

REFERENCES

Ahrend, Rudiger, Boris Cournede, and Robert Price. 2008. "Monetary Policy, Market Excesses, and Financial Turmoil." *OECD Economics Department* working paper no. 597. Paris: Organisation for Economic Co-operation and Development.

Armingeon, Klaus. 2010. "National Fiscal Responses to the Economic Crisis: Domestic Politics and International Organizations." Paper prepared for the Council of European Studies Seventeenth International Conference. Montreal (April 15–17, 2010).

Beck, Thorsten, Diane Coyle, Mathias Dewatripont, Xavier Freixas, and Paul Seabright. 2010. *Bailing out the Banks: Reconciling Stability and Competition.* London: Centre for European Policy Studies.

Beck, Thorsten, Asli Demirgüç-Kunt, and Ross Levine. 2010. "A New Database on Financial Development and Structure." *Research at the World Bank*, November 2010. http://go.worldbank.org/X23UD9QUX0 (accessed February 2011).

British Election Study. 2005. *The British Election Study at the University of Essex.* Essex: University of Essex. Available at: http://www.bes2009-10.org (accessed April 24, 2012).

Burrows, Roger, and Steve Wilcox. 2000. *Half the Poor: Home Owners with Low Incomes.* London: Council of Mortgage Lenders.

Carmassi, Jacopo, Elisabetta Luchetti, and Stefano Micossi. 2010. "Overcoming Too-Big-to-Fail: A Regulatory Framework to Limit Moral Hazard and Free Riding in the Financial Sector." Report of the CEPS-Assonime Task Force on Bank Crisis Resolution. Brussels: Centre for European Policy Studies.

Castles, Francis G. 1998. "The Really Big Trade-off: Home Ownership and the Welfare State in the New World and the Old." *Acta Politica* 33(1): 5–19.

Clark, Colin. 1940. *The Conditions of Economic Progress.* London: Macmillan.

Clarke, Harold D., Nitish Dutt, and Allan Kornberg. 1993. "The Political Economy of Attitudes Toward Polity and Society in Western European Democracies." *Journal of Politics* 55(4): 998–1021.

Coates, David, and Colin Hay. 2000. "Home and Away? The Political Economy of New Labour." Paper presented to 50th Annual Political Studies Association Conference. London (April 10–13, 2000).

Department of Finance. 2009. "Summary of 2009 Budget Measures—Policy Changes." Dublin: Government of Ireland, Central Statistics Office. http://www.budget.gov.ie/Budgets/2009/Summary.aspx (accessed March 11, 2012).

———. 2011. "National Recovery Plan 2011–2014." http://www.budget.gov.ie/RecoveryPlan.aspx (accessed March 11, 2012).

The Economist. 2002. "Going Through the Roof." 362(8266)(March 30–April 5): 65.

Electoral Commission. 2011. "Party Finance Analysis PEF Online Donations Search." Available at: http://www.electoralcommission.org.uk/party-finance/party-finance-analysis (accessed December 20, 2011).

EU-KLEMS Growth and Productivity Accounts Database. 2009. Available at http://www.euklems.net (accessed November 2009).

European Commission. 2011. "The Economic Adjustment Programme for Ireland." *European Economy* occasional paper 76. Brussels: European Commission.

http://ec.europa.eu/economy_finance/publications/occasional_paper/ 2011/pdf/ocp76_en.pdf (accessed February 2011).

Evans, Alan W., and Oliver Marc Hartwich. 2005a. *Unaffordable Housing: Myths and Fables*. London: Policy Exchange.

———. 2005b. *Bigger Better Faster More: Why Some Countries Plan Better than Others*. London: Policy Exchange.

Fisher, A. G. B. 1935. *The Clash of Progress and Security*. London: Macmillan.

Frieden, Jeffry A. 1991. "Invested Interests." *International Organization* 45(4): 425–51.

Gourevitch, Peter. 1986. *Politics in Hard Times: Comparative Responses to Economic Crises*. Ithaca, N.Y.: Cornell University Press.

Gregory, Mary, Wiemer Salverda, and Ronald Schettkat, eds. 2007. *Services and Employment: Explaining the U.S.-European Gap*. Princeton, N.J.: Princeton University Press.

Hall, Peter A., and David Soskice. 2001. *Varieties of Capitalism: The Institutional Foundations of Comparative Advantage*. Oxford: Oxford University Press.

Hardiman, Niamh, and Sebastian Dellepiane. 2011. "Governing the Economy: A Triple Crisis." In *Crisis in Irish Governance*, edited by Niamh Hardiman. Manchester, U.K.: Manchester University Press.

Hicks, Stephen, Craig Lindsay, Donna Livesey, Nick Barford, and Richard Williams. 2005. "Public Sector Employment." London: Office for National Statistics.

HM Revenue and Customs. 2008. "Pre-Budget Report 2008." London: Her Majesty's Government National Archives. Available at: http://webarchive.national archives.gov.uk/20100330144254/http://www.hmrc.gov.uk/pbr2008/index .htm (accessed February 2011).

Honohan, Patrick. 2010. "The Irish Banking Crisis: Regulatory and Financial Stability Policy 2003–2008." Dublin: Commission of Investigation into the Banking Sector in Ireland.

Inklaar, Robert, and Marcel Peter Timmer. 2008. "GGDC Productivity Level Database: International Comparisons of Output, Inputs, and Productivity at the Industry Level." *GGDC* Research Memorandum GD-104. Groningen: University of Groningen.

International Monetary Fund (IMF). 2009. "Ireland: 2009 Article IV Consultation—Staff Report; and Public Information Notice on the Executive Board Discussion." *IMF* Country Report 09/195. Washington, D.C.: IMF.

———. 2010. "Ireland: 2010 Article IV Consultation—Staff Report; and Public Information Notice on the Executive Board Discussion." *IMF* Country Report 10/209. Washington, D.C.: IMF.

Iversen, Torben. 1999. *Contested Economic Institutions*. Cambridge: Cambridge University Press.

Iversen, Torben, and David Soskice 2010. "Real Exchange Rates and Competitiveness: The Political Economy of Skill Formation, Wage Compression, and Electoral Systems." *American Political Science Review* 104(3): 601–23.

Iversen, Torben, and Anne Wren. 1998. "Equality, Employment, and Budgetary Restraint: The Trilemma of the Service Economy." *World Politics* 50(July): 507–46.

Kalwij, Adriaan S., and Stephen Machin. 2007. "Comparative Service Consumption in Six Countries." In *Services and Employment: Explaining the U.S.-European Gap*, edited by Mary Gregory, Wiemer Salverda, and Ronald Schettkat. Princeton, N.J.: Princeton University Press.

Kelly, Elish, Seamus McGuinness, and Philip O'Connell. 2008. "Benchmarking, Social Partnership, and Higher Remuneration: Wage-Setting Institutions and the Public-Private Sector Wage Gap in Ireland." *ESRI* working paper no. 270. Dublin: Economic and Social Research Institute.

Kemeny, Jim. 1980. "Home Ownership and Privatization." *International Journal of Urban and Regional Research* 4(3): 372–88.

———. 2005. "'The Really Big Trade-Off' between Home Ownership and Welfare: Castles' Evaluation of the 1980 Thesis, and a Reformulation 25 Years on." *Housing, Theory, and Society* 22(2): 59–75.

Kitchin, Rob, Justin Gleeson, Karen Keaveney, and Cian O'Callaghan. 2010. "A Haunted Landscape: Housing and Ghost Estates in Post-Celtic Tiger Ireland." *NIRSA* working paper no. 59. Maynooth: National University of Ireland. Available at: http://www.nuim.ie/nirsa/research/documents/WP59-A-Haunted -Landscape.pdf (accessed February 2011).

Kongsrud, Per Mathis, and Isabelle Wanner. 2005. "The Impact of Structural Policies on Trade-Related Adjustment and the Shift to Services." *OECD Economics Department* working paper no. 427. Paris: Organisation for Economic Cooperation and Development.

Lane, Philip. 1998. "Profits and Wages in Ireland, 1997–98." *Journal of the Social and Statistical Inquiry Society of Ireland* 27(5): 223–47.

———. 2011. "The Irish Crisis." *IIIS* discussion paper no. 356. Dublin: Institute for International Integration Studies. Available at: http://http://www.tcd.ie/iiis/ documents/discussion/pdfs/iiisdp356.pdf (accessed February 2011).

Lane, Philip, and Agustin Benetrix. 2010. "International Differences in Fiscal Policy During the Global Crisis." *IIIS* discussion paper no. 336. Dublin: Institute for International Integration Studies. Available at: http://http://www.tcd.ie/ iiis/documents/discussion/pdfs/iiisdp336.pdf (accessed February 2011).

Lane, Philip, and Gian Maria Milesi-Ferretti. 2010. "The Cross-Country Incidence of the Global Crisis." *IMF* working paper 10-171. Washington, D.C.: International Monetary Fund.

Laver, Michael. 2005. "The Voters." In *Politics in the Republic of Ireland*, edited by John Coakley and Michael Gallagher. London: Routledge.

Lee, Simon. 2008. "The British Model of Political Economy." In *Ten Years of New Labour*, edited by Matt Beech and Simon Lee. London: Palgrave Macmillan.

Lyons, Tom, and Brian Carey. 2011. *The Fitzpatrick Tapes*. Dublin: Penguin.

Marsh, Michael, Richard Sinnott, John Garry, and Fiachra Kennedy. 2008. *The Irish Voter: The Nature of Electoral Competition in the Republic of Ireland*. Manchester, U.K.: Manchester University Press.

Mathiason, Nick, and Yuba Bessaoud. 2011. "The Data: The Growth of City Donations to the Conservative Party." London: Bureau of Investigative Journalism. Available at: http://www.thebureauinvestigates.com/2011/02/08/the-data -the-growth-of-city-donations-to-the-conservative-party (accessed February 23, 2011).

Matthews, David. 2010. "Regional Analysis of Public Sector Employment 2010." London: U.K. Office of National Statistics. Available at: http://www.ons.gov .uk/ons/rel/pse/public-sector-employment/2010/index.html (accessed April 24, 2012).

McGuinness, Seamus, Elish Kelly, and Philip O'Connell. 2008. "The Impact of Wage Bargaining Regime on Firm-Level Competitiveness and Wage Inequality: The Case of Ireland." *ESRI* working paper no. 266. Dublin: Economic and Social Research Institute.

Montgomerie, Johnna. 2007. "The Logic of Neo-Liberalism and the Political Economy of Consumer Debt-Led Growth." *Neo-Liberalism, State Power, and Global Governance* 4(2007): 157–72.

Organisation for Economic Co-operation and Development (OECD). 2009. "The Effectiveness and Scope of Fiscal Stimulus." In *OECD Interim Economic Outlook (March 2009)*. Paris: OECD.

Pennington, Mark. 2000. *Planning and the Political Market: Public Choice and the Politics of Government Failure*. London: The Athalone Press.

Regling, Klaus, and Maz Watson. 2010. *A Preliminary Report on the Sources of Ireland's Banking Crisis*. Dublin: Commission of Investigation into the Banking Sector in Ireland.

Schwartz, Herman, and Leonard Seabrooke. 2008. "Varieties of Residential Capitalism in the International Political Economy: Old Welfare States and the New Politics of Housing." *Comparative European Politics* 6(3): 237–61.

Soskice, David. 2007. "Macroeconomics and Varieties of Capitalism." In *Beyond Varieties of Capitalism: Conflict, Contradictions, and Complementarities in the European Economy*, edited by Bob Hancke, Martin Rhodes, and Mark Thatcher. Oxford: Oxford University Press.

Swenson, Peter. 1991. "Bringing Capital Back in, or Social Democracy Reconsidered: Employer Power, Cross-Class Alliances, and Centralization of Industrial Relations in Denmark and Sweden." *World Politics* 43(4): 513–44.

Taylor, John. 2009. "The Financial Crisis and the Policy Responses: An Empirical

Analysis of What Went Wrong." *NBER* working paper no. 14631. Cambridge, Mass.: National Bureau of Economic Research.

Trinity College Dublin. 2007. *Irish National Election Study, 2002–2007*. Dublin: Trinity College Dublin. Available at: http://www.tcd.ie/ines (accessed April 24, 2012).

Walsh, James P., and Jiangyan Yu. 2010. "Determinants of Foreign Direct Investment: A Sectoral and Institutional Approach." IMF working paper no. WP/10/87. Washington, D.C.: IMF.

Warren, Elizabeth, and Amelia W. Tyagi. 2004. *The Two-Income Trap: Why Middle-Class Parents Are Going Broke*. New York: Basic Books.

Watson, Matthew. 2008. "Constituting Monetary Conservatives via the 'Savings Habit': New Labour and the British Housing Market Bubble." *Comparative European Politics* 6(3): 285–304.

Weale, Martin. 2006. "Commentary: The Housing Market and Government Policy." *National Institute Economic Review* 195(1): 4–8.

Williams, Brendan, Brian Hughes, and Patrick Shiels. 2003. "Access to Housing: The Role of Housing Supply and Urban Development Agencies in the Greater Dublin Area." *Journal of Irish Urban Studies* 2(1): 25–52.

Wren, Anne, ed. 2012. "Introduction: The Political Economy of Post-Industrial Societies." In *The Political Economy of the Service Transition*, edited by Anne Wren. Oxford: Oxford University Press.

Wren, Anne, Mate Fodor, and Sotiria Theodoropoulou. 2012. "The Trilemma Revisited: Implications for Inequality and Employment Creation of the ICT Revolution and The Expansion of Service Trade." In *The Political Economy of the Service Transition*, edited by Anne Wren. Oxford: Oxford University Press.

PART III | Cross-National Consequences

Chapter 11 | Crisis as Political Opportunity? Partisan Politics, Housing Cycles, and the Credit Crisis

Ben W. Ansell

THE FINANCIAL CRISIS of the autumn of 2008, sparking fears of a repeat of the Great Depression, produced a dramatic and choreographed set of government responses across the advanced industrial world. Policymakers faced immediate threats requiring urgent action, in particular the teetering financial sector, as well as the impending likelihood of a prolonged slump in broader economic activity. Looking to the longer run, the crisis also galvanized debate about the regulatory framework governing both global finance and domestic lending. Although recent economic events suggest that the worst-case scenarios were held at bay, decisions made by governments in the year following the stock market downturn of October 2008 will have a significant impact on the long-run fiscal health, monetary stability, and regulatory frameworks of most countries. These choices, in fact, differed quite sharply across states. Some, such as the United States and China, implemented large discretionary fiscal stimuli; others, such as Germany and Sweden, with automatic fiscal stabilizers kicking in, were more hesitant to provide discretionary stimuli. Still other countries, such as Greece, Iceland, Ireland, and Hungary, were forced to adopt fiscal austerity measures in response to market fears of their insolvency. In terms of financial stabilization, variance was broad. Central banks and finance ministries differed in the kinds of assets they would accept as collateral, and though some states enacted moves to nationalize banks and regulate traders, others took a more hands-off approach to financial stabilization and regulation.

Despite the importance, and sheer magnitude, of government policies implemented since the financial crisis began, at present scholars lack both a comprehensive cross-national account of how countries differed in their policy responses and an understanding of why these different choices were made. Indeed, remarkably little political science analysis has examined the role of governments in responding to housing booms and busts (but see Schwartz and Seabrooke 2008; Schwartz 2009; Ansell 2011; chapter 10, this volume). Yet housing was the prime cause of the credit crisis—inflated house prices producing the original sin of consumer overleverage. To properly understand how governments responded to this crisis, we need to move from the standard political economy focus on labor market income and class differences to an analysis of how wealth and home ownership affect preferences and policy. This chapter builds on a theory of the political economy of ownership to address two questions: what explains variation in government policy responses to the credit crisis, and the degree to which these responses are part of a broader long-term pattern of government responses to cycles in the housing market.

FROM INCOME TO ASSETS: A THEORETICAL AND EMPIRICAL BACKGROUND

Political economists know a great deal about the political causes and consequences of business cycles in the postwar era. Drawing first on Keynesian economics and the Philips curve, and later on various versions of rational expectations business cycle theories, successive scholars have drawn broad conclusions both about the effects of partisanship and labor market institutions on price inflation and unemployment (Hibbs 1977; Hall and Franzese 1998; Iversen 1999), and about the impact of macroeconomic forces on public policies (Franzese 2002). One irony of this expansive and convincing literature is that just as a broad consensus on the relationship between politics and macroeconomics has emerged, contemporary trends in the business cycle, particularly in price inflation, suggest that the macroeconomic volatility that characterized the mid-twentieth century has been tamed. A variety of scholars, most notably Ben Bernanke (2004), announced that a Great Moderation—with massively reduced volatility in output, employment, and price inflation—has taken place. When we examine price inflation across the OECD, that assertion seems to hold up. Between 1956 and 1985, the average level of price inflation in the Organisation for Economic Co-operation and Development (OECD) was 6.9 percent, with a within-country standard deviation of 4.9 percent. Between 1985 and 2006, the average level of price inflation more than halved to 3.3 percent, as did the standard deviation—to 2.4 percent. Put simply, price inflation has been substantially lower and considerably less volatile over the past few decades.

However, although price inflation of goods and services was dormant, another form of volatility was waking. From the mid-1980s, asset markets in equities and housing became substantially more volatile. Equity markets have been volatile historically, but the same has not been true of house prices. In particular, house prices across the advanced industrial world accelerated in hitherto unseen rates between 2001 and 2007 before plummeting in an unforeseen fashion between 2008 and 2010. The period between 1985 and 2006 saw three times the average level of real house price inflation as that between 1970 and 1985 and, even before 2006 and the downturn in housing prices, a higher level of volatility. This final boom and bust period is unprecedented in modern times (Shiller 2007).

Most analysts agree that the huge housing booms and subsequent busts across the advanced industrial world resulted from a set of policies that enabled cheap credit, including mortgage market and broader financial deregulation, and extended periods of low interest rates (Schwartz 2009). In combination, these policies have produced ever-greater leakage from the housing sector into the health of overall economy. The International Monetary Fund (IMF) estimates that in a number of countries, especially the United States, shocks to house prices and their feedback into consumption and residential investment account for north of 20 percent of variation in national economic output, even though changes in house prices do not directly figure into national income accounts (2008). Moreover, house prices themselves have become ever more sensitive to policy changes. In many states—not only the Anglo American liberal market economies (LMEs) but also coordinated market economies such as Belgium, Norway, Denmark, and Japan—more than 50 percent of house price variation can be accounted for by monetary policy changes. This phenomenon is new. The interest rate elasticity of house prices has increased massively since the 1970s. Whereas in most OECD states, between 1970 and 1982 a 1 percent point increase in interest rates was associated with less than a 1 percent decline in house prices, between 1983 and 2007 the same interest rate change had substantially larger effects: producing a 2 percent decline in house prices in Sweden, Finland, and the United Kingdom, 3.5 percent in the United States and France, and 5 percent in Spain and Holland (IMF 2008). In short, housing was both more strongly affected by macroeconomic policy and a greater cause of ensuing macroeconomic outcomes. The Great Moderation was far from apparent in asset markets. It was likely this shift in volatility from the product to the asset market that blinded policymakers to the underlying weaknesses of the bubble economy of 2003 to 2008 that precipitated the credit crisis. Hence, if we wish to understand comparative political responses to the credit crisis, it is crucial to understand conceptually how asset cycles affect citizens' preferences and the behavior of politicians.

The two periods from 1945 to the early 1980s and from the early 1980s to the present can be characterized as representative of two ideal types, *employment dominance* and *asset dominance*. In the former, macroeconomic policies have larger effects on the product market—in terms of prices, wages and employment—than they do on the value of assets such as equities and housing. Furthermore, citizens in a world of employment dominance rely on wages for their income, and on employer- or government-provided unemployment benefits or pensions for periods where they are out of the labor force, either through involuntary unemployment or voluntary retirement. Asset dominance, by contrast, describes a world in which changes in macroeconomic policies have a larger effect on the value of assets than on product prices, wages, or employment. In this world, citizens depend increasingly on the value of their assets both for day-to-day income (using the value of their asset as collateral) and for unemployment or retirement (a nest egg effect). Whether the shift to asset dominance is final depends to some degree on citizens' reactions to the recent collapses in asset prices—risk-averse individuals may be less willing to own housing, or particularly equities. Nonetheless, the genie of asset dominance will remain out of the bottle because its emergence corresponds to ever-rising flows of international capital since the 1980s. These flows have underpinned both the explosion in asset prices and the volatility in asset valuations as global capital surges and ebbs at a higher intensity and frequency than ever before.[1]

There is some variation in the degree to which different countries more closely approximate each type. Liberal market economies (LMEs) such as Australia, the United Kingdom, and the United States uniformly experienced sizeable credit booms and housing appreciation (chapter 10, this volume). However, although LMEs had similar experiences, coordinated market economies varied: for example, Scandinavian states—such as Denmark and Sweden—had house price growth comparable to LMEs, whereas others—such as Germany and Japan—actually experienced house price declines over the period. Generally, non-LMEs that saw housing booms also had traditions of high homeownership rates, especially the southern European states, such as Spain. Thus, although increased financial interconnection has exposed all countries to global shifts in asset price volatility, these shifts were most pronounced in LMEs, Scandinavia, and southern Europe. What these countries had in common were not only high rates of homeownership but also, especially in the LMEs and southern Europe, very high levels of international capital inflows, largely as a response to persistent current account deficits. Whereas chapter 10 in this volume sees housing booms as a phenomenon largely related to the domestic financial architecture of LMEs, I argue that a broader array of countries were susceptible because of the asymmetry in global capital flows, especially southern European states. Put simply, housing booms had both domestic and international causes.

Theoretically, how would we expect political behavior to differ in these two ideal types? When asset prices—like housing—are rising, I argue that asset-owning citizens will respond by desiring both lower taxes and less publicly provided social insurance (see also Kemeny 1981; Castles 1998; Ansell 2011; chapter 10, this volume). First, increased earnings from assets are likely to make citizens more tax sensitive, either because their assets are directly taxed, as in property taxation, or because they adopt the anti-tax preferences of high-income individuals.[2] Second, because asset owners have privately insured against income loss in unemployment or old age by being able to use their assets—especially housing—as a nest egg, they have less demand for public insurance as a hedge against such risks. Private insurance substitutes for public insurance. These responses to rising asset prices should be mirrored by in the case of decreasing asset prices— producing a reversal of preferences. Arguably, house price crashes should lead to increased demand for social insurance against the vagaries of the market.

The discussion of changes in house prices raises the question of who the relevant political actors are in this argument: after all, price changes themselves do not vote. Homeowners are the obvious beneficiaries of house price appreciation and similarly, renters and potential first-time buyers are the losers. These are essentially latent political interests—large groups of actors with common interests but unlikely to have individual incentives to bear the costs of organizing for this interest. Thus, identifiable interest groups with observable preferences over social policy are difficult to come by, though in countries where the financial and construction sectors are especially sizable, these lobby groups will attempt to secure policies that sustain housing prices. More broadly, we might expect the aggregate national homeownership rate to affect the balance of homeowner versus renter interests in terms of demands on politicians. Specifically, in countries with higher homeownership rates, we would expect homeowners to be more effective at expressing their preferences for reduced social spending and taxation during periods of house price appreciation. Where homeowners are a larger group, they become a more attractive source of votes for politicians. Survey analysis of the United States and the United Kingdom, as opposed to Germany, finds a stronger effect of house price appreciation on policy preferences in the former two high homeownership cases compared to the latter country, well known for its traditionally low homeownership rate (Ansell 2011).

We can think about the connection between homeowners and politicians two ways, the composition of parties and opportunistic policymaking. Broadly, in terms of composition, asset owners tend to have conservative views on social and economic policies and are represented by right-wing parties, as shown by an array of studies since the 1980s (Kingston, Thompson, and Eichar 1984; Pratt 1987; Verberg 2000). This pattern is consistent with the established findings that higher income and older citizens—both more likely to own houses—tend to vote for right-wing parties. This connection is accentuated by the fact that higher income and older citizens are not only more likely to be homeowners but are also disproportionately likely to benefit from increasing house prices. Wealthier citizens tend to own more expensive houses, which for a given percentage increase in aggregate house prices will see larger absolute gains (Edlin 2007). Older citizens also disproportionately benefit from rising house prices because they are likely to downsize or rent in their impending retirement, and thereby cash out their housing gains. Indeed, the effects of house price appreciation on individual preferences over social security are much stronger for right-wing voters than for other citizens (Ansell 2011). Thus the composition of the right-wing electorate is disproportionately made of homeowners who push right-wing parties to cut spending and taxes.

Political opportunism provides a complementary mechanism connecting homeowners and political parties. Instead of responding purely to the composition of their voting base, parties often have consistent policy preferences, insulated somewhat from their constituents, and seek opportunities to enact those preferences conditional on aggregate public opinion moving in their direction. Under this mechanism, because homeowners form a majority of the electorate, during periods of rising house prices, the political climate shifts in the antitax antispending direction favored by right-wing parties. This mechanism further suggests that these effects will be stronger where homeownership is higher and homeowners form an even greater share of aggregate public opinion. Putting these mechanisms together, we should expect to see the preferences of homeowners channeled by right-wing parties during periods of asset price change. Put simply, during house price booms I expect right-wing governments to cut taxes and spending. This pattern should be amplified in countries with high homeownership, which include both LMEs and various Scandinavian and southern European states. In contrast, left-wing governments have both fewer asset owners among their constituents and a baseline preference for increased spending. We might expect such parties to try to

Figure 11.1   Effects of House Price Changes on Social Spending
1980 to 2003

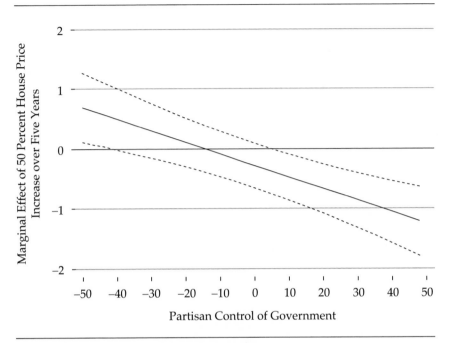

Source: Author's compilation based on Ansell (2011).

increase social insurance spending to target benefits to their constituents who lack the private insurance provided by asset ownership. When asset prices are stagnant, arguably both the opportunistic and compositional motivations driving political parties are attenuated substantially. Thus, the effect of partisanship is conditional on the size of housing price changes.

This pattern is visible in data drawn from the period 1980 to 2003 from eighteen advanced industrial countries. Figure 11.1 shows estimates of the marginal effect on social spending of real house prices increasing, at different levels of partisanship (Ansell 2011).[3] There is a clearly negative slope: as government shifts to the right the effect of house price appreciation on social spending moves from increased spending, at the extreme Left, to decreased spending, for almost all governments on the Right. It is notable that this pattern is most robust for the Right, with significant decreases in spending occurring for almost all right-wing governments. In countries with high levels of homeownership, this pattern is accentuated.

However, the pattern is consistent across both liberal and coordinated market economies. In other words, the effects of homeownership are not duplicative of varieties of capitalism partly because a wide variety of countries have high homeownership rates—not only liberal Britain and America have homeownership rates above 65 percent but also Norway, Spain, and Finland.

Thus across the last few decades, OECD countries do appear to have experienced important effects of housing on the behavior of governments. Does the story of the past decades hold up today? Have right-wing parties responded similarly in the fiscal environment following the credit crash of 2008 and have left-wing parties, for their part, moved in a countervailing direction to shore up spending?

HOUSING BOOMS, PARTISANSHIP, AND THE STIMULUS

The collapse in global house prices that began in earnest in 2007 was the prelude to a sustained decline in industrial output the following year, followed in October 2008 by a collapse in equity valuations and a near collapse of the international financial system. Almost immediately, governments unveiled a set of policies to respond to these challenges. These policies came in three forms: monetary policy easing, fiscal stimulus, and regulatory policies. Monetary policymaking was rapid and uniform across the advanced industrial world. By late October 2008, central banks had coordinated a massive slashing of interest rates. Policies regarding fiscal stimulus and financial regulation, however, took longer to be enacted and varied considerably. In this section and the next, I describe this variation and then examine its determinants. In particular, I focus on the joint role of partisanship and the size of housing booms.

Although the crisis began in earnest in October 2008, most governments took several months to respond fully. In particular, February 2009 saw a rapid spurt of government announcements about fiscal stimuli. The simultaneity of responses appears related to the American Recovery and Reinvestment Act (ARRA) of the Obama administration, enacted on February 17, 2009, having been introduced three weeks earlier. The $787 billion act was the single largest national fiscal stimulus in absolute amount and appears to have set the cross-national fiscal agenda. Arguably, like monetary policy, the pattern of engaging in fiscal stimuli across the OECD displayed a high deal of interdependence, with even the most reluctant countries, such as Germany, engaging in fiscal policy in short order after the U.S. announcement.

Thus, if we are to look for substantive cross-national variation in fiscal responses to the credit crisis, we will not find it terms of the choice to engage in stimulus, which was effectively universal, nor the timing, which was near simultaneous. Instead, we must to turn to examine differences among stimulus policies in terms of their size and composition. Here we do find substantial variation as displayed in table 11.1, which uses data from the OECD (2009a) and presents information on both the cyclical and discretionary elements of the budget deficit and breaks down discretionary policy into the types of tax cuts or spending increases that states employed. The first thing to note is that the massive fiscal deficits carried by most states over 2009 and 2010 were partly produced by collapses in tax revenues and countercyclical increases in spending to cover unemployment insurance and other stabilization expenses. Although the average cyclical effect on government finances was 5.6 percent of GDP, discretionary stimuli averaged at only 1.6 percent of national income. However, the relatively small average discretionary stimulus is a product of several states—Hungary, Iceland, and Ireland—having to engage in massive fiscal retrenchment, producing an anti-stimulus effect in these states. The size of stimuli ranged between less than 1 percent of GDP in France, Portugal, and Switzerland, and around 6 percent in Korea and the United States. Put simply, discretionary government policies reflect substantially greater variation than the degree to which states experienced cyclical deficits.

Variation was also considerable in how the stimuli were structured both in terms of the relative share of taxation and spending and within these categories. Some countries tilted their stimuli toward tax cuts, such as the Czech Republic and New Zealand, whereas others focused on spending increases, such as Australia, Denmark, Korea, and Spain. Some countries focused tax cuts on individual income taxes, as in Australia and Spain. Others focused on cuts to social taxes, as in Germany and the Netherlands, or consumption taxes as in Canada and the United Kingdom. Some focused spending increases on government consumption—Denmark and Sweden—and others on government investment—Australia, Canada, Poland. Still others increased transfers to households, businesses, or subnational entities—respectively, Luxembourg, Japan, and the United States. Clearly variation in both the size and targeting of fiscal stimuli is ample. We now turn to how well the hypothesized interplay between house price booms and partisanship fits this data.

To code partisanship, I use 2007 data derived from the proportion of cabinet seats held by right-wing, center, or left-wing parties (Armingeon et al. 2009). Where control of government changed by the time of the announced stimulus packages in OECD countries, I recoded the cabinet composition using data drawn from a collection of country profiles (Bale and Van Biezen 2009). I use two variables to reflect cabinet partisanship,

Table 11.1   Size and Composition of Fiscal Stimuli across OECD as Percentage of GDP

	Cyclical Change	Stimulus Change	Tax Changes	Individual Tax	Business Tax	Consump. Tax
Australia	–3.4	–5.4	–1.3	–1.1	–0.2	0
Austria	–4.9	–1.2	–0.8	–0.8	–0.1	0
Belgium	–7.7	–1.4	–0.3	0	–0.1	–0.1
Canada	–3.6	–4.1	–2.4	–0.8	–0.3	–1.1
Czech Republic	–6.1	–2.8	–2.5	0	–0.7	–0.4
Denmark	–6.9	–3.3	–0.7	0	0	0
Finland	–6.8	–3.2	–2.7	–1.9	0	–0.3
France	–4.8	–0.7	–0.2	–0.1	–0.1	0
Germany	–6.5	–3.2	–1.6	–0.6	–0.3	0
Greece	—	0.8	0.8	0.8	0	0
Hungary	–7.7	7.7	0.2	–0.6	–0.1	2.3
Iceland	–6.4	7.3	5.7	1	—	—
Ireland	–6.3	8.3	6	4.5	–0.2	0.5
Italy	–5.7	0	0.3	0	0	0.1
Japan	–4.2	–4.7	–0.5	–0.1	–0.1	–0.1
Korea	—	–6.1	–2.8	–1.4	–1.1	–0.2
Luxembourg	–7.5	–3.9	–2.3	–1.5	–0.8	0
Mexico	—	–1.7	–0.4	0	0	–0.4
Netherlands	–5.6	–2.5	–1.6	–0.2	–0.5	–0.1
New Zealand	–3.9	–3.7	–4.1	–4	0	0
Norway	—	–1.2	–0.3	0	–0.3	0
Poland	–4.4	–1.2	–0.4	0	–0.1	–0.2
Portugal	–4.6	–0.8	—	—	—	—
Slovak Republic	—	–1.3	–0.7	–0.5	–0.1	0
Spain	–5.6	–3.9	–1.7	–1.6	0	0
Sweden	–8.7	–3.3	–1.7	–1.3	–0.2	0
Switzerland	–3.7	–0.5	–0.2	–0.2	0	0
Turkey	—	–4.4	–1.5	–0.2	–1.1	–0.2
United Kingdom	–5.1	–1.9	–1.5	–0.5	–0.2	–0.6
United States	–3.1	–5.6	–3.2	–2.4	–0.8	0

Source: Author's compilation based on OECD (2009a).

Social Tax	Spending Changes	Govt. Consump.	Govt. Invest.	Transfers Families	Transfers Business	Transfers Regions
0	4.1	0	3	1.1	0	0
0	0.4	0	0.1	0.2	0	0.1
0	1.1	0	0.1	0.5	0.5	0
−0.1	1.7	0.1	1.3	0.3	0.1	—
−1.4	0.3	−0.1	0.2	0	0.2	0
0	2.6	0.9	0.8	0.1	0	0
−0.4	0.5	0	0.3	0.1	0	0
0	0.6	0	0.2	0.3	0	0
−0.7	1.6	0	0.8	0.3	0.3	0
0	0	−0.4	0.1	0.4	0.1	0
−1.5	−7.5	−3.2	0	−3.4	−0.4	−0.5
—	−1.6	—	—	—	—	—
1.2	−2.2	−1.8	−0.2	−0.1	0	0
0	0.3	0.3	0	0.2	0.1	0
−0.2	4.2	0.2	1.2	0.6	1.5	0.6
0	3.2	0	1.2	0.7	1	0.3
0	1.6	0	0.4	1	0.2	0
0	1.2	0.1	0.7	0.1	0	0
−0.8	0.9	0	0.5	0.1	0	0
0	−0.3	0.1	0.6	−0.6	0	0
0	0.9	0	0.4	0	0	0.3
0	0.8	0	1.3	0.2	0.1	0
—	—	0	0.4	0	0.4	0
−0.1	0.7	0	0	0.1	0.6	0
0	2.2	0.3	0.7	0.5	0.7	0
−0.2	1.7	1.1	0.3	0.1	0	0.2
0	0.3	0.3	0	0	0	0
0	2.9	0.6	1.2	0	0.3	0.6
0	0.4	0	0.4	0.2	0	0
0	2.4	0.7	0.3	0.5	0	0.9

along the lines developed by Klaus Armingeon and his colleagues (2009). First is *right-wing partisanship*—the proportion of the cabinet held by right-wing politicians, following the Armingeon and colleagues' coding of parties by country. Second is *left-wing partisanship*—the proportion of the cabinet held by left-wing politicians. These are not mirror images of one another because a third category—center-party politicians—remains: for example, the Democratic Party in the United States or the FDP in Germany.[4] I run two sets of cross-sectional regressions, one for right-wing partisanship and one for left-wing partisanship.[5] Each time I interact the relevant partisanship variable with a house price variable. This variable is the 2001 to 2006 five-year increase in real house prices, taken from the Bank for International Settlements estimates of house prices adjusted for inflation. The reason for using this span of years is that it best reflects the overall size of the housing boom in most countries, given that by 2007 prices had leveled and indeed begun declining in many countries. Each regression thus contains partisanship, house price appreciation, their interaction, and finally a measure of the cyclical budget deficit in 2008, drawn from table 11.1.

I conduct two sets of regressions, one for the right-wing partisanship measure and one for the left-wing partisanship measure. In each, I examine two broad indicators of discretionary fiscal policy—first aggregate tax changes and second aggregate spending increases. Obviously, most tax changes were negative and spending was positive, because all these states save Ireland engaged in countercyclical stimuli. Because of Ireland's unique status as a retrencher in this cross-section (see chapter 10, this volume), I report results both with and without Ireland. I also show for each tax and spending dependent variable, the effects of examining the direct effect of partisanship in model A and then the effect conditional on house prices in model B. As we shall see, in every case, partisanship matters only in terms of its interaction with housing prices.

Table 11.2 uses the right-wing partisanship variable. Models A through C examine the determinants of discretionary tax policy. Although model A shows no net direct effect of partisanship on the size of tax cuts, models B and C both display an interactive effect of partisanship conditional on the size of the housing boom in each state, albeit not robust in model B. Specifically, where the boom was particularly large, right-wing government led to larger tax cuts. Put differently, states with large housing booms had large tax cuts as part of their discretionary stimuli when government was under right-wing control. The elective affinity of right-wing government, housing boom, and cuts in revenues holds in this cross-sectional analysis. The effect is also apparent in terms of discretionary spending. Right-wing governments in countries with large house booms had much lower spend-

Table 11.2 Percentage of Cabinet from Right and Stimulus Policies

	Model A Tax	Model B Tax	Model C Tax Excluding Ireland	Model D Spending	Model E Spending	Model F Spending Excluding Ireland
Right Government	0.012	0.030**	0.021**	-0.009	0.011	0.015
	(0.012)	(0.015)	(0.008)	(0.009)	(0.012)	(0.010)
House Price Change		0.839	0.556		0.961	1.094
		(0.740)	(0.585)		(1.200)	(1.215)
Right × House Prices		-0.041	-0.040**		-0.046**	-0.047**
		(0.028)	(0.019)		(0.019)	(0.018)
Cyclical	-0.301	-0.335	-0.195	0.201	0.163	0.097
	(0.288)	(0.301)	(0.185)	(0.220)	(0.211)	(0.186)
Constant	-3.266**	-3.798**	-2.923**	2.828*	2.226	1.814
	(1.493)	(1.725)	(1.117)	(1.362)	(1.395)	(1.301)
Observations	17	17	16	17	17	16
R^2	0.117	0.189	0.328	0.107	0.275	0.298

Source: Author's compilation based on Armingeon et al. (2009) and OECD (2009a).
Robust standard errors in parentheses
*** $p < 0.01$, ** $p < 0.05$, * $p < 0.1$

ing increases than either left or center governments or, indeed, right-wing governments in countries without large house price booms.

Table 11.3 shows symmetric results when we turn to measuring cabinet partisanship with the proportion of cabinet seats held by left-wing parties (again following the Armingeon and colleagues definitions of party). In terms of tax stimuli, the results are statistically insignificant. However, the interaction term does have its expected sign—positive—and as we shall see presently, there is evidence of a borderline significant impact of housing booms when left-wing parties are entirely absent from government, in this case producing a reduction in taxes. The analysis of spending does show the expected robust interaction between left-wing cabinet seats and house prices. When left-wing parties held no seats, house booms were associated with spending cuts in stimuli. When they held the entire cabinet, however, house booms were associated with spending increases.

Because interpreting interactive coefficients is difficult, I graph the estimated effects of house price booms at varying levels of cabinet partisanship.[6] Figures 11.2 and 11.3, drawn from models C and F of table 11.2, use the right-wing seats measure and show the estimated interactive effect of house price booms and partisanship on, respectively, discretionary taxes and discretionary spending. The figures show strong conditional effects. In total right-wing control of government, house price booms are robustly associated with a decline in discretionary taxes and with a decline in discretionary spending. Interestingly, the estimated size of tax cuts and spending cuts as a percentage of national income are almost identical—implying that right-wing governments in countries with house price booms did not engage in Keynesian countercyclical policies but instead accompanied tax cuts with spending cuts.[7]

Figures 11.4 and 11.5 show the effects of left-wing control of government. Here we see that when left-wing governments controlled cabinets, the size of the house price boom had no robust effect on discretionary tax policy. The booms were associated with an increase in discretionary spending. Put together, unlike right-wing parties, left-wing parties in countries with housing booms did engage in countercyclical policies with some gusto. However, perhaps surprisingly, this result holds up only when one examines the conditional effect of partisanship and housing prices. Neither left-wing, nor indeed right-wing, partisanship have any direct effect on either discretionary tax or spending policies. The effect of partisanship was moderated by countries' housing experience. Why were these effects only conditional? Where housing booms were moderate or absent, neither the opportunity for parties to engage in politically attractive shifts in policy nor the compositional motivation produced by changing demands from parties' voting bases was in play. Without these inter-

Table 11.3 Percentage of Cabinet from Left and Stimulus Policies

	Model A Tax	Model B Tax	Model C Tax Excluding Ireland	Model D Spending	Model E Spending	Model F Spending Excluding Ireland
Left Government	-0.001	-0.020	-0.015	0.007	-0.026	-0.028
	(0.008)	(0.018)	(0.014)	(0.011)	(0.020)	(0.020)
House Price Change		-1.931	-2.423*		-3.493**	-3.269**
		(1.733)	(1.328)		(1.200)	(1.194)
Left × House Prices		0.038	0.038		0.068**	0.068**
		(0.037)	(0.027)		(0.026)	(0.026)
Cyclical	-0.318	-0.336	-0.191	0.196	0.164	0.098
	(0.281)	(0.296)	(0.183)	(0.224)	(0.218)	(0.187)
Constant	-2.704*	-1.997	-1.604	2.154	3.430**	3.252**
	(1.485)	(1.283)	(1.003)	(1.362)	(1.232)	(1.120)
Observations	17	17	16	17	17	16
R^2	0.059	0.090	0.227	0.077	0.267	0.304

Source: Author's compilation based on Armingeon et al. (2009) and OECD (2009a).

Robust standard errors in parentheses

*** $p < 0.01$, ** $p < 0.05$, * $p < 0.1$

Figure 11.2   Marginal Effects of House Booms on Discretionary
              Taxes, Right-Wing Government

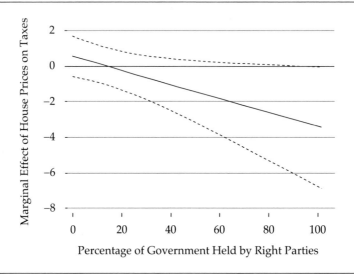

Source: Author's compilation based on author's data.

Figure 11.3   Marginal Effects of House Booms on Discretionary
              Spending, Right-Wing Government

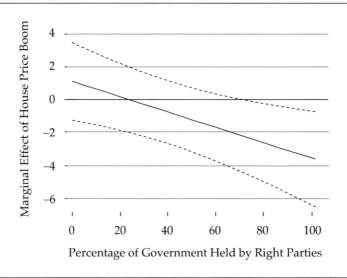

Source: Author's compilation based on author's data.

Figure 11.4   Marginal Effects of House Booms on Discretionary
Taxes, Left-Wing Government

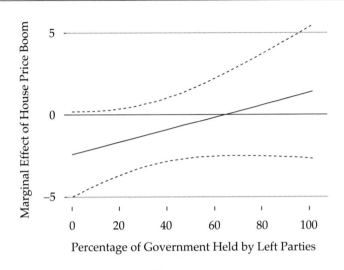

Source: Author's compilation based on author's data.

Figure 11.5   Marginal Effects of House Booms on Discretionary
Spending, Left-Wing Government

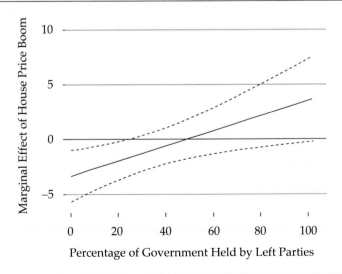

Source: Author's compilation based on author's data.

Figure 11.6   Homeownership Rates and House Price Booms

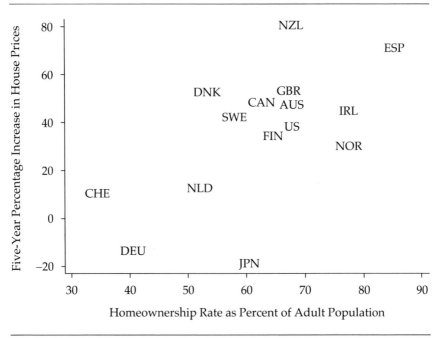

Source: Author's compilation based on Atterhög (2005).

nal and external forces produced by a large group of politically active homeowners, partisan responses were constrained.

Examining homeownership directly supports this conjecture. Home-ownership and the size of the housing boom in the first decade of the new millennium are quite closely related. Figure 11.6 demonstrates this pattern using the five-year house price appreciation variable and a measure of aggregate homeownership drawn from Mikael Atterhög (2005). Countries in the northeast corner of the graph include not only LMEs but also southern European and Scandinavian countries. Parties should respond to the wishes of homeowners more in countries where homeownership is widespread and reflects a larger potential vote pool. Moreover, this effect should be amplified under conditions of rising house prices. Tables 11.4 and 11.5 use two homeownership variables in place of the house price appreciation variable and its interactive term used in the previous analysis. The first measure is the aggregate homeownership rate and the second is that rate multiplied by house price appreciation, thereby measuring the aggregate increase in national housing wealth.

Table 11.4   Right-Wing Partisanship and Homeownership Variables

Variables	(1) Tax	(2) Tax	(3) Spend	(4) Spend	(5) Tax	(6) Tax	(7) Spend	(8) Spend
Right	-0.102	-0.020	0.112*	0.086	0.023*	0.016*	0.017	0.020*
	(0.097)	(0.107)	(0.058)	(0.070)	(0.011)	(0.007)	(0.011)	(0.010)
Ownership	-0.000	0.017	0.041	0.036				
	(0.038)	(0.035)	(0.029)	(0.027)				
Right × Home ownership	0.002	0.000	-0.002*	-0.001				
	(0.002)	(0.002)	(0.001)	(0.001)				
Home Ownership × 5-Year Percent Price Increase					0.007	-0.000	0.017	0.020
					(0.011)	(0.005)	(0.015)	(0.015)
Right × Home Ownership × 5-Year Percent Price Increase					-0.000	-0.001***	-0.001***	-0.001***
					(0.000)	(0.000)	(0.000)	(0.000)
Cyclical	-0.379	-0.320	0.192	0.174	-0.309	-0.105	0.177	0.094
	(0.441)	(0.366)	(0.244)	(0.246)	(0.364)	(0.154)	(0.246)	(0.211)
Constant	-3.161	-3.887	-0.132	0.094	-3.568	-2.374**	2.156	1.672
	(3.849)	(3.280)	(2.360)	(2.188)	(2.014)	(1.029)	(1.624)	(1.486)
Observations	16	15	16	15	14	13	14	13
R²	0.280	0.088	0.356	0.192	0.131	0.576	0.353	0.347

Source: Author's compilation based on Armingeon et al. (2009) and OECD (2009a), and Atterhög (2005).

Table 11.5 Left-Wing Partisanship and Homeownership Variables

Variables	(1) Tax	(2) Tax	(3) Spend	(4) Spend	(5) Tax	(6) Tax	(7) Spend	(8) Spend
Left	0.152	0.017	-0.159*	-0.115	-0.005	-0.007	-0.030	-0.029
	(0.147)	(0.144)	(0.088)	(0.098)	(0.015)	(0.009)	(0.021)	(0.022)
Ownership	0.155	0.020	-0.131	-0.085				
	(0.159)	(0.160)	(0.089)	(0.103)				
Left × Home Ownership	-0.002	-0.000	0.002*	0.002				
	(0.002)	(0.002)	(0.001)	(0.001)				
Home Ownership × 5-Year Percent Price Increase					-0.021	-0.052***	-0.063***	-0.050**
					(0.043)	(0.009)	(0.019)	(0.020)
Left × Home Ownership × 5-Year Percent Price Increase					0.000	0.001**	0.001**	0.001**
					(0.001)	(0.000)	(0.000)	(0.000)
Cyclical	-0.563	-0.348	0.360	0.289	-0.317	-0.086	0.228	0.140
	(0.464)	(0.412)	(0.303)	(0.304)	(0.355)	(0.144)	(0.262)	(0.217)
Constant	-13.645	-4.660	11.256	8.262	-2.436	-1.290	4.057**	3.616**
	(11.226)	(11.263)	(6.658)	(7.426)	(1.759)	(0.836)	(1.389)	(1.263)
Observations	16	15	16	15	14	13	14	13
R^2	0.240	0.124	0.306	0.156	0.068	0.601	0.343	0.322

Source: Author's compilation based on Armingeon et al. (2009) and OECD (2009a), and Atterhög (2005).
Robust standard errors in parentheses
*** $p < 0.01$, ** $p < 0.05$, * $p < 0.1$

The results are broadly similar to those found for house price appreciation, albeit less robust with the homeownership variable and more robust with the homeownership × house price appreciation variable. Putting these results together, it appears that aggregate homeownership rates did indeed matter for fiscal stimulus responses, but much more where house prices had also risen substantially. In terms of overall discretionary tax-cutting or spending increases, we find a consistent conditional effect of partisanship, with housing shaping party responses most where ownership was broad and price appreciation high.

Discretionary taxes and spending are still rather broad categories. It is instructive to examine precisely what kinds of policies governments altered as part of their discretionary stimulus policies. Tables 11.6 and 11.7 examine the determinants of specific components of the stimuli.[8] Examining right-wing partisanship, across individual taxes, business taxes, and social taxes the general interactive pattern we saw for taxes in general holds up—it is, however, robust only in terms of social taxation. Right-wing governments in countries with house price booms appear to have cut social insurance taxes sharply. In terms of spending, there are no robust effects on government consumption or investment, but right-wing parties in housing boom countries were less likely to engage in transfers to households, businesses, or subnational units.

Table 11.7 repeats the exercise for the left-wing partisanship variable. Here we see a similar pattern—except in reverse—to that in table 11.6. Left-wing parties in countries without housing booms reduced social insurance taxes but those in countries with housing booms did not. In terms of spending, some evidence indicates increased government consumption in states with large housing booms and left-wing control of government. But the much stronger effects appear in terms of transfers, especially to businesses and localities, where fully left-wing governments with house booms greatly increased transfers. Overall, it appears that the interactive effects of partisanship and house price booms appear most strongly in terms of social insurance taxation and transfers to households.

Two caveats to this analysis are important. First, we are limited in this section to a cross-section of seventeen states for which we have data for housing prices, government partisanship, and cyclical and discretionary budgetary changes.[9] This kind of cross-sectional data forces us to make rather heroic assumptions that partisan changes across countries are similar to those within them. However, we obviously lack the perfect counterfactual of two political parties in the same country simultaneously responding to the credit crisis.

Second, was the interaction between political parties and house prices in the 2009 stimuli a function of the housing boom or the bust? If the expe-

Table 11.6 Composition of Stimuli and Right Governments

	(1) Indiv Tax	(2) Bus Tax	(3) Soc Tax	(4) Cons Tax	(5) Gov Cons	(6) Gov Inv	(7) Tran HH	(8) Tran Bus	(9) Tran Loc
Right Government	0.012	0.004**	0.006**	-0.001	0.004	-0.001	0.002	0.009*	0.002
	(0.008)	(0.002)	(0.002)	(0.002)	(0.002)	(0.005)	(0.002)	(0.004)	(0.002)
House Price Change	-0.551	0.369	1.041***	-0.151	0.298	0.216	0.564	0.333	0.024
	(0.743)	(0.241)	(0.245)	(0.259)	(0.207)	(0.694)	(0.349)	(0.561)	(0.172)
Right × House Prices	-0.025	-0.005	-0.010***	0.001	-0.004	-0.004	-0.015**	-0.019*	-0.006**
	(0.023)	(0.003)	(0.003)	(0.005)	(0.003)	(0.008)	(0.005)	(0.010)	(0.003)
Cyclical	-0.183	-0.039	0.039*	-0.036	-0.067	0.164	0.019	-0.012	0.052
	(0.177)	(0.040)	(0.021)	(0.054)	(0.083)	(0.132)	(0.046)	(0.050)	(0.059)
Constant	-1.780	-0.640**	-0.409**	-0.238	-0.311	1.575	0.338	-0.031	0.385
	(1.065)	(0.290)	(0.179)	(0.293)	(0.523)	(0.948)	(0.319)	(0.346)	(0.429)
Observations	16	16	16	16	16	16	16	16	15
R^2	0.335	0.418	0.730	0.063	0.179	0.174	0.487	0.502	0.280

Source: Author's compilation based on Armingeon et al. (2009) and OECD (2009a).

Table 11.7 Composition of Stimuli and Left Governments

	(1) Indiv Tax	(2) Bus Tax	(3) Soc Tax	(4) Cons Tax	(5) Gov Cons	(6) Gov Inv	(7) Tran HH	(8) Tran Bus	(9) Tran Loc
Left Government	-0.005	-0.003	-0.007**	0.001	-0.009**	0.009	-0.003	-0.017**	-0.009***
	(0.013)	(0.003)	(0.002)	(0.003)	(0.003)	(0.013)	(0.005)	(0.007)	(0.003)
House Price Change	-2.410	0.023	0.284**	-0.094	-0.099	-0.089	-0.748	-1.522**	-0.545***
	(1.555)	(0.240)	(0.112)	(0.274)	(0.281)	(0.749)	(0.427)	(0.569)	(0.115)
Left × House Prices	0.020	0.006	0.012**	-0.001	0.011*	-0.004	0.015*	0.034**	0.013***
	(0.030)	(0.005)	(0.004)	(0.005)	(0.005)	(0.017)	(0.008)	(0.013)	(0.003)
Cyclical	-0.184	-0.040	0.044*	-0.037	-0.060	0.153	0.018	-0.010	0.065
	(0.173)	(0.046)	(0.023)	(0.057)	(0.073)	(0.113)	(0.054)	(0.049)	(0.053)
Constant	-1.083	-0.386	0.025	-0.301	0.096	1.281	0.556*	0.780*	0.786*
	(0.820)	(0.329)	(0.135)	(0.355)	(0.390)	(0.724)	(0.266)	(0.381)	(0.361)
Observations	16	16	16	16	16	16	16	16	15
R^2	0.305	0.170	0.596	0.051	0.298	0.286	0.390	0.605	0.511

Source: Author's compilation based on Armingeon et al. (2009) and OECD (2009a).

Robust standard errors in parentheses

*** $p < 0.01$, ** $p < 0.05$, * $p < 0.1$

rience of the housing boom is more important, then right-wing parties will choose fiscal responses that cut taxes, whereas left-wing parties will choose those that increase spending. But the parties could have responded to the decline in house prices that began in 2008, making policy in the reverse manner. Why did parties respond to the boom and not to the bust? Most stimuli were decided on just as house prices began to decline rather than after several years of decline, and the empirical results in this section used the five-year change in house prices, which even in 2009 reflected much more boom than bust. Also, as we saw, empirical evidence suggests a hangover of house price booms: right-wing parties continued to respond in the credit crisis in the same tax-cutting, spending-trimming fashion as during the long preceding house boom. However, it is quite possible that over the longer term, if house price declines continue, we could see a reversal of preferences for the political parties.

One way to think about this issue is to examine the cases of Japan and Germany, where house prices had in fact declined between 2001 and 2006. These cases fit closely within the patterns found: that is, far from being outliers, despite having very different (in fact negative) levels of house price appreciation to the rest of the sample, Japan and Germany across the statistical models typically have some of the lowest residuals. Thus, the earlier findings are not being driven purely by house price booms—those countries with stagnating and declining house prices fit the overall pattern rather well. This of course does not directly address the question of how long it takes preferences to reverse. What is the lag between antitax homeowners in good times and pro–social spending homeowners in bad times? At root, this is an empirical question that simple cross-sectional analyses cannot address. That said, it appears that in Japan's case house price declines did eventually force a change in preferences in line with the theory.

The fiscal responses of Australia, New Zealand, Switzerland, and Norway together provide examples of the differential effects of partisanship in boom and nonboom states. Both Australia and New Zealand had major housing booms. Over the five years from 2001 to 2006, house prices increased 50 percent in Australia and nearly 80 percent in New Zealand. Moreover, each country responded to the shock of the credit crisis similarly in terms of their cyclical budget deficit—3.4 percent and 3.9 percent of GDP respectively. Yet their discretionary responses to the credit crisis were vastly different. In Australia, Labour Prime Minister Kevin Rudd increased spending by 4.1 percent of GDP, almost solely in government investment and transfers to households, including $1.2 billion in credits for first-time homebuyers (OECD 2010). Meanwhile, in New Zealand, National Party leader John Key slashed taxes, mostly income tax and small business tax, and in fact cut spending somewhat with the Kiwisaver program by reducing transfers to households (OECD 2009b). Cumulatively, New Zealand's stimulus, some of which began under the previous government, came to 4.1 percent of GDP almost entirely in tax cuts.

Why did both countries respond with such sizable stimuli and why was the composition so different? The housing boom in both countries tipped over into collapsing house prices during 2008, creating a compelling need for politicians to respond. Indeed, both the massive round of tax cuts in New Zealand and the massive spending—especially the credits for homebuyers—in Australia produced a stabilization and ensuing growth in housing prices during 2009. The distinction in their approaches derived from different supporting constituencies. The Australian stimulus was targeted at nonhomeowners buying houses ($1.2 billion) and at low- and middle-income families ($3.2 billion), and social investment policies like education and social housing; the stimulus was, indeed, strongly opposed by the opposition coalition. The New Zealand reforms, however, provided tax cuts to small businesses ($300 million) and reduced top marginal income tax rates.

On some dimensions, Switzerland and Norway might have been expected to respond similarly to Australia and New Zealand. After all, Switzerland, another highly open economy, experienced a very similar cyclical budget shock to the Antipodean countries—3.7 percent of GDP. Yet Sweden and Norway did not show the same kind of pronounced partisan pattern of spending and tax cuts. The Swiss government, largely dominated by right-wing parties, spent just half a percent of GDP on stimuli, half on tax cuts and half on spending (OECD 2009a). The left-wing Norwegian coalition also had a small discretionary stimulus of just over 1 percent of GDP, increasing spending by under 1 percent of GDP, less than a quarter of the amount of their Australian counterparts. Common to both countries was a much more moderate growth in house prices, less than 25 percent over five years. Demands from homeowners for tax relief or spending measures to maintain demand were largely absent because the size of the shock to housing was much smaller. Parties consequently had less electoral raw material with which to fashion opportunistic responses to the crisis: for example, the Swiss coalition may have desired large tax cuts but lacked the opportunity that would have been created by a larger group of homeowners with more at stake in sustaining aggregate demand and house prices. Consequently, partisan politics mattered substantially less in these countries in determining fiscal responses.[10]

FINANCIAL POLICY AND PARTISAN POLITICS

I now move from fiscal policy to a brief analysis of financial policymaking during 2008 and 2009. Perhaps the most pressing issue that governments faced in late 2008 was the threat of a severe banking crisis turning into a complete financial meltdown. Even before fiscal stimuli were developed, many governments had already intervened in the financial sector through regulation and financial support. Of course, many of these rushed regulations amounted to winding back the series of deregulatory reforms adopted since the 1980s, particularly in the case of the United Kingdom and United States (see chapters 11 and 7, this volume). In terms of these re-regulations, governments quickly moved to prohibit certain forms of trading or ring-fenced particular assets. Financial support included government purchase of toxic assets, outright nationalization of banks, and the provision of guarantees and liquidity.

Table 11.8 presents descriptive statistics on these financial policies. The first four columns examine the size of governmental support for the financial sector as a percentage of GDP. These data are drawn from the IMF (2009) and include direct capital injections, the purchase of assets by national treasuries, guarantees backing financial firms provided by governments, and the provisioning of liquidity. In all four cases, governments typically did not have to draw down on the full amount promised, largely because the financial crisis did not prove quite as deep as initially feared. The fifth column reflects the actual size of upfront financing engaged in by governments. Whereas governments guaranteed an average of almost 25 percent of national income, the actual amount of upfront financing provided averaged only around 5 percent of GDP, albeit with substantial variation. For example, whereas the Australian government had to provide only 0.7 percent of GDP in upfront financing, the British government, through its purchases of financial institutions and liquidity provision, spent 20 percent of national income on financial stabilization policies.

A second way of addressing governmental intervention in the financial sector is to simply code in a binary fashion whether the government decided to intervene in particular areas. The OECD has created one such index of financial intervention, with the following components: whether deposit insurance was enhanced, the government bought debt from the financial sector, engaged in direct capital injection to shore up financial firms, nationalized any financial firms, ring-fenced any assets, purchased any toxic assets, decided to fund commercial paper purchases, decided to fund the purchase of securities, and decided to restrict short-selling (2009a). Clearly some of these actions are attempts to shore up financial firms, whereas others restrict the purchase or sale of various assets. Thus, ascertaining exactly how friendly to the financial sector such policies are is difficult—some financial firms benefit from bans on short-selling, whereas others lose. Similarly, some firms benefit from capital injections, whereas others who do not receive them may consider them to be unfair advantages. Generally, this index is thus best interpreted as measuring the

Table 11.8   Financial Regulations and Government Support

	Capital Injection	Treasury Asset Purchase	Guaran-tees	Liquidity	Upfront Govern-ment Financing	Financial Regula-tion
Australia	0	0.7	8.8	—	0.7	3
Austria	5.3	0	30.1	6.4	8.9	5
Belgium	4.8	0	26.4	6.4	4.8	4
Canada	0	10.9	13.5	1.5	10.9	4
Czech Republic	—	—	—	—	—	1
Denmark	—	—	—	—		5
Finland	—	—	—	—		5
France	1.4	1.3	16.4	6.4	1.6	4
Germany	3.8	0.4	18	6.4	3.7	5
Greece	2.1	3.3	6.2	6.4	5.4	3
Hungary	1.1	2.4	1.1	15.7	3.5	3
Iceland	—	—	—	—	—	4
Ireland	5.9	0	198.1	6.4	5.9	5
Italy	0.7	0	0	6.4	0.7	3
Japan	2.4	21.2	7.3	2.9	0.8	5
Korea	2.3	5.5	14.5	4.5	0.8	3
Luxembourg	—	—	—	—	—	3
Mexico	—	—	—	—	—	1
Netherlands	3.4	10.3	33.6	6.4	13.6	5
New Zealand	—	—	—	—	—	2
Norway	2	15.8	0	14.7	15.8	3
Poland	0	0	3.2	5.5	0	2
Portugal	2.4	0	12	6.4	2.4	5
Slovak Republic	—	—	—	—	—	1
Spain	0	3.9	18.3	6.4	3.9	4
Sweden	2.1	4.8	47.5	13.6	5.2	4
Switzerland	1.1	0	0	25.5	1.1	5
Turkey	0	0.3	0	3.1	0	0
United Kingdom	3.9	13.8	49.7	14.4	20	8
United States	5.2	1.3	10.9	8.4	6.7	9
Mean	2.27	4.36	23.44	8.28	5.29	3.80
Standard deviation	1.90	6.12	41.62	5.56	5.47	1.92

Source: Author's compilation based on IMF (2009).

level of aggregate government intervention in the financial sector for stabilization purposes. Again variation is considerable across the OECD in how interventionist governments were. The United States engaged in all of these policies, whereas the Czech Republic banned only short-selling.

To what degree were variations in financial stabilization policies a func-

tion of partisanship, both in terms of the IMF data on the size of intervention, and the OECD data in terms of the range of policies used? In the
previous section, I found that partisanship only explained fiscal stimulus
policy conditional on a country's housing profile. The logic behind this
argument was that home ownership and house price appreciation change
the policy preferences of citizens and that political parties aggregating
these preferences will be responding partly to the shape of a country's
housing market. As we move to financial stabilization policies, the question is whether we expect this pattern to continue to hold.

The pattern might differ for two reasons. First, the fiscal dilemmas
states faced in 2009 were closely connected to domestic housing markets—
countries such as Spain, the United States, and the United Kingdom, which
had experienced large housing booms, suddenly found a major source of
employment, consumption financing, and tax revenues drying up—leading to the need for fiscal responses, whether through tax cuts, on the Right,
or spending, on the Left. However, the threat to financial stability from
collapsing banks affected all countries, regardless of their housing markets, because the stability of banks largely depended on rapid flows of
international capital. German banks were no more immune from this dilemma than British banks were.

Second, the preferences of political parties over financial stabilization
policies are more opaque than over taxing and spending. Financial stabilization can either harm or help banks depending on whether they chafe at
the new regulations or are bailed out by them. Similarly, the fiscal impact
of stabilization measures does not have clear consequences for the voting
public. Higher-income individuals pay higher taxes and bear accordingly
greater shares of the bailout cost. However, because they also hold a larger
share of the nation's wealth in terms of savings and assets, they are also
the chief beneficiaries of explicit and implicit guarantees to the stability of
the financial system. Because interest group and voter preferences are
unclear, partisan attitudes toward financial stabilization might instead
simply reflect different party preferences over state intervention read
broadly—left-wing parties are more supportive than right-wing of government regulation and ownership of the financial market. Our expectations for the effects of partisanship on financial stabilization thus differ
from those on fiscal policy. The conditional effect of partisanship and
housing markets should be considerably less important and the direct effect of partisanship is likely to be determined not by voter preferences per
se but by party preferences over state intervention.

Accordingly, I run two sets of analyses in table 11.9—both with and
without the housing interaction. We find that the effects of partisanship,
unlike those of discretionary stimuli, appear to operate only directly on

Table 11.9   Partisanship and Financial Responses

	Financial Regulation Model A	Capital Injection Model B	Treasury Purchase Model C	Guarantees Model D	Liquidity Model E	Upfront Financing Model F
Bivariate						
Right share of cabinet	-0.018**	-0.013	-0.001	0.090	-0.042**	-0.052*
	(0.008)	(0.009)	(0.031)	(0.202)	(0.019)	(0.026)
Constant	4.675***	2.845***	4.411**	19.408***	10.264***	7.637***
	(0.568)	(0.595)	(1.836)	(4.771)	(1.488)	(1.934)
Observations	30	22	22	22	21	22
R^2	0.156	0.090	0.000	0.009	0.114	0.180
Interactive						
Right government	-0.003	-0.021**	0.091	0.005	-0.017	-0.084*
	(0.010)	(0.009)	(0.061)	(0.200)	(0.069)	(0.046)
House price change	0.245	-2.822	2.878	5.533	0.930	0.079
	(1.797)	(2.026)	(7.390)	(17.673)	(7.370)	(9.538)
Right × house prices	-0.026	0.036	-0.277*	0.777	-0.051	0.082
	(0.022)	(0.033)	(0.137)	(0.757)	(0.155)	(0.130)
Constant	5.165***	3.773***	4.742	17.229**	10.160**	8.627**
	(0.658)	(0.531)	(3.653)	(7.229)	(3.282)	(3.637)
Observations	18	15	15	15	14	15
R^2	0.185	0.104	0.272	0.117	0.064	0.199

Source: Author's compilation based on Armingeon et al. (2009) and OECD (2009a), and IMF (2009).

Robust standard errors in parentheses

*** $p < 0.01$, ** $p < 0.05$, * $p < 0.1$

financial stabilization without an effect conditional on the size of the housing boom. Although some caution should be exercised, because the sample sizes across the simple bivariate and the conditional analyses are distinct, it appears broadly that partisanship has a nonconditional effect on financial stabilization policies. In particular, right-wing control of the cabinet has a negative impact on the OECD composite financial regulation indicator and on both liquidity provisioning and (less robustly) upfront government financing. Interestingly, these effects, except for liquidity provisioning, do not hold up if we use the left-wing government partisanship variable. In other words, right-wing governments behave differently than either left-wing or centrist governments as regards financial stabilization. At the same time, left-wing governments are not appreciably different from centrist and right-wing governments. In fact, it is centrist governments that are most favorable to financial regulation, though this result is mostly driven by the United States and thus depends partly on coding the Democratic Party as centrist rather than as left-wing. Broadly, the bivariate analysis shows that right-wing governments were least likely to engage in either financial regulation or upfront government financing. The multivariate analysis, on the other hand, displays no robust pattern of partisanship interacted with the size of housing booms.[11] Thus, whereas the size of discretionary stimuli appeared to depend on the combination of partisanship and housing boom size, as regards financial stabilization, partisanship simply has a direct effect. It appears that right-wing parties unconditionally chose a less interventionist strategy than did left-wing parties.

CONCLUSION

The credit crisis produced a flurry of activist fiscal policy across the advanced industrial world, the likes of which had not been seen for several decades. Although both the decision to use stimuli and their timing were near uniform across the OECD, variation was in fact significant in the size and composition of fiscal stimuli. I have argued that the interactive effect of government partisanship and the relative size of housing booms experienced by these countries in the pre-crisis fat years explains a good deal of this variation. And indeed, this interactive pattern actually explains broad patterns in social spending across the OECD over the past three decades (Ansell 2011). Put simply, the housing market has an enormous impact on citizens' wealth and on macroeconomic outcomes more generally. It is not surprising that political parties should have internalized this effect in their policymaking. I have shown that housing cycles, through the medium of political partisanship, appear to have strong effects on government spending policies, particularly on social spending. The fiscal stimulus bills of the last few years were no exception.

However, in examining the determinants of financial stabilization policies, I found that the effects of partisanship were unmediated. Right-wing parties, regardless of the size of the housing boom, were less favorable to financial regulation, and provided both less liquidity and less upfront financing to the financial system. This might appear surprising for two reasons. First, the stability of countries' financial sectors was deeply linked to the prevalence of cheap credit and housing booms, hence it is surprising that house booms appear unrelated to financial stabilization measures. Second, many financial stabilization policies could be construed as favorable to the financial sector, raising the question of why left-wing parties engaged in policies that benefited a sector more traditionally associated with the right. The first puzzle can be answered by reference to the high levels of interconnectedness between the financial systems of OECD countries. The second puzzle is rather more opaque because the distributive effects of financial stabilization are mixed. Perhaps left-wing parties are increasingly supported by—or, more cynically, captured by—financial sectors, as in the United Kingdom and the United States. More likely, the greater degree of intervention by left-wing governments is a function of broader left-wing preferences for a larger role for government, even though the beneficiaries of financial stabilization were not typical left-wing constituents.

Bringing both fiscal and regulatory issues together, the varied responses to the credit crisis of 2008 present an important challenge to political economists. To this point, very little theoretical or empirical work has been conducted examining the impact of housing, or asset ownership more generally, on political behavior (for important exceptions, see Schwartz 2009; Schwartz and Seabrooke 2008; Canes-Wrone and Park 2009). Thus we lack a language to help understand how individuals and political parties will respond to business cycle volatility produced by the asset market, as opposed to our traditional focus, the goods market. This chapter provides a bridge linking a set of general theories about asset markets and public spending to the specific case of the credit crisis, finding a good deal of explanatory leverage. An equally intriguing question is how governments will react to an era of stagnant house prices, or perhaps a long bear market, if these events come to pass. Yves Tiberghien argues in chapter 9 of this volume that Japan's response to the credit crisis has been a marked shift toward social democratic reforms—in his argument this is a response to a collapse in exports, but Japan continues to nurse a hangover from a collapse in housing prices during the 1990s, and asset values remain below their previous peaks. Thus the asset market also points toward increasing demand for social insurance. This example raises an intriguing question: will the old partisan patterns of the 1960s and 1970s, driven by labor market cleavages, reemerge in a new form, driven by the inequalities of ownership and the volatility of asset markets?

NOTES

1. Statistical analysis of the determinants of five-year changes in house prices shows a strong positive effect of current account deficits, and hence capital account inflows. Similarly, the interplay between partisanship and housing prices shown in figure 11.1 is accentuated in countries with current account deficits. Hence there is an important global dimension to the emergence of, and variation among countries in, asset dominance.

2. The extensive literature on tax revolts argues that the success of antitax messaging by right-wing parties since the 1970s was galvanized by the discontent of homeowners with property taxes (Martin 2008).

3. The x-axis represents partisanship, where negative fifty signals a government left of a country's mean level of partisanship and positive fifty signals a government to the right. The y-axis represents the effect on total social spending as a percentage of GDP associated with an increase in house prices of 50 percent over five years. The pattern in figure 11.1 is amplified in countries with high rates of homeownership and lesser in countries with low rates, suggesting that house price changes matter more in countries where homeowners form a very large political constituency.

4. Arguably the Democratic Party represents the left wing in the United States. However, because the analysis in this section is cross-sectional, we must be careful not to conflate the Democratic Party with socialist European parties. Furthermore, the final stimulus bill in the United States reflected the necessity of overcoming sixty-vote cloture rules in the Senate, requiring two Republican votes, thereby making the bill more moderate. Rerunning the regressions with Democrats coded as left wing does not alter the results substantially.

5. Similar results are obtained by creating a partisanship index that measures right-wing cabinet proportion minus left-wing cabinet proportion.

6. The marginal change being modeled here is a doubling of house prices between 2001 and 2006. For comparability to figure 11.1, a 50 percent increase in house prices would simply be this marginal effect divided by two.

7. Both graphical and statistical analysis of the net change in countries' fiscal position regressed on partisanship and house prices confirm this hypothesis. Left-wing governments with housing booms, conversely, do appear more likely to have increased budget deficits more when housing booms were larger.

8. All the models exclude Ireland.
9. The BIS housing data only covers eighteen countries. The OECD does not provide data on Norway's cyclical deficit reducing the sample to seventeen. Including Norway and removing the cyclical deficit variable does not alter results substantially.
10. Clearly factors other than housing contribute to explaining the smaller partisan differences, particularly electoral frameworks.
11. Notably similar results are obtained using the homeownership variables in place of the house price appreciation variables.

REFERENCES

Ansell, Ben W. 2011. "Nest Eggs and Negative Equity: The Political Economy of Ownership." Unpublished manuscript, University of Minnesota.

Armingeon, Klaus, David Weisstanner, Sarah Engler, Panajotis Potolidis, Marlène Gerber, and Philipp Leimgruber. 2009. "Comparative Political Dataset I, 1960–2009." Bern: University of Bern Institute of Political Science. Available at: http://www.ipw.unibe.ch/content/team/klaus_armingeon/comparative_political_data_sets/index_ger.html (accessed February 25, 2010).

Atterhög, Mikael. 2005. "Importance of Government Policies for Home Ownership Rates." Working Paper no. 54. Stockholm: Swedish Royal Institute of Technology.

Bale, Tim, and Ingrid Van Biezen. 2009. "Political Data in 2008." *European Journal of Political Research* 48(7-8): 859–73.

Bernanke, Ben. 2004. "The Great Moderation." Remarks at the meetings of the Eastern Economic Association. Washington, D.C. (February 20, 2004).

Canes-Wrone, Brandice, and Jee-Kwang Park. 2009. "Inverse Electoral Business Cycles and the U.S. Housing Market." Paper presented at the Midwest Political Science Association Annual Conference. Chicago (April 4, 2009).

Castles, Francis. 1998. "The Really Big Trade-Off: Home Ownership and the Welfare State in the New World and the Old." *Acta Politica* 33(1): 5–19.

Edlin, Aaron. 2007. "Housing Collapse? Bring It on!" *The Economists Voice* 4(1): 1–3.

Franzese, Robert. 2002. *Macroeconomic Policies of Developed Democracies*. New York: Cambridge University Press.

Hall, Peter A., and Robert Franzese Jr. 1998. "Mixed Signals: Central Bank Independence, Coordinated Wage Bargaining, and European Monetary Union." *International Organization* 52(3): 505–35.

Hibbs, Douglas. 1977. "Political Parties and Macroeconomic Policy." *American Political Science Review* 71(4): 1467–87.

International Monetary Fund (IMF). 2008. "The Changing Housing Cycle and the Implications for Monetary Policy." In *Economic Outlook 2008*. Washington, D.C.: IMF.

————. 2009. *Companion Paper—The State of Public Finances: Outlook and Medium-Term Policies After the 2008 Crisis*. Washington, D.C.: IMF Fiscal Affairs Department.

Iversen, Torben. 1999. *Contested Economic Institutions*. New York: Cambridge University Press.

Kemeny, Jim. 1981. *The Myth of Home Ownership*. London: Routledge.

Kingston, Paul, John Thompson, and Douglas Eichar. 1984. "The Politics of Home Ownership." *American Politics Quarterly* 12(2): 131–50.

Martin, Isaac. 2008. *The Permanent Tax Revolt*. Palo Alto, Calif.: Stanford University Press.

Organisation for Economic Co-operation and Development (OECD). 2009a. "The Effectiveness and Scope of Fiscal Stimulus." In *OECD Economic Interim Outlook (March 2009)*. Paris: OECD. Available at: http://www.oecd.org/dataoecd/3/62/42421337.pdf (accessed February 25, 2010).

————. 2009b. *OECD Economic Surveys: New Zealand*. Paris: OECD.

————. 2010. *OECD Economic Surveys: Australia*. Paris: OECD.

Pratt, Geraldine. 1987. "Class, Home, and Politics." *Canadian Review of Sociology and Anthropology* 24(1): 39–57.

Schwartz, Herman. 2009. *Subprime Nation*. Ithaca, N.Y.: Cornell University Press.

Schwartz, Herman, and Leonard Seabrooke. 2008. "Varieties of Residential Capitalism in the International Political Economy: Old Welfare States and the New Politics of Housing." *Comparative European Politics* 6(3): 237–61.

Shiller, Robert. 2007. *Irrational Exuberance*, 2nd ed. New York: Doubleday.

Verberg, Norine. 2000. "Homeownership and Politics: Testing the Political Incorporation Thesis." *Canadian Journal of Sociology* 25(2): 169–95.

Chapter 12 | West European Welfare States in Times of Crisis

David Rueda

IT IS WELL known that relative poverty has increased dramatically in a number of industrialized democracies in recent times. In a 2008 report, before the effects of the Great Recession had been realized, the Organisation for Economic Co-operation and Development (OECD) observed that the period from 2003 to 2008 had seen growing inequality and poverty in two-thirds of OECD countries (OECD 2008). The report showed that in the mid-2000s, the percentage of people with an income, after taxes and transfers, below 60 percent of the median was higher than 20 percent in Australia, Ireland, Japan, New Zealand, Portugal, Spain, and the United States. Decades of rapid growth, therefore, had failed to make a significant dent on relative poverty. Facing the Great Recession, these developments made Tony Atkinson ask, "If a rising tide does not lift all boats, how will they be affected by an ebbing tide?" (2008, online).

Relative poverty, and its close relation inequality, is frequently invoked as an explanation for a number of critical issues in political science. It is often considered a determinant of processes as diverse as the decline of electoral turnout (Verba, Nie, and Kim 1978; Rosenstone and Hansen 1993), the increase in the support of extreme-right parties (Betz 1994), or the likelihood of political conflict (for a review, see Lichbach 1989). At the same time, work by labor economists demonstrates that supply and demand factors alone cannot account for cross-national variation in inequality (Freeman and Katz 1995; Blau and Kahn 1996; Gottschalk and Smeeding 1997). Most analysts would agree that policy influences relative poverty in significant ways.

The effects of the present economic crisis will be devastating in a number of respects. This chapter focuses on the potential effects of the crisis on relative poverty. It emerges as a reaction to a general impression, in the general press as well as in academia, that the "automatic stabilizers" of the welfare state in most of western Europe will significantly diminish the effect of unemployment on inequality. A very public debate has taken place on the role of temporary fiscal stimulus measures during the crisis, but much less attention has been dedicated to the effects of the automatic stabilizers in the tax and transfer system. There is, in fact, a lack of research in economics on automatic stabilization (Blanchard 2006; for an exception, see Dolls, Fuest, and Peichl 2010). It is true, as I will show, that the welfare state was an effective buffer between unemployment and poverty in the past. As Anthony Atkinson has pointed out, when we look at the distributional impact of unemployment in the recent past, for example, in the mid-1980s, we see that the impact of unemployment on household living standards depended on government policy. In the mid-1980s, unemployment in Europe was around double that in the 1970s and four times that in the 1960s, but "it was not inevitable that unemployment led to mass poverty" (Atkinson 2008, online).

This chapter explores the question of whether we should assume that the welfare state today remains a powerful buffer between unemployment and poverty. The main argument can be stated very simply: we should not. The recent transformation of the welfare state, emphasizing activation and conditionality, has significantly weakened its power to intermediate between unemployment and poverty.

UNEMPLOYMENT, THE WELFARE STATE, AND POVERTY: ARGUMENT AND PREVIOUS EXPERIENCE

It is not controversial to propose that unemployment has the potential to promote relative poverty. The first reason is a direct one. To the extent that the unemployed receive benefits that are lower than the wage they would receive if they were employed, or receive no benefits at all, an economy with large numbers of unemployed people will have more people in relative poverty than one with lower numbers. A majority of households rely on earnings for their income. Unemployment therefore usually represents a large decline in income that will push some people under the poverty line. This may be made worse by the higher vulnerability to unemployment of people already close to the poverty line.

The second effect of unemployment on poverty is more indirect and works through its influence on wages. The basic insight of the literature on labor market segmentation is that unskilled, low-paid workers are more readily substitutable than more skilled, high-paid workers, and consequently that their bargaining position is more immediately and more adversely affected by unemployment (Galbraith 1998; Bradbury 2000). In this framework, the rate of unemployment can be considered a significant measure of the overall demand for labor or, in other words, the tightness of labor markets. Tight labor markets strengthen workers' bargaining power vis-à-vis employers. Because unskilled, low-paid workers are more readily substitutable than more skilled, highly paid workers, their bargaining position is therefore more immediately and more adversely affect by unemployment. By this logic, high unemployment causes wage dispersion that then produces relative poverty.[1]

A number of studies have produced evidence in agreement with the arguments above. Early studies of economic recessions in the United States show that income inequality increased during recessions and decreased during expansions (see, for example, Thurow 1970). Using the framework Alan Blinder and Howard Esaki (1978) developed to analyze the effects of unemployment and inflation on income inequality and poverty, several authors have found unemployment to be significantly inegalitarian (see, for example, Blank and Blinder 1986; Blank and Card 1993; Romer and Romer 1999).

Taking these arguments into consideration, the importance placed on controlling unemployment for the promotion of equality is understandable. In Scandinavia, the low poverty model for the rest of industrialized democracies, politicians have been very explicit in their claims that "nothing is more important for income distribution than keeping the unemployment rate low" (Aaberge et al. 2000, 79). As mentioned in the previous paragraph, however, the inegalitarian effects of unemployment are based on two essential factors: those affected by unemployment suffer significant income losses and the incidence of unemployment is concentrated on low-skill and low-pay workers.

The direct role of the welfare state in influencing the income losses of the unemployed is straightforward. A more generous welfare state will minimize these losses both by having a high replacement rate for social benefits and by covering a large amount of the population under the blanket of social protection. Social benefits provide a way to redistribute wealth to the poor and to insure them against labor market risks (Moene and Wallerstein 2003).[2] As Gøsta Esping-Andersen argues, by insuring the poor against labor market risks, welfare programs reduce people's dependence on employment as a source of income (1990). Some evidence supports these expectations. Using microsimulation models, Mathias Dolls, Clemens Fuest, and Andreas Peichl show that "social transfers, in particular the rather generous systems of unemployment insurance in Europe, play a key role for demand stabilization and explain an important part of the difference in automatic stabilizers between Europe and the US" (2010, 4).

These effects are, however, more ambiguous when we consider the relationship between social policy and unemployment. In theory, an increase in unemployment benefits would increase unemployment by shifting the wage-setting curve upwards, or by weakening job search intensity (for details on the effects of unemployment benefits, see, for example, Carlin and Soskice 2007). And, if high reservation wages increase the income of the lowest paid but also promote higher levels of unemployment, by pricing out low-skilled workers, its effects on income inequality and relative poverty may not be straightforward. Although significant evidence supports the role of social transfers on smoothing the effects of unemployment on disposable income, the actual effects of social benefits on unemployment have been less clear (see Dolls, Fuest, and Peichl 2010). Stephen Nickell and Richard Layard (1999) do indeed find a positive effect of benefit generosity on unemployment and, more specifically, Lane Kenworthy finds the generosity of unemployment benefit replacement rates to be detrimental to employment growth in private-sector consumer services (2004, chap. 5). Jonas Pontusson, on the other hand, finds this relationship not to be immediately apparent (2005, chap. 7).[3]

These paragraphs emphasize the passive side of the welfare state, but active policies have become an important part of the analysis of the effects of unemployment on poverty. Starting in the 1990s, arguments emphasizing the need for activation (or social investment) started to dominate the debate about the welfare state in industrialized democracies. The perception, in the words of Frank Vandenbroucke, former minister for social affairs and pensions in Belgium, was that "the traditional welfare state is, in a sense, predominantly a passive institution. Only once there has been a bad outcome is the safety net spread. It is surely much more sensible for an active state to respond to old and new risks and needs by prevention" (2001, 4). In this view, "social policy should shift from consumption and maintenance-oriented programs to those that invest in people and enhance their capacity to participate in the productive economy" (Jenson and Saint-Martin 2003, 86). Higher levels of active labor market policy were then expected to limit the effects of unemployment on inequality and poverty.

Active labor market policy is particularly important as a part of the welfare state because it is recognized as one of the policy options still open to government in an era characterized by international openness. The effectiveness of traditional demand-management policies is questionable in increasingly open economies, or it was, until the Great Recession. In an open economy, however, some options are still available to governments.

Active labor market policy belongs within the group of supply-side policies that partisan governments can use to promote employment, growth, and equality in an environment characterized by increasing levels of internationalization (see Garrett and Lange 1991; Boix 1998).

The effect of active policies on the relationship between unemployment and inequality is, again, not unambiguous. If activation means more and better training for those with low skills in the labor force, then it will promote higher productivity and, consequently, lower unemployment and income inequality. If activation, on the other hand, means a reduction in the generosity of social benefits and an increase in punitive labor market policies to push individuals into low-pay employment, then it may increase income inequality and poverty as it decreases unemployment. Active measures may be inegalitarian also through their effect on wages. Successful active policy, if directed to promote low-pay jobs, may promote the entry into employment of individuals who simply underbid wage demands and increase low-wage competition (see Saint-Paul 1998; Calmfors 1994).

This line of discussion makes it clear that two things are needed when analyzing the effects of the welfare state on poverty. First, the effects of social policy on unemployment need to be explored. Second, the direct effects of social policy on relative poverty and those of unemployment, conditional on different levels of social policy, need to be assessed. Considering the previous arguments, four scenarios are possible.

Table 12.1 attempts to put into a graphical form the expectations outlined. When passive labor market policies (PLMP) and active labor market policies (ALMP) are both low, the expected effects of policy on unemployment would be muted. With regard to relative poverty, unemployment was hypothesized to increase it, because within the framework of an ungenerous welfare state the unemployed receive benefits that are lower than their potential wages, the poor are vulnerable to more low-wage competition, and there are few active measures to benefit from. When ALMP is high but PLMP is low, it was argued that employment could grow, if activation means more and better training. Whether the combined effects of higher ALMP and lower levels of unemployment would promote less poverty is, however, unclear. The negative effects of unemployment would either be compounded by ALMP, if activation simply pushes people into low-pay jobs, or mitigated by it, if training increases the skills of low-paid workers. When ALMP is low and PLMP is high, on the other hand, unemployment could rise, if higher reservation wages priced out low-skilled workers. Whether the combined effects of higher PLMP and higher levels of unemployment would promote poverty is, again, unclear. As argued, high replacement rates for social benefits combined with high

Table 12.1   Effects of Welfare State

| | | ALMP | |
		Low	High
PLMP	Low	Unemployment increases poverty (no buffer between unemployment and poverty)	Ambiguous effect of unemployment on poverty (ambiguous effect of ALMP on low pay)
	High	Ambiguous effect of unemployment on poverty (possibly negative effect of PLMP on employment, but buffer between unemployment and poverty)	Possible poverty-reducing effect of unemployment (limited effect of policy on employment, greater need of the poor financed by the rich)

Source: Author's summary.

coverage of the population would minimize the effects of unemployment on poverty. High levels of ALMP and PLMP, finally, have unclear direct effects on employment. The possibly negative effects of passive policy could be balanced, or outweighed, by the possible positive effects of active policy (see Pontusson 2005, 178). With the effects of policy on unemployment minimized, the effect of unemployment on poverty would be drastically reduced. In fact, as suggested in the table, the nature of welfare state financing could even reverse these effects. To the extent that social policies are paid for by the rich and effectively insure the poor against income loss from unemployment, greater need may translate into income compression in a generous welfare state: the rich pay more to cover the greater number of unemployed poor.

WELFARE TO WORKFARE

As suggested, the starting point for activation initiatives is the idea that passive labor market policies can produce benefit dependency and increase unemployment.[4] Generous social policies are, in this view, associated with high reservation wages and low job search intensity (Eichhorst and Konle-Seidl 2008, 3). To combat the harmful effects of generous benefits on employment, two solutions are offered through activation. First, activation is meant to push people into employment, particularly low-pay employment, by reducing the attractiveness of social benefits. Second, policies are focused on providing benefit recipients with the skills required to be successful when searching for a job.

In practical policy terms, one aspect of activation has therefore involved limiting social benefits by either reducing their generosity or making eligibility more difficult (that is, increasing conditionality). In this respect, "the core element of activation is the removal of options for labour market exit and unconditional benefit receipt by members of the working-age population" (Eichhorst and Konle-Seidl 2008, 6). A second aspect, what Werner Eichhorst and Regina Konle-Seidl call the enabling side of activation, attempts to develop or strengthen traditional active labor market policies like job search assistance, subsidized employment, training programs and making-work-pay initiatives designed to facilitate entry into the labor market by topping up low-pay jobs (2008). A fundamental characteristic of activation and workfare is the introduction of systematic links between two sides of the welfare state not necessarily connected in the past—social protection and employment promotion (Barbier 2004).

Although it is clear that the transformation toward activation and workfare takes place in several dimensions of policy, the objective of this chapter is to explore the influence of this transformation on the relationship between unemployment and poverty. For this purpose, it would be convenient to create summary measures for the degree of activation experienced in any given country. I do this by exploring the two distinct dimensions of the workfare state explicitly.

First, as mentioned, the workfare state has two defining (and related) characteristics—conditionality and activation. Conditionality is essentially a process that makes social benefits less generous and more difficult to obtain. This demanding side of the workfare state is best captured by a measure of benefit generosity.[5] Perhaps the most straightforward way to measure whether social benefits have become more punitive is to explore the amount of resources a government dedicates to unemployment benefits.

Measures of benefit generosity are not clear cut. It is common to assess the importance of the welfare state by looking at the level of social policy as a percentage of GDP (see, for example, Huber and Stephens 2001). Although this may be a reasonable measure for some purposes, the limitations in its ability to capture benefit generosity are clear. Its most important weakness is that it focuses exclusively on the supply of social policy and ignores the demand side. In this respect, I agree that "measuring the size of the welfare state in terms of social spending as a percentage of GDP, as virtually all of the literature does, is problematic because such measures fail to take account of changes in societal welfare needs" (Clayton and Pontusson 1998, 70). This point is particularly important when trying to capture the influence of conditionality. It would be difficult to measure the effects of workfare without taking into consideration the demand for ben-

Table 12.2   Demanding Workfare

	1985 to 1989	1990 to 1999	2000 to 2005	Demanding Workfare?
Australia	0.14	0.15	0.12	Yes
Austria	0.23	0.29	0.25	No
Belgium	0.27	0.28	0.41	No
Canada	0.19	0.15	0.10	Yes
Denmark	0.57	0.56	0.60	No
Finland	0.23	0.28	0.23	No
France	0.10	0.15	0.17	No
Germany		0.20	0.18	Yes
Greece	0.05	0.04	0.04	Yes
Ireland	0.19	0.14	0.20	No
Italy	0.11	0.06	0.05	Yes
Luxembourg	0.48	0.26	0.32	Yes
Netherlands	0.30	0.41	0.38	No
Norway	0.19	0.19	0.14	Yes
Spain	0.13	0.16	0.20	No
Sweden	0.27	0.30	0.20	Yes
Switzerland	0.31	0.29	0.22	Yes
United Kingdom	0.17	0.10	0.06	Yes
United States	0.08	0.07	0.07	Yes

Source: Author's compilation based on Samanni et al. (2010) and OECD (2006, 2007).
Note: Unemployment benefits as percentage of GDP over unemployment rate as percentage of civilian labor force.

efits. In this chapter, I follow the lead of a number of other authors by measuring benefit generosity as the ratio of unemployment benefits[6] to GDP over the ratio of the unemployed to the civilian labor force (see, for example, Iversen and Cusack 2000). This seems a reasonable way to assess the importance of the demanding side of workfare. When unemployment transfers as a proportion of the total size of the economy rise faster than the unemployment rate, for example, this measure of benefit generosity will increase and conditionality will decrease.

Table 12.2 summarizes the benefit generosity data, measured as unemployment benefits as percentage of GDP over percentage of unemployed, for the OECD countries in this analysis.[7] The high degree of cross-national variation in the table is best illustrated by dividing the countries into three groups, which do not really coincide with the three usual varieties of capitalism, or worlds of welfare capitalism. The Mediterranean and most of the liberal economies—France, Greece, Italy, and Spain, and Australia,

Canada, the United Kingdom, and United States—belong to the group characterized by low levels of benefit generosity. All these countries spend an average of less than 0.15 percent of GDP per 1 percent of unemployed. The group characterized by intermediate levels of benefit generosity includes several non-Mediterranean continental countries (Austria, Germany, and Switzerland), one liberal economy (Ireland), and several Scandinavian states (Finland, Norway, and Sweden). These countries spend an average of more than 0.15 percent but less than 0.30 percent of GDP per 1 percent of unemployment. The final group—Belgium, Luxembourg, the Netherlands, and Denmark—spends the highest average amounts on benefits per 1 percent of unemployed—more than 0.30 percent of GDP.

Although this cross-national variation is interesting, the arguments about activation are also concerned with temporal variation. As explained, conditionality is argued to have transformed the welfare state in these countries regardless of point of origin. Table 12.2 presents some evidence for this, but conditionality is by no means general to all countries. In the fifth column of table 12.2, a summary assessment is presented of whether these countries have experienced a move toward more demanding workfare. In as many as eleven nations, the answer is yes. A reduction in benefit generosity has been experienced in Australia, Canada, Germany, Greece, Italy, Luxembourg, Norway, Sweden, Switzerland, the United Kingdom, and the United States.[8] In most of these countries, the level of generosity from 2000 to 2005 is lower than the averages from 1985 to 1989 and from 1990 to 1999. In one, Luxembourg, the level in the 1990s was lower than in the 2000s. In another, Greece, the level does not change from the 1990s to the 2000s. This leaves only eight countries that have not experienced an increase in the demanding dimension of the workfare state. Belgium, Denmark, France, and Spain saw increases in generosity in each decade in the table. Austria, Finland, and the Netherlands saw increases from the 1980s to the 1990s, and a decline in the 2000s that still leaves generosity at higher levels than they started. In Ireland, generosity decreases from the 1980s to the 1990s but increases significantly in the 2000s.

The decrease in the generosity of the welfare state suggested by table 12.2 is perhaps underestimated, because its general nature has been noted by a number of observers. Walter Korpi and Joachim Palme, for example, analyze net replacement rates in the public insurance systems for sickness, disability, and unemployment for eighteen OECD countries (2003). They find that the welfare state underwent a change between the 1980s and 1990s. They conclude "that the long gradual increase in average benefit levels characterizing developments up to the mid-1970s has not only stopped but turned into a reverse" (Korpi and Palme 2003, 445).

The demanding side of the workfare state could also be explored using an alternative measure Lyle Scruggs and James Allan (2006) developed to explicitly reproduce and improve on Esping-Andersen's commodification index.[9] Their decommodification index is constructed using three major social insurance programs: pensions, unemployment insurance, and sickness benefits. Of these three, the measure of pension generosity is the least related to conditionality. By eliminating this component from a measure of benefit generosity and analyzing the addition of the unemployment insurance and sickness benefits indexes, a picture broadly consistent with the one presented in table 12.2 would emerge.[10] Because the measure includes both unemployment and sickness components, it partially captures the use of sickness and disability benefits to subsidize labor market exit.[11]

The second dimension of the workfare state (activation) relates to its enabling dimension and, as mentioned, to the traditional role of active labor market policies. In this respect, the most straightforward measure for this dimension is provided by the OECD. This measure contains all expenditure aimed at the improvement of an individual's chances of finding employment. It includes spending on public employment services and administration, labor market training, school-to-work youth programs, and employment programs for the disabled. I measure the generosity of active labor market policy as the ratio of spending to GDP over the ratio of the unemployed to the civilian labor force, as I did with the previous measure of spending and for the same reason.

Table 12.3 presents the active labor market policy data for this chapter's analysis. It is possible once again to divide our countries into three groups. In fact, comparing table 12.3 to table 12.2, it is impossible to not notice the similarities. When looking at cross-national differences, levels of generosity in unemployment benefits in table 12.2 seem highly correlated with levels of active labor market policy in table 12.3. Once again, the group characterized by low levels of ALMP generosity includes the Mediterranean and most of the liberal economies—France, Greece, Italy, Spain, Australia, Canada, the United Kingdom, and the United States. All these countries spend an average of less than 0.10 percent of GDP per 1 percent of unemployed. The group characterized by intermediate levels of ALMP generosity includes several non-Mediterranean continental countries (Austria, Belgium, and Germany), one liberal economy (Ireland), and two Scandinavian states (Finland and Norway). These countries spend an average of more than 0.10 percent but less than 0.20 percent of GDP per 1 percent of unemployed.[12] The final group is made up of Denmark, Luxembourg, the Netherlands, Sweden and Switzerland. They spend the highest average amounts on ALMP per 1 percent of unemployed, more than 0.20 percent of GDP.

In table 12.2, a significant number of countries had experienced an in-

Table 12.3   Enabling Workfare

	1985 to 1989	1990 to 1999	2000 to 2005	Enabling Workfare?
Australia	0.04	0.05	0.06	Yes
Austria	0.09	0.10	0.14	Yes
Belgium	0.11	0.10	0.14	Yes
Canada	0.06	0.05	0.05	No
Denmark	0.12	0.21	0.38	Yes
Finland	0.17	0.13	0.10	No
France	0.07	0.10	0.11	Yes
Germany		0.16	0.13	No
Greece	0.02	0.03	0.02	No
Ireland	0.07	0.10	0.18	Yes
Italy		0.03	0.07	Yes
Luxembourg	0.37	0.08	0.15	No
Netherlands	0.10	0.24	0.41	Yes
Norway	0.18	0.20	0.17	No
Spain	0.02	0.03	0.06	Yes
Sweden	0.80	0.39	0.25	No
Switzerland	0.29	0.18	0.19	No
United Kingdom	0.07	0.06	0.09	Yes
United States	0.04	0.03	0.03	No

Source: Author's compilation based on Samanni et al. (2010) and OECD (2006, 2007).
Note: Active labor market policy as percentage of GDP over unemployment rate as percentage of civilian labor force.

crease in the demanding side of workfare. In looking at the enabling side of workfare in table 12.3, the picture is perhaps less consistent. Ten countries have experienced increases in the levels of ALMP per 1 percent unemployed: Australia, Austria, Belgium, Denmark, France, Ireland, Italy, the Netherlands, Spain, and the United Kingdom. Of these countries, the changes in Australia, Spain, and the United Kingdom seem too small to warrant considering them examples of activation: in Australia, the level of ALMP per 1 percent unemployed increased from 0.04 percent of GDP to 0.06, in the United Kingdom from 0.07 to 0.09, and in Spain from 0.02 to 0.06. This leaves us with seven countries of nineteen where activation has been significant at the enabling side. If social investment means increasing the conditionality of passive measures while increasing the resources dedicated to active measures, tables 12.2 and 12.3 make it clear that the model has been adopted by very few countries.

The previous section has made clear that we should not look at the levels of enabling or demanding workfare independently. It is the combination of passive and active labor market policies that contributes to different levels of unemployment and income inequality. We can combine the data in tables 12.2 and 12.3 to explore these combinations.

Figure 12.1 presents two panels depicting the decade averages for active and passive labor market policy in the countries in this chapter's analysis. The first panel presents all the data, and the second focuses on observations less than 0.4 percent of GDP per 1 percent unemployed. A general correlation between active and passive labor market policy generosity is clear. When we look at the means for active and passive labor market policy, reflected by the gridlines, we can also see, however, all quadrants within the panels are populated. Some cases show high levels of active and passive labor market policy: Sweden in 1980s and 1990s, and Denmark in 1990s and 2000s. Others show low levels of active and passive labor market policy: Spain in 1980s, 1990s, and 2000s. Still others show above average passive labor market policy per unemployed, but below average active labor market policy per unemployed: Finland in the 1990s and 2000s. In some cases, passive labor market policy per unemployed is below average, but active labor market policy per unemployed is above average: Norway in the 1980s, 1990s, and 2000s. Finally, temporal movement over the quadrants is evident: for example, Sweden moves from the high active and high passive quadrant in the 1980s and 1990s, to the high active but low passive quadrant in the 2000s. What explains the emergence of these patterns? Providing a full account of the factors influencing the developments outlined is beyond the scope of this chapter (the analysis that follows is dedicated instead to explore whether these patterns are a significant determinant of the relationship between unemployment and poverty), but some general observations can be provided.

The importance of workfare in all industrialized democracies is increasing for several reasons. There is what Colin Hay has called "input convergence" (2000, 514), that is, the concurrence of a number of exogenous factors affecting all these countries. Economic changes—such as the shift from manufacturing to services—and demographic ones—such as the aging of the population, the decline of traditional family structures, and declining birthrates—present new challenges for the welfare state. On the other hand, globalization and, for some countries, European integration limit the degrees of freedom governments enjoy (see, for example, Ferrera and Hemerijck 2003; Pierson 2001a). At the same time, activation has been increasingly accepted as the solution against high unemployment and low employment rates. The transformation of the welfare state into a more active one has been an objective repeatedly endorsed by OECD labor ministers in recent years (see, for example, Larsen 2004). As John Martin points out, it has also become part of the EU's official strategy to decrease unem-

Figure 12.1   Active and Passive Labor Market Policy in the OECD

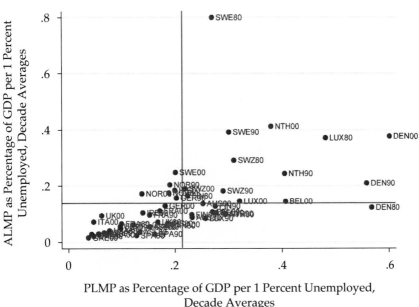

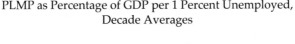

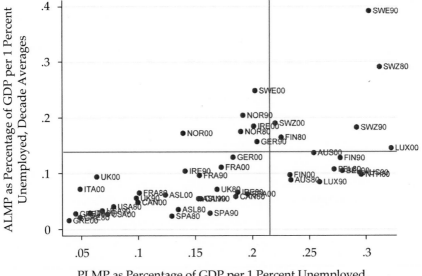

Source: Author's calculation based on Sammani et al. (2010) and OECD (2006, 2007).

ployment since the Essen Summit in December 1994 (1998, 12), reiterated also in the 1997 European Employment Strategy.

It is true that these factors are general enough to reflect an exogenous push for workfare and diverse enough to explain some cross-national differences, but I would like to emphasize another essentially political process affecting workfare: the emergence of insider-outsider differences in the labor market and their interaction with partisan politics. I would argue that the distinction between insiders and outsiders is essential to understanding the politics of workfare since the 1970s. As I explain elsewhere, *insiders* are defined as those members of labor with stable and protected employment, whereas *outsiders* have insecure jobs or no jobs at all (see Rueda 2007). Recent work in comparative political economy has identified the increasing political and economic relevance of this distinction (see, for example, Emmenegger et al. 2011; Palier and Thelen 2010). The potential for conflict between insiders and outsiders is a result of their different vulnerabilities to unemployment. Insiders are less affected by unemployment and therefore less likely to support parties that dedicate substantial resources to employment promotion or benefits for the unemployed. Outsiders are more vulnerable to unemployment because they are either unemployed already or enjoy little employment protection. They are therefore more concerned with the employment strategies of political parties, and favor generous benefits for the unemployed. The implications for the development of workfare seem significant. Insiders, if sufficiently protected from unemployment, have little incentive to oppose demanding workfare. In fact, higher levels of labor market policy, whether active or passive, benefit outsiders, but not well-protected insiders who are more affected by the higher taxes needed to pay for these services and by the low-wage competition these policies can promote. The evolution of labor market policy since the 1970s in most OECD countries is significantly affected by the power of insiders and, in particular, their connections to electorally successful Left parties (see Rueda 2007). The pattern of demanding or enabling workfare policy is no exception.

INFLUENCE OF WORKFARE ON RELATIONSHIP BETWEEN UNEMPLOYMENT AND POVERTY

In this section I describe the measures for unemployment and poverty, the method used to explore their relationship, the control variables introduced into the analysis, and some preliminary results.

In assessing the influence of the workfare state on the relationship between unemployment and poverty. I first consider the direct effects of labor market policy on unemployment. Second, I explore the effects of unemployment on poverty, conditional on different combinations of active and passive labor market policy.

For the second step, it is important to use a measure for poverty that takes into consideration disposable income rather than market income. This measure is taken from the Luxembourg Income Study (LIS). The measure of poverty in this chapter is commonly used: the percentage of people with household disposable income below 60 percent of the median. This is a measure of relative poverty and will change as the median household income changes in any given country-year. As with all relative measures of poverty, this is a measure of inequality. It focuses on the bottom of the distribution but, as it captures the difference between this group and the median, will reflect to some extent whatever affects the general income distribution.

The LIS data take the form of five-year waves with observations pertaining to different years for different countries. This reduces the number of possible observations significantly. It also means that the number of observations per country is not constant. The availability of inequality and generosity data reduces this chapter's analysis to eighty-six country-year observations. The smallest number of observations per country is two, for both Germany and Greece. The highest number is seven, for the United States. Of the nineteen countries in the analysis—Australia, Austria, Belgium, Canada, Denmark, Finland, France, Germany, Greece, Ireland, Italy, Luxembourg, Netherlands, Norway, Spain, Sweden, Switzerland, the United Kingdom, and the United States—the average is 4.5 observations.

Two things limit the analysis of income inequality: the relatively limited number of observations and the shortness of the time series. Given these limitations, the analysis below is necessarily preliminary. I estimate the following equations.

$$U_{it} = \beta_0 + \beta_1 ALMP_{it-1} + \beta_2 PLMP_{it-1} + \beta_3 X_{1it} + \ldots + \beta_n X_{nit} + \varepsilon_{it},$$

where U_{it} is the unemployment rate (measured as percentage of the civilian labor force), β_0 represents a general intercept, $ALMP_{it-1}$ is the one-year lag of the enabling dimension of the welfare state (measured as active labor market policy spending as percentage of GDP per 1 percent unemployed), $PLMP_{it-1}$ is the one-year lag of the demanding dimension of the welfare state (measured as active labor market policy spending as percentage of GDP per 1 percent unemployed),[13] X_1 to X_n are control variables, β_1 to β_n are the slopes of the explanatory variables, and ε_{it} denotes the errors.

$$Y_{it} = \gamma_0 + \gamma_1 U_{it-1} + \gamma_2 ALMP_{it-1} + \gamma_3 U_{it-1}{}^*ALMP_{it-1} + \gamma_4 PLMP_{it-1}$$
$$+ \gamma_5 U_{it-1}{}^*PLMPit_{-1} + \gamma_6 X_{1it} + \dots + \gamma_n X_{nit} + \varepsilon_{it}$$

where Y_{it} is relative poverty, γ_0 represents a general intercept, unemployment has now also been lagged by 1 year ($U_{it-1}{}^*ALMP_{it-1}$ and $U_{it-1}{}^*PLMP_{it-1}$ are the interaction between unemployment and both dimensions of the welfare state), γ_1 to γ_n are the slopes of the explanatory variables, and ε_{it} denotes the errors.

In both models, I estimate random effects and Huber-White standard errors adjusted for within-country correlation. Three sets of estimates are presented for each equation. In the first set of results, the only explanatory variables are the main variables of interest (the two dimensions of the welfare state in the first equation; unemployment, the two dimensions of the welfare state, and the interactions in the second equation). In the second and third set of results, an increasing number of control variables are added. The control variables follow from previous analysis of inequality in the comparative political economy literature (for details and sources, see table 12A.1).

Female labor force participation. Higher female labor force participation has been argued to be associated with higher inequality for several reasons. First is the influence of wage discrimination (Blau and Kahn 2000). Also, to the extent that women are on average less educated or have less work experience than men, an increase in the proportion of the total labor force made up of women can represent an increase in the relative supply of unskilled or less skilled labor (Topel 1994; Svensson 1995).

Private service employment. It is often argued that inequality and private service employment are associated, because the private service sector often represents an increase in the relative supply of unskilled or less skilled labor. As Torben Iversen and Anne Wren point out (1998), the scope for productivity growth in services is limited, pricing closely reflects labor costs, and demand for these services is highly price sensitive.

Union density. Several factors contribute to more compressed income distributions in unionized firms or sectors (see Rueda and Pontusson 2000). Among them, the fact that unions approximate the logic of democratic decision-making and that they have a strong interest in curtailing wage setting based on the subjective decisions of foremen and managers.

Wage bargaining centralization. The standard argument linking centralization to income compression asserts that centralization facilitates the reduction of interfirm and intersectoral income differentials because it means that more firms and sectors are included in a single wage settlement. Additionally, it can be argued that centralization produces income compression by altering the distribution of power among actors (as suggested by Wallerstein 1999, this would follow a median voter logic) and by making bargaining more transparent.

Left government. Governments can influence the income distribution through a number of policies, in addition to unemployment benefits and active labor market measures (see Rueda 2008). Left governments seem more likely to promote higher levels of minimum wage, equal-pay legislation, incomes policy, and a variety of other measures that strengthen the competitive position of women and other disadvantaged groups, such as immigrants, in the labor market.

International trade openness. Adrian Wood (1994) argues that much of the trend toward increased wage inequality in the OECD countries in the 1980s can be attributed to an increase in trade with less developed countries. The basic logic of this analysis is that by importing less skill-intensive goods from low-wage countries, OECD countries are essentially importing low skill labor, which puts downward pressure on the relative wages of the unskilled. I introduce a variable measuring imports plus exports as a percentage of GDP.

The results for the models exploring the determinants of unemployment are presented in table 12.4. The first column presents the estimates when only the two dimensions of workfare are used as explanatory variables. The second and third columns add the control variables. The estimates from all models make it clear that increasing the enabling side of workfare promotes lower unemployment while decreasing the demanding side of workfare, which means increasing the generosity of benefits, has no significant effects. Increasing the percentage of GDP per 1 percent unemployment dedicated to active labor market policy results in significant decreases in unemployment. Decreasing the resources dedicated to passive measures has no effect: it is therefore unclear whether, when we look at our sample, a high reservation wage is in fact associated with less willingness to search for employment.[14]

Going back to table 12.1, it seems then that those quadrants characterized by higher levels of active policy are associated with lower unemployment. The costs of PLMP implied in table 12.1, however, do not seem to

Table 12.4   Determinants of Unemployment in the OECD

	(1)	(2)	(3)
Demanding workfare	**5.047**	**−0.018**	**0.432**
(lag of PLMP)	4.770	3.363	2.823
	0.290	0.996	0.878
Enabling workfare	**−13.295**	**−7.423**	**−6.949**
(lag of ALMP)	3.749	1.496	1.767
	0.000	0.000	0.000
Service employment		**0.328**	**0.424**
		0.073	0.064
		0.000	0.000
Female employment		**−0.750**	**−0.580**
		0.236	0.239
		0.002	0.015
Wage bargaining co-		**−0.590**	**−0.344**
ordination		0.371	0.353
		0.112	0.329
Union density		**0.190**	**0.169**
		0.058	0.058
		0.001	0.004
Left government		**−0.002**	**−0.002**
		0.007	0.007
		0.765	0.748
International openness			**−0.044**
			0.007
			0.000
Intercept	**8.515**	**13.008**	**3.271**
	1.247	8.151	9.201
	0.000	0.110	0.722
R^2	0.175	0.005	0.034
N	389	389	389

Source: Author's calculations based on Samanni et al. (2010), LIS (2007), OECD (2006, 2007, 2010c, 2010d), Armingeon et al. (2011) and UN (2010).

Note: The estimates are FGLS and contain standard errors adjusted for within-country correlation. Numbers in bold are estimated coefficients; numbers in italics are their standard errors; third row of numbers are *p*-values from two-sided *t*-tests.

apply. Some of the argument in earlier sections implied that increases in passive labor market policy would price out low-skilled workers. This effect does not seem to be confirmed by the preliminary analysis in table 12.4.

Table 12.5 presents the second step in this chapter's argument. The determinants of relative poverty are presented in three columns. The first

Table 12.5   Determinants of Poverty in the OECD

	(1)	(2)	(3)
Lag of unemployment	**0.283**	**0.328**	**0.351**
	0.109	*0.104*	*0.100*
	0.009	0.002	0.000
Demanding workfare	**6.327**	**8.148**	**8.282**
(lag of PLMP)	*6.302*	*5.140*	*5.291*
	0.315	0.113	0.117
Workfare (lag of PLMP) ×	**−1.849**	**−1.322**	**−1.318**
Lag of unemployment	*0.607*	*0.482*	*0.446*
	0.002	0.006	0.003
Enabling workfare	**−2.047**	**−2.270**	**−2.162**
(lag of ALMP)	*3.926*	*3.132*	*3.318*
	0.602	0.469	0.515
Workfare (lag of ALMP) ×	**−1.168**	**−1.806**	**−1.918**
Lag of unemployment	*1.064*	*0.551*	*0.566*
	0.272	0.001	0.001
Service employment		**−0.071**	**−0.118**
		0.111	*0.098*
		0.521	0.227
Female employment		**0.423**	**0.430**
		0.230	*0.232*
		0.066	0.064
Wage bargaining		**0.333**	**0.296**
coordination		*0.272*	*0.256*
		0.221	0.248
Union density		**−0.070**	**−0.069**
		0.024	*0.023*
		0.003	0.003
Left government		**−0.002**	**−0.002**
		0.005	*0.004*
		0.663	0.608
International openness			**0.012**
			0.010
			0.245
Intercept	**16.684**	**4.306**	**6.157**
	1.527	*6.082*	*5.889*
	0.000	0.479	0.296
R^2	0.371	0.390	0.375
N	86	86	86

Source: Author's calculations based on Samanni et al. (2010), LIS (2007), OECD (2006, 2007, 2010c, 2010d), Armingeon et al. (2011) and UN (2010).
Note: The estimates are FGLS and contain standard errors adjusted for within-country correlation. Numbers in bold are estimated coefficients; numbers in italics are their standard errors; third row of numbers are *p*-values from two-sided *t*-tests.

column presents the estimates when only unemployment, the two dimensions of workfare, and their interactions with unemployment are used as explanatory variables. The second and third columns add the control variables.

The effects of the variables of interest—unemployment and the different measures of the workfare state—are difficult to interpret from table 12.5. The estimates of the unemployment variable represent the effects of unemployment when both policy measures are zero. We can see from the table that, as expected, at the lowest levels of ALMP and PLMP unemployment significantly increase the levels of poverty. I present conditional effects in a moment, and they tell us more about the effects of unemployment at different levels of welfare policy. For the time being, however, it can also be concluded that the three models do not produce substantially different results. I will use the results with the highest number of control variables as the basis for my calculations. But conditional effects are mostly the same if the other columns were used.

The effect of the control variables is not of interest to the topic of this chapter but I will simply report that some of them are significant. Union density has a strong egalitarian effect over disposable income (see also Rueda and Pontusson 2000). But female labor force participation (although only at the 90 percent confidence level) is associated with higher levels of poverty.

As to the relationship between the variables of interest and poverty, testing hypotheses requires assessing the effects of unemployment at different levels of ALMP and PLMP. The combination of enabling and demanding policies is expected to affect relative poverty. In table 12.1, I hypothesized that the most damaging effects of unemployment on relative poverty would occur when both ALMP and PLMP generosity was low. A less enabling but more demanding welfare state would minimize the effects of social policy as a buffer between unemployment and poverty. Although the effects of unemployment were ambiguous when one dimension of policy was high and the other was low, I argued that high levels of both ALMP and PLMP generosity could perhaps reverse the effects of unemployment.

I now use the results in table 12.5 to calculate the conditional effects of unemployment with different patterns of enabling and demanding workfare. In discussing tables 12.2 and 12.3, I described the average levels of ALMP and PLMP generosity. To illustrate the effects of unemployment conditional on workfare, I have selected a range for each workfare variable reflecting the most common values in the sample. For unemployment benefits as a percentage of GDP over the unemployment rate, around 90 percent of observations are between 0 and 0.4. I have selected 0 as the

Table 12.6   Unemployment Effects Conditional of Workfare Patterns

		Enabling Workfare (ALMP as percentage of GDP per 1 percent Unemployed)		
		Low	Average	High
Demanding workfare (PLMP as percentage of GDP per 1 percent Unemployed)	Low	0.351**	0.159*	−0.129
	Average	0.087	−0.104	−0.392**
	High	−0.176	−0.368**	−0.656**

Source: Author's calculations based on Samanni et al. (2010), LIS (2007), OECD (2006, 2007, 2010c, 2010d), Armingeon et al. (2011), and UN (2010).

Note: Conditional effects from estimating FGLS and standard errors adjusted for within-country correlation. Numbers are estimated coefficients of unemployment variable.

* if statistically significant at 90% level of confidence, ** if statistically significant at 95% level of confidence.

value for low PLMP generosity (a very demanding workfare state), 0.2 as an average value (the actual mean is 0.22), and 0.4 as the value for high PLMP generosity. For ALMP as a percentage of GDP over the unemployment rate, around 90 percent of observations are between 0 and 0.25. I have selected 0 as the value for low ALMP generosity, 0.1 as an average value (the actual mean is 0.12), and 0.25 as the value for high ALMP generosity (a very enabling workfare state). Table 12.6 presents the coefficients and significance levels for the effects of unemployment conditional of these levels of workfare.

Table 12.6 presents some preliminary evidence supporting this chapter's claims. Unemployment is positive and statistically significant at the 99 percent level of confidence when ALMP and PLMP generosity is low. It is also positive and significant, but only at the 90 percent level of confidence, when PLMP generosity is low but ALMP generosity is at the sample mean. The table makes it clear how increasing levels of ALMP generosity (moving to the right within the same row) and increasing levels of PLMP generosity (moving down within a column) mitigate and eventually reverse the effects of unemployment on poverty. At high levels of ALMP and PLMP generosity, unemployment is associated with decreasing levels of poverty. A 1 percent increase in unemployment when 0 percent of GDP per 1 percent unemployed is dedicated to active and passive labor market policies would be associated with a 0.35 percent increase in the number of people with household disposable income below 60 percent of the median. The same increase in unemployment would still be associated with an increase of 0.16 percent in the number of people with household disposable income below 60 percent of the media when 0 percent of GDP per 1 percent unemployed is dedicated to PLMP and 0.1 percent of GDP per 1 percent unemployed (the sample mean) is dedicated to ALMP. To put these numbers in context, the mean level of relative poverty in our sample is 13.4 percent. These increases described are therefore substantial.

Table 12.6 also presents some interesting evidence in favor of the egalitarian effects of unemployment. Low or averages levels of ALMP and average or high levels of PLMP succeed in muting the effects of unemployment on poverty. When one of the policies is high and the other is average or higher, moreover, a reversal of unemployment effects can be perceived. These effects, which are concentrated in the lower right corner of table 12.6, suggest that increases in unemployment in very generous welfare state move households out of poverty. A 1 percent increase in unemployment when both policies are high (0.4 percent of GDP per 1 percent unemployed is dedicated to PLMP, and 0.25 percent to ALMP) would be associated with a 0.66 percent decrease in the number of people with household disposable income below 60 percent of the median. These effects, as suggested earlier, may be a consequence of the way welfare states are financed. In many ways, social policies, whether active or passive, are paid for by the rich to insure the poor. As unemployment grows, the number of those in need of benefits increases, as do the demands on the taxes of those who remain employed. A generous welfare state facing unemployment therefore automatically brings down the top half of the distribution while attempting to keep the bottom half stable, which would decrease the levels of relative poverty.

More important for this analysis, table 12.6 makes clear that workfare has the potential to make unemployment very damaging for poverty. Increasingly demanding workfare policies move welfare states up in the vertical dimension in table 12.6 and therefore make the effect of unemployment increasingly inegalitarian. Enabling workfare would move welfares states to the right in the horizontal dimension in table 12.6 and therefore help limit the effects of unemployment on poverty even if PLMP is low. However, as shown in table 12.3, the move toward more effective active policies has been less general than that toward more demanding passive policies. The figures clearly illustrate that the best way to control or even reverse the effects of unemployment on poverty is for welfare states to increase the generosity of their unemployment benefits at the same time that they increase their levels of ALMP. This is not a prescription of the workfare–social investment framework and, more important, it is not a prescription that is easy to implement in times of crisis.

ECONOMIC CRISIS, UNEMPLOYMENT, AND POVERTY

That the present economic crisis has had and will have dramatic effects on unemployment in most OECD countries is not contested. A look at recent news stories, even if superficial, leaves no doubt about the extraordinary dimensions of the problem. Table 12.7 presents data on harmonized unemployment rates for the countries in our sample from 2007 to 2010 and makes the significance of the problem clear. All countries except Germany and Austria experienced an increase in unemployment during this period. The increases range from the moderate to the spectacular. In Australia, Belgium, Luxembourg, the Netherlands, Norway, and Switzerland, the rate increases by 1 percent or less. In the United Kingdom, the United States, Greece, Ireland, and Spain, the increases range from 2.5 percent to more than 11.8 percent.

It is also possible to present some preliminary data of what kinds of workers have been most affected by the Great Recession. Two economic processes are associated with the recent economic crisis in OECD countries: the bursting of the housing price bubble and an extraordinary decline in international trade. As a consequence, the two sectors most dramatically affected with regard to employment are construction and manufacturing. The OECD calculates that the construction sector is historically 70 percent more vulnerable to the vagaries of the economic cycle than the average across all sectors (2010a, 52). In the present crisis, Ireland and Spain are particularly dramatic examples, showing declines in construction employment of 37 percent and 25 percent respectively over the twelve months, concluding in the second quarter of 2009 (OECD 2010a, 52). Durable goods manufacturing is similarly vulnerable to the economic cycle: according to the OECD, 40 percent more than the average across all sectors.

The employment impact of the Great Recession has also varied across types of workers. Although gender has not been a good predictor of the likelihood of losing one's job in this economic crisis, perhaps because of the concentration of male workers in construction, unemployment has concentrated on what we could call outsiders: immigrants, the young, unskilled, and precariously employed (OECD 2010a). The data are perhaps most telling when looking at youth and skills. In 2009, the OECD average unemployment rate for young people (age fifteen to twenty-four) was 16.4 percent but a much lower 7.3 percent for so-called prime-age workers (age twenty-five to fifty-four).[15] In 2008, the last year we have data for, the OECD average unemployment rate for people with less than an upper secondary education was 8.7 percent, but only 3.2 percent for

Table 12.7   Unemployment During the Crisis

	2007	2008	2009	2010
Australia	4.4	4.2	5.6	5.2
Austria	4.4	3.8	4.8	4.4
Belgium	7.5	7	7.9	8.3
Canada	6	6.1	8.3	8
Denmark	3.8	3.4	6.1	7.4
Finland	6.9	6.4	8.2	8.4
France	8.4	7.8	9.5	9.8
Germany	8.8	7.6	7.7	7.1
Greece	8.3	7.7	9.5	12.6
Ireland	4.6	6.3	11.8	13.7
Italy	6.1	6.8	7.8	8.4
Japan	3.9	4	5.1	5.1
Luxembourg	4.2	4.9	5.2	4.6
Netherlands	3.6	3.1	3.7	4.5
Norway	2.5	2.5	3.1	3.5
Spain	8.3	11.4	18	20.1
Sweden	6.1	6.2	8.3	8.4
Switzerland	3.4	3.2	4.1	4.2
United Kingdom	5.3	5.6	7.6	7.8
United States	4.6	5.8	9.3	9.6

Source: Author's compilation based on OECD (2010d).
Note: Unemployment as percentage of labor force (harmonized).

those with a tertiary education.[16] The effects of the crisis on those who were precariously employed are more difficult to assess systematically. But it is clear that in countries like Spain and Italy, the unemployment consequences of the Great Recession have been concentrated on those with temporary employment.[17]

I have argued that unemployment would promote inequality if those affected by it suffered significant income losses and the incidence of unemployment was concentrated on low-skill and low-pay workers. Given the less than complete generosity and coverage of replacement rates in the OECD countries and the data presented about the incidence of unemployment since 2007, both hypotheses seem justified when analyzing the consequences of the Great Recession.

How have the countries in our sample reacted to these increases in unemployment? The results in table 12.6 suggest that high ALMP generosity combined with high PLMP generosity limit the damaging effects of unemployment on relative poverty. Have OECD countries reacted to the crisis by increasing, or at least maintaining, the levels of PLMP and ALMP? The limited nature of market policy data, available only until 2009, does not allow us to answer these questions systematically. But we can look at the immediate reactions to the crisis.

Table 12.8 presents the levels of ALMP and PLMP generosity with the latest data available. The years 2006 and 2007 serve as a before-the-crisis baseline. The early reaction to the crisis is captured by the 2008 and 2009 data. The most remarkable characteristic of the numbers in table 12.8 is their stability. It is not clear that there has been any reaction to the crisis in these countries. Both ALMP and PLMP generosity stays more or less the same in 2008 and 2009. In some countries it goes up slightly, in some it goes down slightly. But all changes are marginal, that is, less than 0.05 percent of GDP per 1 percent unemployed. The only exception is the United States, where PLMP generosity goes up significantly from around 0.06 percent of GDP per 1 percent unemployed in 2006 and 2007 to 0.14 percent in 2008 and 0.11 percent in 2009. In the rest of the countries, whatever combination of enabling and demanding workfare was reached before the crisis remains in 2008 and 2009.

A less systematic exploration of the policy reactions to the crisis would suggest that, if anything, the welfare state has become less generous both in its demanding and enabling dimensions. In the countries of the European periphery, the crisis has reached dramatic proportions and social policy is just one of the areas that have been the subject of draconian cuts directed to reduce debt. But even in OECD countries that have not been radically affected by the crisis, this decrease in generosity has been clear. I focus on two significant examples, the United Kingdom and Germany.

In the United Kingdom, reducing the generosity of the welfare state seems to have been an objective of recent governments not affected by partisan changes. In the midst of the crisis in July 2008, the then secretary for work and pensions, Labour's James Purnell, published a green paper emphasizing the expansion of compulsory work for the unemployed, targeting in particular the more than 2.5 million claimants of incapacity benefit and those unemployed for more than two years. This policy thrust informed the 2009 welfare reform bill. It promised to abolish income support, to implement a new sanctions regime for those not attending job centers, and to require nonworking mothers whose youngest child is seven or older to sign on. The arrival of the Conservative-Liberal Democrat coalition to power in 2010 reaffirmed this austerity-dominated direction for labor market policy in the United Kingdom. It is difficult to get exact data on budget priorities. For example, no explicit mention was made of welfare policy in the speech by Chancellor of the Exchequer George Osborne's announcement of the 2011 budget. But it seems clear that the plans involve significant cuts in social spending to accomplish the

Table 12.8 Workfare During the Crisis

	ALMP Generosity (ALMP/GDP/Unemployment)				PLMP Generosity (PLMP/GDP/Unemployment)			
	2006	2007	2008	2009	2006	2007	2008	2009
Australia	0.07	0.07	0.07	0.06	0.10	0.09	0.11	0.10
Austria	0.15	0.15	0.18	0.18	0.30	0.28	0.31	0.31
Belgium	0.13	0.16	0.18	0.18	0.26	0.27	0.29	0.30
Canada	0.05	0.05	0.05	0.04	0.09	0.09	0.11	0.12
Denmark	0.39	0.34	0.39	0.27	0.48	0.39	0.36	0.28
Finland	0.12	0.13	0.13	0.11	0.22	0.21	0.21	0.23
France	0.10	0.11	0.11	0.10	0.15	0.15	0.15	0.15
Germany	0.09	0.08	0.11	0.13	0.17	0.15	0.14	0.20
Greece					0.04	0.04	0.06	0.07
Ireland	0.14	0.14	0.11	0.07	0.19	0.20	0.21	0.22
Italy	0.07	0.07	0.07	0.06	0.11	0.11	0.12	0.18
Japan	0.04	0.05	0.07	0.09	0.09	0.07	0.06	0.08
Luxembourg	0.10	0.11	0.09	0.09	0.13	0.12	0.11	0.17
Netherlands	0.28	0.31	0.34	0.33	0.40	0.39	0.42	0.46
Norway	0.17	0.22			0.15	0.17	0.13	0.16
Spain	0.09	0.10	0.07	0.05	0.17	0.17	0.16	0.16
Sweden	0.19	0.18	0.16	0.14	0.13	0.11	0.07	0.09
Switzerland	0.17	0.17			0.20	0.17	0.17	0.24
United Kingdom	0.06	0.06	0.05	0.04	0.03	0.03	0.04	0.04
United States	0.03	0.03	0.03	0.02	0.05	0.07	0.14	0.11

Source: Author's compilation based on OECD (2010d).
Note: Harmonized unemployment rate as percentage of civilian labor force. For the definitions of active and passive policies, see text.

6 percent of GDP reduction in total spending from 2011 to 2015 the coalition is aiming for. The jobseeker's allowance has become more restrictive under the coalition government. In spite of this, rising unemployment will cost the government £700m more than expected in unemployment benefits in 2012, according to the Office for Budget Responsibility.

In Germany, a significant effort toward workfare was undertaken shortly before the economic crisis. In March 2003, the German chancellor, Gerhard Schröder, presented to parliament an ambitious set of reform policies known as Agenda 2010. An important component was a decrease in dismissal costs and a significant reform of social security to increase work incentives and to lower labor costs. With the arrival of the economic crisis, and now with Angela Merkel as chancellor, Germany was initially one of the countries most affected by the downturn (in 2009, the International Monetary Fund considered Germany and Japan to be the worst performing economies in the OECD). This initial shock was confronted with temporary measures like *short-time working* policies—the government partly financing private sector wages in the hope that employers would retain workers with skills that would be needed after the recovery. But these policies coexisted with a continuation of the emphasis on workfare that emerged before the crisis. As in the United Kingdom, the decrease in the generosity of the welfare state has been generally justified by the need for austerity. This way, in June 2010, Merkel announced drastic public spending cuts totalling more than $96 billion over four years. This was part of a sweeping austerity strategy meant to address Germany's budget deficit, which was planned to exceed 5 percent of GDP in 2010. The plan particularly focused on reducing social security and unemployment benefits: increasing their means-tested nature in a workfare-influenced effort explicitly directed to reduce long-term unemployment and raise the rate of employment. Although Merkel's cabinet in November 2010 also approved a plan to increase the basic welfare payments (Hartz IV) by €5, this minimal increase was done again in a context emphasizing workfare. In Merkel's words, "Hartz IV is not a way of life," and the benefits, even in times of crisis, are "meant as a bridge back to employment" (Levitz 2010, online).

The Great Recession has therefore not resulted in policies to mitigate the effects on unemployment on relative poverty. In fact, the economic crisis and the dramatically deteriorating labor market conditions developing since 2007 have been accompanied by a continuation of the workfare emphasis that dominated the previous decade. Despite important national differences, this pattern has affected most OECD countries, not only the United Kingdom and Germany. Deficit reduction has become the goal, from the countries of the European periphery—see the measures proposed by the new PP government in Spain or the Salva Italia spending cuts proposed by Monti—to those less affected by debt-financing problems, like the United States, where the generosity of unemployment benefits is a political hot potato.

The lack of response to the Great Recession is surprising. First, because temporary automatic-stabilizer stimulus to react to a crisis seems to have some economic justification, though it is not receiving much attention at present. This idea goes back to the 1950s (see, for example, Phillips 1954) and it is picked up by Olivier Blanchard, Giovanni Dell'Ariccia, and Paolo Mauro (2010). Blanchard and his colleagues argue that a distinction must be made between truly automatic stabilizers, which by their nature imply a procyclical decrease in transfers or increase in tax revenues, and "rules that allow some transfers or taxes to vary based on prespecified triggers tied to the state of the economic cycle" (2010, 212). An example of an automatic-stabilizer stimulus would be temporary transfers triggered by the crossing of a threshold by a macro variable and targeted at low-income households. Although the first kind of automatic stabilizer is affected by the general debate about the costs and benefits of welfare state generosity, the temporary nature of the second kind makes it an attractive response to the present crisis. Second, because if the story of the Great Recession is that governments have stuck with the reforms they adopted in the 1990s and early 2000s, in very different circumstances, the strategy does not seem politically sustainable. Regarding this issue, however, the literature of dualization may offer an explanation. Although political response to the Great Recession—*indignados* in Spain, Occupy Wall Street in the United States, Occupy London in the United Kingdom, and the like—has been limited, the seemingly unpartisan continuation of workfare in crisis may be the result of the political influence of well-protected insiders who are less vulnerable to unemployment even in times of crisis than they were before the 1980s. Center-left parties in most OECD countries have failed to benefit politically from the economic and employment crisis that has characterized the period after 2007. One reason for this failure is arguably that although unemployment has increased greatly in many industrialized democracies, the increase has not made it is easier for center-left parties to reconcile the interests of insiders and outsiders. It is not possible to win elections without the support of large groups of insider voters, who, in many countries, have not faced a significant risk of unemployment even in the difficult economic circumstances since 2007.[18]

Leaving this preliminary explanation of workfare aside, this chapter has argued that one of the most damaging consequences of such dramatic increases in unemployment, if not mitigated by labor market policy, is their effect on poverty. It is, however, impossible to assess this effect at this point. Data on poverty, much less the LIS data on disposable income poverty, are not available at this early stage. Given the impossibility of exploring the real effects of these increases in unemployment on relative poverty, we must engage in an exercise of prediction in this section of the chapter. I will assume that the previous section has painted an accurate picture of the relationship between unemployment and poverty conditional on different levels of labor market policy. I then use the estimates from these models to predict the potential levels of relative poverty in a couple of different scenarios involving varying degrees of workfare.

I focus on two countries. In 2007, the United Kingdom is an example of low unemployment benefit generosity and low active labor market policy generosity (see table 12.8). It is therefore an example of a country in which the demanding side of workfare is significant, but activation in the enabling side is not. Our second example is Sweden, which in 2007 has high unemployment benefit generosity and high active labor market policy generosity. This is our example of a country in which the demanding side of workfare has not been very significant, but activation in the enabling side has been.

I simulate two scenarios. In one, the generosity of the welfare state increases, meaning more generous unemployment benefits or more generous ALMP. In the other, it decreases, meaning more generous unemployment benefits or less generous ALMP.

To calculate these effects we face a few difficulties. First, we don't have data on disposable income for 2007, the year before the crisis hits. To set up the baseline for the comparison, I simply take the values for inequality for the last year we have available. In the United Kingdom, this is 2004, when 19 percent of the population had household disposable incomes below 60 percent of the median. In Sweden, it is 2005, when only 12 percent of the population did. Second, we have data on benefit generosity in 2006, because we use a one-year lag in our calculations, and can simulate an increase in generosity equal to 0.07 percent of GDP or a decrease in generosity equal to 0.07 percent of GDP. These are not extreme changes in ALMP or PLMP generosity: a standard deviation change would be closer to 1.2 percent in both cases. Third, I take the standardized unemployment rate in 2007 and 2010 from table 12.7. For the United Kingdom, unemployment was 5.3 in 2007 and reached 7.8 in 2010. For Sweden, it was 6.1 in 2007 and 8.4 in 2010. Finally, we use the estimates from column 3 in table 12.5, with all the control variables.

These simulations present us with a clear picture. In the United Kingdom, an increase in the generosity of PLMPs and ALMPs would significantly reduce the impact of the predicted unemployment increase on relative poverty. If the generosity of ALMP and PLMP were to increase by a modest 0.07 percent of GDP per 1 percent unemployed as a reaction to the crisis, the number of those in poverty would only increase, from 19.20

percent to 19.93 percent. If benefits were to be reduced by 0.07 percent of GDP per 1 percent unemployed, a more realistic possibility,[19] relative poverty would increase to a more dramatic 20.29 percent.

Sweden in 2006 was much more generous than the United Kingdom. It dedicated 0.14 percent of GDP per 1 percent unemployed to unemployment benefits and 0.19 percent of GDP to ALMP. The simulated increase in unemployment benefit and ALMP generosity would, as in the United Kingdom, reduce the impact of the predicted unemployment increase on relative poverty. If unemployment benefits and ALMPs were increased by 0.7 percent of GDP per 1 percent unemployed, the number of those in poverty would only increase from 11.97 percent to a still modest 12.68 percent. If benefits were to be reduced by 0.07 percent of GDP per 1 percent unemployed, on the other hand, relative poverty would increase to a higher 12.87 percent of the population.

CONCLUSIONS

In September 2009, OECD employment and labor ministers met in Paris to discuss how the job crisis resulting from the Great Recession should be tackled. They agreed that "the severity of the recession called for decisive and comprehensive actions and endorsed a set of broad guidelines for the labour market and social policy responses that are intended to limit the social costs of the recession while also promoting a return to sound economic growth" (OECD 2010b, 16). Already in 2010, the OECD report analyzing the concrete labor market reactions to the crisis had mixed conclusions. Many governments hoped to expand or at least hold constant the resources devoted to PLMP and ALMP compared with those in 2009. But "countries facing especially large government budget deficits or where an already high unemployment rate is projected to remain stable or decline are more likely to envisage beginning to trim back some of the increases in spending that were taken in response to the crisis" (OECD 2010b, 18). In 2011, the commitment to mitigate the effects of the crisis on unemployment and the effects of unemployment on poverty seems to have grown weaker still. Budgetary concerns and fiscal discipline have replaced unemployment as the main concern in the media, and most academic analyses.

This chapter is meant to reverse this increasing apathy toward the implications of the crisis with regard to unemployment by making two main points. The first is that, without the buffering effects of the welfare state, unemployment has a significant effect on relative poverty. We ignore the political costs of potential increases in poverty and inequality—in terms of electoral turnout, support for anti-system parties, or political conflict—at our peril. The second point is that focusing on the relative changes in social policy from the levels reached in 2007 overestimates the power of the welfare state to mitigate the effects of unemployment. By the mid-2000s, the welfare state in most OECD countries had gone through a profound change. Conditionality had transformed social benefits and welfare policies had become more demanding. An emphasis on enabling activation, on the other hand, had not been adopted equally. This workfare transformation has grave consequences for poverty in industrialized democracies. The story of the Great Recession is that governments have stuck with the reforms they adopted in the 1990s and early 2000s. We should not assume that the welfare state today remains a powerful buffer between unemployment and poverty and we should be concerned about the consequences of the present economic crisis.

Table 12A.1   Variables Used in the Analysis

Variable	Definition
Relative poverty	Percentage of the population earning less than 60 percent of the median disposable household income.
Unemployment	Unemployment rate (percentage of civilian labor force)
Unemployment benefits	Unemployment expenditure, public, total as percentage of GDP
ALMP	Active labour market programs total, percentage GDP
Service employment	Civilian employment in services as percentage of civilian employment
Female employment	Female labor force participation as percentage of civilian employment
Wage bargaining coordination	Coordination of wage bargaining: 5 = economy-wide bargaining, based on a) enforceable agreements between the central organizations of unions and employers affecting the entire economy or entire private sector, or on b) government imposition of a wage schedule, freeze, or ceiling; 4 = mixed industry and economy-wide bargaining: a) central organizations negotiate non-enforceable central agreements (guidelines) and/or b) key unions and employers associations set pattern for the entire economy; 3 = industry bargaining with no or irregular pattern setting, limited involvement of central organizations and limited freedoms for company bargaining; 2 = mixed industry- and firm level bargaining, with weak enforceability of industry agreement; 1 = none of the above, fragmented bargaining, mostly at company level

Table 12A.1   (continued)

Variable	Definition
Union density	Trade union density, the percentage of wage and salary earners that are trade union members, divided by the total number of wage and salary earners—calculated using survey data, wherever possible, and administrative data adjusted for non-active and self-employed members otherwise
Left government	Cabinet composition: social democratic and other left-wing parties as a percentage of total cabinet posts, weighted by the number of days the government was in office in a given year
International openness	Openness to Trade (imports plus exports) as percentage of GDP, Constant 1990 Prices

Source: Author's compilation. Relative poverty: Samanni et al. (2010) and LIS (2007); Unemployment: Samanni et al. (2010) and OECD (2006); Unemployment benefits and ALMP: Samanni et al. (2010) and OECD (2007); Service employment, female employment, and union density: OECD (2010c); Wage bargaining coordination: Visser (2009); Left government: Armingeon et al. (2011); International openness: Samanni et al. (2010), UN (2010), and OECD (2010d).

NOTES

1. It could also be argued that the causal relationship between unemployment and wages outlined above could in fact be reversed. A number of studies suggest that employers are more likely to lay off unskilled workers than skilled workers during economic downturns, and to the extent that an increase of unemployment entails a disproportionate loss of low-paid jobs, it should be associated with less wage inequality (for some evidence, see Rueda and Pontusson 2000). Even if this was the case, however, the effect of unemployment on household disposable income inequality and relative poverty (as it will be explained, this is the measure of interest for this chapter) would still be positive.

2. To the degree that social benefits, whether active or passive, are paid by the rich to pay/insure the poor they may also promote equality in a different way: as a result of unemployment they may automatically bring down the top half of the distribution (who have to pay higher taxes) to protect an increasing number of unemployed people at the bottom. I will return to this idea when discussing the results.

3. In line with Jonas Pontusson (2005), Nickell (1997) argues that the effects of benefit generosity on unemployment are limited when accompanied by activation.

4. The terms *welfare-to-work* and *workfare* are often used to describe particular aspects of activation and conditionality policies commonly identified with the Anglo Saxon model. In this section, it encompasses a more general set of policies.

5. In some of the literature on activation, this punitive side of policy is often simply described as workfare (see Serrano Pascual 2007).

6. This measure of unemployment benefits includes all public cash expenditures to the unemployed. It includes redundancy payments out of the public budget as well as some early-retirement "pension" expenditure to unemployed beneficiaries before they reach the standard pensionable age.

7. To control for the distorting effects of the Great Recession, the data in this section end in 2005. The evolution of demanding and enabling workfare during the crisis is discussed in the following section.

8. Even leaving aside Australia, France, Greece, and the United States, where the decreases have not been substantial, we still have seven countries where benefit generosity has decreased significantly.

9. For Gøsta Esping-Andersen, decommodification was defined as the emancipation of the individual from market dependence by promoting the provision of social services as a matter of right (1990, 22). In a very real sense, therefore, the evolution toward activation and workfare has represented a move toward the recommodification of the welfare state, making individuals more dependent on the market and the provision of benefits more conditional.

10. Cross-nationally, this measure is highly correlated with the one in table 12.2. When looking at temporal variation, however, the correlation is lower. Figures are available from the author.

11. Until the 1980s, many OECD countries had relied on policies to reduce labor supply to combat unemployment. These included early retirement initiatives and the use of incapacity and sickness benefits as valid substitutes for other social benefits. But, in the era of permanent fiscal austerity, solutions relying on the promotion of labor market exit have become much more difficult. Cost containment emerges as a top priority in all industrialized democracies, even if national strategies to address this goal are quite diverse (Pierson 2001b).

12. The exceptions when comparing with table 12.1 are Belgium, which has high levels of unemployment generosity but intermediate ones of ALMP; and Switzerland and Sweden, which have intermediate levels of unemployment generosity but belong to the more generous group when looking at ALMP.

13. The policy variables are lagged in both equations because of concerns about endogeneity. If not lagged, the results of the policy variables could be suspected to be themselves the result of unemployment, in the first equation, or poverty, in the second. For similar reasons I also lag unemployment in the second equation. By lagging these variables, I am trying to capture their

causal effect over time on contemporary unemployment, first equation, and contemporary poverty, second equation. The presented results are robust to the estimation of lags of different duration, as well as of five-year moving averages.

14. Although not the focus of this chapter, the results in table 12.4 also show that higher level of service employment, lower levels of female labor force participation, higher union density, and less international openness all promote higher unemployment levels.

15. These OECD averages hide a high degree of national variation. In 2009, countries like Spain exhibit particularly dramatic youth unemployment rates: 37.9 percent unemployment for young people, versus 16.5 percent for prime-age workers. But even in the case of Sweden, where last-in first-out rules are followed for layoffs, the numbers are significant: 25.0 percent unemployment for young people versus 6.2 percent for prime age workers (see OECD 2010b).

16. In terms of education effects, the United States is a particularly unequal country. The unemployment rate for those with less than an upper secondary education was 10.1 percent, versus 2.4 percent for those with a tertiary education.

17. In Spain, 85 percent of job losses affected people with temporary employment (OECD 2010a, 54).

18. This argument is developed in more detail, and illustrated with electoral data from Sweden, in Johannes Lindvall and David Rueda (2012).

19. This is not as significant a change as in simulation for Sweden. In Sweden, the decrease is 0.07 percent. But in 2006 data, the United Kingdom spent only 0.04 percent of GDP per 1 percent unemployed on unemployment benefits and 0.06 of GDP on ALMPs. The simulated decreases simply take the values to 0.

REFERENCES

Aaberge, Rolf, Anders Björklund, Markus Jäntti, Peder J. Pedersen, Nina Smith, and Tom Wennemo. 2000. "Unemployment Shocks and Income Distribution: How Did the Nordic Countries Fare During Their Crises?" *Scandinavian Journal of Economics* 102(1): 77–99.

Armingean, Klaus, David Weisstanner, Sarah Engler, Panajotis Potolidis, Marlène Gerber, and Philipp Leimgruber. 2011. "Comparative Political Data Set, 1960–2009. " Bern, Switzerland: Institute of Political Science, University of Bern.

Atkinson, Anthony B. 2008. "Unequal Growth, Unequal Recession?" *OECD Observer* 270/271. http://www.oecdobserver.org/news/fullstory.php/aid/2751 (accessed January 2012).

Barbier, Jean Claude. 2004. "Systems of Social Protection in Europe." In *Labour and Employment Regulations in Europe*, edited by Jens Lind, Herman Knudsen, and Henning Joergensen. Brussels: Peter Lang.

Betz, Hans-Georg. 1994. *Radical Right-Wing Populism in Western Europe*. New York: St. Martin's Press.

Blanchard, Olivier. 2006. "Comments on 'The Case Against the Case Against Discretionary Policy,' by Alan Blinder." In *The Macroeconomics of Fiscal Policy*, edited by Richard Kopcke, Geoffrey Tootell, and Robert Triest. Cambridge, Mass.: MIT Press.

Blanchard, Olivier, Giovanni Dell'Ariccia, and Paolo Mauro. 2010. "Rethinking Macroeconomic Policy." *Journal of Money, Credit, and Banking* 42(6): 199–215.

Blank, Rebecca, and Alan S. Blinder. 1986. "Macroeconomics, Income Distribution, and Poverty." In *Fighting Poverty: What Works and What Doesn't*, edited by Sheldon Danziger and Daniel Weinberg. Cambridge, Mass.: Harvard University Press.

Blank, Rebecca, and David Card. 1993. "Poverty, Income Distribution, and Growth: Are They Still Connected?" Brookings Papers on Economic Activity, Economic Studies Program, Brookings Institution 24(2): 285–340.

Blau, Francine, and Lawrence Kahn. 1996. "International Differences in Male Wage Inequality." *Journal of Political Economy* 104(4): 791–836.

———. 2000. "Gender Differences in Pay." *Journal of Economic Perspectives* 14(4): 75–99.

Blinder, Alan S., and Howard Y. Esaki. 1978. "Macroeconomic Activity and Income Distribution in the Postwar United States." *Review of Economics and Statistics* 60: 604–9.

Boix, Carles. 1998. *Political Parties, Growth, and Equality*. New York: Cambridge University Press.

Bradbury, Katherine. 2000. "Rising Tide in the Labor Market: To What degree Do Expansions Benefit the Disadvantaged." *New England Economic Review* 32(1): 3–33.

Calmfors, Lars. 1994. "Active Labour Market Policy and Unemployment: A Framework for the Analysis of Crucial Design Features." *OECD Economic Studies* 22(1): 7–47.

Carlin, Wendy, and David Soskice. 2007. *Macroeconomics: Imperfections, Institutions, and Policies*. Oxford: Oxford University Press.

Clayton, Richard, and Jonas Pontusson. 1998. "Welfare State Retrenchment Revisited." *World Politics* 51(1): 67–98.

Dolls, Mathias, Clemens Fuest, and Andreas Peichl. 2010. "Automatic Stabilizers and Economic Crisis: U.S. vs. Europe." *NBER* working paper 16275. Cambridge, Mass.: National Bureau of Economic Research.

Eichhorst, Werner, and Regina Konle-Seidl. 2008. "Contingent Convergence: A Comparative Analysis of Activation Policies." *IZA* discussion paper no. 3905. Bonn: Institute for the Study of Labor.

Emmenegger, Patrick, Silja Haeusermann, Bruno Palier, and Martin Seeleib-Kaiser, eds. 2011. *The Age of Dualization*. Oxford: Oxford University Press.

Esping-Andersen, Gøsta. 1990. *The Three Worlds of Welfare Capitalism*. Cambridge: Polity Press.

Ferrera, Maurizio, and Anton Hemerijck. 2003. "Recalibrating Europe's Welfare Regimes." In *Governing Work and Welfare in a New Economy*, edited by Jonathan Zeitlin and David Trubek. Oxford: Oxford University Press.

Freeman, Richard, and Lawrence Katz, eds. 1995. *Differences and Changes in Wage Structures*. Chicago: University of Chicago Press.

Galbraith, James. 1998. *Created Unequal*. New York: The Free Press.

Garrett, Geoffrey, and Peter Lange. 1991. "Political Responses to Interdependence: What's 'Left' for the Left?" *International Organization* 45(4): 539–64.

Gottschalk, Peter, and Timothy Smeeding. 1997. "Cross-National Comparisons of Earnings and Income Inequality." *Journal of Economic Literature* 35(June): 633–87.

Hay, Colin. 2000. "Contemporary Capitalism, Globalization, Regionalization, and the Persistance of National Variation." *Review of International Studies* 26(4): 509–31.

Huber, Evelyne, and John Stephens. 2001. *Development and Crisis of the Welfare State*. Chicago: University of Chicago Press.

Iverson, Torben, and Thomas R. Cusack. 2000. "The Causes of Welfare State Expansion." *World Politics* 52(3): 313–49.

Iversen, Torben, and Anne Wren. 1998. "Equality, Employment, and Budgetary Restraint." *World Politics* 50(4): 507–46.

Jenson, Jane, and Denis Saint-Martin. 2003. "New Routes to Social Cohesion? Citizenship and the Social Investment State." *Canadian Journal of Sociology* 28(1): 77–99.

Kenworthy, Lane. 2004. *Egalitarian Capitalism*. New York: Russell Sage Foundation.

Korpi, Walter, and Joakim Palme. 2003. "New Politics and Class Politics in the Context of Austerity and Globalization: Welfare State Regress in 18 Countries, 1975–95." *American Political Science Review* 97(3): 425–46.

Larsen, Jørgen Elm. 2004. "The Active Society and Activation Policy: Ideologies, Contexts, and Effects." In *The New Face of Welfare*, edited by Jörgen Goul Andersen, Anne-Marie Guillemard, Per H. Jensen, and Birgit Pfau-Effinger. Bristol: Policy Press.

Levitz, David. 2010. "Merkel's Cabinet Approves Reform to Unemployment Benefits." *Deutsche Welle*, October 20, 2010. Available at: http://www.dw.de/dw/article/0,,6132990,00.html (accessed April 25, 2012).

Lichbach, Mark. 1989. "An Evaluation of 'Does Economic Inequality Breed Political Conflict?' Studies." *World Politics* 41(4): 431–70.

Lindvall, Johannes, and David Rueda. 2012. "The Insider-Outsider Dilemma." Unpublished manuscript. Department of Politics and IR, Oxford University.

Luxembourg Income Study (LIS). 2007. *Luxembourg Income Study Database*. Available at: www.lisdatacenter.org (accessed June 20, 2012). Luxembourg: LIS.

Martin, John. 1998. "What Works Among Active Labour Market Policies: Evidence from OECD Countries' Experiences." *OECD Labour Market and Social Policy* occasional paper 35. Paris: Organisation for Economic Co-operation and Development.

Moene, Karl Ove, and Michael Wallerstein. 2003. "Earnings Inequality and Welfare Spending." *World Politics* 55(4): 485–516.

Nickell, Stephen. 1997. "Unemployment and Labor Market Rigidities: Europe versus North America." *Journal of Economic Perspectives* 11(3): 55–74.

Nickell, Stephen, and Richard Layard. 1999. "Labor Market Institutions and Economic Performance." In *Handbook of Labor Economics* vol. 3, edited by Orley Ashenfelter and David Card. Amsterdam: Elsevier Science.

Organisation for Economic Co-operation and Development (OECD). 2006. *Population and Labour Force Statistics. Vol. 2006* release 02. Paris: Organisation for Economic Co-operation and Development. Available at: http://www.oecd.org/std/labour (accessed June 20, 2012).

———. 2007. *The Social Expenditure Database*. Paris: Organisation for Economic Co-operation and Development. Available at: http://stats.oecd.org/wbos/default.aspx?datasetcode=SOCX_AGG (accessed June 20, 2012).

———. 2008. *Growing Unequal?* Paris: OECD.

———. 2010a. *From Crisis to Recovery*. Paris: OECD.

———. 2010b. *Employment Outlook: Moving Beyond the Job Crisis*. Paris: OECD.

———. 2010c. *Labour Force Statistics*. Paris: Organisation for Economic Co-operation and Development.

———. 2010d. *Economic Outlook*. Paris: Organisation for Economic Co-operation And Development.

Palier, Bruno, and Kathleen Thelen. 2010. "Institutionalizing Dualism." *Politics & Society* 38(1): 119–48.

Phillips, Alban W. 1954. "Stabilization Policy in a Closed Economy." *Economic Journal* 64(254): 290–323.

Pierson, Paul. ed. 2001a. *The New Politics of the Welfare State*. Oxford: Oxford University Press.

———. 2001b. "Coping with Permanent Austerity: Welfare State Restructuring in Affluent Democracies." In *The New Politics of the Welfare State*, edited by Paul Pierson. Oxford: Oxford University Press.

Pontusson, Jonas. 2005. *Inequality and Prosperity: Social Europe vs. Liberal America*. Ithaca, N.Y.: Cornell University Press.

Romer, Christina D., and David H. Romer. 1999. "Monetary Policy and the Well-being of the Poor." *Federal Reserve Bank of Kansas City Economic Review* Q(I): 21–49.

Rosenstone, Steven, and John Mark Hansen. 1993. *Mobilization, Participation, and Democracy in America*. New York: Macmillan.

Rueda, David. 2007. *Social Democracy Inside Out: Partisanship and Labor Market Policy in Industrialized Democracies*. Oxford: Oxford University Press.

———. 2008. "Left Government, Policy, and Corporatism: Explaining the Influence of Partisanship on Inequality." *World Politics* 60(April): 349–89.

Rueda, David, and Jonas Pontusson. 2000. "Wage Inequality and Varieties of Capitalism." *World Politics* 52(3): 350–83.

Saint-Paul, Gilles. 1998. "A Framework for Analysing the Political Support for Active Labor Market Policy." *Journal of Public Economics* 67(1998): 151–65.

Samanni, Marcus, Jan Teorell, Staffan Kumlin, and Bo Rothstein. 2010. The QoG Social Policy Dataset, version 22Feb10. University of Gothenburg: The Quality of Government Institute. Available at: http://www.qog.pol.gu.se (accessed June 20, 2012).

Scruggs, Lyle, and James Allan. 2006. "Welfare-State Decommodification in 18 OECD Countries: A Replication and Revision." *Journal of European Social Policy* 16(1): 55–72.

Serrano Pascual, Amparo. 2007. "Reshaping Welfare States: Activation Regimes in Europe." In *Reshaping Welfare States and Activation Regimes in Europe*, edited by Amparo Serrano Pascual and Lars Magnusson. Brussels: Peter Lang.

Svensson, Lennart. 1995. *Closing the Gender Gap*. Lund: Ekonomisk-Historiska Föreningen.

Thurow, Lester. 1970. "Analyzing the American Income Distribution." *American Economic Review* 60(2): 261–69.

Topel, Robert. 1994. "Wage Inequality and Regional Labor Market Performance in the United States." In *Labour Market and Economic Performance*, edited by Toshiaki Tachibanaki. New York: St. Martin's Press.

United Nations (UN). 2010. *National Accounts*. New York: United Nations Publications.

Vandenbroucke, Frank. 2001. "The Active Welfare State: A Social-Democratic Ambition for Europe." *Policy Network Journal* 1(March). http://oud.frankvandenbroucke.be/html/soc/PU010213.htm (accessed March 12, 2012).

Verba, Sidney, Norman Nie, and Jae-On Kim. 1978. *Participation and Political Equality*. New York: Cambridge University Press.

Visser, Jelle. 2009. *The ICTWSS Database: Database on Institutional Characteristics of Trade Unions, Wage Setting, State Intervention, and Social Pacts in 34 countries Between 1960 and 2007*. Version 2, January 2009. Amsterdam Institute for Advanced Labour Studies, University of Amsterdam. Available at: http://www.uva-aias.net/207 (accessed June 20, 2012).

Wallerstein, Michael. 1999. "Wage-Setting Institutions and Pay Inequality in Advanced Industrial Societies." *American Journal of Political Science* 43(3): 649–80.

Wood, Adrian. 1994. *North-South Trade, Employment, and Inequality*. Oxford: Clarendon Press.

Index